e Language and Literature

'*The Routledge Language and Literature Reader* is the most important stylistics collection in a decade. The essays included represent some of the best work of the past forty years and cover a wide range of approaches to poetry, prose, and drama from standard literary linguistics to cognitive stylistics, text world theory, and quantitative stylistics. It is sure to become a standard text on courses.'

David L. Hoover, *New York University, USA*

The Language and Literature Reader is an invaluable resource for students of English literature, language and linguistics. Bringing together the most significant work in the field with integrated editorial material, this Reader is a structured and accessible tool for the student and scholar.

Divided into three main parts, *Foundations, Developments* and *New Directions,* the Reader provides an overview of the discipline from the early stages in the 1960s and 1970s, through the new theories and practices of the 1980s and 1990s, to the most recent and contemporary work in the field. Each chapter contains a brief introduction by the editors situating it in the context of developing work in the discipline and glossing it in terms of the part and of the book as a whole. A final part concludes with a 'retrospect and prospect', written by the editors, which places developments in the area of stylistics within a brief history of the field and offers a polemical perspective on the future of a growing and influential discipline.

Extracts from: Ronald Carter, Guy Cook, Catherine Emmott, Roger Fowler, Joanna Gavins, Ray Gibbs, Keith Green, Michael Halliday, Geoffrey Leech, David Lodge, Dan McIntyre, Walter Nash, Mary Louise Pratt, Elena Semino, Mick Short, Paul Simpson, John Sinclair, Violeta Sotirova, Peter Stockwell, Michael Stubbs, Alison Tate, Michael Toolan, Elizabeth Closs Traugott, Willie van Peer, Katie Wales, Paul Werth, Jean Jacques Weber and Henry Widdowson.

Ronald Carter is Professor of Modern English Language at the University of Nottingham. His books include the co-authored *Working with Texts* (3rd edition, 2007), *The Routledge History of Literature in English* (2nd edition, 2001) and *Language and Creativity: The Art of Common Talk* (2004).

Peter Stockwell is Professor of Literary Linguistics at the University of Nottingham. His recent titles include *Sociolinguistics* (2nd edition, 2007), *Cognitive Poetics* (2002) and the co-authored *Language in Theory* (2004).

The Language and Literature Reader

Edited by Ronald Carter and
Peter Stockwell

Routledge
Taylor & Francis Group

LONDON AND NEW YORK

First published 2008
by Routledge
2 Park Square, Milton Park, Abingdon, Oxon OX14 4RN

Simultaneously published in the USA and Canada
by Routledge
270 Madison Ave, New York, NY 10006

Routledge is an imprint of the Taylor & Francis Group, an informa business

© 2008. This collection and editorial matter
© Ronald Carter and Peter Stockwell
Individual essays © individual contributors

Typeset in Perpetua and Bell Gothic by
Swales & Willis Ltd, Exeter, Devon
Printed and bound in Great Britain by
The Cromwell Press, Trowbridge, Wiltshire

British Library Cataloguing in Publication Data
A catalogue record for this book is available from the British Library

Library of Congress Cataloging in Publication Data
The language and literature reader/[compiled by] Ronald Carter and Peter Stockwell.
p. cm.
Includes index.
1. Philology, Modern. I. Carter, Ronald, 1947– II. Stockwell, Peter.
PB41.L356 2008
801′.95–dc22
2007043072

ISBN 10: 0–415–41002–9 (hbk)
ISBN 10: 0–415–41003–7 (pbk)

ISBN 13: 978–0–415–41002–1 (hbk)
ISBN 13: 978–0–415–41003–8 (pbk)

CONTENTS

PREFACE

THIS READER PRESENTS SIGNIFICANT work in the field of language and literary studies over the course of the past 40 years. It is organised into three main sections, in all cases exemplifying seminal innovations in the development of theory and analytical practice. Each chapter contains a brief introduction by the editors to individual papers, situating them in the context of developing work in the field and, where appropriate, glossing them in terms of the part and of the book as a whole. Most articles have been edited for length and textual focus.

The first part exemplifies, from an historical perspective, the *Foundations* of the discipline as developed in the 1960s and 1970s by drawing on the work of major founding figures in the field of both language and literary studies; a second part, entitled *Developments*, underlines the strengths of the discipline across major literary genres as new theories and practices were developed in the 1980s and 1990s; and a third part illustrates a range of *New Directions* and future possibilities for language and literature studies, drawing in particular on recent work in narrative studies, literary linguistic analysis of point of view, the relationship between language and literary context, corpus stylistics and research with a cognitive poetic orientation. The final section contains a specially written 'retrospect and prospect', situating developments in the field of stylistics in the light of a brief history and also offering perspectives on the future of a discipline that has grown even more exponentially in the last ten years.

Choosing the title *Language and Literature* for this Reader was not easy, for choices are closely bound up with the criteria adopted for the selection of papers and with the multiple designations that exist to describe work in the field. Other terms used to embrace the interface between language and literary studies include: stylistics, literary stylistics, literary linguistics, literary pragmatics, linguistic criticism and literary semantics. For example, the prominent professional organisation in this field (PALA) is called the Poetics and Linguistics Association. There are a range of major journals, including *Style*; *Language and Style*; *Poetics*; *Poetica*; *Language and Literature*; *Journal of Literary Semantics* and an even wider range of series and titles embracing such work from leading international publishers, all revealing different variations in their designation. The terms *language* and *literature* are, of course, themselves both highly problematic. 'Language' has innumerable inflections that in turn embrace different descriptive and theoretical orientations; and the term 'literature' continues to be endlessly problematised in both theory and practice.

The focus of most of the papers in this volume is, however, on applications of language analysis to a range of mostly canonical literary texts. This focus does not eschew discussion of the strengths and limitations of different linguistic analytical frameworks, and does not disqualify questions about canonicity and literariness. Neither does it mean that authors of articles are inattentive to issues in linguistic and literary theory. It does mean, however, that the main purpose of the Reader is to illustrate work in which texts are analysed primarily as verbal artefacts, drawing, where appropriate, on stylistic theory and linguistic descriptive frameworks in order to make that analysis as detailed, systematic and replicable as possible and to argue that interpretations, however ideologically positioned, cannot be divorced from the particular linguistic texture of the literary text.

RC and PS, Nottingham

ACKNOWLEDGEMENTS

The editors and publishers would like to thank the following for permission to reproduce copyright work:

Sinclair, J.M. 'Taking a poem to pieces' in Fowler, R. *Essays on Style and Language*,
Copyright © 1966 Routledge, Kegan Paul. Reproduced by permission of Taylor &
Francis Books UK.

Permission from estate of Philip Larkin for 'First Sight' in *The Whitsun Weddings*, 1964,
Faber and Faber Ltd. Reproduced by kind permission of the publisher.

Reprinted by permission of Farrar, Straus and Giroux, LLC: 'First sight' in *Collected
Poems* by Philip Larkin. Copyright © 1988, 2003 by the Estate of Philip Larkin.

Lodge, D. 'Stylistics' in *The Language of Fiction*, Copyright © 1966 Routledge, Kegan
Paul. Reproduced by permission of Taylor & Francis Books UK.

Halliday, M.A.K. (1973) 'Linguistic Function and Literary Style: An Inquiry into the
Language of William Golding's *The Inheritors*' in Chatman, S. *Literary Style: A
Symposium* © 1972 Oxford University Press, pp. 330–68. Extracts reproduced by
kind permission of the publishers.

Extracts from William Golding, *The Inheritors* (1955) by kind permission of the publishers, Faber and Faber Ltd.

Widdowson, H.G. (1972) 'On the deviance of literary discourse', *Style*, VI, 3: 294–306.
Reproduced by kind permission of *Style* journal.

Traugott, E.C. and Pratt, M.L. (1977) 'Applying linguistics' in *Linguistics for Students of
Literature* (NY: Harcourt Brace Jovanovich), pp. 19–34. Reproduced by kind permission of Elizabeth Traugott.

'love is more thicker than forget' is reprinted from *Complete Poems 1904–1962*, by E.E.
Cummings, edited by George J. Firmage, by permission of W.W. Norton &
Company. Copyright © 1991 by the Trustees from the E.E. Cummings Trust and
George James Firmage.

Extracts from Samuel Beckett, *Murphy* (1938) extracts reproduced by kind permission
of the publishers Grove Press Inc.

Fowler, R. (1981) 'Linguistic criticism' in *Literature as Social Discourse* (London: Batsford), pp. 24–45. Reproduced by kind permission of Mrs Paddy Pipe-Fowler.

Leech, G.N. *A Linguistic Guide to English Poetry* (Longman, 1969), pp. 103–11. Pearson
Education Ltd. Reprinted with permission.

Short, M.H. (1980) 'Discourse analysis and drama' *Applied Linguistics*, II, 2: 180–202.
Reprinted by permission of Oxford University Press and the author.

Pinter, H. 'Trouble in the Works' from *Collected Shorter Plays*, Volume II. Copyright © 1977 by H. Pinter, Ltd. Used by permission of Grove/Atlantic, Inc. and Faber and Faber Ltd.

Toolan, M. (1986) 'Poem, reader, response: Making sense with "Skunk Hour"', in Nicholson, C. and Chaterjee, R. (eds). *Tropic Crucible* (Singapore: Singapore Univ Press), pp. 84–97. Reproduced by permission of National University of Singapore Press (www.nus.edu.sg/npu).

Reprinted by permission of Farrar, Straus and Giroux, LLC: 'Skunk Hour' from *Collected Poems* by Robert Lowell. Copyright © 2003 by Harriet Lowell and Sheridan Lowell.

'Style and interpretation in Hemingway's "Cat in the Rain"', pp. 65–80 from Carter, R. (ed.) *Language and Literature*, Copyright © 1982 Routledge. Reproduced by permission of Taylor & Francis Books UK.

'Cat in the Rain' reprinted with the permission of Scribner, an imprint of Simon & Schuster Adult Publishing Group, from *In Our Time* by Ernest Hemingway. Copyright 1925 Charles Scribner's Sons. Copyright renewed 1953 by Ernest Hemingway.

'Cat in the Rain' from the *Complete Short Stories* published by Jonathan Cape. Reprinted by permission of The Random House Group Ltd.

Nash, W. 'Changing the guard at Elsinore' pp. 23–41 from Carter, R. and Simpson, P. (eds) *Language, Discourse and Literature*, Copyright © 1989 Routledge. Reproduced by permission of Taylor & Francis Books UK.

Van Peer, W. 'But what is literature?: Toward a descriptive definition of literature', pp. 127–41 from Sell, R. (ed.) *Literary Pragmatics*, Copyright © 1990 Routledge. Reproduced by permission of Taylor & Francis Books UK.

Reproduced with permission from Green, K. 'Deixis and the poetic persona', *Language and Literature* I, 2: 121–34. Copyright © 1992, by permission of the author and Sage Publications Ltd.

Tate, A. (1994) 'Bakhtin, addressivity, and the poetics of objectivity' in Sell, R. and Verdonk, P. *Literature and the New Interdisciplinarity* (Amsterdam: Rodopi), pp. 135–50. Reproduced by permission of the publisher.

Williams, W.C. 'The Red Wheelbarrow' from *Collected Poems: 1909–1939*, Volume I, copyright © 1938 by New Directions Publishing Corp. Reprinted by permission of New Directions Publishing Corp and Pollinger Ltd.

Wales, K. 'Teach yourself rhetoric: an analysis of Philip Larkin's "Church Going"', pp. 134–58 from Verdonk, P. (ed.) *Twentieth Century Poetry: From Text to Context*, Copyright © 1993 Routledge. Reproduced by permission of Taylor & Francis Books UK.

Larkin, P. 'Church Going' is reprinted from *The Less Deceived* by permission of The Marvell Press, England and Australia.

Werth, P. '"World Enough and Time": deictic space and the interpretation of prose', pp. 181–205 from Verdonk, P. and Weber, J-J. (eds) *Twentieth Century Fiction: From Text to Context*, Copyright © 1995 Routledge. Reproduced by permission of Taylor & Francis Books UK.

Cook, G. (1996) 'Making the subtle difference: literature and non-literature in the classroom' in Carter, R. and McRae, J. (eds) *Language, Literature and the Learner* (Longman: Pearson Education Ltd), pp. 151–65. Reprinted with permission.

Cinzano advert reproduced by permission of Cellar Trends (http://www.cellartrends.co.uk).

Weber, J.-J. (2000) 'Educating the reader: narrative technique and evaluation in Charlotte Perkins Gilman's *Herland*' in Bex, T., Burke, M. and Stockwell, P. (eds) *Contextualized Stylistics* (Amsterdam: Rodopi), pp. 181–94. Reproduced by permission of the publisher.

Gilman, C.P. *Herland* extracts reproduced by kind permission of the publishers The Women's Press, London (1997)

Simpson, P. (2000) 'Satirical humour and cultural context: with a note on the curious case of Father Todd Unctuous', in Bex, T., Burke, M. and Stockwell, P. (eds) *Contextualized Stylistics* (Amsterdam: Rodopi), pp. 243–66. Reproduced by permission of the publisher.

Stockwell, P. '(Sur)real stylistics: from text to contextualizing' in Bex, T., Burke, M. and Stockwell, P. (eds) *Contextualized Stylistics* (Amsterdam: Rodopi), pp. 15–38. Reproduced by permission of the publisher.

Poem by Hugh Sykes Davies, copyright not located.

Gibbs, R.W. (2002) 'Feeling moved by metaphor', in Csabi S. and Zerkowitz, J. (eds) *Textual Secrets* (Budapest: Eotvos Lorand University), pp. 13–28. Reproduced by kind permission of Ray Gibbs.

Reproduced with permission from McIntyre, D. 'Point of view in drama: a sociopragmatic analysis of Dennis Potter's *Brimstone and Treacle*', *Language and Literature* XIII, 2: 139–60. Copyright © 2004, by permission of the author and Sage Publications Ltd.

Extract from Dennis Potter's *Brimstone and Treacle*, 1978, Eyre Methuen Publishing Ltd. Reproduced by kind permission of Judy Daish Associates Ltd.

Reproduced from Stubbs, M. 'Conrad in the computer', *Language and Literature* 14: 5–24. Copyright © 2005, by permission of the author and Sage Publications Ltd.

Emmott, C. '"Split selves" in fiction and in medical "life stories": cognitive linguistic theory and narrative practice' in Semino, E. and Culpeper, J. (eds) *Cognitive Stylistics*, 2002, pp.153–81. With kind permission by John Benjamins Publishing Company, Amsterdam/Philadelphia. www.benjamins.com, and the Foundation of Language.

Gavins, J. 'Too much blague? An exploration of the text worlds of Donald Barthelme's *Snow White*', pp. 129–44 from Gavins, J. and Steen, G. (eds) *Cognitive Poetics in Practice*, Copyright © 2003 Routledge. Reproduced by permission of Taylor & Francis Books Ltd.

Excerpts reprinted with the permission of Scribner, an imprint of Simon & Schuster Adult Publishing Group, and SLL/Sterling Lord Literistic, Inc. from *Snow White* by Donald Barthelme. Copyright © 1967 by Donald Barthelme. All rights reserved.

Semino, E. 'A cognitive stylistic approach to mind style in narrative fiction' in Semino, E. and Culpeper, J. (eds) *Cognitive Stylistics*, 2002, pp.95–122. With kind permission by John Benjamins Publishing Company, Amsterdam/Philadelphia. www.benjamins.com, and the Foundation of Language.

Reproduced from Sotirova, V. 'Connectives in free indirect style; continuity or shift?' *Language and Literature* XIII, 3: 216–34. Copyright © 2004, by permission of the author and Sage Publications Ltd.

PART ONE

Foundations

Chapter 1

Taking a poem to pieces

JOHN SINCLAIR

This paper explores the foundations to a linguistic analysis of a literary text by focusing on the syntax of a poem, arguing that such features of language organisation often go unnoticed or uncommented on in traditional literary analyses. Sinclair acknowledges the consequent mismatches between the linguist's and the literary critic's terminologies but guards against naive correlations between descriptive terms and interpretations of meaning. In fact, the paper is resistant to interpretive and especially evaluative readings, arguing that no reading is possible until the language of the text is analysed explicitly and systematically and Sinclair deliberately and provocatively stops short of any such interpretation. Papers such as this led to numerous debates in the late 1960s between literary and language specialists, with literary critics bemoaning the reductiveness of such analysis and linguists bemoaning the absence or, at best, the impressionistic nature of much literary criticism and commentary of such texts.

For further developments in the study of syntax in poetry see Sinclair (1982), Austin (1985) and several papers in Carter (1982). The paper is one in a line of linguistic studies of Larkin's poetry – see Wales, Chapter 15, this volume – where linguists are drawn to analyse the seeming ordinariness of his syntax and use of language in general.

THIS CHAPTER IS DESIGNED to carry the reader of literature to the brink of linguistics. In recent years a number of linguists have attempted to describe linguistic features as they occur in literary texts, hoping that their descriptions might help a reader to understand and appreciate the text (for example, Halliday 1964, Hill 1955, Levin 1962). I have chosen a short, recent, lyric poem. It contains no magnetic peculiarities of language; in fact most critics, I imagine, would ignore the language altogether. My hypothesis is that the grammatical and other patterns are giving meaning in a more complex and tightly packed way than we expect from our familiarity with traditional methods of describing language. Modern methods of linguistic analysis, based on more comprehensive and detailed theories of language, can at least tackle the problem of describing literature. In this paper the accent will be on grammar; there is little to say about the vocabulary of such a short text when we have no proper description of English vocabulary patterns to use as a basis; the phonology and orthography (the study of the sound- and letter-sequences and combinations) are also largely ignored – with reluctance – for reasons of space and simplicity.

First sight

1   Lambs that learn to walk in snow
When their bleating clouds the air
Meet a vast unwelcome, know
Nothing but a sunless glare.
5   Newly stumbling to and fro
All they find, outside the fold,
Is a wretched width of cold.
As they wait beside the ewe,
Her fleeces wetly caked, there lies
10   Hidden round them, waiting too,
Earth's immeasurable surprise.
They could not grasp it if they knew,
What so soon will wake and grow
Utterly unlike the snow.

Philip Larkin

[. . .] Moving on to the structure of the sentences, we recognize two elements, in the primary analysis; what we call a *free* clause and what we call a *bound* clause (for more detailed information the reader is referred to Halliday 1961). *They could not grasp it* is a typical free clause, and *when their bleating clouds the air* or *newly stumbling to and fro* are bound clauses. No distinction is made at this depth of detail between clauses containing a finite or a non-finite verb, since their operation in the structure of sentences is almost identical. Using just this one distinction, we can plot the occurrence of these clauses relative to each other and relative to the lines in the poem. (See Table 1.1, opposite.)

It will be seen that no account has been taken of two clauses in the poem; in the first line, *that learn to walk in snow* and in the sixth, *they find*. These clauses are not operating in sentence structure at all; instead they are forming part of the structure of what we are going to call *nominal groups*. If they operated directly in sentence structure then *all, outside the fold, is a wretched width of cold* would be isolated as a complete clause. There is nothing in the shape of this word-sequence to prohibit it standing as a clause, but it is not the one in the poem. Clauses which do not form discrete elements of the structure of sentences are called *rankshifted* clauses.

In everyday English, in the mass of sentences which contain α and β the sequence αβ is most common. Discontinuity, i.e. α[β] is rarer, and so is the sequence βα. The last sentence in the poem is a good example of the αβ type. It is the only one. The other three have discontinuous α, βα sequence, and both, in that order. But we can refine the idea of discontinuity a little with reference to a particular text like this one. As we read along the lines, we can say at certain points that we confidently expect something else to finish off a structure. If at the bottom of a page one reads *He put* one expects on the next page to read about not only something to put but somewhere to put it. If one reads *He*

Table 1.1 Sentence structure

Exponents of 'α'	Line No.	Sentence structure line	Exponents of 'β'	Sentence structure
Lambs that learn to walk in snow	1	α –		
	2	β	When their bleating clouds the air	α[β]α
Meet a vast unwelcome, know	3	(– α)α –		
Nothing but a sunless glare.	4	(– α)		
	5	β	Newly stumbling to and fro	βα
All they find, outside the fold,	6	α –		
Is a wretched width of cold.	7	(– α)		
	8	β	As they wait beside the ewe,	βα[ββ]
	9	βα –	Her fleeces wetly caked,	
there lies	10	ββ	Hidden round them, waiting too,	
Earth's immeasurable surprise.	11	(– α)		
They could not grasp it	12	αβ	if they knew,	αββ
	13	β –	What so soon will wake and grow	
	14	(– β)	Utterly unlike the snow.	

α and β are elements of sentence structure expounded by free and bound clauses respectively. To account for interruptions, the symbols α – and β – in column 3 indicate that a clause is interrupted by a line-ending or another clause, and (– α) and (– β) indicate the conclusion of an interrupted clause. In column 5 is given the structure of the four sentences, with square brackets surrounding the symbol for a clause which occurs inside the one whose symbol precedes the bracket.

played one is a lot less certain what will follow; in fact, if it was not contrary to normal printers' practice we would not be surprised if the next page started with a period. Now the effect which we can presume an intruding element to have will depend in any instance on the strength of the current expectations. It is clear that strong expectations have been set up in both the cases of discontinuous clauses here: *lambs that learn to walk in snow* . . . and *there lies*. . . . It is interesting, too, that both occurrences of the item *wait* are in bound clauses which either precede or interrupt free ones. Here there is a serious difficulty in terminology. A term is needed to indicate a sentence in which the onset of a predictable α is delayed or in which its progress is interrupted. Unfortunately, whatever term is coined is liable to be construed as a contextually meaningful label. I want to use the term *arrest* for this type of structure, without wishing to suggest that *any* occurrence of this structure produces an 'effect' of arrestment. Pseudo-linguistic literature is already too full of naive correlations between a noise or a structure and explicit meanings. I wish my terms to carry only as much contextual meaning as terms like *finite, predicate*. With this in mind, let us say that the first three sentences in the poem are *arrested*, whereas the last one is not.

In sentence 1, then (structure α[β]α), the progress of the first α is interrupted by the β. Sentence 2 (βα) by beginning with β, delays the onset of the α. Both these exponents of arrest appear in sentence 3 (βα[ββ]) where the solitary α has its onset delayed and its progress interrupted.

Next we must consider the structure of the clauses in this poem. We recognize four primary elements of clause structure, the subject (S), predicator (P), complement (C) and adjunct (A). Every part of every clause must be ascribed to one or other of these four elements (the exceptions are irrelevant to our present purpose). The subject and complement(s) are usually nominal groups, the predicator a verbal group, and adjuncts are adverbial groups. Let us plot the structure of clauses in much the same way as we did the structure of sentences. In this diagram the slanting line (/) denotes the place where an intruding clause appears and the vertical line (|) denotes where a line boundary occurs. The rankshifted clauses in both cases are part of the subject of another clause (see Table 1.2).

As with the sentences, let us see how well the clauses fit the lines. Here there is a clear difference between free and bound clauses. Though simple in structure, all the free clauses except the last have a line boundary in the middle, and in the last bound one there is a line boundary.

What is the meaning of a line-boundary? Clearly its meaning depends upon its relation to the surrounding grammar. If it occurs between sentences (as at the end of lines 4 and 11) it is *congruent* with the grammar, and its meaning is of reinforcement, or the like. If it occurs between clauses or at any lower rank, then its meaning is dependent on the nature of the predictions that have been set up. Thus a line boundary occurring between α and β in most cases simply reinforces, emphasizes the structural boundary. It adds, perhaps, a slight element of surprise to the occurrence of the β. On the other hand, a line boundary occurring between β and α will reinforce the prediction of the β, will reinforce the *arrest* that was mentioned above.

A line boundary within a clause will follow the same pattern, according to the amount of prediction that precedes it. Table 1.3 shows the line boundaries in this poem classified by

(*a*)   Grammatical rank; sentence, clause and group.
(*b*)   Type, i.e. *arresting* (when predictions have been set up)
        releasing (where there are no remaining *grammatical* predictions).

It is clear from Tables 1.2 and 1.3 that in the first three sentences the free clauses are all arrested, whereas in the last sentence the free clause is neutral and a bound one is

Table 1.2 Clause structure

Exponent	Free	Bound	Rankshifted
Lambs that learn to walk in snow/| meet a vast unwelcome	S/|PC		
that learn to walk in snow			SPA
When their bleating clouds the air		ASPC	
know | Nothing but a sunless glare.	P|C		
Newly stumbling to and fro		APA	
All they find outside the fold | Is a wretched width of cold.	SA|PC		
they find			SP
As they wait beside the ewe		ASPA	
Her fleeces wetly caked		SAP	
There lies / | Earth's immeasurable surprise.	SP/|C		
Hidden round them,		PA	
waiting too		PA	
They could not grasp it	SPC		
if they knew,		ASP	
What so soon will wake and grow | Utterly unlike the snow.		SAP|A	

Table 1.3 Line boundaries (including stanza boundary)

Line ref.	Rank	Between structures	Arrest/Release
4	Sentence	Sentence/sentence	
7	Sentence	Sentence/sentence	
11	Sentence	Sentence/sentence	
2	Clause	β/α	Arrest
5	Clause	β/α	Arrest
8	Clause	β/α	Arrest
10	Clause	β/α	Arrest
12	Clause	β/ β	Release
1	Group	S/P	Arrest
3	Group	P/C	Arrest
6	Group	A/P	Arrest
9	Group	P/C	Arrest
13	Group	P/A	Release

released. The only reason we have to expect the last line in the poem is a metrical one. Again the last sentence is quite different from the others.

One common feature of English grammar is not represented in the clause or sentence structure of this poem. This is *linkage*, words like *and*, *but*, *however*, *in fact* which occur so often in conversation and writing. In this poem, each sentence, and each free or bound clause, stands rather separate. The only examples of such words, the *but* of line 4 and *and* of line 13, link items inside clauses, and do not affect the isolation of clauses and sentences.

All the free clauses are affirmative. No interrogatives, exclamations, imperatives. Also, all free clauses are transitive, and only one bound clause is (line 2). So transitivity is here carried almost entirely by the free clauses. [. . .] The sequence of the elements of clause structure is pretty much what would be expected in everyday English. Unusual sequences of elements of clause structure form a familiar set of devices in the language of poetry, but in this poem it must be noted that the adjuncts scarcely ever occur in other than the commonest position for them. *Newly* (line 5) and *outside the fold* (6) are slightly unusual and are discussed further below; *so soon* (line 13) is perhaps slightly in advance of its commonest position.

Two points must be made, in greater detail, in regard to the punctuation of adjuncts.

(a) Line 6 *outside the fold*. Note the comma preceding this adjunct. Without it one would naturally tend to regard *outside the fold* as part of the rankshifted clause and analyse as follows:

$$S \qquad\qquad P \qquad\qquad C$$
all they find outside the fold / is / a wretched width of cold.

The element 5 would be uttered with one intonation contour with its most prominent point on the last syllable, *fold*. But because of the comma, we analyse

$$S \qquad\quad A \qquad\quad P \qquad\quad C$$
all they find / outside the fold / is / a wretched width of cold

and there are now two separate intonation contours, a falling one, most prominent on *find*, and a slightly rising one, most prominent on *fold*.

The difference in meaning is slight, here, between presence or absence of the comma. A point is made about the lambs actually going outside the fold. Compare the difference using the verb *see*.

all they see outside the fold, is a wretched width of cold.
all they see, outside the fold, is a wretched width of cold.

Since the adjunct, in part of the surrounding non-rankshifted clause, is out of position, the total contrast is similar to the contrast between

John, outside the office, found it nice.
and
John found it nice outside the office.

(b) Line 13. There is no comma after *grow*, but there is a line boundary, which has something of a parallel effect, of separating one piece of language from another. Here the difference in meaning is considerable. Compare

> I want him to grow like me (i.e. assuming he will grow, specifying direction)
> I want him to grow, like me (i.e. specifying growth and drawing a parallel)

Because the text has an ambiguous structure at this point, the adjunct 'utterly unlike the snow' is, in my interpretation, made to do double duty. A rough paraphrase might run thus:

> The snow will not grow but something else will, and when it does it will grow to look utterly unlike the snow.

These are, of course, not the only points of punctuation. For example, some readers may disagree with the analysis of lines 9–10, on the grounds that *lies hidden* is a unit which cannot be divided by a clause boundary; again the absence of a comma supports this, whereas the occurrence of a line-end suggests the division. The poet has the advantage here also of a combination of the alternative meanings.

We may now consider structure at the next rank below clause, the *group*, the unit out of which clauses are made. It may consist of one or more words, and groups have a direct relation to elements of clause structure. There are three kinds of group, as we have already noted, *nominal*, *verbal* and *adverbial* (see Table 1.4). Verbal groups are the simplest kind in this text, since nearly all the verbal groups are single-word, present-tense items. This is only remarkable when one thinks of the enormous variety of choices available, e.g. *might have come, could have been coming, wasn't going to come, came sailing, came to talk, oughtn't to have been going to be avoiding coming to see*. With such a restricted selection, the variations are liable to be quite striking, and as one might expect they distinguish sentence 4 from the others. None of the verbs in this sentence are 'simple present' items. Two contain *modal verbs*, i.e. *could* and *will*; one of these is negative and the other 'double-headed' – *wake and grow*. The third is a 'simple past' item in a bound clause. The only other complication in verbal groups is the *learn to walk* in line 1.

The adverbial groups are not very prominent. The three main kinds of adverbial group are the grammatical binding groups like *when, if*, the adverbs like *newly* and *so soon*, and the prepositional groups like *in snow*. In this poem the main point again is their simplicity. Of the second and third types, there is no distinction made in the poem that is not covered by facts already adduced and not worth repeating. It is useful, though, to note that free clauses are almost devoid of adjuncts. *Outside the fold*, which has already been discussed, is the only one. In contrast, and excluding *when, as* and *if*, there are eight adjuncts in bound clauses. So the free clauses have complements but not adjuncts, and the bound ones adjuncts but not complements.

The selection of *newly* deserves a note. Although an adverb, *newly* is not one that is commonly found in a free clause structure. Its commonest place is as a verbal modifier when that verb is itself a nominal modifier; as in *a newly-advertised product, a newly-made dress*. I suppose that the average reader notes that there is something a little odd about the line, but has no difficulty, of course, in understanding it.

Before passing on to the nominal group, which has the most variety at this rank, let

Table 1.4 Groups

Nominal	Verbal	Adverbial
Lambs that learn to walk in snow⎤	learn to walk	in snow
that snow⎦	---	When
their bleating the air	clouds	
a vast unwelcome	Meet know	
Nothing but a sunless glare.		
	stumbling	Newly to and fro
All they find the fold⎤	find	outside the fold
they ⎦	---	
a wretched width of cold⎤	Is	
cold⎦		
they the ewe	wait	As beside the ewe
Her fleeces there	caked lies	wetly
them	Hidden waiting	round them too
Earth's immeasurable surprise.		
They it they	could not grasp knew	if
What	will wake and grow	so soon
the snow		Utterly unlike the snow

us note a pattern in the relation between group and line. The first line is one element of clause structure (though containing a rankshifted clause), the fourth is also, and the seventh, apart from the unstressed initial syllable. Line 11 is one group, and so is line 14. So the last line in each sentence contains but one element of clause structure: although the average length of an element is a third of a line.

Although the nominal groups are interesting, they are not nearly as complex as we are accustomed to meeting with quite frequently in normal conversation. Here is a table of them [see Table 1.5].

There are no numerals, and no nouns occurring pre-head (like *stone* in *stone wall*). There is never more than one adjective, and not many of those, and only in complements. Subjects are simplest; six out of the ten of them are single pronouns, and the others are the two *hq* structures and two *dh*, the exponent of *d* being a possessive deictic. Those two *dh* groups are subjects in bound clauses.

Rankshifted nominal groups are those which occur as elements in the structure of other nominal groups, or as the 'objects' of prepositions. In this poem they are again simple in structure, and regularly consist of a single lexical item, with or without a non-possessive deictic.

The complements are most complex. The single *dh* structure is complement to the only transitive bound clause, and the single *h* structure is, as one might expect, in the last sentence. This leaves us with the four complements involving adjectives, and is an interesting place to pause for a moment because these four complements also contain most of the unusual vocabulary juxtapositions to be found in the poem. *Vast unwelcome* is very unusual, so also *a wretched width of cold, width* being the odd man out. *Sunless glare* is less striking, perhaps because *sun* and *glare* are common enough together; *immeasurable*

Table 1.5 Nominal group structure

In subject		In complement		Rankshifted	
hq	(lambs that learn to walk in snow)	dh	(the air)	h	(snow)
h	(that)	deh	(a vast unwelcome)		
dh	(their bleating)	h + deh	(nothing but a glare)	dh	(the fold)
hq	(all they find)	dehq	(a wretched width of cold)	h	(cold)
h	(they)	deh	(earth's surprise)	dh	(the ewe)
h	(they)				
dh	(her fleeces)	h	(it)	h	(earth)
				dh	(the snow)
h	(they)				
h	(they)				
h	(what)				

Symbols used

h = headword, round which the rest pivots.

d = deictic, a word like *the*, *a*, *which*, coming at the beginning of the group.

e = an adjective.

q = anything which comes after the headword (in this poem the only exponents of q are rank-shifted clauses – see 'subject' column – and a prepositional group – see 'complement' column).

surprise is unusual particularly with *Earth's* in front. Any two of the three words might pass unnoticed, but these three in this particular grammatical arrangement look very odd indeed.

The paucity of lexical comment reflects the fact that objective description of vocabulary patterns is still impossible. It happens that our present text does not contain many strong lexical patterns; apart from those mentioned above, perhaps *bleating clouds* in line 2 is the only one that invites attention.

Parallel to the note on *newly*, above, should be a note on *unwelcome*. This word is commonly an adjective, and one of the features of an adjective is that it is incapable of being headword in a group modified by *a*, *an*. Here an unusual effect is created by the occurrence of just such a nominal group, forcing us to accept *unwelcome* as a noun. The prefix perhaps regains some of the meaning it could have in Old English.

The structure of the words in this poem brings out a pattern which is worthy of tentative consideration. If we study the *affixes*, it is fairly easy to divide the *inflectional* (e.g. lamb*s*, stumbl*ing*, cloud*s*, lie*s*, fleece*s*) from the others. Of the others, there are a few that mark a different word-class from the same item without the affix, e.g. *wetly*, *newly*, *utterly*, *width*. Lastly there is a small group where the affix drastically affects the meaning of the word:

unwelcome, sun*less*, *im*measurable, *un*like

There is a similarity about these four, so that they may be labelled *reversing affixes*, though here the classification is less rigorous than before. One way or another, these affixes reverse the meaning of the rest of the word of which they form a part. What can we say about the contribution of such word structure in poetry, and in this poem? In poetry it is possible both to have one's cake and eat it, rather more so than in other varieties of a language. But when, for example, a trade union official said recently: 'We are not yet talking about strike action', he contrived to be ominous. The paradox of a sentence like 'I will never mention the name of John Smith' has a meaning which can be used in poetry. We could describe it as bipartite: in the present case

(*a*)   A statement about the speaker's future intentions. At least one possibility is cut out. By knowing something of what the speaker is *not* going to do, we also know a little about what he *is* going to do. Very little, very vaguely, but by no means negligible.

(*b*)   The accomplishment of the utterance, including the mention of John Smith's name. The physical fact of the utterance can never be ignored in literary writing.

According to the same argument, the last line of this poem contrives to begin to say something about the appearance of whatever is about to wake and grow, and it also manages to mention the snow. The importance of the latter half of the meaning is borne out by the rarity, in love poetry, of lines like:

> Her smile was not in the least like the grin of a decomposing vampire however notionally accurate they may be.

Three out of the four complex nominal groups in this poem, then, show a reversing affix. On both grammatical and lexical grounds we have shown that these places are important. The fourth,

> a wretched width of cold

contents itself with a word-class affix and unusual lexis and grammar.

The last line in the poem also shows this feature of reversal, and the structure of the line above it shows another device, common enough in poetry, which gives the reader only a vague meaning. It is the traditional 'brush-off' structure. 'Something I'd prefer not to talk about' 'Nothing you won't know all about in time' 'What doesn't concern you . . .'

The grammar has led us briefly into lexical and contextual matters, but only sporadically. There is still a great deal unsaid about the structure of this little poem, and even what has been said suffers by being in the nature of commentary. Grammar deals with contrasts, multiple choices from a great many systems simultaneously, and the meaning of a grammatical statement can only be fully elicited with reference to the total grammatical description. Nevertheless, the exercise shows how some aspects of the meaning of the poem can be described quite independently of evaluation.

References

Austin, T. (1985) *Language Crafted: Linguistic Theory of Poetic Syntax*. Bloomington: Indiana University Press.

Carter, R. (ed.) (1982) *Language and Literature: An Introductory Reader in Stylistics*. London: Allen and Unwin/Routledge.

Halliday, M.A.K. (1961) 'Categories of the theory of grammar', *Word* 17: 241–92.

Halliday, M.A.K. (1964) 'The linguistic analysis of literary texts', Proceedings of the IXth Congress of Linguists (The Hague).

Hill, A.A. (1955) 'An analysis of "The Windhover": an experiment in structural method', *PMLA* 70 (5): 968–78.

Levin, S.R. (1962) *Linguistic Structures in Poetry*. The Hague: Mouton.

Sinclair, J. (1982) 'Lines about lines', in R. Carter (ed.) *Language and Literature: An Introductory Reader in Stylistics*, London: Allen and Unwin/Routledge, pp. 163–78.

Extracted from John Sinclair (1966) 'Taking a poem to pieces', in R. Fowler (ed.) *Essays on Style and Language*, London: RKP, pp. 68–81.

Chapter 2

Stylistics

DAVID LODGE

In this paper, extracted from his classic *Language of Fiction* (1966), David Lodge takes a broad historical view of the development of close verbal analysis of literary texts, leading the reader through some key positions in twentieth-century textual analysis. Lodge was one of the first literary critics to propose a more systematic, less impressionistic account of the verbal workings of literary texts, especially the novel. Lodge reminds us that stylistics has important and influential historical antecedents in work by Leo Spitzer and discusses the varying emphases on different aspects of style in different traditions of European stylistics and Anglo-American New Criticism. For Lodge at that time the role of evaluation and the part played by texts in history are key factors for literary critics that are neglected by stylisticians.

This Reader covers work over an approximately 40-year period but for further reading in the history of stylistics and for further discussion of East European and Russian Formalist traditions in the twentieth century, see Birch (1989), Sebeok (1960), Epstein (1978) and Bennett (1990).

M ODERN STYLISTICS HAS ADDRESSED itself to several interrelated tasks: to clarify the concept of style, to establish for 'style' a central place in the study of literature, and to develop more precise, inclusive, and objective methods of describing style than the impressionistic generalizations of traditional criticism. The first thing that must be said about modern stylistics is that it is largely a Continental phenomenon. Stylistics as such scarcely exists as an influential force in Anglo-American criticism of literature in English. We have no Spitzer, no Auerbach, no Ullman. We have no body of work comparable to that revealed by a glance through Hatzfeld's *Critical Bibliography of the New Stylistics Applied to the Romance Literatures 1900–1952* (1953). There is in this respect a chasm between Anglo-American studies and modern language studies which is rarely bridged. The loss has, I think, been mutual. Anglo-American criticism has ignored valuable developments in methods of accounting for the literary use of language flexible enough to take in both poetry and prose. English criticism, in particular, has maintained a somewhat provincial mistrust of formal grammatical analysis and description from which its own characteristically intuitive and empirical approach could benefit. Continental stylistics, on the other hand, generally yields up thinner results in terms of interpretation and evaluation of individual texts, than the best Anglo-American criticism. It has not really asked itself the fundamental questions about the nature of literary discourse, [. . .] which are the commonplaces of literary theorizing in England and America. It remains blandly convinced of a success which is not altogether apparent to an outsider.

Both the virtues and the limitations of Continental stylistics can be traced in its origins. It developed rapidly after the First World War, to fill a vacuum existing in the humanities in Europe between, on the on the one hand, a dryly academic philology preoccupied with the formulation of laws to explain phonological and semantic change, and on the other a peculiarly barren form of literary history which was interested in every question about a work except 'what does it mean?' Leo Spitzer has graphically described this situation, and his own response to it, in his essay, *Linguistics and Literary History*. His solution to the problem was stylistics: 'Stylistics, I thought, might bridge the gap between linguistics and literary history.'

Spitzer is usually considered to have been the father of 'the New Stylistics' (Spitzer 1948). His achievement was twofold. Firstly, he asserted and demonstrated that in causally relating a particular literary effect to a particular ordering of language, criticism takes a significant step forward from impressionistic appreciation – goes perhaps as far as it can go in 'explaining' the effectiveness of a literary text. Winifred Nowottny (1962) cites a particularly forceful example of this in her book, *The Language Poets Use*:

> Many people have observed the sublime effect of the passage (Genesis i. 3.) – And God said, let there be light; and there was light', but it was left to Spitzer to trace the sublime effect to its cause – in the fact that the syntax in which the fulfilment of God's command is described is as close as possible to the syntax of the command itself. (In the original Hebrew, as Spitzer points out, the parallelism of command and fulfilment is even closer: *jehi aur vajehi aur*.)

Spitzer's second main achievement was his development of a method for dealing with the style of long and complex structures, such as novels. It has been described as the 'linguistic' or 'philological circle'. Here is Spitzer's own description of the genesis of the method:

> In my reading of modern French novels, I had acquired the habit of underlining expressions which struck me as aberrant from general usage, and it often happened that the underlined passages, taken together, seemed to offer a certain consistency. I wondered if it would not be possible to establish a common denominator for all or most of these deviations: could not the common spiritual etymon, the psychological root of several individual 'traits of style' in a writer be found, just as we have found an etymon common to various fanciful word formations?

In reading a novel of the Parisian underworld, *Bubu de Montparnasse* by Charles

Louis-Philipe, Spitzer is struck by a particular use of '*a cause de*', suggesting causality, where the average person would see only coincidence. Further examination reveals a similarly individual use of '*parce que*' and '*car*':

> Now I submit the hypothesis that all these expansions of causal usages in Philippe cannot be due to chance: there must be 'something the matter' with his conception of causality. And now we must pass from Philippe's style to the psychological etymon, to the radix in his soul. I have called the phenomenon in question 'pseudo-objective motivation': Philippe, when presenting causality as binding for his characters, seems to recognize a rather objective cogency in their sometimes awkward, sometimes plati-tudinous, sometimes semi-poetic reasonings; his attitude shows a fatalistic, half-critical, half-understanding, humorous sympathy with the necessary errors and thwarted strivings of these underworld beings dwarfed by inexorable social forces. The pseudo-objective motivation, manifest in his style, is the clue to Philippe's *Weltanschauung*; he sees, as has also been observed by literary critics, without revolt but with deep grief and a Christian spirit of contemplativity, the world functioning wrongly with an appearance of tightness, of objective logic. The different word-usages, grouped together . . . lead towards the psychological *etymon*, which is at the bottom of the linguistic as well as of the literary inspiration of Philippe.

I am not competent to assess the validity of this interpretation, and quote it merely to illustrate the nature of Spitzer's method. As a method it is perhaps vulnerable, and I want to make quite clear what to me seems valuable and what questionable, in it. In the general idea of a movement of critical response from particular example to a hypo-thetical general interpretation, and back again to further examples which confirm or modify the hypothesis, Spitzer provides a sound model for critical procedure, its novelty inhering mainly in its application to linguistic usage. What is unsatisfactory about Spitzer's method – to an English critic, at least – is its orientation to psychological explanation and interpretation of the artist, and to the formulation of those grand sche-matic theories about cultural change and the history of ideas so dear to the Germanic scholarly mind. Not that either kind of speculation is invalid, but they can obscure the unique interest and value of the particular text with which the critic starts. The linguistic circle, in other words, will be most useful if it works with a hypothesis about the text considered as a whole, and not except by inference, with a hypothesis about the psyche of the author or about his age.

Spitzer's method has been criticized for being insufficiently objective and scientific. But a true 'science' of stylistics is a chimera as I shall argue later. Few men have borne more persuasive witness than Spitzer to the necessary part played by intuition in literary criticism. Criticism can be more objective, more 'scientific' if you wish, than it often is; but in the last resort we rely on 'talent, experience, and faith'.

There is, however, in Spitzer's method a certain bias which it is important to recognize. This is, very naturally, a philological bias. The linguistic features which interest Spitzer are those which deviate from the norm: 'I had acquired the habit of under-lining expressions which struck me as aberrant from general usage.' And this explains why Spitzer's interest is in connecting – not linguistics and literary criticism – but linguistics and literary history: 'The individual stylistic deviation from the general norm must represent a historical step taken by the author, I argued: it must reveal a shift of the soul of the epoch, a shift of which the writer has become conscious and which he would translate into a necessarily new linguistic form.' This may be true but it by no means follows that what strikes the philologically-trained reader as an important deviation from normal linguistic usage is equally important in determining the literary identity of a given text; still less that deviation thus conceived is the sole area of stylistic activity. As René Wellek has pointed out: 'often the commonplace, the most normal linguistic elements are the constituents of literary structure.'

This built-in philological bias and its contingent emphasis on deviation is characteristic of the 'Continental' school of Stylistics (or New Stylistics as it is sometimes called). Consider, for instance Professor Stephen Ullmann's study *Style in the French Novel* (1957). Ullmann belongs to a later generation than Spitzer's and offers a more sophisticated theoretical apparatus, and one more congenial to the English critic. He recognizes, for instance, that the same device of style may give rise to a variety of effects, and that 'to study the integration of a stylistic device into the structure of a novel, one must examine it at the level of the entire work of art.' But the interests, the principles behind the book are essentially philological. Ullmann isolates certain stylistic devices such as free indirect speech, and inversion, and examines with great subtlety and perception their functioning in the work of certain French novelists. But he starts with a philological rather than a critical response: the devices are selected for close examination, it would appear, because they relate crucially to his reading of particular texts, but because they interest him as deviations from normal usage. And in exploring the function of such devices, Ullmann relies heavily on the consensus of existing critical opinion about his authors, on which his findings constitute a kind of philological gloss.

'The tasks of stylistics are . . . primarily descriptive,' says Ullmann. This follows logically from the philological principles of stylistics of this type; but it suggests that stylistics can never become a fully comprehensive method of literary criticism. The difference may be stated in this way: for both stylistician and critic, the interest and meaning of any linguistic element is determined by its context; but for the latter the context is, in the first place, the individual text considered as a whole, while for the former it is the language considered as a whole.

There is a further and more important distinction: the stylistician seems to be obliged to rely upon an implied or accepted scale of value, or to put aside questions of value altogether; whereas the literary critic undertakes to combine analysis with evaluation.

References

Bennett, T. (1990) *Formalism and Marxism*. London: Routledge.

Birch, D. (1989) *Language, Literature and Critical Practice*. London: Routledge.

Epstein, E.L. (1978) *Language and Style*. London: Methuen.

Hatzfeld, H.A. (1955) *A Critical Bibliography of the New Stylistics Applied to the Romance Literatures 1900–1952*. Chapel Hill: University of North Carolina.

Nowottny, W. (1962) *The Language Poets Use*. London: Athlone Press.

Sebeok, T. (ed.) (1960) *Style in Language*. Cambridge, MA: MIT Press.

Spitzer, L. (1948) *Linguistics and Literary History: Essays in Stylistics*. Princeton, NJ: Princeton University Press.

Ullman, S. (1957) *Style in the French Novel*. Cambridge: Cambridge University Press.

Extracted from David Lodge (1966) 'Stylistics', in *The Language of Fiction*. London: RKP, pp. 52–8.

Chapter 3

Linguistic function and literary style: an inquiry into the language of William Golding's *The Inheritors*

M.A.K. HALLIDAY

This is one of the groundbreaking analyses in stylistics. Written and presented at a symposium on literary style in August 1969, Halliday uses his own developing systemic-functional model of language to demonstrate the establishment of a peculiar world-view in William Golding's *The Inheritors*. He shows how relatively simple stylistic features set up a norm from which the novel can then deviate. The chapter is important as a modern linguistic delineation of the nature of foregrounding as being both a textual and an interpretative matter: though the sense of a text is dependent on stylistic features, any single set of features can create a norm and also be used to deviate from it. The hallmarks of stylistics are already present in this chapter: engagement with literary criticism, a rigorous and tested analytical model, a concern for interpretative as well as textual matters, and an openness to falsifiability.

Halliday was here drawing on his own work (Halliday 1967a, 1967b, 1968, 1970, fully developed in 2004), which has been hugely influential in stylistics over the past 40 years. For further examples of analyses that draw on systemic-functional linguistics, see Simpson (1993), Carter (1997) and Toolan (1998).

[. . .]

*T*HE *INHERITORS* PROVIDES A remarkable illustration of how grammar can convey levels of meaning in literature; and this relates closely to the notion of linguistic functions [. . .]. The foregrounded patterns, in this instance, are ideational ones, whose meaning resides in the representation of experience; as such they express not only the content of the narrative but also the abstract structure of the reality through which that content is interpreted. [. . .]

The book is, in my opinion, a highly successful piece of imaginative prose writing; in the words of Kinkead-Weekes and Gregor (1967) in their penetrating critical study, it is a 'reaching out through the imagination into the unknown.' The persons of the story are a small band of Neanderthal people, initially eight strong, who refer to themselves as 'the people'; their world is then invaded by a group of more advanced stock, a fragment of a tribe, whom they call at first 'others' and later 'the new people.' This casual impact – casual, that is, from the tribe's point of view – proves to be the end of the people's world, and of the people themselves. At first, and for more than nine-tenths of the book (pp. 1–216), we share the life of the people and their view of the world, and also their view of the tribe: for a long passage (pp. 137–80) the principal character, Lok, is hidden in a tree watching the tribe in their work, their ritual and their play, and the account of their doings is confined within the limits of Lok's understanding, requiring at times a considerable effort of 'interpretation.' At the very end (pp. 216–38) the standpoint shifts to that of the tribe, the inheritors, and the world becomes recognizable as our own, or something very like it. I propose to examine an aspect of the linguistic resources as they are used first to characterize the people's world and then to effect the shift of world-view.

For this purpose I shall look closely at three passages taken from different parts of the book; [two of] these are reproduced [below]. Passage A is representative of the first, and longest, section, the narrative of the people; it is taken from the long account of Lok's vigil in the tree. Passage C is taken from the short final section, concerned with the tribe; while [there is a transitional] passage B [not reproduced in this book . . .]. Linguistically, A and C differ in rather significant ways [. . .].

Passage A (*The Inheritors*, pp. 106–7)

The bushes twitched again. Lok steadied by the tree and gazed. A head and a chest faced him, half-hidden. There were white bone things behind the leaves and hair. The man had white bone things above his eyes and under the mouth so that his face was longer than a face should be. The man turned sideways in the bushes and looked at Lok along his shoulder. A stick rose upright and there was a lump of bone in the middle. Lok peered at the stick and the lump of bone and the small eyes in the bone things over the face. Suddenly Lok understood that the man was holding the stick out to him but neither he nor Lok could reach across the river. He would have laughed if it were not for the echo of the screaming in his head. The stick began to grow shorter at both ends. Then it shot out to full length again.

The dead tree by Lok's ear acquired a voice.

'Clop!'

His ears twitched and he turned to the tree. By his face there had grown a twig: a twig that smelt of other, and of goose, and of the bitter berries that Lok's stomach told him he must not eat. This twig had a white bone at the end. There were hooks in the bone and sticky brown stuff hung in the crooks. His nose examined this stuff and did not like it. He smelled along the shaft of the twig. The leaves on the twig were red feathers and reminded him of goose. He was lost in a generalized astonishment and excitement. He shouted at the green drifts across the glittering water and heard Liku crying out in answer but could not catch the words. They were cut off suddenly as though someone had clapped a hand over her mouth. He rushed to the edge of the water and came back. On either side of the open bank the bushes grew thickly in the flood; they waded out until at their farthest some of the leaves were opening under water; and these bushes leaned over.

The echo of Liku's voice in his head sent him trembling at this perilous way of bushes towards the island. He dashed at them where normally they would have been rooted on dry land and his feet splashed. He threw himself forward and grabbed at the branches with hands and feet. He shouted:

'I am coming!'

[Halliday goes on to cite passage B (*The Inheritors*, pp. 215–17), which is not reproduced here.]

Passage C (*The Inheritors*, pp. 228–9)

The sail glowed red-brown. Tuami glanced back at the gap through the mountain and saw that it was full of golden light and the sun was sitting in it. As if they were obeying some signal the people began to stir, to sit up and look across the water at the green hills. Twal bent over Tanakil and kissed her and murmured to her. Tanakils lips parted. Her voice was harsh and came from far away in the night.

'Liku!'

Tuami heard Marlan whisper to him from by the mast.

'That is the devil's name. Only she may speak it.'

Now Vivani was really waking. They heard her huge, luxurious yawn and the bear skin was thrown off. She sat up, shook back her loose hair and looked first at Marlan then at Tuami. At once he was filled again with lust and hate. If she had been what she was, if Marlan, if her man, if she had saved her baby in the storm on the salt water –

'My breasts are paining me.'

If she had not wanted the child as a plaything, if I had not saved the other as a joke – He began to talk high and fast.

'There are plains beyond those hills, Marlan, for they grow less; and there will be herds for hunting. Let us steer in towards the shore. Have we water – but of course we have water! Did the women bring the food? Did you bring the food, Twal?'

Twal lifted her face towards him and it was twisted with grief and hate.

'What have I to do with food, master? You and he gave my child to the devils and they have given me back a changeling who does not see or speak.'

The sand was swirling in Tuami's brain. He thought in panic: they have given me back a changed Tuami; what shall I do? Only Marlan is the same — smaller, weaker but the same. He peered forward to find the changeless one as something he could hold on to. The sun was blazing on the red sail and Marlan was red. His arms and legs were contracted, his hair stood out and his beard, his teeth were wolf's teeth and his eyes like blind stones. The mouth was opening and shutting.

'They cannot follow us, I tell you. They cannot pass over water.'

The clauses of passage A (56 in total, numbers in brackets that follow show occurrences) are mainly clauses of action (21), location (including possession) (14), or mental process (16); the remainder (5) are attributive. Usually the process is expressed by a finite verb in simple past tense (46). Almost all of the action clauses (19) describe simple movements (*turn*, *rise*, *hold*, *reach*, *throw forward*, etc.); and of these the majority (15) are intransitive; the exceptions are *the man was holding the stick*, *as though someone had clapped a hand over her mouth*, *he threw himself forward*, and *the echo of Liku's voice in his head sent him trembling at this perilous way of bushes towards the island*. The typical pattern is exemplified by the first two clauses, *the bushes twitched again* and *Lok steadied by the tree*, and there is no clear line, here, between action and location: both types have some reference in space, and both have one participant only. The clauses of movement usually (16) also specify location, e.g. *the man turned sideways in the bushes*, *he rushed to the edge of the water*; and on the other hand, in addition to what is clearly movement, as in *a stick rose upright*, and what is clearly location, as in *there were hooks in the bone*, there is an intermediate type exemplified by *(the bushes) waded out*, where the verb is of the movement type but the subject is immobile.

The picture is one in which people act, but they do not act on things; they move, but they move only themselves, not other objects. Even such normally transitive verbs as *grab* occur intransitively: *he grabbed at the branches* is just another clause of movement (cf. *he smelled along the shaft of the twig*). Moreover a high proportion (exactly half) of the subjects are not people; they are either parts of the body (8) or inanimate objects (20), and of the human subjects half again (14) are found in clauses which are not clauses of action. Even among the four transitive action clauses, cited above, one has an inanimate subject and one is reflexive. There is a stress set up, a kind of syntactic counterpoint, between verbs of movement in their most active and dynamic form, that of finite verb in independent clause, in the simple past tense characteristic of the direct narrative of events in a time sequence, on the one hand, and on the other hand the preference for non-human subjects and the almost total absence of transitive clauses. It is particularly the lack of transitive clauses of action with human subjects (there are only two clauses in which a person acts on an external object) that creates an atmosphere of ineffectual activity: the scene is one of constant movement, but movement which is as much inanimate as human and in which only the mover is affected – nothing else changes. The syntactic tension expresses this combination of activity and helplessness.

No doubt this is a fair summary of the life of Neanderthal man. But passage A is not a description of the people. The section from which it is taken is one in which Lok is observing and, to a certain extent, interacting with the tribe; they have captured one of the people, and it is for the most part their doings that are being described. And the tribe are not helpless. The transitivity patterns are not imposed by the subject-matter; they are the reflection of the underlying theme, or rather of one of the underlying themes – the inherent limitations of understanding, whether cultural or biological, of Lok and his people, and their consequent inability to survive when confronted with beings at a higher stage of development. In terms of the processes and events as we would interpret them, and encode them in our grammar, there is no immediate justification for the predominance of intransitives; this is the result of their being expressed through the medium of the semantic structure of Lok's universe. In our interpretation, a goal-directed process (or, as I shall suggest below, an externally caused process) took place: someone held up a bow and drew it. In Lok's interpretation, the process was undirected (or, again, self-caused): *a stick rose upright* and *began to grow shorter at both ends*. (I would differ slightly here from Kinkead-Weekes and Gregor, who suggest, I think, that the form of Lok's vision is perception and no more. There may be very little processing, but there surely is some; Lok has a theory – as he must have, because he has language.)

Thus it is the syntax as such, rather than the syntactic reflection of the subject-matter, to which we are responding. This would not emerge if we had no account of the activities of the tribe, since elsewhere – in the description of the people's own doings, or of natural phenomena – the intransitiveness of the syntax would have been no more than a feature of the events themselves, and of the people's ineffectual manipulation of their environment. For this reason the vigil of Lok is a central element in the novel. We find, in its syntax, both levels of meaning side by side: Lok is now actor, now interpreter, and it is his potential in both these roles that is realized by the overall patterns of prominence that we have observed, the intransitives, the non-human subjects, and the like. This is the dominant mode of expression. At the same time, in passage A, among the clauses that have human subjects, there are just two in which the subject is acting on something external to himself, and in both these the subject is a member of the tribe; it is not Lok. There is no instance in which Lok's own actions extend beyond himself; but there is a brief hint that such extension is conceivable. The syntactic foregrounding, of which this passage provides a typical example, thus has a complex significance: the predominance of intransitives reflects, first, the limitations of the people's own actions; second, the people's world view, which in general cannot transcend these limitations – but within which there may arise, thirdly, a dim apprehension of the superior powers of the 'others,' represented by the rare intrusion of a transitive clause such as *the man was holding the stick out to him*. Here the syntax leads us into a third level of meaning, Golding's concern with the nature of humanity; the intellectual and spiritual developments that contribute to the present human condition, and the conflicts that arise within it, are realized in the form of conflicts between the stages of that development – and, syntactically, between the types of transitivity.

Passage A is both text and sample. It is not only these particular sentences and their meanings that determine our response, but the fact that they are part of a general syntactic and semantic scheme. That this passage is representative in its transitivity patterns can be seen from comparison with other extracts. It also exemplifies certain other relevant features of the language of this part of the book. We have seen that there is a strong preference for processes having only one participant: in general there is only one nominal element in the structure of the clause, which is therefore the subject. But while there are very few complements, there is an abundance of adjuncts (44); and most of these (40) have some spatial reference. Specifically, they are (a) static (25), of which most (21) are place adjuncts consisting of preposition plus noun, the noun being either an inanimate object of the immediate natural environment (e.g. *bush*) or a part of the body, the remainder (4) being localizers (*at their farthest*, *at the end*, etc.); and (b) dynamic (15), of which the majority (10) are of direction or non-terminal motion (*sideways*, *(rose) upright*, *at the branches*, *towards the island*, etc.) and the remainder (5) perception, or at least circumstantial to some process that is not a physical one (e.g. *(looked at Lok) along his shoulder*, *(shouted) at the green drifts*). Thus with the dynamic type, either the movement is purely perceptual or, if physical, it never reaches a goal: the nearest thing to terminal motion is *he rushed to the edge of the water* (which is followed by *and came back!*).

The restriction to a single participant also applies to mental process clauses (16). This category includes perception, cognition, and reaction, as well as the rather distinct sub-category of verbalization; and such clauses in English typically contain a 'phenomenon,' that which is seen, understood, liked, etc. Here however the phenomenon is often (8) either not expressed at all (e.g. *(Lok) gazed*) or expressed indirectly through a preposition, as in *he smelled along the shaft of the twig*; and sometimes (3) the subject is not a human being but a sense organ (*his nose examined this stuff and did not like it*). There is the same reluctance to envisage the 'whole man' (as distinct from a part of his body) participating in a process in which other entities are involved.

There is very little modification of nouns (10, out of about 100); and all modifiers are non-defining (e.g. *green drifts*, *glittering water*) except where (2) the modifier is the only semantically significant element in the nominal, the head noun being a mere carrier demanded by the rules of English grammar (*white bone things*, *sticky brown stuff*). In terms of the immediate situation, things have defining attributes only if these attributes are their sole properties; at the more abstract level, in Lok's understanding the complex taxonomic ordering of natural phenomena that is implied by the use of defining modifiers is lacking, or is only rudimentary.

We can now formulate a description of a typical clause of what we may call 'Language A,' the language in which the major part of the book is written and of which passage A is a sample, in terms of its process, participants and circumstances:

(1)   There is one participant only, which is therefore subject; this is:

    (a)   actor in a non-directed action (action clauses are intransitive), or participant in a mental process (the one who perceives, etc.), or simply the bearer of some attribute or some spatial property;

    (b)   a person (*Lok, the man, he*, etc.), or a part of the body, or an inanimate object of the immediate and tangible natural environment (*bush, water, twig*, etc.); unmodified, other than by a determiner which is either an anaphoric demonstrative (*this, that*) or, with parts of the body, a personal possessive (*his*, etc.).

(2)   The process is:

    (a)   action (which is always movement in space), or location-possession (including e.g. *the man had white bone things above his eyes* = 'above the man's eyes there were . . .'), or mental process (thinking and talking as well as seeing and feeling – a 'cunning brain'! – but often with a part of the body as subject);

    (b)   active, non-modalized, finite, in simple past tense (one of a linear sequence of mutually independent processes).

(3)   There are often other elements which are adjuncts, i.e. treated as circumstances attendant on the process, not as participants in it; these are:

    (a)   static expressions of place (in the form of prepositional phrases), or, if dynamic, expressions of direction (adverbs only) or of non-terminal motion, or of directionality of perception (e.g. *peered at the stick*);

    (b)   often obligatory, occurring in clauses which are purely locational (e.g. *there were hooks in the bone*).

A grammar of Language A would tell us not merely what clauses occurred in the text but also what clauses could occur in that language (see Thorne 1965). For example, as far as I know, the clause *a branch curved downwards over the water* does not occur in the book; neither does *his hands felt along the base of the rock*. But both of them could have. On the other hand, *he had very quickly broken off the lowest branches* breaks four rules: it has a human actor with a transitive verb, a tense other than simple past, a defining modifier, and a non-spatial adjunct. This is not to say that it could not occur. Each of these features is improbable, and their combination is very improbable; but they are not impossible. They are improbable in that they occur with significantly lower frequency than in other varieties of English (such as, for example, the final section of *The Inheritors*).

Before leaving this passage, let us briefly reconsider the transitivity features in the light of a somewhat different analysis of transitivity in English. [. . .] In these terms, the entire transitivity structure of Language A can be summed up by saying that there is no cause and effect. More specifically: in this language, processes are seldom represented as resulting from an external cause; in those instances where they are, the 'agent' is seldom a human being; and where it is a human being, it is seldom one of the people. Whatever the type of process, there tends to be only one participant; any other entities are involved only indirectly, as circumstantial elements (syntactically, through the mediation of a preposition). It is as if doing was as passive as seeing, and things no more affected by actions than by perceptions: their role is as in clauses of mental process, where the object of perception is not in any sense 'acted on' – it is in fact the perceiver that is the 'affected' participant, not the thing perceived – and likewise tends to be expressed circumstantially (e.g. *Lok peered at the stick*). There is no effective relation between persons and objects: people do not bring about events in which anything other than they themselves, or parts of their bodies, are implicated.

There are, moreover, a great many, an excessive number, of these circumstantial elements; they are the objects in the natural environment, which as it were take the place of participants, and act as curbs and limitations on the process. People do not act on the things around them; they act within the limitations imposed by the things. The frustration of the struggle with the environment, of a life 'poised . . . between the future and the past,' is embodied in the syntax: many of the intransitive clauses have potentially transitive verbs in them, but instead of a direct object there is a prepositional phrase. The feeling of frustration is perhaps further reinforced by the constant reference to complex mental activities of cognition and verbalization. Although there are very few abstract nouns, there are very many clauses of speaking, knowing and understanding (e.g. *Lok understood that the man was holding the stick out to him*); and a recurrent theme, an obsession almost, is the difficulty of communicating memories and images (*I cannot see this picture*) – of transmitting experience through language, the vital step towards that social learning which would be a precondition of their further advance.

Such are some of the characteristics of Language A, the language which tells the story of the people. There is no such thing as a 'Language B.' [There] is simply the point of transition between the two parts of the book. There is a 'Language C': this is the language of the last sixteen pages of the novel, and it is exemplified by the extract shown as passage C [above . . .]. [T]he switch is extremely sudden, being established in [. . .] three words [. . .] when Lok, with whom we have become closely identified, suddenly becomes *the red creature*.

[. . .]

By the time we reach passage C, the transition is complete. Here, for the first time, the majority of the clauses (48 out of 67) have a human subject; of these, more than half (25) are clauses of action, and most of these (19) are transitive. Leaving aside two in which the thing 'affected' is a part of the body, there is still a significant increase in the number of instances (17, contrasting with 5 in the whole of A and B together) in which a human agent is acting on an external object. The world of the inheritors is organized as ours is; or at least in a way that we can recognize. Among these are two clauses in which the subject is *they*, referring to the people ('the devils': e.g. *they have given me back a changeling*); in the tribe's scheme of things, the people are by no means powerless. There is a parallel here with the earlier part. In passage A the actions of the tribe are encoded in terms of the world-view of the people, so that [there is a] predominance of intransitive clauses [. . .]. Similarly, in passage C references to the people are encoded in terms of the world-view of the tribe, and transitive structures predominate; yet the only member of the people who is present – the only one to survive – is the captured baby, whose infant behaviour is described in largely intransitive terms (pp. 230–1). And the references to the people, in the dialogue, include such formulations as '*They cannot follow us, I tell you. They cannot pass over water*,' which is a [. . .] reassurance that, in a [. . .] world of cause and effect whose causes are often unseen and unknown, there are at least limits to the devils' power.

[. . .]

While there are still inanimate subjects in the clause (11), as there always are in English, there is no single instance in passage C of an inanimate agent. In A and B we had *the echo of Liku's voice in his head sent him trembling . . .*, *the branches took her, the water had scooped a bowl out of the rock*; in C we have only *the sail glowed, the sun was sitting in it, the hills grow less*. Likewise all clauses with parts of the body as subject (8) are now intransitive, and none of them is a clause of mental process. Parts of the body no longer feel or perceive; they have attributes ascribed to them (e.g. *his teeth were wolf's teeth*) or they move (*the lips parted, the mouth was opening and shutting*). The limbs may move and posture, but only the whole man perceives and reacts to his environment. Now, he also shapes his environment: his actions have become more varied – no longer simply movements; we find here *save*, *obey*, and *kiss* – and they produce results. Something, or someone, is affected by them.

Just as man's relation to his environment has altered, so his perception of it has changed; the environment has become enlarged. The objects in it are no longer the *twig*, *stick*, *bush*, *branch* of Language A, nor even the larger but still tangible *river*, *water*, *scars in the earth*. In [. . .] C we have *the mountain . . . full of golden light*, *the sun was blazing*, *the sand was swirling* (the last metaphorically); and also human artifacts: *the sail*, *the mast*. Nature is not tamed: the features of the natural environment may no longer be agents in the transitivity patterns, but neither are they direct objects. What has happened is that the horizons have broadened. Where the people were bounded by tree and river and rock, the tribe are bounded by sky and sea and mountain. Although they are not yet conquered, the features that surround them no longer circumscribe all action and all contemplation. Whereas Lok *rushed to the edge of the water and came back*, the new people *steer in towards the shore*, and *look across the water at the green hills*.

The Inheritors has provided a perspective for a linguistic inquiry of a kind whose relevance and significance is notoriously difficult to assess: an inquiry into the language of a full-length prose work. In this situation syntactic analysis is unlikely to offer anything in the way of new interpretations of particular sentences in terms of their subject-matter; the language as a whole is not deviant, and the difficulties of understanding are at the level of interpretation – or rather perhaps, in the present instance, re-interpretation, as when we insist on translating *the stick began to grow shorter at both ends* as 'the man drew the bow.' I have not, in this study, emphasized the use of linguistic analysis as a key; I doubt whether it has this function. What it can do is to establish certain regular patterns, on a comparative basis, in the form of differences which appear significant over a broad canvas. In *The Inheritors* these appear as differences within the text itself, between what we have called 'Language A' and 'Language C.' In terms of this novel, if either of these is to be regarded as a departure, it will be Language C, which appears only briefly at the very end; but in the context of modern English as a whole it is Language A which constitutes the departure and Language C the norm. There is thus a double shift of standpoint in the move from global to local norm, but one which brings us back to more or less where we started.

[. . .]

The establishment of a syntactic norm (for this is what it is) is thus a way of expressing one of the levels of meaning of the work: the fact that a particular pattern constitutes a norm *is* the meaning. The linguistic function of the pattern is therefore of some importance. The features that we have seen to be foregrounded in *The Inheritors* derive from the ideational component in the language system; hence they represent, at the level at which they constitute a norm, a world-view, a structuring of experience that is significant because there is no *a priori* reason why the experience should have been structured in this way rather than in another. More particularly, the foregrounded features were selections in transitivity. Transitivity is the set of options whereby the speaker encodes his experience of the processes of the external world, and of the internal world of his own consciousness, together with the participants in these processes and their attendant circumstances; and it embodies a very basic distinction of processes into two types, those that are regarded as due to an external cause, an agency other than the person or object involved, and those that are not. There are, in addition, many further categories and subtypes. Transitivity is really the cornerstone of the semantic organization of experience; and it is at one level what *The Inheritors* is about. The theme of the entire novel, in a sense, is transitivity: man's interpretation of his experience of the world, his understanding of its processes and of his own participation in them. This is the motivation for Golding's syntactic originality; it is because of this that the syntax is effective as a 'mode of meaning.' (See Firth 1957.)

The particular transitivity patterns that stand out in the text contribute to the artistic whole through the functional significance, in the language system, of the semantic options which they express. [. . .]

In *The Inheritors*, the syntax is part of the story. As readers, we are reacting to the whole of the writer's creative use of 'meaning potential'; and the nature of language is such that he can convey, in a line of print, a complex of simultaneous themes, reflecting the variety of functions that language is required to serve. And because the elements of the language, the words and phrases and syntactic structures, tend to have multiple values, any one theme may have more than one interpretation: in expressing some content, for example, the writer may invite us at the same time to interpret it in quite a different functional context – as a cry of despair, perhaps. It is the same property of language that enables us to react to hints, to take offence and do all the other things that display the rhetoric of everyday verbal interaction. A theme that is strongly foregrounded is especially likely to be interpreted at more than one level. In *The Inheritors* it is the linguistic representation of experience, through the syntactic resources of transitivity, that is especially brought into relief, although there may be other themes not mentioned here that stand out in the same way. Every work achieves a unique balance among the types and components of meaning, and embodies the writer's individual exploration of the functional diversity of language.

References

Carter, R. (1997) *Investigating English Discourse*. London: Routledge.

Firth, J.R. (1957) 'Modes of meaning', in *Papers in Linguistics* 1934–1951, London: Longmans, pp. 190–215 [original in *Essays and Studies* (*The English Association*, 1951)].

Halliday, M.A.K. (1967a) *Grammar, Society and the Noun*. London: H.K. Lewis.

Halliday, M.A.K. (1967b) 'Notes on transitivity and theme in English (Part I)', *Journal of Linguistics* 3: 37–81.

Halliday, M.A.K. (1968) 'Notes on transitivity and theme in English (Part II)', *Journal of Linguistics* 4: 179–215.

Halliday, M.A.K. (1970) 'Language structure and language function', in J. Lyons (ed.) *New Horizons in Linguistics*, Harmondsworth: Penguin, pp. 140–65.

Halliday, M.A.K. (2004) *An Introduction to Functional Grammar* (3rd edition, revised by C. Matthiessen). London: Arnold.

Kinkead-Weekes, M. and Gregor, I. (1967) *William Golding: A Critical Study*. London: Faber.

Simpson, P. (1993) *Language, Ideology and Point of View*. London: Routledge.

Thorne, J.P. (1965) 'Stylistics and generative grammars', *Journal of Linguistics* 1: 49–59.

Toolan, M. (1998) *Language in Literature*. London: Arnold.

Extracted from M.A.K. Halliday (1971) 'Linguistic function and literary style: an inquiry into the language of William Golding's *The Inheritors*', in S. Chatman (ed.) *Literary Style: A Symposium*, Oxford: Oxford University Press, pp. 330–68.

Chapter 4

On the deviance of literary discourse

HENRY WIDDOWSON

In this chapter from the early 1970s, Henry Widdowson asserts that linguists and literary critics look at literary texts for fundamentally different purposes. Elsewhere, Widdowson (1975) provocatively characterises stylistics as a discipline and 'English' as a subject. Here, he sets out an accommodation for stylisticians and literary scholars, identifying the area of common ground as he sees it between the two traditions, by focusing on the significance of special uses of language. Stylistics has commonly been regarded as placing an undue emphasis on linguistic deviance, and it is true that stylisticians for many years have been attracted to odd and unusual examples of language use in literature. Widdowson differentiates linguistic deviance from literary deflection, in order to demonstrate that stylisticians can have things to say about literary value and significance.

For further discussions of the status of deviance in stylistics, see Cook (1994), Carter (1997), van Peer (1986, 2007) and Bortolussi and Dixon (2003).

A GOOD DEAL OF WORK in literary stylistics has been concerned with the essentially descriptive linguistics problem of how to account for expressions which would normally be assigned an * (or perhaps a ? or even a ??) to designate deviance from well-formedness, but which occur fairly commonly in actual communication. The problem is that such expressions are interpretable in spite of the fact that they do not correspond with the well-formed strings generated by a grammar which is meant to represent the speaker's knowledge of his language. In other words, if a grammar accounts for the knowledge a language user has of his language, how does it come about that he knows how to interpret sentences which are not generated by the grammar? Discussion of this question (see Chomsky 1961, Katz 1964, Ziff 1964, Levin 1962, Thorne 1965, Fowler 1969, Butters 1970), as its history might indicate, has led to a consideration of literary texts as exemplification of the problem, and from there to a suggestion that the meaning of literary texts may in some sense be explicated in terms of grammatical statements.

Some of this work on deviant sentences and their interpretation has provided interesting insights into the way language is manipulated in literary writing (particularly, in my opinion, in the work of Thorne [. . .] 1965, 1970, 1971). But as I have suggested elsewhere (Widdowson 1972), much of it has a curiously irrelevant air about it. We are shown how literary texts can be described in linguistic terms, but such descriptions often seem to lead back to the grammar from which they came rather than towards any conclusions about the way the language functions to achieve a literary effect. The linguistic properties of the texts stand out in well-defined clarity, but their literary properties seem in consequence to be peripheral and out of focus. What I want to do in this paper is to suggest a different orientation to stylistic analysis: one which represents it not simply as a grammarian's problem-solving operation but as an attempt to explain how language is put to a unique communicative purpose in literary discourse.

It is important to recognize that stylistic analysis which derives from an interest in deviant sentences adopts an orientation to literature which is essentially different from that of the literary scholar, and that its findings have no necessary relevance to the concerns of literary criticism. Both the linguist and the literary scholar have an interest in literary texts, but their interests are different. The linguist sees them as data providing evidence of the operation of grammatical rules other than those of the standard grammar. The literary scholar sees them as aesthetic objects sufficient in themselves and having, as it were, [quoting Wordsworth] 'no need of a remoter charm, by thought supplied,' nor any interest unborrowed from their own intuitive judgements. Where the linguist tends to see a collection of sentences, the literary scholar sees a unique message.

Literary scholars have not been slow in pointing out this lack of coincidence of interest (see, for example, Hough 1969). It reveals itself in the way linguists bring their attention to bear on texts like *anyone lived in a pretty how town* and *A grief ago,* which many literary scholars would regard as little deserving of such scrutiny, rather than on texts which approximate more closely to 'normal' uses of language. As Wellek has pointed out: 'The danger of linguistic stylistics is its focus on deviations from, and distortions of, the linguistic norm. We get a kind of counter-grammar, a science of discards. . . . But often the most commonplace, the most normal, linguistic elements are the constituents of literary structure. A literary stylistics will concentrate on the aesthetic purpose of every linguistic device, the way it serves a totality, and will beware of the atomism and isolation which is the pitfall of much stylistic analysis' (Wellek 1960: 417–18). There have been a number of similar objections to the linguistic approach to stylistic analysis on the grounds that statements about linguistic structures, whether deviant or not, frequently fail to account for features of literary texts which make an essential contribution to their meaning. Thus Hendricks (1969) shows that there are aspects of the Shakespeare sonnet analysed in Levin (1964) in terms of equivalent structures which defy structural analysis in such terms. Again, Riffaterre (1966), discussing the analysis of Baudelaire's *Les Chats* in Jakobson and Lévi-Strauss (1962), makes the comment: 'No grammatical analysis of a poem can give us more than the grammar of the poem.'

The linguist then is interested primarily in making linguistic statements about texts which because of their structural peculiarities represent attractive data. Such statements may have implications for exegesis, which is what the literary scholar is aiming at, but it is not the purpose of such statements that they should. Even less is it the purpose of the linguist to point them out. After the linguist has finished his analysis, there remains the major task of establishing its significance. We should not be surprised if its significance turns out to be marginal.

What I am suggesting is that the linguist and the literary scholar, though both having an interest in literary texts, see these texts as two different kinds of phenomena. My view is that only when there is an agreement as to which phenomenon might profitably be the common concern of both are there likely to be any significant advances in stylistics studies. Part of my purpose in this paper is to suggest what this phenomenon might be.

[. . .] The first step is to consider the distinction between two kinds of abnormality: that which can be accounted for in terms of violations of grammatical rules, and that which can only be accounted for in terms of departure from some norm of usage. Following Halliday (1971), we might call the first of these *deviations* and the second *deflections*. The point about deflections is that they are grammatically impeccable: indeed they are often cited as illustrations of the recursive properties of a grammar. For example, it is an essential feature of a generative grammar of the familiar algebraic kind that no limit is imposed on the number of relative clauses that can be embedded into a noun phrase. The following therefore is a perfectly, almost ostentatiously, grammatical structure.

> A man who had been soaked in water, and /who had been/ smothered in mud, and /who had been/ lamed by stones, and /who had been/ cut by flints and /who had been/ stung by nettles, and /who had been/ torn by briars. . . . etc . . .
> (Where the slant lines indicate optional deletions).

The operation of recursive rules of this kind has the effect of combining into syntagmatic sequence elements which are paradigmatically related and which normally represent alternative choices for filling a place in syntactic structure. This shift from the paradigmatic to the syntagmatic is pointed out in Jakobson (1960), who sees it as a defining feature of the poetic function of language. It can be illustrated by arranging the passage given above (an extract from *Great Expectations*) into the familiar substitution table as follows:

A man who had been			
	soaked	in	water
	smothered		mud
	lamed	by	stones
	cut		flints
	stung		nettles
	torn		briars

The items ranged vertically in the columns are in paradigmatic relationship in that any could be selected to make up the given structure, and in this sense are equivalent. If we select all the alternatives, we thereby project this equivalence into the syntagmatic plane to produce the Dickens passage:

> A man who had been soaked in water, and smothered in mud, and lamed by stones, and cut by flints, and stung by nettles, and torn by briars . . .

Levin's work on the linguistic structures of poetry (Levin 1964) is a study of deflections in that it shows how poetry exploits grammatical rules to create patterns of language over and above those which the grammar itself requires. Patterns of 'arrest' and 'release' as discussed in Sinclair (1966) are again instances of deflection, and have nothing to do with the violation of grammatical constraints.

The essential point is that the study of deflection leads to a recognition that there are regularities of language in literary texts which are rhetorical rather than grammatical in nature, and which have to do with the structure of the texts as pieces of communication. These are regularities which are realized in the message itself rather than projected from the code. But when we come to look at deviations we find, as is observed in Thorne (1965), Leech (1965), Levin (1965), and Halliday (1971), that they do not occur in isolation but pattern in with other features of the text. Indeed, if they did not it would often be impossible to impose any interpretation on them. It would appear that deviations must also be regarded as rhetorical features in so far as they occur in regular patterns, even though as isolated phenomena they can be discussed in grammatical terms. We can now, I think, begin to see why grammatical statements do not necessarily provide insights into how literary texts are to be interpreted. Since a grammar is a characterization of sentences, all that grammatical statements can do is to indicate how the sentences of a text conform or do not conform to those generated by a grammar. But a text is a use of sentences in the performance of an act of communication, and if one wishes to understand what is being communicated one has to discover how individual grammatical features contribute to the message of the text as a whole. In other words, it is only when one recognizes the rhetorical function of linguistic forms that one can assess their significance. Deviations and deflections are both rhetorical functions: it happens that only the former are also subject to grammatical comment. But it is only when they are seen as fulfilling a rhetorical function that their relevance to exegesis can be appreciated.

It seems to me that a good deal of work on both deviance and deflection has often appeared inconsequential because it has resulted in essentially linguistic statements without any suggestion as to how these relate to the communicative properties of the texts in question. In the early work of Halliday (e.g. Halliday 1964) texts are anatomized into arrays of linguistic constituents but we are left in the dark as to what their communicative import might be. Levin (1964) in presenting his analysis of a Shakespeare sonnet makes the comment: 'The analysis . . . is not an attempt at a full-scale interpretation; it is an attempt to reveal the role that couplings play in the total organization of the poem.' But, as the criticism of Hendricks [1969] indicates, the role that couplings play cannot be understood until it is related to other linguistic aspects of the poem. And the 'total organization' of the poem can only mean its total rhetorical organization, of which couplings are only one part. One may sympathize with the reluctance of the linguist to involve himself in the problems of interpretation of texts (he has, after all, been trained to see language primarily in terms of isolated sentences out of context). But the fact remains that if he wishes to say anything enlightening about texts he cannot just treat them as exemplification of linguistic categories. Sooner or later he must say something about how and what they communicate since it is of the nature of texts that they do communicate meanings and are not simply patterns of formal objects.

It seems to me that the question that any textual analyst should be concerned with is not 'What are the linguistic peculiarities of this text and how can they be accounted for in grammatical terms?' but rather 'What is being communicated in this text and how are the resources of the language being used to bring this communication about?' In other words, if the linguist's exercises in stylistics are to be of relevance to literary studies, they can no longer be restricted to a consideration of texts as collections of tokens of grammatical types, but must focus on those aspects of literary texts which are of interest to the literary scholar – viz. their communicative properties as pieces of discourse. It is not text as a grammatical phenomenon but as a rhetorical phenomenon that must be the object of stylistic study. There are a number of signs that this is now being recognized as linguists are increasingly turning their attention to the social functions of language. It is interesting to compare Halliday's earlier stylistic work (as in Halliday 1964) with his recent analysis of the language of William Golding's *The Inheritors* (Halliday 1971 [and Chapter 3 in this volume]), and Ohmann's shift of emphasis from the consideration of literature as sentences (Ohmann 1966) to an analysis in terms of illocutionary acts (Ohmann 1971).

Once we make the adjustment to thinking of literature as communication, we can see a way of reconciling the two observations referred to above, that literary effects seem to depend in some way on linguistic deviance, and yet literary effects can often be achieved without doing violence to grammatical rules. I would suggest that it is a defining feature of literature that it is always deviant as communication but that this does not necessarily involve grammatical deviance. This point can be illustrated by reference to recent observations in G. Lakoff (1970) and R. Lakoff (1969): G. Lakoff considers the following sentences:

> I mentioned that Sam smoked pot last night.
> Last night, I mentioned that Sam smoked pot.

He points out that sentence (1) is open to two interpretations: one in which the time adverbial relates to the verb *mentioned* in the main sentence and the other in which it relates to the verb *smoked* in the subordinate sentence. Sentence (2) is only grammatical in relation to the first reading in spite of the fact that, in isolation, it is a well-formed sentence. In consequence one has to accept the possibility of context-dependent grammaticalness. R. Lakoff makes the same point in connection with sentences like the following:

> The boy is over there.
> A boy is over there.

She comments: '. . . it is impossible to state a rule using as the environment the superficial form of the sentence alone to predict whether (3) or (4) will be correct in a given sentence.'

We may leave aside what problems this view of grammaticalness is likely to create for the grammarian. What is of relevance to the present discussion is the fact that an utterance may have all the marks of correspondence to a well-formed sentence, and yet be deviant as an utterance in a given context. Consider, for example, the following exchange. If one is treating it simply as an exemplification of grammatical units, it may be said to consist of two well-formed sentences. If one considers it as a use of language, however, it is deviant:

A: Where is the boy?
B: She is over there.

If (as I myself would wish to do) one restricts grammatical statements to the structural properties of sentences, one is obliged to accept that grammatical sentences may be used to perform deviant communicative acts, and that there is no necessary correspondence between grammatical and communicative deviance.

My choice of the deviant use of a personal pronoun as illustration was deliberate because what I want to suggest now is that the clue to the deviance of literary discourse is to be found in the way personal pronouns are used. Grammarians have long recognized that the category of person functions as a connection whereby the linguistic system is plugged in, as it were, to the situation in which language is used. As Palmer, for example, has recently put it, 'Person is probably the one linguistic category that has clearly defined reference to non-linguistic entities' (Palmer 1971: 89). This connecting-up function of person is brought out in the observation by Jakobson (1963) that the first and second person pronouns (which he refers to as 'shifters') can only be partially described in terms of either code or message, but are in fact elements of dual character which represent an overlap of the two. Commenting on Jakobson's remarks, Barthes suggests that it might be through a study of such pronoun shifters 'that we should seek the semiological definition of the messages which stand on the frontiers of language, notably certain forms of literary discourse' (Barthes 1967: 23). What I wish to do is to take up this suggestion and to make a move in the direction of such a definition.

First and second person define the communication situation. Physically, so to speak, the first person is the sender and the second person the receiver; and socially the first person is the addresser and the second person the addressee. In normal circumstances the sender/addresser and the receiver/addressee are not distinct, so that the communication situation may be represented as follows:

I		**II**
Sender	_____	Receiver
Addresser		Addressee

In literary writing, as has often been observed, the first person is commonly used to refer to someone/something other than the writer, and the second person to someone/something other than the reader. Thus all kinds of animate and inanimate entities, which are clearly incapable of sending or receiving messages, assume the roles of addresser and addressee: these include the moon, sun, stars, night, clouds, brooks, mountains, birds, a spade, a Grecian urn, and the beautiful railway bridge over the silv'ry Tay, to mention but a few. With reference to literary communication, then, the situation might be represented as follows:

I_1_____	I_2_____	II_2_____	II_1_____
Sender	Addresser	Addressee	Receiver

One of the consequences of this dual focus situation, of course, is that the sender is freed of the constraints imposed upon him by normal communication conditions and can express ideas and experiences without, as it were, ontological commitments. Consider the following line from Wilfred Owen's poem *Strange Meeting:* 'I am the enemy you killed, my friend.' Obviously, such an utterance is impossible in normal communication conditions since the minimal requirement made of sender is that he should be alive. But notice that if we replace the first person with the third person we get a perfectly normal utterance: 'He is the enemy you killed, my friend.' It will not do, of course, simply to say that the literary first person corresponds to the conventional third person. It does not. In Owen's poem, for instance, the dead soldier speaks of an experience which no observer could be conscious of and which requires a first person addresser. Similarly, when the third person occurs in literary texts experiences which could never normally be predicated of a third person are expressed. But we cannot set up a correspondence between literary third person and conventional first person since, again, a third person observer is presupposed. Consider, for example, the description of Tom Brangwen's death in D.H. Lawrence's *The Rainbow*:

> As he staggered something in the water struck his legs, and he fell. Instantly he was in the turmoil of suffocation. He fought in the black horror of suffocation, fighting, wrestling, but always borne down, borne inevitably down. Still he wrestled and fought to get himself free, in the unutterable struggle of suffocation, but he always fell again deeper. Something struck his head, a great wonder of anguish went over him, then the blackness covered him entirely.
>
> In the utter darkness, the unconscious, drowning body was rolled along, the water pouring, washing, filling in the place. . . .

We might say that in the first paragraph of this passage we are, as it were, inside Tom Brangwen and the description is from the first person point of view, whereas in the second paragraph we are outside Tom Brangwen and the description is from the third person point of view. But there is no sense of incongruity about this because the pronoun *he* refers neither to the third nor to the first person in the conventional sense but to some unique amalgam of the two. This synthesis of 1st and 3rd person is related to the hybrid form of speech presentation in fiction which Bally (1912) called *le style indirect libre*. A discussion of Dickens' use of this device is to be found in Gregory (1965), and a comment on the use made of it by Jane Austen appears in Hough (1969). See also Ullmann (1957).

It is easy to see that similar arguments could be used to relate the second and third persons. Thus, for example, the elaborate vocatives in poems like Keats's *Ode to the Nightingale* and Shelley's *Ode to the West Wind* clearly incorporate a third person element; and this must be the case with any address to a non-human entity. The use of the third person pronoun with second person implications is perhaps less common, though it occurs fairly frequently in love poems which are clearly addressed to the object of affection but employ the third person pronoun, and, perhaps less obviously, in satire.

We might represent the relationship between the conventional and literary use of person as follows:

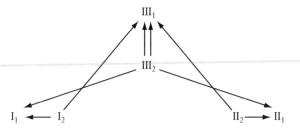

It is possible then to distinguish four types of person operating in the 'detached' communication situation within which literature functions, deriving from the three normal types in the following way.

1st person	I / III
2nd person	II / III
3rd person	III / I
4th person	III / II

If it is accepted that the category of person defines a communication situation, then it is clear that the irregular realization of this category in literary writing establishes communicative deviance. I would suggest that any use of language which assumes the dual focus situation as outlined above is by definition deviant, even though it may not be overtly marked as such by structural abnormality. It follows that any linguistic element, no matter how 'normal' it might appear to be, may take on a value in a literary text, by virtue of the way it patterns with other elements in the text, which may not correspond with the value it would normally assume in conventional communication. Put another way, one can never be certain that any expression in a literary text is used in a conventional sense. As with the meanings of the personal pronouns discussed above, the meaning of any literary expression is a function of the relationship between the meaning it assumes in conventional discourse and the meaning it assumes as an element of a pattern within a literary text. In other words, because a literary text is deviant as communication the values of conventional communication no longer apply. Consequently the literary text depends upon a unique patterning of language to provide linguistic elements with new values over and above those which these elements carry with them from conventional use. It is in this sense that literary texts create their own language and thereby necessarily express a reality other than that which is communicable by conventional means.

References

Bally, C. (1912) 'Le style indirect libre en français moderne', *Germanisch-Romanische Monatshift* 4: 549–56, 597–606.

Barthes, R. (1967) *Elements of Semiology*. London: Jonathan Cape (trans. from R. Barthes (1967) *Eléments de Sémiologie*. Paris: Editions de Seuil).

Bortolussi, M. and Dixon, P. (2003) *Psychonarratology: Foundations for the Empirical Study of Literary Response*. Cambridge: Cambridge University Press.

Butters, R.R. (1970) 'On the interpretation of "deviant utterances" ', *Journal of Linguistics* 6 (1): 105–10.

Carter, R. (1997) *Investigating English Discourse*. London: Routledge.

Chomsky, N. (1961) 'Some methodological remarks on generative grammar', *Word* 17: 219–39 (Reprinted as 'Degrees of grammaticalness', in J. Fodor and J. Katz (eds) (1964) *The Structure of Language*. Englewood Cliffs, NJ: Prentice Hall, pp. 119–36).

Cook, G. (1994) *Discourse and Literature*. Oxford: Oxford University Press.

Fowler, R. (1969) 'On the interpretation of "nonsense strings"', *Journal of Linguistics* 5 (1): 75–83 (Reprinted in R. Fowler (1971) *The Languages of Literature*. London: Routledge and Kegan Paul).

Gregory, M. (1965) 'Old Bailey speech in *A Tale of Two Cities*', *A Review of English Literature* 6 (2): 42–55.

Halliday, M.A.K. (1964) 'Descriptive linguistics in literary studies', in G.I. Duthie (ed.) *English Studies Today, Third Series*. Edinburgh: University Press, pp. 25–39 (Reprinted in M.A.K. Halliday and A. McIntosh (1966) *Patterns of Language*. London: Longman, and in D.C. Freeman (ed.) (1970) *Linguistics and Literary Style*. New York: Holt, Rinehart and Winston, pp. 57–72).

Halliday, M.A.K. (1971) 'Linguistic function and literary style: an inquiry into the language of William Golding's *The Inheritors*', in S. Chatman (ed.) *Literary Style: A Symposium*. New York: Oxford University Press, pp. 330–68.

Hendricks, W.O. (1969) 'Three models for the description of poetry', *Journal of Linguistics* 5 (1): 1–22.

Jakobson, R. (1960) 'Closing statement: linguistics and poetics', in T.A. Sebeok (ed.) *Style in Language*, Cambridge, MA: MIT Press, pp. 350–77.

Jakobson, R. (1963) 'Shifters, verbal categories and the Russian verb', in *Essais de Linguistic Générale*, Paris: Editions de Minuit, pp. 5–21.

Jakobson, R. and Lévi-Strauss, C. (1962) ' "Les Chats" de Charles Baudelaire', *L'Homme* 2.

Hough, G. (1969) *Style and Stylistics*. London: Routledge and Kegan Paul.

Katz, J. (1964) 'Semi-sentences', in J. Fodor and J. Katz (eds) *The Structure of Language*, Englewood Cliffs, NJ: Prentice Hall, pp. 400–16.

Lakoff, G. (1970) *Linguistics and Natural Logic*. Ann Arbor: University of Michigan.

Lakoff, R. (1969) 'Transformational grammar and language teaching', *Language Learning* 19 (1/2): 117–40.

Leech, G. (1965) ' "This bread I break": language and interpretation', *A Review of English Literature* 6 (2), 66–75 (Reprinted in D.C. Freeman (ed.) (1970) *Linguistics and Literary Style*, New York: Holt, Rinehart and Winston).

Levin, S.R. (1962) 'Poetry and grammaticalness', in M. Halle (ed.) *Preprints of Papers for the 9th International Congress of Linguists*, Cambridge, MA: Congress of Linguists, pp. 308–14 (Reprinted in S. Chatman and S.R. Levin (eds) (1967) *Essays on the Language of Literature*. Boston: Houghton Mifflin).

Levin, S.R. (1964) *Linguistic Structures in Poetry*. The Hague: Mouton.

Levin, S.R. (1965) 'Internal and external deviation in poetry', *Word* 21: 225–37.

Ohmann, R. (1966) 'Literature as sentences', *College English* January (Reprinted in S. Chatman and S.R. Levin (eds) (1967) *Essays on the Language of Literature*. Boston: Houghton Mifflin).

Ohmann, R. (1971) 'Speech, action and style', in S. Chatman (ed.) *Literary Style: A Symposium*, New York: Oxford University Press, pp. 261–6.

Palmer, F. (1971) *Grammar*. London: Penguin.

Riffaterre, M. (1966) 'Describing poetic structures: two approaches to Baudelaire's "Les Chats"', *Yale French Studies* 36 and 37: 200–42.

Sinclair, J.McH. (1966) 'Taking a poem to pieces', in R. Fowler (ed.) *Essays on Style and Language*, London: Routledge and Kegan Paul, pp. 68–81.

Thorne, J.P. (1965) 'Stylistics and generative grammars', *Journal of Linguistics* 1 (1): 49–59 (Reprinted in D.C. Freeman (ed.) (1970) *Linguistics and Literary Style*. New York: Holt, Rinehart and Winston).

Thorne, J.P. (1970) 'Generative grammar and stylistic analysis', in J. Lyons (ed.) *New Horizons in Linguistics*, London: Penguin, pp. 185–97.

Thorne, J.P. (1971) 'The grammar of jealousy: a note on the character of Leontes', in A.J. Aitken, A. McIntosh and H. Palsson (eds) *Edinburgh Studies in English and Scots*, London: Longman, pp. 55–65.

Ullmann, S. (1957) *Style in the French Novel*. Oxford: Blackwell.

van Peer, W. (1986) *Stylistics and Psychology: Investigations of Foregrounding*. London: Croom Helm.

van Peer, W. (ed.) (2007) 'Special issue: foregrounding', *Language and Literature* 16 (2).

Wellek, R. (1960) 'Closing statement from the viewpoint of literary criticism', in T.A. Sebeok (ed.) *Style in Language*, Cambridge, MA: MIT Press, pp. 408–18.

Widdowson, H.G. (1972) 'Deviance and poetic communication', *Work in Progress*, Department of Linguistics, University of Edinburgh, pp. 107–9.

Widdowson, H.G. (1975) *Stylistics and the Teaching of Literature*. London: Longman.

Ziff, P. (1964) 'On understanding "Understanding utterances" ', in J. Fodor and J. Katz (eds) *The Structure of Language*, Englewood Cliffs, NJ: Prentice Hall.

Extracted from Henry Widdowson (1972) 'On the deviance of literary discourse', *Style* 6 (3): 294–306.

Chapter 5

Language, linguistics and literary analysis

ELIZABETH CLOSS TRAUGOTT AND MARY LOUISE PRATT

This chapter is taken from Traugott and Pratt's 1970s textbook *Linguistics for Students of Literature*. The linguistics it drew on included generative grammar, which few stylisticians today regard as being very useful in stylistic analysis. However, by analogy, Traugott and Pratt here expound the notion that a literary text sets up its own 'grammar', which the reader learns and uses to develop a richer insight into the literary work. This is linked with the classic stylistic notions of deviance and fore-grounding. All of these issues are interesting for the way that Traugott and Pratt draw a firm thread from linguistic analysis to aesthetics and literary appreciation. The book is also remarkable for the richness of its stylistic discussions from a time when the use of linguistics in literary study was popular in the US, an approach which is only now being rediscovered in North America.

For an interesting debate on the status of stylistics, see Fish (1980) and Toolan (1990, 1996).

'Applying' linguistics

[. . .]

THE STUDY OF STYLE and the language of literature is one of the most traditional applications of linguistics, one which has been given new impetus by the rapid new developments in linguistics since the development of generative grammar. At the present time, linguistic analysis of literature is one of the most active and creative areas of literary studies. As is the case with its other areas of application, linguistics is not essential to the study of literature. Certainly one does not need to know linguistics in order to read and understand literary works; and critical analysis has long been carried out without formal linguistic apparatus. However, linguistics can contribute a great deal to our understanding of a text. It can help us become aware of *why* it is that we experience what we do when we read a literary work, and it can help us talk about it, by providing us with a vocabulary and a methodology through which we can show how our experience of a work is in part derived from its verbal structure. Linguistics may also

help us solve problems of interpretation by showing us in rigorous ways why one structure is possible but not another. Above all, however, linguistics can give us a point of view,
a way of looking at a text that will help us develop a consistent analysis, and prompt us
to ask questions about the language of the text that we might otherwise ignore. Since
texts are the primary data for all literary criticism, adequate means of textual description are essential if any criticism is to be properly founded. Linguistics helps ensure a
proper foundation for analysis, by enabling the critic to recognize the systematic regularities in the language of a text. In fact, we can use linguistics to construct a theory about
the language of a text in the form of a 'grammar of the text.' In this sense, although
linguistics does not encompass literary criticism, it is relevant to all criticism.

Literature as a type of discourse

Though we sometimes tend to think of literature as a realm of free, individual expression, it is in many respects highly conventionalized, like everything else in language. One
important set of conventions are those governing literary genre. In linguistics, the term
'genre' is used to refer not only to types of literary works, but also to any identifiable
type of discourse, whether literary or not. In this sense, the lecture, the casual conversation, and the interview are all genres, just as the novel and short story are. This broader
view of genre is valuable in that it helps us conceptually to bridge the traditional gap
between literary and nonliterary discourse. It enables us to view literature as a particular
range of genres or discourse types, that is, as a particular subset of the repertory of
genres existing in a given speech community. In our own culture, there is some disagreement about exactly which genres constitute literature. There is little consensus, for
example, on the status of the limerick or the nursery rhyme; the distinction sometimes
drawn between literature and folklore is dubious at best; a religious poem might be
considered literature when it appears in a poetry anthology, but not when it appears in a
hymn book. [. . .]

Among characteristics of literature as a range of genres is that it is generally public,
not private, discourse. In addition, written literature is discourse that may be read at a
far distance in time and place from its origin. This means that the relationship that holds
between speaker/author and hearer/reader in written literature is of a very special sort
and one that is a particularly important aspect of what can be called 'literary pragmatics.' Furthermore, literary discourse is often fictional. One of the pragmatic conventions of fictional narrative is that the speaking *I* of the speech act is understood not to be
the author of the work, but an intermediate narrator or addresser who has been created
by the author. Within the fictional world of the story, the narrator (or addresser), not
the author (or speaker), is held immediately responsible for what is said. Thus we speak
of reliable and unreliable *narrators*, not authors. The author is responsible as speaker,
however, when the fiction comes to be judged by the external world, as in criticism,
libel suits, censorship cases, or Pulitzer Prizes.

Aside from genre conventions, literary discourse has many other general linguistic
characteristics for which the linguist can provide tools of analysis. Certain kinds of
phonological, syntactic, and semantic phenomena occur with much greater frequency in
literature than in other kinds of discourse. For example, 'poetic' devices like metaphor,
alliteration, and archaism are commonly associated with literature, although they are, of
course, not unique to it. The conventions of rhyme and metre constitute elaborate

formal constraints on phonology, syntax, and vocabulary, and the study of grammars can help show exactly what these constraints are. One of the most important characteristics of literary discourse is its recurrent linguistic patterning, or 'cohesion,' a patterning which may be found to operate at all levels of the grammar; and it is here especially that the linguist can throw light on the language of a text, demonstrating both what the linguistic system in the work is and how it operates in that particular text.

Cohesion

The idea of cohesion was first developed in detail by Roman Jakobson, one of the leading linguists of the twentieth century and a pioneer in the application of linguistics to literature. In 1960 Jakobson characterized, with reference to poetry, a notion basic to the analysis of literary texts: that they have cohesion or internal patterning and repetition far exceeding that of most nonliterary texts. Cohesion in poetry is usually discussed in terms of repeated refrains, regular stanzas, rhymes, alliteration, metre, and similar devices. Jakobson's interest lay not so much in these well-known features but in rather less frequently discussed linguistic features, especially linguistic cohesiveness created between elements at different levels of the grammar, such as parallels between meaning and sentence structure, or between sentence structure and sound structure (and, of course, their interplay with other specifically poetic features, such as metre).

Jakobson [1960: 358] describes the phenomenon of cohesion as follows: 'The poetic function projects the principle of equivalence from the axis of selection into the axis of combination.' A difficult sentence, but probably the one most often quoted in linguistic approaches to literature. What he means by this is that, in poetry, structures which are roughly equivalent in sound, or sentence structure, or grammatical category, or some other aspect tend to be combined in a linear order or sequence. Poetry, in other words, involves partial repetition, whether of metrical patterns, rhymes, or sentence structures. Jakobson cites Caesar's famous *veni, vidi, vici* as an example. This sentence combines in sequence three words of the same grammatical category (verbs), same inflection (first person singular past tense), same number of syllables, same stress pattern, and very similar sound structure (rhyme and alliteration). This extraordinary cohesiveness is what makes the sentence so memorable. In the English *I came, I saw, I conquered*, some of the effect is lost because of the /s/ versus /k/, and the two syllables of *conquered* versus the single syllables of the other words, but the sentence is still strikingly cohesive. At the semantic level, the cohesion has a particularly interesting effect. By seeming to equate the acts of coming, seeing, and conquering, Caesar's sentence implies that the last act was as easy for him as the first two. Hence, the impression of majestic arrogance it produces.

Political slogans and advertisements thrive on the principle of cohesion, in part because it makes them easier to remember. For example, among advertisements we find *Turn on Schick, turn out chic* for a Schick hair styler and *Silk and Silver turns grey to great* for Silk and Silver hair colouring. These both involve cohesion in phonology, vocabulary, and meaning associations. In poetry the principle is usually exploited in a more subtle way; but cohesion is present at least to some degree, except in some experimental poetry that deliberately rejects it.

A relatively simple literary example of cohesion is provided by Rober Browning's well-known song from 'Pippa Passes':

The year's at the spring
And day's at the morn;
Morning's at seven;
The hillside's dew-pearled;
The lark's on the wing;
The snail's on the thorn;
God's in his heaven —
All's right with the world!

Patterning is evident at every level in this poem, and at the same time we can see how patterns are varied to avoid monotony. One of the most obvious cohesive patterns here is the syntax – each line is a single clause consisting of [noun + 's + X], and X consists of a prepositional phrase everywhere except in lines 4 and 8 where the pattern is varied. (But note that this variation itself is cohesive, in that it occurs at the same point in each pair of four lines, and involves an adjective in both cases). The syntactic cohesion coincides with semantic cohesion among the nouns. In the first four lines, we find a series of time nouns in order of increasing specificity: *year*, *spring*, *day*, *morn*, *morning*, *seven*, joined by the preposition *at*. This extremely tight patterning is loosened and played upon in the second four where *lark* and *snail* are linked both by semantic likeness (two animals) and contrast ('higher' versus 'lower' animals). With *on the wing* and *on the thorn*, syntactic and lexical likeness interplay with semantic difference (*on* has the same form but different meaning in each case). In line 7, *God* is forcibly incorporated into the pattern and thus unexpectedly placed on the same level of existence as *lark* and *snail*, while the change of prepositions from *on* to *in* keeps the parallelism from being complete.

Metrical patterning in the poem interacts rather subtly with lexical and syntactic patterns. In each part, the first, second, and fourth lines have the pattern $\breve{} / \breve{}\breve{} /$ (where / means a stressed syllable and $\breve{}$ an unstressed one), while the third line has the mirror image $/ \breve{}\breve{} / \breve{}$. Thus, though the last line of each part breaks syntactic and lexical patterns, it does conform metrically, while metrical variation is used in the third and seventh lines and helps counteract any monotony arising from the syntactic and lexical cohesiveness.

At yet another level, the internal regularity of this poem is itself counterbalanced by the fact that, with respect to normal spoken English, many of the poem's expressions are decidedly 'irregular.' We do not say that years are 'at the spring' or days 'at the morn.' These expressions illustrate the fact that literature often uses expressions that are not, or are no longer, common in spoken conversational language. Moreover, in this poem, the fictional singer, Pippa, is a young Italian woman, and the song, fictionally, is being sung in Italian. Doubtless, Browning wants to remind us of this by estranging us from the English in the text.

The phenomenon of cohesion in literature obviously has everything to do with the fact that literature is art, that literary texts are constructed to produce in us the kinds of experience we speak of as 'aesthetic,' in which symmetry and interplay of sameness and difference play a major role. A complete understanding of cohesion will depend on further understanding of aesthetic experience and perception.

One of the secrets of good poetry is to be cohesive, and yet not too much so. Too rigid an equivalence leads readily to doggerel. While the literary critic may want to evaluate the cohesiveness in a text, the linguist's task is not so much to evaluate as to demonstrate exactly what is present and what is not. It is also the linguist's task to show where there are differences as well as similarities, or where there is some variation in a pattern or some kind of opposition between surface and underlying patterns. [. . .]

The idea of the 'grammar' of a text

From the point of view of generative grammar, discovering the systematic regularities in the language of a text is only a partial step toward a full account of the text's linguistic structure. Rather than limiting an account of a text to observed regularities, we can go on to make generalizations about the text's phonological, syntactic, and semantic structure and its pragmatic characteristics, generalizations which will reveal the text's stylistic traits and tendencies and the principles on which it is structured. Such generalizations resemble those that constitute the grammar of a language. It has therefore become customary to extend the term 'grammar' from 'grammar of a language' to 'grammar of a text.' Constructing a grammar of a text, then, is a way of hypothesizing about its overall internal structure. It enables the critic to make stylistic observations in an organized way about the most detailed facts of language.

One of the most interesting ways to use a grammar of a text is to compare it with the overall grammar of the language in which it is written. Such comparison can reveal, for example, what grammatical categories and options have and have not been used, and in what ways the text departs from normal usage. Indeed, a grammar of a text provides the only rigorous basis for comparing the language of an individual text with 'the language as a whole.'

[. . .]

Of course, constructing a grammar of a simple text is not exactly the same thing as constructing a grammar of a language. Grammars of languages have to account not just for the available data in a language, but also for the potentially available data, the infinite number of sentences that could be produced in the language. Because they have this predictive power, grammars of languages can always be tested against new data in the language. With individual text grammars, there are no other potentially available data against which the analysis could be tested. Still, in theory, a grammar of a text would enable us to characterize a text specifically enough to produce another text stylistically indistinguishable from it. In practice this is seldom completely possible, because literary works are often highly individualized and because their internal structure depends on factors other than purely linguistic ones. But the possibility that one can know the structure of a text well enough to produce something similar is one on which pastiche and caricature operate, and the idea that a grammar can characterize the language of the text in full detail underlies computerized poetry, since the program which produces such poetry is a grammar of the text it produces.

Describing a text in terms of its grammar involves viewing it as a single whole in which certain structures are simultaneously present. Likewise, to speak of cohesion as the presence of internal patterns is to treat the text as an object possessing certain properties, rather than as a temporal progression. Such a view is necessarily incomplete, for a text is also a temporal sequence. A written text is laid out in space because expressed language is a temporal thing. The act of reading takes time; the experience of a literary work is temporal. So of course is the author's act of writing. There are critics who maintain that the only valid way of approaching a literary text is through description of the temporal experience of reading [for example, Fish 1976]. Others claim a text must be viewed as a dynamic structure constantly transforming itself as the work progresses [see, for example, Iser 1975]. In fact we need all these perspectives.

Style as choice

It is customary not only to talk about the language of a text or author, but more specifically about the 'style.' People speak of racy, pompous, formal, colloquial, inflammatory, or even nominal and verbal styles. How can such generalizations be characterized linguistically? One way is to say that style results from a tendency of a speaker or writer to consistently choose certain structures over others available in the language. With this view, we can distinguish between 'style' and 'language' by saying that language is the sum total of the structures available to the speaker, while style concerns the characteristic choices in a given context. In this sense, in writing a grammar of a text, we will probably be more concerned with the style than with the language, for it is not so much that every possible structure available is interesting, as those which dominate a text, or part of it.

To claim that style is choice is not, of course, to claim that it is always conscious choice. Indeed, if one had to make all phonological, syntactic, semantic, and pragmatic choices consciously, it would take a very long time to say anything at all. In literature, as in all discourse, a sense of the 'best way of putting something' can be intuitive or conscious; the result as far as the reader is concerned will be much the same.

Stylistic choice is usually regarded as a matter of form or expression, that is, as choice among different ways of expressing an invariant or predetermined content. But this view is misleading, for writers obviously choose content too. In our grammar, with its semantic and pragmatic components, both content and expression can be viewed as matters of choice. Choice of content involves choice of semantic structures; choice of expression involves choice of pragmatic functions and contextual features (such as what relation a speaker adopts toward the hearer, what inferences are to be conveyed, what assumptions made). Choices in both these components of the grammar are in turn the basis for phonological, syntactic, and lexical choices. This approach provides us with a new way of thinking about whether there is or is not a duality between form and content. This issue has been discussed in philosophy and aesthetics for centuries. A large number of critics and stylisticians acknowledge such a duality, saying that given some particular content ('meaning') a variety of surface forms are possible. In this view it is possible for there to be sentences that are synonymous, even though they have different forms. The opposing position is that every difference in form brings a difference in meaning and that synonymy is therefore impossible. Now it is clearly useful to say that *My twenty-three year old brother is a bachelor* is synonymous with (has the same meaning as) *My twenty-three year old brother is unmarried*. Yet they are not exactly equivalent. For example, one would scarcely say the first sentence to a child because *bachelor* is a technical term, while one might say the second. The difference is pragmatic, not semantic. In terms of our grammar, in choosing between these two sentences, the speaker makes a pragmatic, contextually motivated choice between two semantically equivalent surface forms. Thus the grammar allows for synonymy (thereby maintaining a form/ content distinction) and at the same time accounts for the fact that synonymous surface forms are not exactly equivalent.

The interplay between semantic sameness and pragmatic difference is exploited by Samuel Beckett in the following passage from his novel, *Murphy*. In the climactic scene of this novel, the ill-adjusted and alienated protagonist, who works as an orderly in a mental hospital, looks deep into the eyes of a singularly withdrawn patient, Mr. Endon, and encounters nothing but his own reflection. Endon's complete unawareness of his presence profoundly shakes Murphy's confidence in his own existence. We read:

> Kneeling at the bedside, the hair starting in thick black ridges between his fingers, his lips, nose and forehead almost touching Mr. Endon's, seeing himself stigmatised in those eyes that did not see him, Murphy heard words demanding so strongly to be spoken that he spoke them, right into Mr. Endon's face, Murphy who did not speak at all in the ordinary way unless spoken to, and not always even then.
>
> > 'the last at last seen of him
> > himself unseen by him
> > and of himself'
>
> A rest.
> 'The last Mr. Murphy saw of Mr. Endon was Mr. Murphy unseen by Mr. Endon. This was also the last Murphy saw of Murphy.'
> A rest.
> 'The relation between Mr. Murphy and Mr. Endon could not have been better summed up than by the former's sorrow at seeing himself in the latter's immunity from seeing anything but himself.'
> A long rest.
> 'Mr. Murphy is a speck in Mr. Endon's unseen.'
> That was the whole extent of the little afflatulence. He replaced Mr. Endon's head firmly on the pillow, rose from his knees, left the cell, and the building, without reluctance and without relief.
>
> (Beckett 1957: 249–50)

Here Beckett gives us several different formulations of the same rather complicated content. The first, highly elliptical, is set out like a poem; the second is an explanatory paraphrase of the first using complete sentences and no pronominalization; the third, reminiscent of nineteenth-century novelistic style, adds some emotive content ('the former's sorrow'), which is removed in the final aphoristic summary of the situation, where a metaphor ('a speck in Mr. Endon's unseen') is introduced. Notice too the way this passage dramatizes the process of choice of surface form. The four versions seem to be a series of (pragmatic) attempts on Murphy's part to arrive at a shortest, clearest formulation. Alternatively, Murphy may be (equally pragmatically) providing several versions to meet the needs of a variety of hypothetical hearers, so that they may do the choosing. Incidentally, this passage also provides a novelistic example of cohesion, being based on the linear sequencing of equivalent units.

A further concept of style, one that has been favoured by the generative frame of reference, is the concept of style as deviance, the idea that style is constituted by departures from linguistic norms. Like the concept of style as choice, the concept of style as deviance is by no means new. One of its chief proponents in this century was Jan Mukarovsky, a leading linguist and literary critic in Prague in the 1930s. He speaks of style as 'foregrounding,' bringing to attention, making new: 'The violation of the norm of the standard, its systematic violation is what makes possible the poetic utilization of language; without this possibility there would be no poetry' [Mukarovsky 1970: 42]. Everyday usage, according to Mukarovsky, 'automatizes' or conventionalizes language to the point that its users no longer perceive its expressive or aesthetic potential; poetry must de-automatize or 'foreground' language by violating the norms of everyday language. [. . .] Rhyme, repetition, archaic and foreign words de-automatize the spoken norm and mark the language as literary, but at the same time they are conventional or automatized features of literary language. In applying the idea of foregrounding, we must carefully distinguish these levels of analysis. Of course such automatized literary conventions are themselves subject to de-automatization. Indeed, for Mukafovsky, it was essential for literature to continuously rejuvenate itself by violating its own norms. [. . .]

At another level of analysis, any structure, particularly a highly cohesive one, may be said to automatize the language within the work, however deviant it may be from the standard. This is the case in the poem 'love is more thicker than forget' by e.e. cummings (as he spelled his name):

> love is more thicker than forget
> more thinner than recall
> more seldom than a wave is wet
> more frequent than to fail
>
> it is most mad and moonly
> and less it shall unbe
> than all the sea which only
> is deeper than the sea
>
> love is less always than to win
> less never than alive
> less bigger than the least begin
> less littler than forgive
>
> it is most sane and sunly
> and more it cannot die
> than all the sky which only
> is higher than the sky
>   [cummings 1954: 381]

There is obviously a very real sense in which this poem startles us into seeing the conventional side of love in a totally new light. But if we understand it, it is largely because there is a pattern so consistent that we could venture to set up a mathematical formula for it. Cohesion within this poem is based on the pairing of antonyms.

Stanza 1 is based on the lexical antonyms *thicker-thinner, forget-recall, seldom-frequent*, and made syntactically cohesive by a *more-than* construction. Stanza 3 is structured in the same way by the antonyms *always-never, bigger-littler*, and is made syntactically cohesive by a *less-than* construction. This *less-than* construction is antonymous to *more-than* in stanza 1 and so completes the parallel between them. Stanzas 2 and 4 have no antonyms within themselves, but are antonymous line by line with each other. The first, third, and fourth lines of stanzas 2 and 4 are antonymous in their nouns and adjectives (*mad-sane*, *moonly-sunly*, *sea-sky*, *deeper-higher*), but not in their comparatives and superlatives. *Most-less* and *most-more* contrast, but are not opposites, and therefore are not antonyms. The second lines break the pattern, but less so than might appear at first sight. The difference is that here the auxiliary verbs *shall* and *cannot*, not the main verbs, are antonymous. The main verbs are synonymous. Since *un-*, when attached to a verb, indicates reversal (as in *undo*, *untie*, *unscrew*, *unscramble*), *unbe* must mean 'cease to exist,' which is essentially the same thing as *die*, except that it emphasizes dying as a reversal of state.

Texts like the cummings' poem, in which deviant language is automatized, are especially well-suited to the grammar-of-a-text approach. If we take a deviant text (and cummings is often a target of such analysis, since he is so overtly interested in language and creating a deviant language) and treat its deviance simply as a lack of internal structure, we are left with no way to explain how the text (a) is comprehensible to us, (b) is consistent, (c) sets up its own world in which structures can be deviant. If, however, we try to establish a 'grammar' of a deviant text, we can show how it is internally consistent and exactly what is deviant and, therefore, how we understand it.

The study of style as deviance helps us to clinch the idea of a grammar of a text and to keep in mind that the language of literature is not always entirely that of everyday usage. It helps us focus on cohesion and on recognizing that what may be perfectly automatic and normal in one text, or for one author, or even one period may be abnormal in another. However, the idea of style as deviance has the disadvantage of encouraging the linguist to look at the language of grammatically highly deviant authors like cummings at the expense of relatively nondeviant ones [. . .]. More generally it tends to undervalue all nondeviant language, both within literature and without. The theoretical claim that aesthetic effects can only be achieved through deviance assumes that normal usage is somehow in principle un- or anti-aesthetic, and even suggests that linguistic systems themselves are by nature hostile to poetry. This is certainly not the case. In the end, the idea of style as deviance always leads back to the broader view that style is choice, where choice includes selecting or not selecting deviant structures. Style as choice subsumes style as deviance, for deviance is only one aspect of the language of literature.

To speak of style as choice, one must recognize not only that there is freedom of choice, but also that there are constraints on choice. In our approach, linguistic choice is made on the basis of the total options available in the grammar, that is, the total options available in the syntactic, semantic, phonological, and pragmatic systems. The first three systems specify the range of structural possibilities which can be chosen from or deviated from. The fourth specifies in part the contextual basis for choice, including such factors as intended audience, topic, genre, channel, degree of formality. Some people might think that a view of style as choice given a preexisting range of potentialities is incompatible with our usual view of the artist as a creator, or that it undervalues the originality of the artist. But this is not the case. If anything, the view of style as choice enables us to appreciate artistic creativity more fully by understanding better wherein it lies. As we discussed at the beginning of this chapter, though the linguistic system is finite, the range of actual utterances possible in language is infinite even at the level of the single sentence, to say nothing of the possibilities at the level of longer discourse. The more one understands the linguistic system, the more one appreciates the infinity and variety of possible choices and combinations of choices available, and the more one appreciates the genius of an artist who, by making and combining choices, creates structures that are deeply meaningful, imaginatively fulfilling, and expressive of our most fundamental concerns as human beings.

References

Beckett, S. (1957) *Murphy*. New York: Grove Press.

cummings, e.e. (1954) *Poems, 1923–1954*. New York: Harcourt Brace Jovanovich.

Fish, S. (1976) 'How to do things with Austin and Searle: speech act theory and literary criticism', *Modern Language Notes* 91: 983–1025.

Fish, S. (1980) *Is There a Text in This Class?* Cambridge, MA: Harvard University Press.

Iser, W. (1975) 'The reality of fiction: a functionalist approach to literature', *New Literary History* 7: 7–38.

Jakobson, R. (1960) 'Closing statement: linguistics and poetics', in T.A. Sebeok (ed.) *Style in Language*, Cambridge, MA: MIT Press, pp. 350–77.

Mukarovsky, J. (1970) 'Standard language and poetic language', in D.C. Freeman (ed.) *Linguistics and Literary Style*, New York: Holt, Rinehart and Winston, pp. 40–56.

Toolan, M. (1990) *The Stylistics of Fiction*. London: Routledge.

Toolan, M. (1996) *Total Speech*. Durham, NC: Duke University Press.

Extracted from Elizabeth Closs Traugott and Mary Louise Pratt (1977) 'Applying linguistics', in *Linguistics for Students of Literature*, New York: Harcourt Brace Jovanovich, pp. 19–34.

Chapter 6

Linguistic criticism

ROGER FOWLER

This chapter is a revised version of Roger Fowler's inaugural lecture as Professor of English and Linguistics, from the mid-1970s. It deals mainly with non-literary language, though he begins by asserting the continuities between literary and non-literary discourse. The *critical linguistics* that Fowler developed was to have a profound effect on literary linguistics in general, bringing ideology and social awareness into stylistic analyses in a more principled manner than had existed previously. The term *stylistics* tends now to be synonymous with *literary linguistics*, though in Fowler's day and for some modern stylisticians it is the study of the language of all discourse-types, including non-literary ones such as political, business, institutional, advertising and humorous discourse. More commonly, non-literary stylistics is now subsumed as *(critical) discourse analysis*, the field that has its roots in Fowler's original work. A highly productive and rich mutual feedback loop has emerged between critical discourse analysis and stylistics over the years.

For further developments in critical discourse analysis, see Fowler's later work (1991, 1996) and also Fairclough (1995, 2001, 2003), Chilton (2003), Pennycook (2001), Toolan (2001) and Wodak and Chilton (2005).

T HE HEADING 'LINGUISTIC CRITICISM' is meant to abbreviate a range of meanings. It means, first of all, criticism of language. To spell it out, critical analysis of the social practices that are managed through the use of language. Next, my title means criticism which employs the concepts and methodology of linguistics: it is possible, but undesirable, to talk about language non-linguistically, a procedure which is guaranteed to get you into trouble. Third, the phrase 'linguistic criticism' is intended to recall the phrase 'literary criticism'. One of my most enduring academic interests has been the linguistic analysis of literary texts. Since it is well known that I have a strong dislike of the motives and practices of literary criticism as carried out by literary critics, you will realise that I'm offering linguistic criticism as an alternative to and improvement on literary criticism. I will be discussing the linguistic criticism of 'literary' texts [very briefly at the end of this chapter], after illustrating the analysis and expounding the theory in relation to a variety of texts that would not normally be called 'literary'. Let me make it clear, however, that I don't believe any special assumptions have to be made about 'literature'. There isn't any special 'literary language' qualitatively distinct from 'ordinary language', so the methods of linguistic criticism can be applied to literary texts without any special adjustment. There are of course some peculiar conventions concerning the ways readers are supposed to respond to 'literary works', and these need to be kept in mind. However, they are conventions in the social psychology of literary communication, and don't affect the nature of the texts as language. The techniques of linguistic criticism apply universally, whatever the genre of the text under consideration.

To appreciate the necessity of criticism, and the importance of linguistic criticism, we need to consider some basic principles in the sociology of knowledge. The world of perception and cognition – the world as we know it – is an artifice, a social construct. We have a variety of names for this world: commonsense, everyday life, the natural attitude, ideology. All of these designations refer to the world as we take it for granted, the habitualized world. Cultural anthropologists have observed the extreme variability of everyday life in different civilizations, and it is from these observations that the principle of a socially constructed commonsense has arisen. A popular account of the processes involved is Berger and Luckmann's book *The Social Construction of Reality* (Berger and Luckman 1976). Berger and Luckmann give a picture of each human society transforming and structuring its environment by a process which they call 'objectification'. Typical and repeated patterns of interaction, technological procedures and the development of roles and institutions cause the members of a society to represent the world as a system of recognisable objects: habituated categories of perception and action which simplify the society's management of itself and of its habitat. These categories are not the deliberately contrived instruments of scientific analysis (though some may have started life as such) but automatically assimilated ways of dividing up the world. Together, the complete set of objectivations in a culture constitutes the representation of reality, or world-view, enjoyed by the community and its members. In a nutshell, we see the world in terms of the categories through which we and our society have constituted it.

Berger and Luckmann acknowledge the power of symbolic systems, and especially language, in the social construction of reality. Language provides labels for the objects which a culture has determined are relevant to its functioning: the existence of linguistic signs ensures the identity of the objects we call 'trees', 'government', 'riots', 'imagination', 'literature', 'girls', 'inaugural lectures', etc.: vocabulary *segments* the world into culture-relevant categories. Language also *classifies* these objectivations by groupings into lexical sets, e.g. kinship terminologies or the jargons of specific occupations or fields of knowledge such as medicine. As Berger and Luckmann observe, occupational jargons are of paramount importance in maintaining the identity of specialized groups and their members: swearing like a trouper or talking like a book maintains the position of the individual as a soldier or an intellectual, and preserves the role of his group within society. Furthermore, because language is a systematic code and not just a random list of labels, it facilitates the storage and the transmission of concepts. Finally, since language is used in interaction between people as well as being a form of knowledge possessed by people, concepts can be negotiated in communication between people. For instance, two persons can discuss whether a third is a 'girl', or a 'woman', or a 'lady', and in so doing they are necessarily exchanging and formulating the social concepts encoded in the words.

How does criticism apply to these processes? By 'criticism' I don't mean the appreciative, supportive role played by the flood of writings about texts and authors which calls itself literary criticism. Nor do I intend the sense of intolerant unreasoned fault-finding, as when someone tells me that I am being very critical today. I mean a careful analytic interrogation of the ideological categories, and the roles and institutions and so on, through which a society constitutes and maintains itself and the consciousness of its members. As we have seen, all knowledge, all objects, are constructs: criticism analyses the processes of construction and, acknowledging the artificial quality of the categories concerned, offers the possibility that we might profitably conceive of the world in some alternative way. [. . .]

[. . . Here are] some choice examples from newspapers [of the 1970s] as examples 1 and 2.

1. (a) NUS REGRETS FURY OVER JOSEPH
    (b) STUDENT LEADERS CONDEMN INSULT TO KEITH JOSEPH
    (c) STUDENT CHIEFS 'REGRET' ATTACK ON SIR KEITH
2. (a) LEYLAND PLANS FOR SURVIVAL REJECTED
        British Leyland's plan for survival was rejected yesterday by senior shop stewards representing 165,000 workers.
    (b) STEWARDS DEFY BL CLOSURE THREAT
        Shop stewards from all BLs plants yesterday rejected overwhelmingly the redundancy programme drawn up by chairman Sir Michael Edwardes.

I'm not going to analyse these fragments. [You could . . .] consider whether they are interchangeable. I don't think so: the paper which headlined the confrontation of Keith Joseph and the NUS as l(a) could never print l(c), and vice-versa.

Our intuitions about these newspaper headlines tell us that each is located in a specific recognisable system of beliefs. 2(a), for instance – LEYLAND PLANS FOR SURVIVAL REJECTED – can only be uttered by someone who believes that any commercial concern, even a company as unsuccessful as British Leyland, is to be credited with taking a laudable initiative if it proposes to sack large numbers of its workers. 2(b), by contrast, is prepared to grant union officials the right to resist management's plans on the grounds that they involve sackings, regardless of the prediction that such redundancies might be the condition of successful commercial continuation. Our knowledge of economic practices and institutions in British society leads us to associate the beliefs implied by these sentences with certain positions in socio-economic structure. The readership of the newspaper which supplied 2(a) is committed to industry and commerce financially as well as ideologically, and is actively hostile to trades unions.

It comes as no surprise that there is a manifest relationship between socio-economic structure and ideology. More important in this context of linguistic criticism is the role of language in mediating the relationship. From the point of view of the sociologist, linguistic analysis provides a novel point of entry for investigating the relationships between belief systems and social structures. Despite the acknowledgement of the importance of language by theorists like Berger and Luckmann, there has so far been little detailed linguistic research into sociologically and ideologically interesting language. Language has been mined for *content,* or used to elicit content, with insufficient recognition of the power of structural arrangements in the shaping and slanting of propositions. As for sociolinguistics, linguistic variation has been studied largely as an index of such sociological variables as stratification, role and status. Semantically empty variables such as single phonemes have been observed by linguists such as William Labov, with little attention to the mediation of social *meanings* by varying linguistic structures. (For typical examples of indexical or correlational sociolinguistics, see Labov 1972 and Trudgill 1974).

So there is an analytic methodology to be developed. Examples 1 and 2 suggest that, although the belief-system embodied by a piece of text may be easily read off by anyone who is attuned to the relevant vibrations, the structural mechanisms involved in shaping the ideas are extremely delicate. Examples l(a)–(c), though very evidently different in tone when they are set alongside one another, don't differ grossly in structure. There are profound but not easily visible differences such as, for instance, the different case-relationships implied by the nominalized predicates *fury, insult* and *attack,* or the reflexivity of *regret* versus the transitivity of *condemn.* Such structural minutiae must be established within the methodological scope of linguistic criticism.

[. . .] Our interest in this question has been partly theoretical and methodological – as linguists and sociologists – and partly practical – as socialists. Trying to describe and interpret the linguistic constructions through which people and institutions articulate their views of the world, we became impressed with the inadequacy of existing linguistic theories for handling the questions we were asking. So with the help of our students, doing textual analysis on a large scale and across a great variety of texts, we developed a suitable technique of analysis. Our starting-point was the functional linguistic model of M.A.K. Halliday (1970, 1978a). In Halliday's own words,

> The particular form taken by the grammatical system of language is closely related to the social and personal needs that language is required to serve.

Linguistic structure is not arbitrary, but is determined by, or motivated by, the functions it performs. Furthermore, *all* parts of language are functional in this sense, not just the structures that explicitly serve social and interpersonal ends like personal pronouns, address forms, speech acts and so on. It follows for the interpretation of discourse that any choice of words and syntactic constructions can have some significance assigned to it. But not randomly: within a given community, particular ranges of significances tend to be conventionally attached to specific types of construction. Not in a one-to-one relationship: each construction we have studied has offered different meanings depending on the contexts in which it is used. There is, necessarily, a degree of unpredictability, so that we can't supply a dictionary of ideological significances. [. . .]

Formalizing the linguistic apparatus is an urgent priority for our future work. A major attraction of linguistic criticism is that it offers precise, potentially formal, descriptions of patterns of language: it differs in this respect from various less plausible existing alternatives, including content analysis and impressionistic practical criticism.

Returning to our practical motives, we have been studying the meanings and functions of public discourse in a divided society, a society based on inequalities of power and opportunity: contemporary British society. The title of our recent book, *Language and Control* (Fowler, Kress, Hodge and Trew 1979) indicates the topic to which we have directed our version of the language-and-ideology thesis. Given the nature of the society we live in, much communication is concerned with establishing and maintaining unequal power relationships between individuals, and between institutions and individuals. Our studies of various genres of discourse argue that this practice is carried out through a much wider variety of language usages and speech acts than just the rules and directives by which interpersonal control is obviously managed. Because language *must* continuously articulate ideology, and because ideology is simultaneously social product and social practice, all our language and that of others expresses theories of the way the world is organized, and the expression of these theories contributes to the legitimation of this theorized organization. [. . .] I'd like now to give you an example, adapted from *Language and Control*, of how linguistic style simultaneously expresses and constructs an ideology. Since criticism is supposed to be reflexive, that is, to engage in critique of the critic's own location within the language-thought-society nexus, the most appropriate example for this university occasion is the examination I did of [the University of East Anglia] UEA's General Regulations for Students; [here] is an extract:

General Regulations for Students

PREAMBLE

The University can function effectively only if all its members can work peaceably in conditions which permit freedom of study, thought and expression within a framework of respect for other persons. The General Regulations exist to maintain these conditions:

> by the protection of free speech and lawful assembly within the University.
> by the protection of the right of all members or officers or employees of the University to discharge their duties.
> by the protection of the safety and property of all members or officers or employees of the University while engaged in their duties or academic pursuits.
> by the protection of the property of the University.

All students matriculating in the University shall, so long as they remain in attendance, be bound by the following Regulations and by such other Regulations as the University may from time to time determine.

1 AGE OF ADMISSION

Those who intend to follow courses for University degrees and diplomas are not normally admitted if they are under the age of seventeen years on 1 October of the year of admission.

2 MATRICULATION

Matriculation is the act of placing a student's name upon the *matricula* or roll of members of the University. Before being allowed to matriculate a student must have fulfilled the examination requirements laid down by the University in respect of general entrance requirements and in respect of course requirements for the programme of study which the student wishes to pursue.

All persons entering the University as students in residence shall sign a Declaration of Obedience to the Authorities of the University, in the following terms: 'I hereby promise to conform to the discipline of the University, and to all Statutes, Regulations and rules in force for the time being, in so far as they concern me'.

Although this text is lacking in directive speech acts, it is clearly intended to be an instrument in controlling behaviour. This control is to be achieved not by regulating specific actions, but by enforcing a set of attitudes. By adopting a familiar bureaucratic style of 'impersonality' (ready-made and available generally for institutions, not invented by UEA) the people responsible for publishing the text have obscured the fact that they intend to control the behaviour of the people to whom the text is addressed. But there is a degree of over-kill; the writer is absolutely unidentifiable, and the addressees are absolutely depersonalized. In these respects, the language is so unlike any discourse which might be spoken by one person to another person that the text is alienating, symbolic of an utter separation of the interests of the source and the addressees (while both parties are, after all, members of the same university community).

Not only is the nature of the power relationship obscured or mystified by the language, so also is the content which is being communicated. The addressee is given very little specific guidance about what activities are approved and what proscribed, and yet the structure of the language expresses an implicit and demanding orthodoxy, a special system of attitudes required of members of the community.

The text is impersonal in the way that rate demands, government circulars, official notices are, and this impersonality has the same linguistic origins, and the same causes in the needs of institutions to interact with individuals in a formal manner. But the subject-matter, and the act of speech, are in fact far from impersonal. The Regulations have for their topic a set of relationships between institution and addressee – rights and obligations, permitted and proscribed behaviour. In these circumstances the impersonality of the language is exceedingly conspicuous. There are no 'you's', and the only first-person pronouns which occur are the 'I' and 'me' in the quoted 'Declaration of Obedience'. The 'you' addressed by this text is consistently transformed into third person: 'a student', 'students', 'persons', 'those', 'they', etc. The effect is to turn the person who is being addressed into someone who is being talked about; like a child whose parents talk about her to other people in her own presence. There is no 'I' in this text; only 'the Authorities of the University' and 'the University', with 'the General Regulations' serving as an intermediary between source and addressee. Notice how both the source and the addressee are expressed in plural form: 'the Authorities', 'students'. Pluralization aggrandizes and obscures the source, as with the royal plural. Pluralization of the addressee, on the other hand, confirms the source's refusal to treat the individual addressee as an individual person.

Impersonality also arises from the avoidance of any explicit command structure:

there are no requests or imperatives. However, a weighty burden of authority is carried by the modal verbs 'shall', 'must' and 'may'. 'Shall' suggests an inexorable obligation, usually imposed on the student but, occasionally, in later paragraphs, the obligation of the university: 'The days on which students register shall be announced annually by the University . . .' 'Must' means an absolute condition. One revealing modal attached to 'the University' is 'may', which ascribes a right, not an obligation: the University may if it chooses dispense with some condition, or has the right, if it chooses, to punish the breach of a regulation.

In most styles that people find 'formal' and 'impersonal', two syntactic constructions are prevalent: *nominalization* and *passivization*. Both abound in this passage. Passives include 'engaged in their duties', 'bound by the following Regulations', 'not normally admitted', 'allowed to matriculate', etc. Nominalization is a transformation which reduces a whole clause to its verb, and turns that into a noun. For example, the noun 'freedom' is derived from 'someone is free', 'study' from 'someone studies something', 'thought' from 'someone thinks', 'Regulations' from 'someone regulates somebody else', and so on. Many derived nominals can be spotted by their ending in *-ion, -ience, -ness*, etc., and many are learned words of classical origin: 'expression', 'protection', 'regulation', 'matriculation', 'declaration'. The impression of formality derives partly from their etymological pedigree, partly from the fact that large numbers of scientific and technical terms have this form.

Nominalization facilitates *relexicalization*, the coding of new, specialized, sets of concepts in new sets of lexical terms (see Halliday 1978b). The student can conform to the Regulations only by learning a new technical vocabulary which expresses the relationships of which the regulations speak. The word 'matriculation' illustrates the essence of this process. This arcane term, meaning admission to the register of students when entering the university for the first time, or the ceremony associated therewith, refers to one sole experience in the life of a person who goes to college. By its intense specialization of reference, the word becomes talismanic in the relationship of student and university. Apparently the student must acquire the meaning of this word as a precondition for a well-formed relationship between the parties: a patently ritual function of language.

Another example, which illustrates how relexicalization generates *systems* of new terms, is the series 'examination requirements', 'course requirements', 'general entrance requirements'. Since the series is productive, the student may feel some unease lest it spawns other terms, unexpressed here and perhaps to be unleashed elsewhere – 'residence requirements', 'political affiliation requirements', 'dietary requirements' are all too plausible offspring of the system.

Nominalization has syntactic as well as lexical repercussions. The personal participants, the 'someones' whoever they may be, are deleted as a clause turns into a noun; so is modality (thus many potential 'may's' and 'shall's' disappear). The deletion of references to persons is entirely compatible with the strategy of suppressing 'I' and 'you': the single word 'Regulation', and all other words like it ('requirement', 'obedience', etc.) is effectively a euphemism, the nominalization allowing the university to avoid telling the truth in its full syntactic form: 'I, the university, require you, the student, to do such-and-such'; 'you, the student, obey me, the university'. Similarly with passives: 'not normally admitted' really means 'the University does not normally admit' – the passive structure, allowing agent-deletion, permits a discreet silence about *who* might refuse to admit the applicant. Usually the agents and patients can be retrieved in an analytic reading, though of course the style discourages such analysis. Sometimes nominalization or passivization makes it extremely difficult to infer the persons associated with the underlying verb: 'matriculation' is a case in point: it is not clear, even if you read the sentences concerned carefully, who does what to whom, in this ritual. 'The act of placing a student's name . . .' suggests that matriculation is something done *to* the student, but the next sentence, 'Before being allowed to matriculate' implies that matriculation is reflexive, something a student does to himself. As the whole text is about the responsibilities and obligations of the two parties, this is a crucial ambivalence.

Syntax may do something even more treacherous. Rather than just clouding the relational responsibilities of the deep structure (who does what to whom), it may actually *reverse* the distribution of rights and duties. Thus someone who has something done to him by another can be made to seem responsible for what happens to him. Consider, for example, the sentence

> All students matriculating in the University shall, so long as they remain in attendance, be bound by the following Regulations and by such other Regulations as the University may from time to time determine.

The deep structure is actually something like 'The University binds all students by Regulations'. But in the passive surface structure, the nominal designating the object ('all students') has been placed in the position of theme, i.e. the left-most noun phrase in the sentence, a position normally associated with the agent. The syntax strongly encourages one to read the first part of this sentence with the expectation that it is going to mention some action carried out by 'all students'; this illusion is heightened by the presence of an active verb of a subordinate clause ('matriculating') immediately following 'all students'; and by the extreme distance between the subject 'all students' and the main verb 'be bound', a distance which forces the reader to cling on to a hypothesis about the way the sentence is going to turn out. The easiest hypothesis is that we are waiting for a main verb which will tell us what action 'all students' perform; but this hypothesis will prove incorrect, since it is actually the university which is doing something.

A linguistic style is 'constitutive': an important function of rules-style is to systematize the special concepts of the society they regulate. Now there is something very odd about the way this text's language analyses the community it refers to. The General Regulations apply to individuals living and working in a large, complex community which encourages and stages a great variety of academic, social and domestic work and interaction. A university, particularly a residential one, is a hive of activity. But this language is used to neutralize the activity, and gives no sense of transaction or productivity. The avoidance of transitive verbs, the use of abstractions as subjects, and pervasive nominalization, account for a large part of the effect. Nominalization permits deletion of reference to the persons responsible for and affected by the processes described by the verbs; nominalization can depersonalize, depopulate. It can also drain the language of actional vitality – an effect recognised in style handbooks which teach aspiring writers to prefer verbs to nouns. The processes and work which go on within the university are presented as nouns (study, assembly, academic pursuits); thinking, talking, writing, etc. become, grotesquely, static 'things' located in a peaceful, stable landscape.

Nominalization transforms the processes of studying and working into objects possessed by the institution, capital items to be accumulated, counted, deployed. The alternative view, that intellectual progress springs from work, dialogue, even conflict, is tacitly discouraged by this style.

My lettrist colleagues may by this point be starting to get a little bothered. This 'linguistic criticism' is labelled as if it were a form of literary criticism, but it seems rather to be a branch of sociolinguistics or discourse analysis. My examples, taken from regulations and from newspapers, may confirm your belief that linguistic criticism is a secular or even profane trade which doesn't apply to literature. If you believe that – and I know that many people do – then you need reminding that literature is indeed a secular institution: a social and economic practice through which cultural values are transmitted, a body of texts which encode and transform belief-systems, a whole set of industries for regulating the conditions of production and consumption of the texts, with a profession of ideologues – yourselves – employed to administer the practice of literature within the educational system.

What I have just said was meant merely as the starting-point for an analysis of the institution of literature which I don't actually intend to pursue [. . .]. If it sounds antagonistic to you, my antagonism is directed to the institution and not to the texts which the institution administers. On the other hand, my interest in literature, and my implicit respect for the texts, doesn't mean that I believe, as linguistic poeticians such as Jakobson and Culler do, that there is some essential property of literariness which makes literary works 'special' (see Culler 1975, Fowler 1979). I have argued against these claims in a number of recent papers and there is no need for me to rehearse the arguments here.

Jakobson's claim of a special, distinctive poetic language forced him and his followers into a very narrow concept of significant literary patterning and consequently they paid attention to a quite restricted range of linguistic features presumed to be the exponents of these patterns. I have found no good reason to separate off literature from other kinds of discourse, and so can open up linguistic investigation to the study of any parts of textual structure.

There is some redressing of balance to be done. The extreme formalism of Jakobson's syntactic and phonetic descriptions meant an equally extreme neglect of interpersonal, expressive and referential dimensions of literary works (Jakobson 1960). Jakobson never offers interpretations of a degree of richness which would satisfy literary critics or literary historians; he exercises such caution in his statements about the relationships of texts to the world around them that one would hardly think there is a world around them. Interestingly, Jakobson's calvinistic formalism is in accord with the prevailing anti-historical, anti-kinetic dogmas of modern literary criticism as expressed by the 'New Critics' and their successors.

The present model of linguistic criticism attacks these limitations on two fronts. To take the simpler part of my proposal first. In formalist poetics, and in traditional and even transformational linguistics, there is very little recognition of *interpersonal* aspects of language. [. . .] several different theoretical categories need to be distinguished in this area: modality, speech acts, implicatures, categories of address, naming, and soon. And these abstract categories are provided with several complicated systems of surface structure forms. The Fowler-Hodge-Kress-Trew model would relate all of these categories to dimensions of social structure, after the fashion of Brown and Gilman's treatment of 'The Pronouns of Power and Solidarity' *(vous* and *tu* in French, etc.) (Brown and Gilman 1960), so on our theory they are of massive significance for interpretation. But a more elementary step in this study is simply to get interpersonal features noticed in practical criticism. In my undergraduate teaching, therefore, it is a particular emphasis: poems like 'My Last Duchess', the more argumentative and exclamatory lyrics of Donne, and almost anything by Blake or by Yeats, are a revelation to students, who generally have little conception of the complexity of the structures which are needed to constitute a written text as a representation of a speech act. [. . .]

I'd like to mention briefly a [. . .] literary topic involving interpersonal structures which particularly interests me and on which I have done some work: the characterization of narrators, implied authors and implied readers in prose fiction texts. So far, I have studied only very overtly characterised narrators, in Fielding, Sterne and George Eliot, narrators, or authors' personae, who draw attention to themselves and to their relationships with their implied readers (Fowler 1977). Pronouns, address forms, modality, speech acts (or pretend ones) and many other interpersonal structures are involved in the characterization of narrators and readers. Description of the languages of narration and reader-creation connects with Wolfgang Iser's stimulating but pre-linguistic work. I think that theories of reception and of the rhetoric of fiction are crying out for the solidity and precision of linguistic description. Iser's recent work (Iser 1974, 1978) is much concerned with ideology: with the ways in which the semantic repertoire of a text interacts with the systems of ideas of a community. This is a central preoccupation of linguistic criticism in my sense, and, to conclude my lecture, I'd like to sketch an example, taken from work in progress, of the study of language and ideology in fictional texts (specifically, novels). [. . .]

I do not take the vulgar Marxist position that the language of a novel reproduces the ideology of the society that, through the author, produced the novel-text. Rather, I want to say that a novel is a linguistically constructed system of beliefs which bears some interesting, usually critical and defamiliarizing, relationship to the numerous ideologies current at its time, in our time, and encoded in the earlier texts in the genre. If this sounds bland, well, I'm sorry, but you have to interpret the claim in the light of the theoretical and methodological innovations I have suggested in the earlier part of this lecture. The linguistic critic must suspect that each and every stylistic choice carries a socially interpretable meaning, and his analytic method dictates a searching, minute and systematic empirical study of the texture of, in this case, very long texts. What is more, linguistic analysis by itself will not give the answers that are required: this analysis must be accompanied by historical research to validate the interpretations which the critic offers. [. . .]

References

Berger, L. and Luckmann, T. (1976) *The Social Construction of Reality* [original 1966]. Harmondsworth: Penguin.

Brown, R. and Gilman, A. (1960) 'The pronouns of power and solidarity', in T.A. Sebeok (ed.) *Style in Language*, Cambridge, MA: MIT Press, pp. 58–71.

Chilton, P. (2003) *Analysing Political Discourse*. London: Routledge.

Culler, J. (1975) *Structuralist Poetics.* London: Routledge and Kegan Paul.

Fairclough, N. (1995) *Critical Discourse Analysis*. London: Longman.

Fairclough, N. (2001) *Language and Power* (2nd edition). London: Longman.

Fairclough, N. (2003) *Analysing Discourse: Textual Analysis for Social Research*. London: Routledge.

Fowler, R. (1977) *Linguistics and the Novel*. London: Methuen.

Fowler, R. (1979) 'Linguistics and, and versus, poetics', *Journal of Literary Semantics* 8: 3–21.

Fowler, R. (1991) *Language in the News: Discourse and Ideology in the Press*. London: Routledge.

Fowler, R. (1996) *Linguistic Criticism* (2nd edition). Oxford: Oxford University Press.

Fowler, R., Hodge, R., Kress, G. and Trew, T. (1979) *Language and Control*. London: Routledge and Kegan Paul.

Halliday, M.A.K. (1970) 'Language structure and language function', in J. Lyons (ed.) *New Horizons in Linguistics*, Harmondsworth: Penguin, pp. 140–65.

Halliday, M.A.K. (1978a) *Language as Social Semiotic*. London: Edward Arnold.

Halliday, M.A.K. (1978b) 'Antilanguages', in *Language as Social Semiotic*, London: Edward Arnold, pp. 165 ff.

Iser, W. (1974) *The Implied Reader*. Baltimore: Johns Hopkins University Press.

Iser, W. (1978) *The Act of Reading*. Baltimore: Johns Hopkins University Press.

Jakobson, R. (1960) 'Closing statement: linguistics and poetics', in T.A. Sebeok (ed.) *Style in Language*, Cambridge, MA: MIT Press, pp. 350–77.

Labov, W. (1972) *Sociolinguistic Patterns*. Philadelphia: University of Pennsylvania Press.

Pennycook, A. (2001) *Critical Applied Linguistics*. Mahwah, NJ: Lawrence Erlbaum.

Toolan, M. (2001) *Narrative: A Critical Linguistic Introduction* (2nd edition). London: Routledge.

Trudgill, P. (1974) *Sociolinguistics: An Introduction* (2nd edition, 1995). Harmondsworth: Penguin.

Wodak, R. and Chilton, P. (2005) *Methods of Critical Discourse Analysis*. London: Sage.

Extracted from Roger Fowler (1981) 'Linguistic criticism', in *Literature as Social Discourse*, London: Batsford, pp. 24–45.

Chapter 7

Metre

GEOFFREY LEECH

Geoffrey Leech's (1969) *A Linguistic Guide to English Poetry* is a landmark of early stylistics. In this chapter, he attempts a more rigorous sketch of metrics than was being widely used in literary criticism at the time, drawing not only on phonetics and phonology, but also with an eye on pragmatic issues of performance and an ear open for readerly matters of interpretation and affect. The discussion is set out by stylistic features, and the chapter is wide-ranging in the sources of its quotations, demonstrating the familiar double-advantage of stylistics as a contribution to linguistic theory and to literary criticism simultaneously.

The linguistic treatment of metrics has had something of a renaissance in recent years. For further work, see Attridge (1995), Fabb (1997, 2002) and Carper and Attridge (2003).

P ROSODY (THE STUDY OF VERSIFICATION) is an area which, like grammar and rhetoric, has suffered from scholars' disillusionment with traditional theory, and their failure to replace it with an agreed alternative. Harvey Gross is a spokesman of current perplexity on this subject when he says at the beginning of his book *Sound and Form in Modern Poetry*: 'The prosodist attempting the hazards of modern poetry finds his way blocked by the beasts of confusion. Like Dante he wavers at the very outset of his journey. He finds four beasts: no general agreement on what *prosody* means and what subject matter properly belongs to it; no apparent dominant metrical convention such as obtained in the centuries previous to this one; no accepted theory about how prosody functions in a poem; and no critical agreement about the scansion of the English meters' (Gross 1964: 3). Certainly matters are not so clear-cut as they were when the rules of Latin scansion were religiously applied to English verse, on the mistaken assumption that the accentual rhythm of English could be handled in the same terms as the quantitative rhythm of Latin. This is an age which has learnt to question official dogmas rather than to accept them – in the case of prosody, with good reason. And yet out of the doubt of recent years there has emerged a certain amount of agreement on the nature of verse structure.

Rhythm and metre

It has become widely accepted, for instance, that versification is a question of the interplay between two planes of structure: the ideally regular, quasi-mathematical pattern called *metre*, and the actual rhythm the language insists on, sometimes called the *prose rhythm*. (In this development Eastern European prosodists have anticipated the thinking of scholars in the West. See the discussion of the Russian 'formalists' in Welleck and Warren's *Theory of Literature* (1949: 173–4). A most thorough and interesting theoretical and practical study of metre is Chatman 1965).

The difference between the two, as imaginatively felt by the poet himself, is expressed by W.B. Yeats (*A General Introduction for my Work*) as follows: 'If I repeat the first line of *Paradise Lost* so as to emphasize its five feet, I am among the folk-singers – "Of mán's first dísobédience ánd the frúit", but speak it as I should I cross it with another emphasis, that of passionate prose – "Of mán's first disobédience ánd the frúit"; . . . the folk song is still there, but a ghostly voice, an unvariable possibility, an unconscious norm.' Actually, Yeats is not comparing 'prose rhythm' with metre directly in this passage, but rather with a type of rendition – that of the folk-singer – which reproduces the metrical regularity at the expense of 'prose rhythm'. However, there is no better way of describing the metrical pattern than by the image of a 'ghostly voice' in the background.

A third factor is sometimes distinguished: that of the *performance* of a particular recitation. This is clearly extraneous to the poem, for the poem is what is given on the printed page, in abstraction from any special inflections, modulations, etc., which a performer might read into it, just as the play *Hamlet* exists independently of actual performances and actual theatrical productions. But performance is related to 'prose rhythm' in the following way. 'Prose rhythm' is not any one particular way of saying a piece of poetry, but rather the potentiality of performance according to the rules of English rhythm. Two different Mark Antony's might render the line 'If yóu have téars, prepáre to shéd them nów' either as just marked, or with a different placing on the first stress thus: 'Íf you have téars, prepáre to shéd them nów'. Either would be permissible according to the rules of normal English pronunciation. Thus performance may be regarded as a particular choice from the aggregate of possible pronunciations in keeping with the normal rhythm of spoken English.

The distinction between metre and rhythm (the qualification of '*prose* rhythm' is unnecessary, and perhaps misleading) suggests a clear strategy for investigating the pattern of English verse. According to the principle 'divide and rule', we may consider in turn (a) the rhythm of English speech, (b) the metrics of English verse tradition, and (c) the relation between the two. We also need to examine the relation between verse form and other aspects of linguistic structure. Naturally one chapter devoted to such a large area of study can only deal with each topic in brief outline: metrics is a complicated subject which has filled many volumes.

The rhythm of English

Underlying any talk of 'rhythm' is the notion of a regular periodic beat; and the very fact that we apply this term to language means that some analogy is drawn between a property of language, and the ticking of a clock, the beat of a heart, the step of a walker, and other regularly recurrent happenings in time. In phonological discussion, the grandiose term *isochronism* ('equal-time-ness') is attached to this simple principle. To attribute the isochronic principle to a language is to suppose that on some level of analysis, an utterance in that language can be split into segments which are *in some sense of equal duration*. In certain languages, such as French, this segment is the syllable. In others, such as English, it is a unit which is usually larger than the syllable, and which contains one stressed syllable, marking the recurrent beat, and optionally, a number of unstressed syllables. This is the unit that I have previously called the (rhythmic) *measure*. Thus English and French are representatives of two classes of language, the 'stress-timed' and the 'syllable-timed' respectively.

I have emphasized the qualification '*in some sense* of equal duration', because the rhythm of language is not isochronic in terms of crude physical measurement. Rather, the equality is psychological, and lies in the way in which the ear interprets the recurrence of stress in connected speech. Here there is a helpful analogy between speech and music. A piece of music is never performed in public with the mechanical rhythm of the metronome, and yet despite various variations in tempo, some obvious and deliberate, some scarcely perceptible, rhythmicality is still felt to be a basic principle of the music and its performance. The gap between strict metronomic rhythm and loose 'psychological' rhythm also exists in language, where there are even more factors to interfere with the ideal of isochronism. For example, the duration of the measure (corresponding to the musical bar) tends to be squashed or stretched according to the number of unstressed syllables that are inserted between one stress and the next, and according to the complexity of those syllables. In this, a speaker of English is rather like a would-be virtuoso who slows down when he comes to difficult, fast-moving passages of semi-quavers, and accelerates on reaching easy successions of crochets and minims. Although some people reject the principle of isochronism because of the lack of objective support for it, I shall treat it here as a reasonable postulate without which a meaningful analysis of rhythm cannot be made. What we call 'stress', by the way, cannot be merely reduced to the single physical factor of loudness: pitch and length also have a part to play. Stress is an abstract, linguistic concept, not a purely acoustic one.

The measure: the unit of rhythm

As the rhythm of English is based on a roughly equal lapse of time between one stressed syllable and another, it is convenient, taking the comparison with music further, to think of an utterance as divided into 'bars' or (as I have already called them) *measures*, each of which begins with a stressed syllable, corresponding to the musical downbeat, A number of unstressed syllables, varying from nil to about four, can occur between one stressed syllable and the next, and the duration of any individual syllable depends largely upon the number of other syllables in the same measure. If we assign the value of a crochet to each measure, then a measure of three syllables can be approximately represented by a triplet of quavers, a measure of four syllables by four semi-quavers, etc. [. . .]

Which syllables are stressed?

To analyse a passage into measures in this way, we need to be able to judge which syllables are normally stressed. Although there are plenty of exceptions, it is a useful general rule that proper nouns and lexical words (most nouns, verbs, adjectives, and adverbs) bear stress in connected speech, whereas grammatical words (prepositions, auxiliaries, articles, pronouns, etc.), particularly monosyllabic grammatical words, usually do not. In reading aloud the sentence 'John is the manager', we scarcely have any choice about where to place the stresses: they fall naturally in two places – viz. on *John* and the first syllable of *manager*. The rhythm is therefore ♫|♫. Now if the sentence is rearranged to read 'The manager is John', the stresses still fall on *manager* and *John*, but the rhythm is radically changed to something like ♪|♫♫|♩. In each case, the grammatical words *is* and *the* remain unstressed. Thus the placing of stress in English is strongly conditioned, though not absolutely determined, by grammar and lexicon.

Some polysyllabic lexical words, like *trepidátion* and *cóunterféiter*, have two stresses; and if the word is uttered in isolation or at the end of a sentence, one of these stresses takes precedence over the other in bearing the nucleus of the intonation pattern: *trepiDAtion*, *cóunterféiter*. In certain treatments of the subject, this extra prominence is described as an extra degree of stress. However, for the purpose of metrics, we can ignore it, and be content to regard *trepidation* and *counterfeiter* as rhythmically alike.

Words which normally have no stress can be stressed for some special purpose; to my knowledge, Hopkins is the only major English poet to mark special stresses in his text; for example 'Yes I cán tell such a key' (*The Leaden Echo and the Golden Echo*). Elsewhere, one generally refrains from reading into a poem unusual stresses of this kind, unless the context clearly demands it.

The system of musical notation as so far developed gives only a rough picture of the rhythmic values of syllables. It is possible to add various refinements, of which two are considered in the following two sections.

Pauses

In music, pauses are marked by rests of various lengths and it is easy to adapt this notation to the purpose of recording rhythmic values in poetry. Pauses are often felt necessary at the end of larger syntactic units – sentences, clauses, and some phrases – in fact, at the boundaries of intonation units. Allowance must be made both for pauses in the middle or at the end of a measure, and for pauses at the beginning of a measure, standing in place of a stressed syllable. Such 'silent stresses' can occur within a line of poetry, at a point where the traditional prosodist would mark a caesura.

Syllable length

It is clear from examples given so far that syllables within the same measure do not all have to have the same length. In writing a three-syllable measure ♫♪, for instance, we may slightly misrepresent a rhythm which is closer to ♩♫ or ♫♩. (In symbolizing three-syllable measures, I shall omit the triplet-sign from now on.) Ezra Pound notes in his *A.B.C. of Reading* that syllables have 'original weights and durations', as well as 'weights and durations that seem naturally imposed on them by other syllable groups around them' (Pound 1951: 198–9). We may translate this observation into terms suitable for the present discussion as follows: one syllable may be longer than another (a) because it is in a measure containing fewer syllables, or (b) because of its internal structure in terms of vowels and consonants. Some vowel nuclei, including all diphthongs, tend to be long (as in *bite*, *bait*, *beat*, *bought*) whereas others tend to be short (*bit*, *bet*, *bat*, *but*). Moreover, the type of final consonant influences the length of the vowel: *beat* is shorter than *bead*, *bead* than *bees*, etc. If there is more than one final consonant, this again contributes to the length of the syllable: *bend* is longer, in relative terms, than *bed* or *Ben*. All these factors show that syllables vary in intrinsic length, as well as in the length imposed on them by the rhythmic beat. The duration of a measure is not equally divided, therefore, but is apportioned amongst its syllables according to their relative weights. Consider, for example, the rhythmic difference between the words *boldly*, *second*, and *comfort*, when spoken in isolation (each constituting a complete measure). The proportional lengths of the syllables can be represented, with tolerable accuracy, as ♩♪, ♪♩ and ♫ that is, as long + short, short + long, and equal + equal.

Syntax, too, has an important bearing on syllable quantity. It seems to be a general principle that an unstressed syllable is especially short if it more closely relates, in syntax, to the stressed syllable following it. This means that unstressed prefixes, and words like *the*, *a* and *is*, tend to be pronounced quickly in comparison with unstressed suffixes. We may call the syntactically forward-looking unstressed syllables 'leading syllables', and the backward-looking syllables 'trailing syllables'.

A convincing illustration of this contrast is found in the two phrases 'some addresses' and 'summer dresses', which are identical in pronunciation except for a difference of rhythm, in slow delivery at least, due to the different position of the word-boundary. The *a-* of *addresses* is a leading syllable, whereas the *-er* of *summer* is a trailing syllable; for this reason the first two syllables of 'some addresses' are long + short, whereas those of 'summer dresses' are equal + equal. [. . .]

The interaction of rhythm and verse form

Yeats was right to describe the 'ghostly voice' of metre as 'an unconscious norm'. Just as poetic language deviates, in other spheres, from norms operating within the language as a whole, so within poetic language itself, verse form, and especially metre, constitutes a secondary norm, an expected standard from which deviation is possible. In poetry, that is, a particular verse pattern (say, blank verse), although foregrounded against the background of everyday 'prose rhythm', is itself taken as a background against which further foregrounding may take place.

Defeated expectancy

Any noticeable deviation from a verse convention, as a disturbance of the pattern which the reader or listener has been conditioned to expect, produces an effect of *defeated expectancy*. A flippant illustration of this effect is provided by the following piece of verse, which, although it scans like a limerick, contains none of the usual rhymes on which a limerick depends for much of its point:

There was an old man from Dunoon,
Who always ate soup with a fork;
   For he said, 'As I eat
   Neither fish, fowl, nor flesh,
I should finish my dinner too quick'.

The temporary sense of disorientation, almost of shock, caused by deviation from a verse pattern may have a clear artistic purpose, as in the sudden interposition of a two-syllable line in this speech by Othello:

O, that the slave had forty thousand lives!
One is too poor, too weak for my revenge.
Now do I see 'tis true. Look here, Iago;
All my fond love thus do I blow to heaven:
'Tis gone.
Arise, black vengeance, from thy hollow cell!
Yield up, O love, thy crown and hearted throne
To tyrannous hate! Swell, bosom, with thy fraught,
For 'tis of aspics' tongues!
                         [*Othello*, III.iii]

On a practical level, it allows time, assuming a strict apportionment of six measures per iambic pentameter, for the speaker's symbolic gesture to be carried out. But in addition, the prominence given to the words ' 'Tis gone' by this check in the movement of the verse adds force to the gesture, and draws attention to it as a landmark, introducing a new and terrible phase of Othello's psychological development.

The power of defeated expectancy as a poetic device depends, naturally enough, on the rigidity of the verse form as it is established in the reader's mind. A truncated line of blank verse such as that just quoted would be less obtrusive in one of the Elizabethan or Jacobean plays in which metrical conventions are handled with greater laxity than in *Othello*. There is a great deal of difference, in principle and in effect, between occasionally violating a well-defined verse pattern, and gently stretching the pattern, so that it tolerates a greater degree of variation.

Metrical variation

As with other kinds of linguistic deviation, it is necessary to distinguish unpredictable licences of versification from 'routine licences' which are themselves allowed by prosodic convention. In the first of these categories belongs *metrical variation*, or acceptable deviation from the metrical norm in terms of the distribution of stressed and unstressed syllables.

Metrical variation can be conveniently studied in this passage from Canto I of Pope's *The Rape of the Lock:*

Of thése am Í, who thỳ protéction cláim,   105
A wátchful spríte, and Áriel ìs my náme.
Láte, as I ránged the crýstal wílds of áir,

In the cléar mírror òf thy rúling stár
I sáw, alás! some dréad evént impénd,
Ére to the máin this mórning sún descénd;   110
But héaven revéals not whát, or hów, or whére:
Wárn'd by the sýlph, óh, píous máid, bewáre!

Perhaps the most frequent of all deviations from the perfect iambic pattern (× / × / × / × / × /) is the reversal of the stressed and unstressed syllable of a foot, especially at the beginning of a line. This is seen in lines 107 ('Late, as I ranged . . .') and 112 ('Warn'd by the sylph . . .'), both of which begin with the configuration / × × / instead of × / × /. A similar, but less common irregularity is the reversal of the order of successive syllables which belong to different feet, as at the beginning of line 108, where the stress values of the second and third syllables are exchanged: 'In the clear mirror . . .' (× × / / × is the most natural pronunciation).

Almost as important as the rearrangement of stress and unstress is another kind of variation: the substitution of a stressed for an unstressed syllable, or *vice versa*. There is an example of the introduction of an extra stress in the last line of the passage, if the word *oh* is pronounced, as one supposes it normally would be, as a stressed syllable. The rhythmic pattern of the line, so rendered, goes: / × × / / / × / × /. A replacement in the other direction is likely in lines 105, 106, and 108, where *thy*, *is*, and *of*, words normally without stress, are placed in a position of metrical stress. Such substitutions seem to violate the metrical design more drastically than rearrangements. The reason for this is that they alter the number of stresses per line, break up the pattern of an even number of stresses, and so disturb the musical continuity of the verse. The introduction of an extra stress holds back the movement because it introduces an extra measure; whereas the subtraction of a stress has the opposite effect of hurrying the line on. Line 108, for instance, can be read as a four-measure line × × / / × × × / × /.

[. . .] Metrical variation involves the conflict between two sets of expectations: the expectations of normal English speech rhythm, and the expectations of conformity to the metrical design. In recitation, we may insist that the metre yield entirely to 'prose rhythm', or we may strike a compromise, by speaking the lines in a somewhat poetic manner, with a special verse rhythm; or we may even sacrifice 'prose rhythm' entirely to metre, reciting in the artificial manner of Yeats's folk-singer. However the poem is performed, a tension between the two standards remains in the text, and is a fruitful source of rhetorical emphasis, onomatopoeia, and other artistic effects. Metrical variation need not, however, have any function apart from making the task of metrical composition less confining, and providing relief from the monotony which would arise from a too rigid adherence to the metrical pattern. [. . .]

The 'verse paragraph'

One of the important functions of enjambment is its role in building up expansive structures known as *verse paragraphs*. This term has been applied to successions of blank verse lines which seem cemented into one long, monumental unit of expression. To the skilful construction of verse paragraphs is attributed much of the epic grandeur of Milton's blank verse. In describing these structures, it is difficult to avoid architectural metaphors: one thinks of a multitude of assorted stone blocks interlocking to form a mighty edifice.

The verse paragraph is neither a unit of syntax nor a unit of verse: it is rather a structure which arises from the interrelation of the two. To see this, let us examine a famous passage in which Milton writes of his own blindness, from the beginning of Book III of *Paradise Lost*:

> Yet not the more
> Cease I to wander where the Muses haunt
> Clear spring, or shady grove, or sunny hill,
> Smit with the love of sacred song; but chief
> Thee, Sion! and the flowery brooks beneath,   30
> That wash thy hallowed feet, and warbling flow,
> Nightly I visit, nor sometimes forget
> Those other two equalled with me in fate,
> So were I equalled with them in renown,
> Blind Thamyris, and blind Mæonides,
> And Tiresias, and Phineus, prophets old:
> Then feed on thoughts, that voluntary move
> Harmonious numbers; as the wakeful bird
> Sings darkling, and in shadiest covert hid
> Tunes her nocturnal note.   40

The essence of the verse paragraph is an avoidance of finality. But what does 'finality' mean? In prose there are various degrees of syntactic finality (end of phrase, end of clause, etc.), leading up to the absolute finality of the end of a sentence. In verse there is also the metrical finality of a line-division. In blank verse, a point of complete rest is only reached when a sentence boundary and a line boundary coincide. If either occurs without the other, some structural expectation is still unfulfilled; the reader has, as it were, arrived at a halting-place, not a destination. Perhaps we may refer to the various kinds of medial stopping place as 'points of arrest', reserving the term 'point of release' for the ultimate point of rest: the coincidence of line-end and sentence-end. The verse paragraph can then be seen as the piece of language intervening between one point of rest and another.

What is remarkable about Milton's style of blank verse is first of all the length of his verse paragraphs – indeed, rarely outside Miltonic blank verse does the unit extend far enough to make the term 'paragraph' applicable. The piece quoted is evidently only an excision from the middle of one of these units of expression, for although it constitutes a complete sentence, it begins and ends at a point of metrical incompleteness – i.e. in the middle of a line. It is also worth noting how Milton deprives the reader of the comfort of relaxing at intermediate stopping places. This is partly brought about by the frequency of enjambment (in this passage, lines 26, 27, 29, etc.), with its corollary, the placement of heavy breaks in the middle of the line. Thus when the metre bids the reader pause, the syntax urges him on, and *vice versa*.

Another factor is the Latin syntax of the periodic sentence, protracted by parentheses, lists, and involved structures of dependence. A particular contribution to the onward-thrusting movement of the language is the way in which anticipatory structure sets up syntactic expectations which are kept in suspense over a long stretch of verse.

For example, 'Thee, Sion! . . .' at the beginning of line 30 above requires completion by a transitive verb which is not supplied until the third word of line 32: 'Nightly I visit'. A more striking illustration comes at the very beginning of *Paradise Lost*, quoted below. Thus three factors – medial sentence boundaries, enjambment, and periodic syntax – combine to provide the tension, the unstaying forward impetus of Milton's blank verse, and (to revert to the architectural simile) make up the cement with which these massive linguistic structures are held together.

Often in Milton's blank verse, as in that of the later Shakespeare, enjambment is so frequent that the line-divisions can scarcely be followed by the ear unaided by the eye. Yet the blank verse mould, I feel, must be continually felt beneath the overlapping syntax: otherwise one misses the effect of criss-crossing patterns, the counterpoint in which lies so much of the power of this kind of verse. Without a feeling for the underlying pentameter scheme, moreover, one fails to appreciate the relaxation of a resolved conflict when the poem at length is brought to a 'point of release'. This profoundly satisfying effect can be likened to that produced by the perfect cadence at the end of a Bach fugue. Sometimes, as in the first twenty-six lines of *Paradise Lost*, the release of tension is enhanced by an uncharacteristic sequence of end-stopped lines, the last of which, in addition, is (also uncharacteristically) a regular pentameter free of metrical variation:

> Of man's first disobedience, and the fruit
> Of that forbidden tree, whose mortal taste
> Brought death into the world, and all our woe,
> . . .
> . . . What in me is dark,
> Illumine! what is low, raise and support!
> That to the heighth of this great argument
> I may assert eternal Providence,
> And justify the ways of God to men.

It is clearly wrong to talk of this as a return to the 'norm' in any statistical sense of that word, for there are more run-on lines than end-stopped lines at the beginning of *Paradise Lost*. Indeed, here the concept of norm and deviation as applied to verse pattern is turned on its head: the irregularity becomes the rule, and the reversion to end-stopped lines becomes telling in contrast.

I may seem to have devoted more attention to an individual poet's style here than is justified. But of course, the Miltonic manner, far from being restricted to Milton, is a wide-ranging influence in English poetry. (Two valuable studies of Milton's verse technique and language are Sprott 1953 and Ricks 1963). Besides, this brief study of Milton has revealed deeper applications of notions like deviation, variation, and defeated expectancy: applications not limited to Milton and those who wittingly or unwittingly come under his influence. It would be instructive, for example, to investigate enjambment and resolution in the work of a poet like T.S. Eliot, who expressly repudiates the Miltonic manner.

References

Attridge, D. (1995) *Poetic Rhythm: An Introduction*. Cambridge: Cambridge University Press.

Carper, T. and Attridge, D. (2003) *Meter and Meaning*. London: Routledge.

Chatman, S. (1965) *A Theory of Metre*. Mouton: The Hague.

Fabb, N. (1997) *Linguistics and Literature: Language in the Verbal Arts of the World*. Oxford: Blackwell.

Fabb, N. (2002) *Language and Literary Structure: The Linguistic Analysis of Form in Verse and Narrative*. Cambridge: Cambridge University Press.

Gross, H. (1964) *Sound and Form in Modern Poetry* (2nd edition, 1996). Ann Arbor: University of Michigan Press.

Leech, G.N. (1969) *A Linguistic Guide to English Poetry*. London: Longman.

Pound, E. (1951) *ABC of Reading*. London: Faber and Faber.

Ricks, C. (1963) *Milton's Grand Style*. Oxford: Clarendon Press.

Sprott, S.E. (1953) *Milton's Art of Prosody*. Oxford: Basil Blackwell.

Welleck, R. and Warren, A. (1949) *Theory of Literature*. London: Jonathan Cape.

Extracted from Geoffrey Leech (1969) *A Linguistic Guide to English Poetry*. London: Longman.

Chapter 8

Discourse analysis and drama

MICK SHORT

Much previously published stylistic analysis focused on grammatical, lexical and phonological features of prose and poetry. Mick Short's influential paper, first published in 1981, is one of the first to show the relevance of stylistic analyses to drama texts and in so doing to make use of recent developments in the 1970s in speech act theory and linguistic discourse analysis. The main aim of his paper is to show that a variety of forms of analysis can be applied to short extracts from a range of dramatic texts from different historical periods. His description of each type of analysis is deliberately relatively brief and informal in order to show the range of possibilities but he clearly illustrates the potential in many aspects. He concludes with a fuller discussion of a complete play, *Trouble in the Works* by Harold Pinter, underlining that key features in the development of the relationship between the two characters cannot be fully explained without reference to linguistic features of the conversational dynamic.

Further examples of the applications of discourse analysis and pragmatics to a range of literary texts where dialogue is central can be found in Carter and Simpson (1989), Short (1996) and Culpeper *et al.* (1998). See also papers in this volume by Nash (Chapter 11) and McIntyre (Chapter 22).

Discourse analysis and its application to dramatic texts

Speech acts

THE THEORY OF SPEECH acts (Austin 1962; Searle 1965, 1969) has drawn attention to the fact that when we produce various utterances we actually do things. Thus when A says to B 'I promise to bring it tomorrow', under normal circumstances A actually makes a promise. In this case the action is made obvious by the presence of the performative verb 'promise'. However, 'I will bring it tomorrow' can also be a promise, given the right contextual circumstances. The introduction of context is important because it is this (what Searle 1969: Ch. 3, calls preparatory and sincerity conditions) which helps us to capture the important observation that the same sentence may in different circumstances perform different acts. Thus 'I will bring it tomorrow' is a promise when the action mentioned is beneficial to B and when A knows this. If it is obviously not of benefit then the speech act status changes to that of a threat or warning – where it is a court summons, for example. [. . .] This is dramatically important at the beginnings of plays and when new characters are introduced, as it allows us immediately to grasp important social relations. Thus when Jonson's *The Alchemist* opens with:

Face:	Believ't I will.
Subtle:	Thy worst. I fart at thee.
Dol Common:	Ha' you your wits? Why gentlemen! For love –
Face:	Sirrah, I'll strip you – (I, i, 1–4)

it is quite apparent, even without the stage direction that tells us so, that Face and Subtle are quarrelling, because they are abusing and threatening each other. On stage the actors would have to produce appropriate actions and tone of voice, which might be actualized in a number of different ways. But the intended meaning and effect are clear from the text and general knowledge (for example, that being stripped is usually unpleasant) alone. The fact that Face and Subtle are threatening each other also allows us to deduce that they are of roughly equal social status. A servant cannot, given normal circumstances, threaten a master. If he does so in play, it signals a change in their relationship.

Commands, like threats, are not accessible to all of the participants in a particular speech situation and therefore also mark clear social relationships. One of the most obvious examples is the first entrance of Lucky and Pozzo in Beckett's *Waiting for Godot*, where the master–servant relationship is marked before Pozzo even appears on the stage:

Enter Pozzo and Lucky, Pozzo drives Lucky by means of a rope passed round his neck, so that Lucky is the first to appear, followed by the rope which is long enough to allow him to reach the middle of the stage before Pozzo appears. Lucky carries a heavy bag, a folding stool, picnic basket and a greatcoat. Pozzo a whip.

Pozzo: (Off.) On! (Crack of whip. Pozzo appears.)

This is also a good example of the prescribed visual and verbal aspects supporting each other to reinforce the significance of the deduction that one makes.

The felicity conditions that have been explored so far have all concerned factors prior to the speech event. But Searle notes that post-conditions also apply. Thus, if you make a promise and then fail to carry it out, you have broken that promise (unless outside circumstances have prevented you). At the end of each act of *Waiting for Godot* Vladimir and Estragon make an agreement, which on both occasions they fail to carry out:

Vladimir: Well, shall we go?
Estragon: Yes, Let's go. (They do not move) (p. 94)

It is the fact that they agree to go and then do not which the critic has to explain.

Presumably they either wilfully break agreements, in which case the value of agreeing in their world is different from ours, or they are prevented from doing what they want by some unknown internal or external force. Which way one jumps interpretatively will depend on other information. For example, the fact that Pozzo also has difficulty in leaving when he apparently intends to is likely to incline us to the second of the two types of possibility outlined above. What is important to note here is that it is our knowledge of the normal production of speech acts which allows us to deduce contextual information when that production is apparently normal and which also allows us to perceive deviant speech act production and interpret it. (For a discussion of the status of speech acts in fiction, see Searle 1975a.)

Presuppositions

The work on presuppositions within both linguistics and philosophy is assuming voluminous proportions, and there is considerable dispute as to how to analyse and categorize them. See, for example, Keenan (1971), Kempson (1975) and Leech (1974). It will be noted that presuppositions often form part of the preconditions for the felicitous production of speech acts. Here I wish to discuss overlapping kinds of presupposition: existential, linguistic and pragmatic.

The notion of existential presupposition was first developed by Strawson (1952) to cope with the philosophical question whether statements like 'The present king of France is wise' could be deemed to be true or false. He claimed that such a sentence presupposed that the king of France existed and therefore could only have a truth value when the presupposition was true. In fictions there are of course many sentences which have false presuppositions; while we experience such fictions, we conventionally assume that such presuppositions are true and it is this convention amongst others that allows us to 'enter into' the world of the novel or play. Thus when, at the beginning of Marlowe's play, Faustus says:

> How I am glutted with conceit of this!
> Shall I make spirits fetch me what I please,
> Resolve me of all ambiguities.
> Perform what desperate enterprise I will?
> I'll have them fly to India for gold (*Doctor Faustus*, I, i, 77–81)

we conventionally enter a world where spirits exist, in spite of the fact that we may not believe in such things at all. 'Spirits' in this quotation can be interpreted as non-referential, as it is generic and in an interrogative sentence. But 'them' in the last line of the quotation does have definite reference, and co-refers to 'spirits'.

Once the world of the play is established we expect to see and hear things consistent with that world. Inconsistencies produce a jarring which the critic is likely to explain either by ascribing demerit to the work or by changing his mind as to the kind of work in front of him. Arguably, the first obvious indication of the absurd nature of *Waiting for Godot* involves a clash between the existential presuppositions held by us and those held by one of the characters. On the first page, Estragon replies by asking 'Am I?' Here Estragon challenges a presupposition, namely that he exists, that we assume he must hold.

The distinction which Strawson makes between what a sentence asserts and what it presupposes is useful for explaining the communicative effect of much embedded material in English sentences. [. . .] In plays such presuppositions are often used to establish the world of the play, and in absurd drama much of the absurdity can come from a clash between presuppositions held by the characters and those held by the audience. Hence, in N.F. Simpson's *One Way Pendulum*, Mrs Groomkirby says:

> If you were to do your proper share of the eating between you, instead of leaving it all to me, I shouldn't have to have Mrs Gantry in anything like so often. (Pause) Paying out good money all the time. (Pause) If it weren't for your father's parking meters we just shouldn't be able to run it. Then we should have to get it eaten ourselves.

Mrs Groomkirby's third sentence presupposes that her husband owns a string of parking meters from which he gains revenue. Her assumption goes unchallenged by the other characters and therefore is presumably shared by them. However, it is obviously at odds with the presuppositions which we as onlookers hold. In our world parking meters are only owned by town councils and the like. But perhaps the most astounding feature of this quotation is Mrs Groomkirby's remarks about eating. The noun phrase 'your proper share of the eating' presupposes that eating is a chore to be shared by the whole family. This linguistic presupposition in concert with other assumptions allows us to take part in a complex and crazy chain of inference whereby we deduce that all food has to be eaten, and that you have to pay a professional to finish up what you cannot finish. Presumably, without Groomkirby's parking meters they would not have been able to buy the food that they have to get rid of, let alone pay Mrs Gantry to eat it!

The term 'pragmatic' is usually reserved for presuppositions relating to immediate context and immediate social relations [. . .] The preconditions for the production of the threats in the extract from *The Alchemist* discussed above are obvious examples of pragmatic presuppositions. Another interesting example comes from the first scene of *King Lear*, where Lear as king is in an obvious position of authority. Kent continually tries to intercede on Cordelia's behalf, thus using his status as adviser. Lear slaps him down on each occasion, forcing Kent to produce more and more obvious intercessions, ranging from mere vocatives like 'good my liege' through questions and opposing statements and finally to the very explicit commands and warnings which provoke his banishment:

> *Kent*: Revoke thy gift,
> Or, whilst I can vent clamour from my throat
> I'll tell thee thou dost evil.
> *Lear*: Hear me recreant
>   . . . if, on the tenth day following
> Thy banish'd trunk be found in our dominions,
> The moment is thy death (I, i, 164–78)

Each time Kent tries to protect Cordelia he is prevented. This forces him to use speech acts carrying pragmatic presuppositions (reinforced by the insulting use of *thee*) which assume social relations more and more at odds with those that in fact exist, until the role relations become apparently almost reversed. It is at this point that Lear finally banishes him.

[. . .]

The co-operative principle in conversation

Grice (1975) is one of the first attempts to account for meaning as it develops in conversation. To this end he distinguishes between what a sentence means and what someone means by uttering that sentence. Hence in the following possible dialogue:

A: Did you enjoy the play?
B: Well, I thought the ice creams they sold in the interval were good.

it is quite apparent that B is saying in an indirect and therefore relatively polite way that he did not enjoy the play, even though he does not actually say so. In ordinary language terms we might say that B implied that he did not like the play even though he did not say so. In order to avoid confusion over the term 'imply', which has a more technical use within philosophical logic, Grice coins the term 'implicature' for this kind of indirect, context-determined meaning. Hence, in the above example, B implicates that he did not enjoy the play.

Grice distinguishes first between what he calls conventional and conversational implicature. Conventional implicature has to do with the conventional as opposed to the logical meaning of certain words, particularly connectors. Hence, if someone says 'She comes from Oxford, so she must be a snob', the word *so* apparently makes an implicative relation between coming from Oxford and being a snob, in spite of the fact that when asked the speaker is hardly likely to want to say that everyone from Oxford is a snob.

An interesting example of the use of conventional implicature comes from Act III of Oscar Wilde's *The Importance of Being Earnest*. Jack is trying to persuade Lady Bracknell of the eligibility of Cecily Cardew:

Jack: Miss Cardew's family solicitors are Messrs. Markby, Markby and Markby.

Lady Bracknell: Markby, Markby and Markby? A firm of the very highest position in their profession. Indeed I am told that one of the Mr Markbys is occasionally to be seen at dinner parties. So far I am satisfied. (III, 139–44)

The sentence relating one of the Mr Markby's presence at dinner parties is obviously meant to be a reason for suggesting that the firm is 'of the very highest in their profession'. This is apparent from Lady Bracknell's use of the adverb 'indeed'. For her, someone's professional reputation can be judged by which table he sits at. However, this is unlikely to be the case for the audience and the use of 'indeed' points up the ironic contrast between us and her.

The distinction between what one says and what one means is also apparent in conversational implicature, where inferred interpretations cannot be ascribed to the conventional meanings of words like *so* and *indeed*. In explanation of this kind of meaning Grice claims that people entering into conversation with each other tacitly agree to co-operate towards mutual communicative ends, thus obeying the co-operative principle and its regulative conventions. He calls these conventions *maxims*, and has suggested that at least the following four obtain:

(1)   the *maxim* of quantity: make your contribution as informative as is required – don't give too much or too little information;

(2)   the *maxim* of quality: make your contribution one that you believe to be true;

(3)   the *maxim* of relation: be relevant;

(4)   the *maxim* of manner: avoid unnecessary prolixity, obscurity of expression and ambiguity, and be orderly.

Maxims are not, however, as strongly regulative as grammatical rules, and are therefore broken quite often. Grice outlines four such cases:

(i)   A speaker may unostentatiously *violate* a maxim; this accounts for lies and deceits.

(ii)   He may *opt out* of the co-operative principle, as, for example, members of government do when they refuse to answer questions on the ground that the information is classified.

(iii)   He may be faced with a clash, and will have therefore to break one maxim or another.

(iv)   He may ostentatiously *flout* a maxim.

It is under the final specification that conversational implicature occurs. Hence in the dialogue between A and B cited above, where maxims (1), (3) and (4) are broken, it is quite apparent to A that B could answer directly, relevantly and more economically whether or not he enjoyed the play. A assumes that B is still obeying the co-operative principle and that B knows that he will assume this. Given this set of assumptions, A then works out the implicature, namely that B did not enjoy the play but does not want to say so in a direct and relatively impolite way. [. . .]

It should be apparent that even the initial work in this area has considerable relevance for the study of literary texts in general and dramatic texts in particular (for other initial suggestions in this area see Pratt 1977; chs 4, 5). Hamlet's reply of 'Words, words, words' to Polonius is an obvious flouting of the maxim of quantity, as it merely gives Polonius information which he patently already possesses. The flouting of the maxim of quantity often seems to be rude, as can be seen from the first scene of *Romeo and Juliet*, where Gregory and Sampson are picking a quarrel with Abraham and Balthasar:

Abraham: Do you bite your thumb at us, sir?
Sampson: I do bite my thumb, sir. (I, i, 43–4)

It is arguable that Sampson's reply breaks the maxim of relation as well, and the repetition and parallelism also help mark the aggression. But what is important to notice here is that Shakespeare exploits the co-operative principle to help establish very quickly indeed the state of near war between the Capulets and Montagues. [. . .]

An example of the breaking of the maxim of relation can be seen in Tom Stoppard's *Enter a Free Man*:

> Riley: (sharply) Give me that tape.
> Brown: I haven't got one!
> Riley: My patience is not inexhaustible!

Brown explicitly rejects the presupposition contained in Riley's first utterance that he has got a tape. Riley interprets this as being an avoidance strategy, and in effect threatens him when he says: 'My patience is not inexhaustible'. We infer that this is a threat because Riley's statement about his patience, although not strictly relevant to the conversation at this point, can be interpreted as an indication that an important pre-condition for violent action on his part, namely the losing of his temper, is about to be fulfilled. Riley's statement also breaks the maxim of manner because of its indirect, double negative form. Interestingly enough, if the *indeed* was removed from the Oscar Wilde example quoted above, the ironic contrast between the workings of our world and Lady Bracknell's would still be apparent. It is thus possible that Grice's category of conventional implicature is really a special, explicit case of the maxim of relation.

This maxim is also problematical in other ways, because it is sometimes difficult to determine if it is broken when a speaker tries to change the topic of a conversation. Consider, for example, the following interchange in Act I of Robert Bolt's *A Man For All Seasons*. More and his daughter are talking just after the exit of Roper:

> Margaret: You're very gay. Did he talk about the divorce?
> More: Mm? You know I think we've been on the wrong track with Will.
>   It's no good arguing with a Roper.
> Margaret: Father, did he?
> More: *Old* Roper was just the same. Now let him think he's going *with*
>   the swim and he'll turn around and start swimming in the oppos-
>   ite direction.

It is quite apparent that More wants to change the subject in order not to talk about the royal divorce and hence refuses to answer Margaret's questions. She, on the other hand, is anxious to know what happened and therefore makes her second question unrelatable to his utterance by echoing her first question. More avoids it. Do implicatures pass between the characters here, are they just ignoring each other's contribution in order to gain topic control, or are both of these things happening? The possible ambiguity arises partly because of the embedded nature of dramatic discourse. What is an implicature for us, the audience, is not necessarily one for More's addressee. Does More want Margaret to realize his intention or not? [. . .]

For some reason it is fairly difficult to find clear examples of the flouting of the maxim of manner, especially in isolation. Another extract from *A Man For All Seasons* is particularly interesting, however. Norfolk is quizzing Rich in Act II about the cup which More gave to Rich in Act I, and which Cromwell wants to use as evidence of More accepting bribes:

> Norfolk: When did Thomas give you this thing?

Rich: I don't exactly remember.
Norfolk: Well, make an effort. Wait! I can tell you! I can tell you – it was
           that Spring – it was that night we were together. You had a cup
           with you when we left; was that it?
           (*Rich looks to Cromwell for guidance but gets none.*)
Rich: It may have been.
Norfolk: Did he often give you cups?
Rich: I don't suppose so. Your Grace.

First, it should be noted that this text contains examples of someone unostentatiously breaking the maxim of quality. Rich does not want to admit the details of the gift to Norfolk. But his replies are also more indirect than they need be. The modification of 'I don't remember' by 'exactly' and the use of 'I don't suppose so' are obvious examples. Rich's purpose in breaking the maxim of manner is not to convey implicatures to Norfolk. Quite the contrary. But at the higher level of discourse Bolt demonstrates to his audience/reader Rich's discomfiture in attempting to conceal the truth. [. . .]

Trouble in the Works

I now turn to an examination of a complete short text, a sketch by Harold Pinter called *Trouble in the Works*. For ease of reference the full text is given below along with sentence numbering. A full analysis would have to be more systematic than that which appears below, and would need to be supplemented by a full stylistic analysis of the more traditional kind.

(An office in a factory. (1) Mr Fibbs at the desk. (2) A knock at the door. (3) Enter Mr Wills. (4))

Fibbs: Ah, Wills. (5) Good. (6) Come in. (7) Sit down will you? (8)
Wills: Thanks, Mr Fibbs. (9)
Fibbs: You got my message? (10)
Wills: I just got it. (11)
Fibbs: Good. (12) Good. (13)
         (Pause. (14))
         Good. (15) Well now . . . (16) Have a cigar? (17)
Wills: No, thanks, not for me, Mr Fibbs. (18)
Fibbs: Well, now, Wills, I hear there's been a little trouble in the
         factory. (19)
Wills: Yes, I . . . I suppose you could call it that, Mr Fibbs. (20)
Fibbs: Well, what in heaven's name is it all about? (21)
Wills: Well, I don't exactly know how to put it, Mr Fibbs. (22)
Fibbs: Now come on, Wills . . . I've got to know what it is, before I can do
         anything about it. (23)
Wills: Well, Mr Fibbs, it's simply a matter that the men have . . . well . . .
         they seem to have taken a turn against some of the products. (24)
Fibbs: Taken a turn? (25)
Wills: They just don't seem to like them any more. (26)

Fibbs: Don't like them? (27) But we've got the reputation of having the finest machine part turnover in the country. (28) They're the best paid men in the industry. (29) We've got the cheapest canteen in Yorkshire. (30) No two menus are alike. (31) We've got a billiard hall, haven't we, on the premises, we've got a swimming pool for the use of staff. (32) And what about the long-playing record room? (33) And you tell me they're dissatisfied? (34)

Wills: Oh, the men are very grateful for all the amenities, sir. (35) They just don't like the products. (36)

Fibbs: But they're beautiful products. (37) I've been in the business a lifetime. (38) I've never seen such beautiful products. (39)

Wills: There it is, sir. (40)

Fibbs: Which ones don't they like? (41)

Wills: Well, there's the brass pet cock, for instance. (42)

Fibbs: The brass pet cock? (43) What's the matter with the brass pet cock? (44)

Wills: They just don't seem to like it any more. (45)

Fibbs: But what exactly don't they like about it? (46)

Wills: Perhaps it's just the look of it. (47)

Fibbs: That brass pet cock? (48) But I tell you it's perfection. (49) Nothing short of perfection. (50)

Wills: They've just gone right off it. (51)

Fibbs: Well, I'm flabbergasted. (52)

Wills: It's not only the brass pet cock, Mr Fibbs. (53)

Fibbs: What else? (54)

Wills: There's the hemi unibal spherical rod end. (55)

Fibbs: The hemi unibal spherical rod end? (56) But where could you find a finer rod end? (57)

Wills: There are rod ends and rod ends, Mr Fibbs. (58)

Fibbs: I know there are rod ends and rod ends. (59) But where could find a finer hemi unibal spherical rod end? (60)

Wills: They just don't want to have anything more to do with it. (61)

Fibbs: This is shattering. (62) Shattering. (63) What else? (64) Come on Wills. (65) There's no point in hiding anything from me. (66)

Wills: Well, I hate to say it, but they've gone very vicious about the high speed taper shank spiral flute reamers. (67)

Fibbs: The high speed taper shank spiral flute reamers! (68) But that's absolutely ridiculous! (69) What could they possibly have against the high speed taper shank spiral flute reamers? (70)

Wills: All I can say is they're in a state of very bad agitation about them. (71) And then there's the gunmetal side outlet relief with handwheel. (72)

Fibbs: What! (73)

Wills: There's the nippled connector and the nippled adapter and the vertical mechanical comparator. (74)

Fibbs: No! (75)

Wills: And the one they can't speak about without trembling is the jaw for Jacob's chuck for use on portable drill. (76)

Fibbs: My own Jacob's chuck? (77) Not my very own Jacob's chuck? (78)

Wills: They've just taken a turn against the whole lot of them, I tell you. (79) Male elbow adaptors, tubing nuts, grub screws, internal fan washers, dog points, half dog points, white metal bushes – (80)

Fibbs: But not, surely not, my lovely parallel male stud couplings. (81)

Wills: They hate and detest your lovely parallel male stud couplings, and the straight flange pump connectors, and back nuts, and front nuts, *and* the bronzedraw off cock with handwheel and the bronzedraw off cock without handwheel! (82)

Fibbs: Not the bronzedraw off cock with handwheel? (83)

Wills: And without handwheel. (84)

Fibbs: Without handwheel? (85)

Wills: And with handwheel. (86)

Fibbs: Not with handwheel? (87)

Wills: And without handwheel. (88)

Fibbs: Without handwheel? (89)

Wills: With handwheel *and* without handwheel? (90)

Fibbs: With handwheel *and* without handwheel? (91)

Wills: With or without! (92)

(Pause. (93))

Fibbs: (Broken) Tell me. (94) What do they want to make in its place? (95)

Wills: Brandy balls. (96)

[. . .] The role relations of the two characters will be marked on stage by their dress, seating position etc. They are also indicated by the vocatives. Fibbs always uses last name only, whereas Wills uses either title plus last name or 'sir'. In the first part of the sketch Fibbs speaks first and initiates the conversational exchanges (see Coulthard 1977: 95–6). He also uses the speech acts of commanding and questioning, which correlate with the pragmatic presupposition that he is socially superior to Wills. Wills, for his part, at the beginning of the piece answers the questions exactly, producing no extra comments of his own, uses lexical items introduced by Fibbs rather than bringing in his own, and does not initiate new topics (cf. the pregnant pause (14)).

Wills's unease is indicated largely by his flouting of the maxim of manner. In sentence 20 he might have replied with 'Yes', but that would have broken the maxim of quality, as there has obviously been more than a little trouble. Instead, he uses the modal verb 'could' (which allows the possibility of *couldn't*) embedded under the non-factive 'suppose'. In 22 he breaks both manner and relation. In 24 he hesitates and has to reformulate his sentence, and then gives the essential information that the men have 'taken a turn' against some of the products, embedded under another non-factive, 'seem'. This circumlocution allied to the use of 'seem' is also used in 26 and 45. The turn-around in relations in the sketch occurs as Fibbs discovers how intransigent the men are towards the products he is so attached to. This takes place gradually in the middle of the sketch. I therefore want to suggest a division of the text into three main sections, corresponding approximately to the following sentence numbers: I = 1–35; II = 36–71; III = 72–96. In terms of numbers of sentences these sections are roughly equal. The first shows Fibbs dominant over Wills and exhibits all of the features outlined above, the third shows Wills dominant over Fibbs, and the second provides the mediation for the change. I have selected sentence 36 as the hinge point between sections I and II because it is here that Wills initiates a conversational exchange for the first time in the sketch. First he replies to Fibbs's question and then he adds a new comment, taking the subject back to that of his previous utterance (26). In so doing, he also denies the presupposition in Fibbs's question, namely that employees cannot be dissatisfied if they have good amenities. Section II shows the two men exchanging control of the conversation. Fibbs takes back the initiative in 41, Wills attempts to take control in 53, Fibbs takes it back in 54, and so on. Section III, on the other hand, is marked by the fact that from the point at which Wills takes back the initiative in 72 he never loses it. As the sketch progresses through this last section Wills's lexis also becomes dominant, so that at the end, in the sequence about the bronzedraw off cock with and without handwheel, Fibbs, in his disbelief, merely repeats the main part of Wills's previous utterance.

The last section is also completely denuded of vocatives marking their 'official' status relations. If we compare the density of status-marking vocatives in sections I and II we find that in section I there are five instances of 'Mr Fibbs' and three occasions where Wills calls Fibbs 'sir' and three occasions where Fibbs uses 'Wills' – i.e. there is a status-marking vocative once every three and a half sentences. In section II there are two instances of 'Mr Fibbs', one of 'sir' and none of 'Wills' – i.e. one every ten sentences. Section III has none at all. We have already noticed that the conversational initiative changes hands relatively often only in the middle section. Hence there is a fairly gradual change in the relations exhibited between the two men. It is also interesting to note in this respect that as the middle section develops Wills breaks the maxim of manner less and less, becoming more and more direct in his replies. The battle for dominance can be neatly illustrated in sentences 55–61.

By now the linguistic basis for the turn-around in the situation should be clear. This leads to the absurd position whereby the manager at the end of the sketch is at the mercy of his shop steward. But this is not the only thing which makes the sketch unreal. It is also the case that there is a series of existential presuppositional clashes between characters and audience. Wills and Fibbs spend their time discussing items about whose existence we must have considerable doubt. A good example is 'high speed taper shank spiral flute reamers'. Like the other products in the sketch they are referred to partly by the use of a noun–noun sequence, this time an extremely long one. [. . .] Because of the wide range of semantic relations associated with such sequences, the longer they get the more uninterpretable they become. Even 'spiral flute reamer' would present problems. Is it something spiral which reams flutes, or a reamer with a spiral flute? And so on. This problem of interpretability is made worse by the use of technical terms like 'comparator', 'flange' and 'bronzedraw', and the fact that a good few of the words and phrases carry overt sexual connotations, for example, 'parallel male stud couplings', 'off cock', 'pet cock'. [. . .] We thus have a situation where the two men are becoming very heated over items whose existence we doubt. But it should be apparent that discourse analysis can be usefully applied in this example to account for much of the sketch's absurdity and 'dramatic' nature, a quality which is quite apparent even if one has never seen the piece enacted.

Conclusion

There are of course problems in using the kind of analyses outlined above. Not least is the fact that the linguistic theory used for analysis is still open to discussion and modification. In spite of initial work by Searle (1975b) it is by no means clear how conversational implicature fits in exactly with the more general notion of indirect speech acts. Moreover, because the original categorization, although not as informal as my treatment, is still relatively informal, it is difficult in some cases to know whether a particular maxim is broken or not, or whether a 'meaning' of which one is intuitively aware can be explained by the implicature theory. A related problem is that of the relative uncontrollability of speaker intention in what has sometimes been called a communication-intention theory of meaning. A speaker might break the maxim of manner, for example, either to implicate something or to try to disguise something from his interlocutor, as Rich does in the example from *A Man For All Seasons*. A complete theory will need to determine which case applies where. The maxim of quality often appears to be broken in casual conversation, where people quite frequently repeat what has already been said in another form. But the 'meaning' of such behaviour is more likely to be part of the general expression of social cohesion than implicature-like in type. Ordinary conversation is also more meandering than the strict application of the maxim of relation would allow.

The problem as to what level of discourse implicatures operate at is a good indication of the need for a fuller and more formal account; and to count as a reasonable and observable analysis almost all the passages I have looked at would require more detailed and explicit treatment. [. . .] But these are questions which always dog the stylistician. There will always be arguments over how detailed and explicit critical analysis should be. And as no area of linguistic analysis can ever really be said to be complete, the stylistician has always to take the analysis he applies partly on trust. Otherwise he would never begin his work at all.

References

Austin, J.L. (1962) *How to Do Things with Words*. Oxford: Oxford University Press.

Carter, R. and Simpson, P. (eds) (1989) *Language, Discourse and Literature: An Introductory Reader in Discourse Stylistics*. London: Allen and Unwin/Routledge.

Coulthard, M. (1977) *An Introduction to Discourse Analysis*. Harlow: Longman.

Culpeper, J., Short, M. and Verdonk, P. (eds) (1998) *Exploring the Language of Drama: From Text to Context*. London: Routledge.

Grice, H.P. (1975) 'Logic and conversation', in P. Cole and J. Morgan (eds) *Syntax and Semantics, Vol 3, Speech Acts*, New York: Academic Press, pp. 41–58.

Keenan, E.L. (1971) 'Two kinds of presupposition in natural language', in C.J. Fillmore and D.T. Langendoen (eds) *Studies in Linguistic Semantics*, New York: Holt, Rinehart and Winston, pp. 45–54.

Kempson, R. (1975) *Presupposition and the Delimitation of Semantics*. Cambridge: Cambridge University Press.

Leech, G.N. (1974) *Semantics*. Harmondsworth: Penguin.

Pratt, M.L. (1977) *Toward a Speech Act Theory of Literary Discourse*. Bloomington: Indiana University Press.

Searle, J. (1965) 'What is a speech act?' in M. Black (ed.) *Philosophy in America*, London: Allen and Unwin, pp. 221–39.

Searle, J. (1969) *Speech Acts: An Essay in the Philosophy of Language*. Cambridge: Cambridge University Press.

Searle, J. (1975a) 'The logical status of fictional discourse', *New Literary History*, 6: 19–32.

Searle, J. (1975b) 'Indirect speech acts', in P. Cole and J. Morgan (eds) *Syntax and Semantics, Vol 3, Speech Acts*, New York: Academic Press, pp. 59–82.

Short, M. (1996) *Exploring the Language of Poetry, Prose and Plays*. Harlow: Longman.

Strawson, P. (1952) *Introduction to Logical Theory*. London: Methuen.

Extracted from M.H. Short (1980) 'Discourse analysis and drama', *Applied Linguistics* 2 (2): 180–202.

PART TWO

Developments

Chapter 9

Poem, reader, response: making sense with *Skunk Hour*

MICHAEL TOOLAN

Stylistics has many different threads: it can be artisanal and practical, with an emphasis on the textual mechanics of a piece of literature, and it can be theoretically sophisticated, with an emphasis on the philosophy of language in general; it can be statistically rigorous and quantitative, and also highly personal; it can be narrowly linguistic, and broadly sociolinguistic. In this chapter, Michael Toolan begins with a philosophical positioning, and elucidates his viewpoint through a close stylistic reading of a poem by Robert Lowell. As the argument develops, it moves away from the sorts of features that any language-aware reader might notice explicitly, towards a more systematic analysis typical of the stylistician. In doing so, Toolan argues for a careful engagement with actual language, not a theoretical ideal of language, and he adapts his methods with principled pragmatism and eclecticism. It might be, as he says, 'shaky' and 'provisional', but it is honest.

The chapter was originally written in the mid-1980s. Toolan went on to develop his thinking expressed here in *The Stylistics of Fiction* (1990) and *Total Speech* (1996).

[. . . W]HAT DO I MEAN by 'a stylistic reading of *Skunk Hour*' [by Robert Lowell]? What is the status of this process and product? These are difficult, perhaps impossible questions to answer satisfactorily – because they are the wrong questions to ask. And yet they are (along with 'But what's the point of all this? Where is either the linguistic justification, or the literary pay-off in an enriched interpretation, for your claims?'), the commonest dismissive rejoinders from both linguists and literary critics. I believe these are false or mistaken questions [. . .]: they are premised on the illusion of linguistics as a scientific study of a fixed bi-planar structural system, on the one hand, and on the received orthodoxy of literary criticism that it is the sensitive open-minded pursuit of *an* essentialist (richest) interpretation of a well-wrought fixed icon of significations (the inalienable property of the text, not the reader). Conventional – prevailing – linguistics and criticism, then, have both miscast the relations between the individual and the community: linguistics assumes that meanings and interpretations are shared, or shareable, just as words are; and professional criticism, while paying lip-service to the facts of private, individual reading and interpretation, typically proceeds, through teaching, examinations, journal- and book-publishing, to disallow much of the rich variety of proferred readings, to foster in readers a self-censorship of the 'eccentric', and to privilege one (perhaps two or three, if it's a classic text) allegedly rich, allegedly 'widely-accepted' interpretation. Both enterprises suppress the active role of the individual.

I thus want to view stylistics as a way rather than a method, a confessedly partial or oriented act of intervention, a reading which is strategic, as all readings necessarily are, whose attraction for me lies in its attempt at public-ness, even as it acknowledges private-ness, unpredictability. If that is an unhappy compromise, I can think of no happier one, nor of any less compromised happiness. If we resist the privileging of undecidability of the 'wild' deconstructionists (Derrida himself seems not to be of their number), engaged in their private revels of pure textuality, we must inevitably grapple with (we may avoid succumbing to) what Christopher Norris has called 'the normative constraints of effective communication' (1982: 113). Be he never so radical in his reading, the published critic's interpretation of a poem is necessarily norm-shaping. The acts of publication, inviting readers to read your views, entail struggling to compel or persuade readers to privilege your reading of a poem over theirs – or at least to engage with your reading and (too often) submit to it through exhaustion, inertia, pressure of other demands. Hence the professional's double bind: he's damned if he doesn't publish, by effecting little intervention in his communities (to say nothing of the pressure to publish or perish – i.e., cease to be a professional); he's damned if he does (prey to charges of authoritarian prescription, coercion of readers and students). The solution – insofar as this is a problem requiring a 'solution' – may lie in renewed self-critical awareness of the provisionality of one's reading, the roots of description in rhetorical persuasion, the bogus and/or non-literary determinants of much that constitutes the academic discipline of literature, a renewed recognition that *professing* literature is too often lost sight of within the literary profession.

My reading then is in part an artifact shaped by the adopted model and theory (not wholly determined – the model is too leaky, and some of the holes are my own work). But there is no alternative to this. There is no absolute or essential reading/ interpretation of *Skunk Hour* since there are no absolute, context-free models or theories. Interpretation and persuasion are everywhere and always at work. Perhaps the most important interpretive act in this essay is one which appears to have cost little intellectual effort on my part: the simple picking out of a particular poem, *Skunk Hour*, by a particular poet, Lowell, and my thrusting it on the attention of readers: a foregrounding or deautomatisation of that particular brief discourse from the vast city of texts jostling for recognition and attention in the arena of 'language and literature'.

If interpretation is ubiquitous the question then becomes, why this particular interpretation? We may adopt Stanley Fish's (1981) notion that *this* particular interpretation, masquerading as original but in fact largely predictable/predicted, derives from or is constituted, validated and sustained by a particular community of interpreters, some group of indefinite extent from whom derives, in whom resides, the authority (provisional, local, community-bound) for such readings.

Much of this is helpful, but it resists one dominant set of myths in literary criticism and the reading of literature (namely that authorial intentions are crucial, the major goal of study; that there is an ideal, 'full' reading of any text – like a Platonic form – in relation to which the dissonant versions of lesser critics are only an approximation), only to arrive us at a position which, while potentially plausible, lacks a great deal of essential examination and critique. We must ask what and where these communities are, how they are constituted, influenced, and changed, and so on. There are perspectives from sociolinguistics, social theory, and cultural criticism, which can enrich our understanding of these phenomena (see the work of Goffman 1971, Halliday 1978, Berger and Luckmann 1967, Said 1982, and Foucault 1972).

In what follows I will present my impressions of what are important patterns and features (motivated prominences, in Halliday's terms) in *Skunk Hour*. As I've implied before, this is the way I use stylistics as *I* make sense of the poem (but I won't deny that I'd like to persuade you). I shall make some attempt to order my observations around established linguistic domains – grammar, syntax, cohesion, semantic oddity or absurdity, transitivity, rhyme and line structure – but hope to resist becoming over-constrained by those 'categories'. Calling to mind traditional grammatical description entails in itself a kind of foregrounding: one foregrounds the nouniness of certain words, the verbiness of others, the proper naminess of some nouny words, not others, the abstractness of some nouny words besides the concreteness of others, and so on. But traditional grammatical categorisations are not entirely arbitrary: they arise and are sustained partly because language-users (often chiefly with pedagogical or rhetorical concerns) find that the patterns of distribution and usage of items in those categories do justify acknowledging samenesses and differences.

Skunk Hour (for Elizabeth Bishop)

Nautilus Island's hermit
heiress still lives through winter in her Spartan cottage;
her sheep still graze above the sea.
Her son's a bishop. Her farmer
is first selectman in our village,
She's in her dotage.

Thirsting for
the hierarchic privacy
of Queen Victoria's century,
she buys up all
the eyesores facing her shore,
and lets them fall.

The season's ill –
we've lost our summer millionaire,
who seemed to leap from an L.L. Bean
catalogue. His nine-knot yawl
was auctioned off to lobstermen.
A red fox stain covers Blue Hill.

And now our fairy
decorator brightens his shop for fall,

his fishnet's filled with orange cork,
orange, his cobbler's awl,
there is no money in his work,
he'd rather marry.

One dark night,
my Tudor Ford climbed the hill's skull,
I watched for love-cars. Lights turned down,
they lay together, hull to hull,
where the graveyard shelves on the town . . .
My mind's not right.

A car radio bleats,
'Love, O careless Love . . .' I hear
my ill-spirit sob in each blood cell,
as if my hand were at its throat . . .
I myself am hell,
nobody's here –

only skunks, that search
in the moonlight for a bite to eat.
They march on their soles up Main Street:
white stripes, moonstruck eyes' red fire
under the chalk-dry and spar spire
of the Trinitarian Church

I stand on top
of our back steps and breathe the rich air –
a mother skunk with her column of kittens swills the
garbage pail.
She jabs her wedge-head in a cup
of sour cream, drops her ostrich tail,
and will not scare.

(Lowell 1977)

When I look at nouns in this poem I notice that there are several proper names – Nautilus, Spartan, Queen Victoria, L.L. Bean, Blue Hill, Tudor Ford, Main St, Trinitarian Church – which I take to be establishing a setting, 'placing' an action, and fostering a mood. The environments that these indexical names severally evoke are potentially quite removed from each other (historically, geographically, culturally). But in this poem that disparateness may be part of a dilemma to be resolved. The lack of fit, connection, coherence in the world the speaker dramatises is implied by such heterogeneity: the question may then arise as to whether this heterogeneity, this disparateness, is a 'problem' to be solved. While still thinking of nouns, one might remark that the three personae of the first half of the poem (which we may wish to set against the 'I' and the skunks of the second half) are all, definitionally, rather exotic individuals: a hermit heiress, a summer millionaire, and a fairy decorator. I believe it important to register such facile, banal observations – despite the contemptuous resistance of traditional critics – precisely because for me – and, I suspect, many others – such immediately-perceived characteristics, noted on a first reading, are very influential on the shape of the elaborated interpretation that comes with repeated readings: I am now *disposed* to expect more – or more about – eccentric individuals, and oddity (even grotesqueness) in their behaviour or the speakers' description of it.

As for the finite verbs, those in the first six stanzas are marked by their connotations of dullness and passivity: *lives, graze, 's, is, 's, buys, lets, 's, 've lost*, and so on. By contrast, when the skunks appear the verbs characteristically express purposive action: *search, march, stand, breathe, swills, jabs, drops, will . . . scare*. In addition note that these are monosyllabic and present tense, and always carry prosodic stress. They may be contrasted with the switched tenses of the earlier stanzas, and, more particularly, the commonest present tense verb of that section, the contracted *'s* form. Using that form has two important effects: it promotes both conversational informality between persona and reader, and a non-syllabic (therefore stress-less) reading of the verb.

Focussing on tense, I see a progression from the extended-relevance or -validity present tense forms of stanzas one to four; to the past tense of stanza five (except the final, confessional line); to the immediate present tense of stanzas six to eight, concluding in the final line with modal *will* (modals being a closed system of verbs with a cluster of especially reserved meanings: here I take the *will* to convey both prediction and insistence).

At the level of syntax what appears prominent is the frequency of short declarative clauses, which often seem conjoined rather abruptly (a point I shall return to when discussing thematic structure and theme-switching). Again, only in the last two stanzas – only (my interpretive aspect would suggest) under the influence of focussing on the planned, purposeful activity of the skunks – do we find the run of clauses genuinely cohering in a sequential discourse. And there is very little embedding of finite clauses: asyndetically-coordinated independent clauses seem to be the norm. This prompts the judgement that here is a series of disparate statements, not closely or hierarchically related to each other. Even where we *suspect* causal connections of purpose or result (between events or states, or between an observation and an evaluation of the self/mind that has made that observation), as at various points in stanzas five and six, explicit connectives signalling logical relations are conspicuously absent. Again, this is conversational, intimate, reflective, self-oriented, and perhaps dangerously uncontrolled, disordered.

Clausal embedding is rare then in this poem. My stylistic approach will nevertheless tend to be attentive to the nature and distribution of any such embedding that does occur. The only subordinated or embedded clauses in the poem are the following:

1. An A clause on *buys* in stanza 2.
2. A Rel clause on *eyesores* in stanza 2.
3. A Rel clause on *millionaire* in stanza 3.
4. An A clause on *lay* in stanza 5.
5. An A clause on *sob* in stanza 6.
6. A Rel clause on *skunks* in stanza 7.

In addition, we should distinguish between top-level Adverbial constituents, which are strictly only subordinate in the sentences in which they occur, and clauses dependent on other top-level clause constituents, hence fully embedded. Here, only the relative clauses, items 2, 3, and 6, are true embeddings. And what is noticeable is that comparatively, the embedding under *skunks*, in line 1 of stanza 7, is one level more complex than the other earlier two subordinate clauses. For it itself has, as Object, a non-finite nominal clause (*a bite to eat*). In other words, I am arguing that *skunks, that search in the moonlight for a bite to eat* is structurally noticeably more complex than either *eyesores facing her shore* or *our summer millionaire, who seemed to leap from an L.L. Bean catalogue.* And that increased structural complexity coincides with many other impressions of a development of order, pattern, coherence, perceived and comprehended complexity, in the final stanzas of the poem – no more than that. (One might also reflect on what – if grammarians are to be trusted – seems an atypical use of *that* as introducer of what I take to be a *non*-restrictive relative clause. Typically *that* is said to be limited to use in introducing restrictive (defining) relative clauses – but not here.)

If we turn now to consideration of the discoursal level of cohesion, and its patternings in this poem, we find a stark absence of intersentential grammatical cohesion. In other words there are few grammatical links between the sentences of this text. On the other hand there is plenty of 'structural' connectedness – which is cohesion in a broader use of that term – via subtle alliterative and assonantal ties between lines. Sometimes, as in the pairing of *in our village* and *in her dotage* in stanza one –

> Her farmer
> is first selectman in our village,
> she's in her dotage.

– this may deepen a tacit mordant scorn of characters. But the richness of connectedness via sound patterning in, particularly, the final four lines of both stanzas seven and eight, conveys nothing so much as a renewed awareness of the complexity of particularity, the relevance of the apparently contingent and unrelated, hidden congruence. The absence of conventional cohesion – even at the lexical level – is one source of the strong impression of brokenness, disjointedness, absence of ordinary thematic unity. Instead, there seems to be a restless flitting, disorderedly, from topic to topic as the stanzas pass.

While there is no conventional lexical cohesion, we may begin to perceive certain lexical interrelations, noticeable for the contradictions, absurdities, the bizarre comparisons or associations they suggest. These are so frequent as to suggest a motivated highlighting of semantic oddity:

1. The *heiress* lives in a *Spartan* cottage.
2. Mention of sheep in l.3 is followed by mention of the son, a bishop (shepherd of a flock?).
3. The faintly ludicrous sheep connotations are kept in play in stanza six, where 'a car radio *bleats*'.
4. The heiress buys up houses only to let them fall.
5. The millionaire's yawl, a boat bought as a plaything, is auctioned off to lobstermen. In a strange reversal of the conventional progression (degeneration?), what was originally a toy becomes a work-tool.
6. Even the descriptions of the early characters contain classifiers which sit ill with the nouns themselves: hermit heiress is a familiar enough breach of the predictable; more suggestive is 'summer millionaire' (is this wealth bound to an annual

cycle?), while 'fairy decorator' teases chiefly since, until recently, 'fairy' would have conventionally been thought of as something which itself decorates, rather than as designating part of the nature of the decorator.

7.   *Blue* Hill is covered by a *red* fox stain.

8.   The decorator '*brightens* his shop for *fall*' (my emphases). A literalist reading may see this as a kind of commercial counteracting of the cold and gloom prevalent in winter months, the shop as a haven of light and warmth – sound business sense. But are there no overtones of decadence, of an advertised carnivalesque delight in the decline of the year, if not a more general decline? A brazen flouting of the proprieties of the seasonal rhythms?

9.   Extending the topic broached in stanza three, of trivial play versus serious work, we are told of the decorator:

> his fishnet's filled with orange cork,
> orange, his cobbler's bench and awl,
> there is no money in his work,
> he'd rather marry.

Despite the possessive pronouns, we know he is neither fisherman nor cobbler – *his fishnet* and *his bench* must be recognised as of quite different status than *his work*. The speaker's elliptical turn of phrase is deliberately misleading, deliberately highlights the gulf between these traditional productive means of employment, and the parasitic imitative 'creativity' of the decorator. It is this latter parasitism in which there is 'no money', rather than the humble primary trades which that parasitism mimics and plays at (literally) domesticating. It remains only to cap these evasions with an absurdity which mocks conventional sexual institutions, and conjures a form of self-prostitution: the homosexual would 'rather marry'.

10. It is not *lovers* who lie together in stanza five, but cars, 'hull to hull'.

11. The 'love' song of stanza six is followed by an image of desperate, murderous insanity.

What, the literary critic asks, does the stylistician make of all this? My answer to this will be developed in a later section of integrative interpretation, but it must be stressed that it is not a question of first finding pure forms, then supplying pure meanings – 'here the form, there the interpretation', to adapt Wittgenstein (1953). The picking out of just these alleged absurdities, bizarreries, grotesqueries, and ironies itself rests on a complex matrix of interpretations, related to how the world habitually is, how language habitually behaves (or rather how speakers habitually use language) *according to me*.

One of the most suggestive linguistic descriptions to have been applied to literary – and other – texts is that of Hallidayan transitivity, the analysis of clauses into certain basic types, and examination of the participant relations within those clauses. It might be complained that the Hallidayan transitivity I propose to apply here is an offshoot of the fixed-code structuralism I have earlier rejected. But whatever the original objectives, in practice Hallidayan transitivity 'systems', like traditional accounts of grammatical word-classes and categories, are quite unlike structuralist grammars, being rhetoric-oriented descriptions focussed on users' unpredictable meaning potential (rather than a 'rule-bound creativity'). In terms of the basic clause options – Action, Mental Process and Relational – it emerges that, in the early stanzas, Relationals are particularly common ('Her son's a bishop. Her farmer / is first selectman in our village, / She's in her dotage', etc.), while there are also several Action clauses – but with negative connotations:

> we've lost our summer millionaire
> His . . . yawl / was auctioned off to lobstermen

Throughout the poem Mental Process clauses are rare. This may seem surprising, given that Lowell is recognised as a confessional poet who skilfully and vividly dramatised his very personal angst, his mental turbulences and passions – and certainly *Skunk Hour* is centrally to do with the grounds for and implications of the speaker's disclosure 'My mind's not right'. It may be that part of the impact of the great confessional poems of the sixties inheres in their avoidance of the leaden literalism that is borne by such direct disclosure as 'I think x', etc., i.e., direct expression of private perceptions, cognitions, and reactions. (In an earlier draft of the poem, entitled 'Inspiration', there are several Mental Process clauses with the speaker as Subject – including the memorable line 'I hate the summer' – which have not survived Lowell's rewriting.) If, as is sometimes claimed, the best confessional poets offer more than self-indulgent, self-regarding therapy, by *metaphorising* their personal distress, an avoidance of MP clauses in favour of Action and Relational ones may be one marker of that metaphorising.

Concerning the speaker of the poem as textual participant, the progression in clause types is from the passivity of MP and R clauses (some with a body part as Affected participant, rather than the whole individual), to a one-participant Action clause, and, finally, a transitive 2-participant Action clause. The speaker figures within the poem only in the final four stanzas. The very first mention of his involvement is eloquent of his initial passivity, submission: 'my Tudor Ford climbed the hill's skull', not 'I drove my Tudor Ford. . . .' Subsequent clauses involving the speaker appear in the following sequence:

I watched for love-cars	MP
My mind's not right	R body-part
I hear my ill-spirit sob	MP body-part
as if my hand were at its throat	R body-part
I myself am hell	R
I stand on top . . .	A 1-part
and breathe the rich air	A 2-part

There is a progression through the poem, then, from focus on mental events and passive reporting of states, to purposeful, speaker-initiated, speaker-controlled action. Using the vocabulary of stylistics I hope to have indicated some of the patterns I perceive to be constitutive of my own interpretation of the poem. But the patternings or progressions mentioned so far are only part of the story. There are many other phenomena in the poem which make important impressions on me – though these are sometimes resistant to assimilation to the conventional descriptive methods of conventional stylistics. This does not make stylistics 'wrong', it simply confirms that in its traditional form it is insufficient: either we radically change stylistics, or we continue to view it as only a part of the way of interpretation. Among these other phenomena I would include the enigmatic rhyme scheme – schematic since (in all but the first stanza, which in addition – like stanza six – has a half-rhyme between lines one and four) there is an ingenious manipulation of a rhyme on each of three distinct syllables, resistant to schematisation in the persistent irregularity or unpredictability of where those rhymes will fall.

abcabb	abbcac	abcdca	abcbca	abcbca	abcacb	abbcca	abcacb
1	2	3	4	5	6	7	8

Again, with sufficient grasp of the dynamics of rhyme and metre, one might uncover an elaborate rhetoric at work here, but what strikes my attention, without such a penetrative analysis, is that enigmatic effect of apparent attention to formal euphony coupled with apparent openness which defies predictability of the pattern. On a more pedestrian note, for what it's worth, it may be that other readers besides me are struck by the number of weak or imperfect rhymes in the early stanzas, often due to their occurrence on disyllabic words with main stress on the first syllable – *hermit/farmer*, *cottage/village/ dotage*, *privacy/century*, *fairy/marry* – by contrast with the consistently full rhymes of the final monosyllabics in the final two stanzas – *search/Church*, *eat/street*, and so on.

Even more removed from traditional stylistics will be my observations on stanza five, where the imagery of love and death compels reflection on the theme of the interconnectedness of love and death. Set on 'one dark night' which, in the context of this poem and of Lowell's known religious convictions, may evoke the 'dark night of the soul' experienced by St John of the Cross and other Christian mystics on their passionate *via* towards inner light, the speaker climbs 'the hill's skull'. Besides the self-evident mortality brought to mind by the word 'skull', the phrase may also echo the sites of Christ's own passion and death – the hill of Calvary, and Golgotha, the place of the skull. Night, itself, connotes both death and the time of love-making, but there is something deliberately grotesque about their conflation here. As noted earlier, it is not the lovers themselves who lie together here, but their cars. But the cars, too, are metonymically reduced, to 'hulls', evocative of empty dead shells. In addition, the sentence progression here –

> they lay together, hull to hull,
> where the graveyard shelves on the town . . .

effects a series of juxtapositions: the lovers to each other, (implicitly) the dead to each other and to the lovers, the graveyard dead to the town living. The lover's hill is, literally, the graveyard; Christ's passion and death were the extreme act of love; and so on. If anything, the analogies and argument are too naked, too desperate, as the speaker acknowledges: 'My mind's not right'. What is established is the sense of a psyche close to disintegration, an impression sustained perhaps by the instances of incomplete, or awkwardly-formed sentence structures in stanza six.

Reflecting the thematic and psychological shift in the last two stanzas, only between stanzas six and seven ('nobody's here – // only skunks') is there structural run-on or connectedness. It's an opening-out which involves amending the earlier wholly negative and absurdist outlook. And the sentence itself, internally, presents an amended view: *nobody's here – // only skunks.*

Lowell was perhaps the greatest of the self-disclosing confessional poets: and yet this poem seems to be largely about others, the heiress, the fairy decorator, the skunks. But in a deeper way we may feel this to be a holding-up of a mirror to the speaker himself. As is acknowledged in stanza six, 'nobody's here' except the speaker – describing, interpreting, conveying his sense of alienation-from-self through his morbid, bitter dwelling on the pathetic, wasted, futile lives of his neighbours. What can be done with this waste? Well, skunks cope with it, exploit it, *make sense* of the mad waste – and the speaker shares the skunks' improvisatory and purposeful activity.

There are several suggestions that the speaker sees some common cause with the skunks – especially the mother skunk. Thus the structuring of the final stanza, line 3, describing the skunks, may be read as a figurative or metaphorical appositional clause describing the 'I' figure breathing the rich air:

> I stand on top
> of our back steps and breathe the rich air –
> a mother skunk with her column of kittens swills the garbage pail.

At any rate, there is a structural and thematic parallel between (1) the speaker breathing in the rich air (note, not *smelly* air!), and (2) the skunks swilling the garbage pail. And with that parallelism (if not identification) in mind, again structurally, the final line, 'and will not scare', can become an affirmation about the speaker as well as the skunk.

At a very general level, then, there is a progression here from loveless self-destruction and voyeurism and perversity, to a limited sense of sharing, community, with the skunks. The humans have money, but appear unresourceful, passive, infertile, arid; the skunks must scavenge, but are active and resourceful. By contrast with the clauses of implicit failure, decline, dehumanising anachronistic yearning in stanzas one to six, the skunks occupy Subject position in clauses with verbs of purposeful, positive action: *search, march, swill, jab, drop, (not) scare.*

A final word on 'She . . . will not scare'. How may we interpret this? A first assumption may be that we simply have an ellipted passive version, 'derived' from:

> She will not be scared by x

But should we exclude an alternative reading, which the syntax certainly invites:

> She will not scare x (where x: me, the speaker)?

The dual reading sustains the identification of skunk and speaker implied elsewhere, and further suggests that the latter is no longer terrified, powerless prey to his own 'ill-spirit'.

It only remains for me to record my deep dissatisfaction with the foregoing determined reading of *Skunk Hour*, my sense of failed communication, even to myself as reader, of how the poem truly works on me. My problem is not that I've failed to understand Lowell's mind: it is that I don't know my own mind. Just as Barthes celebrated the poem which could mean many things to one reader, interpretive stylistics as a way of reading arrives one at mirages of closure only to remind that the way, the text, continues. [. . .]

Those sceptical of Fish's [1981] notions that the authority of interpretations rests with communities, and that interpretation is all, often ask what these acts of interpreting are interpretations *of*. For those wedded to a goal of comprehensive description of the 'interpretive competence' of an interpretive community, there is the awful prospect of an infinite regress (note the loadedness of that word!), reading as entering the abyss. Once a belief is 'unpicked', its interpretive roots specified (to the extent that this is possible), it ceases to be the *fons et origo* of one's interpretive practices – the roots now are, instead.

What then of stylistics, and its interpretive foundations in language? Cannot language description, like any other descriptive-cum-interpretive base, be unpicked, analysed, dissolved? In principle, yes. But not in practice, if we continue to want to see poems as a public discourse, shareable to a degree by different readers. The lunar pull of convention, collectivity, normativity, social cohesion and accommodation, interacts dialectically with individualism and *self*-consciousness. Our eyes are moonstruck, whatever our private intentions. Speaking relatively, and personally, there can be no willed forgetting of this language game. And so the soiled 'truths' of structuralism return, to lead a better life and be of service to the community: our shaky, provisional structures of writing and reading (as of speaking and listening), these projects of our desires, are seen for what they always and necessarily are: the work of bricoleurs, not engineers.

References

Berger, P. and Luckmann, T. (1967) *The Social Construction of Reality*. Harmondsworth: Penguin.

Fish, S. (1980) *Is There a Text in This Class?* New York: Oxford University Press.,

Foucault, M. (1972) *The Archaeology of Knowledge*. London: Tavistock.

Goffman, E. (1971) *Relations in Public*. Harmondsworth: Penguin.

Halliday, M.A.K. (1978) *Language as Social Semiotic*. London: Edward Arnold.

Lowell, R. (1977) 'Skunk hour', in *Selected Poems*, New York: Farrar, Straus & Giroux, p. 95.

Norris, C. (1982) *Deconstruction*. London: Methuen.

Said, E. (1982) 'The world, the text, the critic', in *The Horizon of Literature* (ed. P. Hernadi), Lincoln: University of Nebraska Press, pp. 31–53.

Toolan, M. (1990) *The Stylistics of Fiction: A Literary-Linguistic Approach*. London: Routledge.

Toolan, M. (1996) *Total Speech: An Integrational Linguistic Approach to Language*. Durham, NC: Duke University Press.

Wittgenstein, L. (1953) *Philosophical Investigations* (trans. G.E.M. Anscombe). Oxford: Basil Blackwell.

Extracted from Michael Toolan (1986) 'Poem, reader, response: making sense with "Skunk Hour" ', in C. Nicholson and R. Chaterjee (eds) *Tropic Crucible*, Singapore: Singapore University Press, pp. 84–97.

Chapter 10

Style and interpretation in Hemingway's 'Cat in the Rain'

RONALD CARTER

In this paper Carter analyses a short story with reference to those linguistic features that are especially prominent in the text, using these same features as a basis for the construction of an interpretation of the story. The analysis is cautious and does not claim a validity for an interpretation solely on the basis of linguistic features (see Lodge 1980 for a more 'pluralistic' analysis) but Carter does argue that the foregrounded linguistic features that he identifies cannot be discounted in any interpretation. Carter makes clear that he works from his own intuitions about the meaning of the story and offers therefore a discussion that aims to be explicit, retrievable and systematic only in terms of those intuitions. The paper is an exercise in what has been termed, by analogy with practical criticism, *practical stylistics*, with a consistent attention to the connection between form and meaning but with the degree of attention to linguistic features being a significant difference in the approach.

Work in a section of this paper on the stylistic analysis of free indirect speech and speech representation in fiction, was inspired in the 1980s by Leech and Short (1981). It has subsequently been taken further in numerous studies, including Short (1996), Semino *et al.* (1997), Toolan (2001), Semino and Short (2004) and Sotirova in this volume (Chapter 27).

HERE IS THE STORY:

There were only two Americans stopping at the hotel. They did not know any of the people they passed on the stairs on their way to and from their room. Their room was on the second floor facing the sea. It also faced the public garden and the war monument. There were big palms and green benches in the public garden. In the good weather there was always an artist with his easel. Artists liked the way the palms grew and the bright colours of the hotels facing the gardens and the sea. Italians came from a long way off to look up at the war monument. It was made of bronze and glistened in the rain. It was raining. The rain dripped from the palm trees. Water stood in pools on the gravel paths. The sea broke in a long line in the rain and slipped back down the beach to come up and break again in a long line in the rain. The motor-cars were gone from the square by the war monument. Across the square in the doorway of the cafe a waiter stood looking out at the empty square.

The American wife stood at the window looking out. Outside right under their window a cat was crouched under one of the dripping green tables. The cat was trying to make herself so compact that she would not be dripped on.

'I'm going down to get that kitty,' the American wife said.

'I'll do it,' her husband offered from the bed.

'No, I'll get it. The poor kitty out trying to keep dry under a table.'

The husband went on reading, lying propped up with the two pillows at the foot of the bed.

'Don't get wet,' he said.

The wife went downstairs and the hotel owner stood up and bowed to her as she passed the office. His desk was at the far end of the office. He was an old man and very tall.

'Il piove,' the wife said. She liked the hotel-keeper.

'Si, si, Signora, brutto tempo. It is very bad weather.'

He stood behind his desk in the far end of the dim room. The wife liked him. She liked the deadly serious way he received any complaints. She liked his dignity. She liked the way he wanted to serve her. She liked the way he felt about being a hotel-keeper. She liked his old, heavy face and big hands.

Liking him she opened the door and looked out. It was raining harder. A man in a rubber cape was crossing the empty square to the cafe. The cat would be around to the right. Perhaps she could go along under the eaves. As she stood in the doorway an umbrella opened behind her. It was the maid who looked after their room.

'You must not get wet,' she smiled, speaking Italian. Of course, the hotel-keeper had sent her.

With the maid holding the umbrella over her, she walked along the gravel path until she was under their window. The table was there, washed bright green in the rain, but the cat was gone. She was suddenly disappointed. The maid looked up at her.

'Ha perduto qualque cosa, Signora?'

'There was a cat,' said the American girl.

'A cat?'

'Si, il gatto.'

'A cat?' the maid laughed. 'A cat in the rain?'

'Yes,' she said, 'under the table.' Then, 'Oh, I wanted it so much. I wanted a kitty.'

When she talked English the maid's face tightened.

'Come, Signora,' she said. 'We must get back inside. You will be wet.'

'I suppose so,' said the American girl.

They went back along the gravel path and passed in the door. The maid stayed outside to close the umbrella. As the American girl passed the office, the padrone bowed from his desk. Something felt very small and tight inside the girl. The padrone made her feel very small and at the same time really important. She had a momentary feeling of being of supreme importance. She went on up the stairs. She opened the door of the room. George was on the bed, reading.

'Did you get the cat?' he asked, putting the book down.

'It was gone.'

'Wonder where it went to?' he said, resting his eyes from reading.

She sat down on the bed.

'I wanted it so much,' she said. 'I don't know why I wanted it so much. I wanted that poor kitty. It isn't any fun to be a poor kitty out in the rain.'

George was reading again.

She went over and sat in front of the mirror of the dressing-table, looking at herself with the hand glass. She studied her profile, first one side and then the other. Then she studied the back of her head and her neck.

'Don't you think it would be a good idea if I let my hair grow out?' she asked, looking at her profile again.

George looked up and saw the back of her neck, clipped close like a boy's.

'I like it the way it is.'

'I get so tired of it,' she said. 'I get so tired of looking like a boy.'

George shifted his position in the bed. He hadn't looked away from her since she started to speak.

'You look pretty darn nice,' he said.

She laid the mirror down on the dresser and went over to the window and looked out. It was getting dark.

'I want to pull my hair back tight and smooth and make a big knot at the back that I can feel,' she said. 'I want to have a kitty to sit on my lap and purr when I stroke her.'

'Yeah?' George said from the bed.

'And I want to eat at a table with my own silver and I want candles. And I want it to be spring and I want to brush my hair out in front of a mirror and I want a kitty and I want some new clothes.'

'Oh, shut up and get something to read,' George said. He was reading again.

His wife was looking out of the window. It was quite dark now and still raining in the palm trees.

'Anyway, I want a cat,' she said. 'I want a cat. I want a cat now. If I can't have long hair or any fun, I can have a cat.'

George was not listening. He was reading his book. His wife looked out of the window where the light had come on in the square.

Someone knocked at the door.

'Avanti,' George said. He looked up from his book.

In the doorway stood the maid. She held a big tortoise-shell cat pressed tight against her and swung down against her body.

'Excuse me,' she said, 'the padrone asked me to bring this for the Signora.'

[. . .] I shall begin this chapter by making a number of observations about some effects produced by this short text. The observations correspond to the main intuitions I have felt in reading and rereading the story a number of times. Needless to say, my intuitions may be different from those of others, and, therefore, what I want to investigate here will be limited by and to those intuitions. I then go on to suggest some questions relevant to an interpretation of the story which those same intuitions give rise to. The central core of the chapter is taken up by a linguistic examination of those parts of the text which seem most prominently to produce the effects I have noticed. The 'hidden' assumption in all this is that some linguistic analysis of a literary text is essential if something other than a merely intuitive or impressionistic account of the story is to be given.

I have three main intuitions about the story:

(1)   The style is very simple and straightforward but it produces complex effects. I am left with a feeling of uncertainty and ambiguity at the end.
(2)   The story is 'about' some kind of rift in the relationship between the two Americans. Without ever mentioning the word or related words Hemingway conveys a feeling of 'the American wife's' *frustration*.
(3)   The 'cat' of the title is somehow made to stand for something else. For want of a better word, I might say that it is symbolic.

Perhaps it will be thought that only intuition (1) has anything to do with the way in which the language of 'Cat in the Rain' is patterned. I hope to demonstrate that (2) and (3) are to a large extent conditioned by linguistic patterning. In any case, I certainly do not feel I can account for them by reference only to singularly literary co-ordinates such as 'theme', 'symbolism', 'plot', or 'character'.

In the course of a stylistic analysis of this story I shall be referring to a number of different features of the text's linguistic structure. Among these are: the role of modal verbs in the story; cohesion, and cohesion by repetition; the function of a narrative device which has come to be termed 'free indirect speech'. Above all, I want to try to show that a primary locus for stylistic effects in 'Cat in the Rain' is to be found in the structure of nominal groups and in the links between them (Berry 1975: ch. 5; Sinclair 1972: ch. 3).

Put simply, a nominal group can be defined as those features which are in a relationship with *nouns*. These linguistic features may be conveniently divided into three main areas for exploration:

Nominal group structure
Verbal structures and free indirect speech
Cohesion, repetition and ambiguity.

The features are selected because they are particularly striking and because they seem, in varying degrees, to be responsible for the effects I have outlined.

Nominal group structure

Most critical writing about Hemingway's 'style' tends to converge on a limited range of adjectives by which it is characterised. 'Clipped', 'laconic', 'bare', 'colourless', 'simple' appear to be among the most frequent. Perhaps the most striking aspect of this 'simple style' can be found in the opening paragraph of our text (lines 1–14).

I am struck here above all by a preponderance of the definite article. 'The' occurs twenty-seven times in that relatively short paragraph. It occurs, too, in nominal groups where there is little between the definite article and the noun (what can be termed minimal modification of the headword) and in groups where there is little which follows or further defines the noun to which the definite article points (termed qualification of the headword). Take, for example, a sentence such as the following which I have invented for purposes of comparison and contrast:

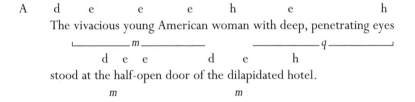

The nominal groups contain definite articles *(d)*, headwords *(h)*, epithets *(e)*, noun-modifiers *(n)* and structures which modify *(m)* and qualify *(q)* those same headwords. Compare these with what are typical structures in the paragraph in question:

B
(i) The rain dropped from the palm trees
(ii) The motor-cars were gone from the square by the war-monument
(iii) There were big palms and green benches in the public garden

One structure in particular – that of definite article *(d)* and headword *(h)* – is largely repeated in other nominal groups:

the hotel	*dh*
the beach	*dh*
the café	*dh*
the square	*dh*
the empty square	*deh*
the hotels facing the gardens	*dh/dh/dh*
	q
and the sea	

I am not, of course, saying that sentence A is in itself necessarily 'normal', but the comparison does allow us to draw some conclusions about the 'style' being used. The kind of structures in B allow a description to emerge where objects or things appear without any particular characteristics. It is as 'bare' as the square is 'empty'. But isolating the nominal group structures in this way does not explain all the effects produced in this opening paragraph.

Looking back at the nominal groups in Section B above produces an impression of what might be termed 'familiarity'. It is a familiarity which comes from knowing what is referred to. In encountering 'the hotel', 'the room facing the sea', 'the beach', 'the bright colours of the hotels facing the gardens and the sea', the 'palms . . . in the public garden' I am faced with a typical scene – one I might find on picture postcards or read about in a not dissimilar' style' in numerous travel brochures. In other words, I somehow do not need to be told more than the writer reveals because, given these props, I, as it were, supply or fill in the details myself. It is as if Hemingway is saying that such a setting is something that we all know so well, it needs no elaboration. In a related way, we might infer that this is the type of hotel typical Americans abroad would stay at. Given this opening paragraph, the reader might be forgiven for expecting that a description of a typical or stereotyped relationship between 'the American wife' and 'her husband' will follow. In any case, the paragraph gives a good example of the complex range of effects which can be brought about by this apparently simple style.

Basically, our observations for the first paragraph hold for the remaining paragraphs. For example, some representative 'structures' are as follows: the umbrella; the cat; the door; the gravel path; the maid; the hotel-keeper; the office; the doorway; the book; the padrone; the signora; the dressing table; the hand-glass – though it should be noted that the repetition of items is not quite so concentrated after the first paragraph. But there is still no marked deviation from the 'simple style' and the particular effects established in that significant opening.

This is not to say that there are no variations on the norm created by the text. In fact, where they do occur, variations are all the more foregrounded. For example:

> She liked his old, heavy face and big hands.
> a cat
> a big, tortoise-shell cat . . . swung down against her body
> cat in the rain

Here we have the greatest degrees of modification in the text applied to a description of the hotel-keeper and the cat respectively. We also notice the indefinite article used in relation to what is elsewhere predominantly *the* cat; connected with 'cat', too, is the title where the noun has no definite article in front of it.

In fact, not only are the hotel-keeper and the cat brought into some degree of prominence, but marked stylistic patterns are also noticeable with reference to the other main 'subjects' of the story:

The Wife	The Cat	The Husband
the American wife (1.15)	cat (in the rain)	her husband (1.25)
the wife (1.28)	the cat (1.17)	the husband (1.28)
the American girl (1.47)	the kitty (1.21)	George (1.73)
his wife (1.94)	a big tortoise-shell cat (1.102)	

In particular, we might note that George – the name of the husband – recurs unaltered from the middle to the end of the story.

Discussion of the kind of meanings elicited by such patterns must await corresponding analysis of other structures, but:

(1) Contact with the 'kitty' seems to equate with the wife being referred to as a 'girl'. In the hotel room she is 'the wife' or 'the American wife'.

(2) The husband remains unaffected. By contrast, the wife, who at the end is referred to as *his* wife, remains nameless throughout. There is a clear contrast in the identities they are given.

(3) The tortoise-shell cat may not be identical with the 'kitty' the woman was searching for. In any case, the cat seems both definite and indefinite.

(4) The 'setting' for the story is made to seem a familiar and expected one.

Verbal structures and free indirect speech

[. . .] It is noticeable how, in this story, a limited range of verbs are employed in a relatively limited range of structures. The main pattern for most verbal groups in the text is as follows:

> The wife *went* downstairs and the hotel owner *stood up* and *bowed* to her as she *passed* the office. His desk *was* at the far end of the office. He *was* an old man and very tall.

That is, a sentence contains either one (usually) or more than one (occasionally) main verb in either simple past or past progressive tense (e.g. 'was reading'). It is a feature which contributes to our impression of the simplicity of the story's style. They are also the basic and expected tenses for conveying narrative action. But what are we to make of those structures which draw attention to themselves by deviation from this expected pattern?

The presence of both auxiliary or modal verbs which add a different 'colouring' to the basic structure and/or switches in tense should be noted. For example:

> C Liking him she opened the door and looked out. It was raining harder. A man in a rubber cape was crossing the empty square to the cafe. The cat would be around to the right. Perhaps she could go along under the eaves. As she stood in the doorway an umbrella opened behind her. It was the maid who looked after their room. 'You must not get wet,' she smiled, speaking Italian. Of course, the hotel-keeper had sent her.

This is the first time modal verbs occur in the text. We have 'could', 'would', 'must' – and a switch in *tense*, 'had sent'. Their occurrence, I would argue, coincides with a moment of excitement in the story, aroused by the woman's proximity to the cat and by the kindness shown her by the hotel-keeper (see lines 25–34). As a result, this passage stands out from the otherwise flat and repetitive narrative. In fact, the 'wife' in the story becomes, as it were, 'associated' with modal verbs in contrast to her husband, whose actions and talk remain very much on the same plane:

> D 'Anyway, I want a cat', she said. 'I want a cat. I want a cat now. If I can't have long hair or any fun, I can have a cat.'

> George was not listening. He was reading his book.

We can also note near the end of the story an important switch to the present tense in 'I want a cat' from 'I wanted that poor kitty' and observe a corresponding shift from reference to a particular kitty she had looked for to an expression which is both more general and indefinite.

But, most of all, I am struck in passage C by the fact that the emotional contours of the wife's 'state' are rendered by a stylistic device known as 'free indirect speech'. It is a feature which works largely to confirm and extend what has already been said about verbal group organisation.

At this juncture some explanation of the notion of 'free indirect speech' is needed. Consider the following three sentences:

(1)   He stopped and said to himself: 'Is that the car I saw here yesterday?' – DIRECT SPEECH
(2)   He stopped and asked himself if that was the car he had seen there the day before – INDIRECT SPEECH
(3)   He stopped. Was that the car he had seen yesterday? – FREE INDIRECT SPEECH

Free indirect speech finds itself somewhere between direct and indirect speech. In literary terms this puts it between an author's reproduction of a character's actual dialogue or speech and a (reported) account of what a character has said. With a free indirect speech, or FIS, a kind of fusion takes place between authorial and character viewpoint in which the shape and texture of the character's voice can be preserved without any loss of the narrator's objective interpretation of events. Pascal (1977), in an extensive study of this narrative device, has aptly termed it 'the dual voice'. In passage C the locutions

Perhaps she could go along under the eaves.
The cat would be around to the right.
Of course, the hotel-keeper had sent her.

are examples of FIS and mark a point in the text – the only point, it should be added – where there is a momentary identification of viewpoint in both Hemingway, as narrator, and 'the American wife'.

The convergence of FIS and a foregrounded concentration of modal verbs marks this as a moment of particular significance in the story. It also reveals this to be a not wholly objective narrative presentation. However 'colourless' or 'neutral' is the style overall, Hemingway seems to allow a merging of his point of view with that of his protagonist. And immediately subsequent to passage C the 'American wife' is transformed into 'the American girl'. The FIS 'fusion' enables us to conclude that *viewpoint* may be a significant contributory factor in any interpretation of this ambiguous and open-ended text. Do we sympathise with the woman and her plight? To what extent is the rift in the relationship attributable to the husband's failure to 'orient' himself to her needs? Or is her longing too vague and indefinite to evoke sympathy? The presence of 'free indirect speech' here seems to tip the scales slightly towards some identification with the 'American *girl*'.

Cohesion, repetition and ambiguity

The first aspect of cohesion with which I wish to deal concerns the nature of the suprasentential organisation in the opening paragraph. Here I shall return to those definite articles. Firstly, however, a brief digression is needed.

Basically, in English, 'the' can fulfil a number of functions. These can be approximately demarcated as follows:

(1)   *The* school is worth supporting.
(2)   *The* moon is covered by clouds.
(3)   It was raining. *The* rain was cold.

Put simply: (1) is *exophoric*; that is, if it has not been mentioned previously in the text, it refers outwards to information or knowledge which listeners or readers can be presumed to share; (2) is *homophoric* and similarly outward-pointing, but the referent is in such cases singular and unique; (3) is *anaphoric* in that it points backwards to information which has already preceded. In each case, 'the' works to establish co-ordinates within and across sentences so that, in particular, when they are linked, the links are cohesive. It can be noted here, too, that verbal repetition can work similarly in establishing the cohesive texture of a passage.

On this basis we might usefully ask what are the effects produced by cohesion in this stretch of text from the middle of the first paragraph:

> E In the good weather there was always an artist with his easel. Artists liked the way the palms grew and the bright colours of the hotels facing the gardens and the sea. Italians came from a long way off to look up at the war monument. It was made of bronze and glistened in the rain. It was raining. The rain dripped from the palm trees.

This passage contains definite articles occurring anaphorically (the rain; the palm trees) and as a result of verbal repetition (rain; palms; artists); a number of items, too, have already been established previously in the text by exophoric reference (the hotel; the sea; the gardens). What we seem to have, therefore, is a passage which is especially cohesive and harmonious. These inter-sentential cohesive effects operate to strengthen and reinforce expectations. It is achieved by quite simple and conventional means. But, again, I suggest that a number of quite complex literary effects are brought about by this patterning. A major effect is, paradoxically, that expectations are *deflated* as well as confirmed. How exactly is this done? One main way in which it is done is for lexical items in the nominal groups to be repeated verbatim. Where reference to 'the hotel', 'the square', 'the palm trees', 'the war monument' recurs, we expect, I think, that there will be variation in the way cohesive links are established. For example, they could be substituted by a pronoun, be further modified or qualified or be replaced by a synonym or hyponym. But nothing changes. There is cohesive fit, but the discourse does not actually go anywhere.

Another example of this 'deflation' is provided by the sentence:

> The sea broke in a long line in the rain and slipped back down the beach to come up and break again in a long line in the rain.

The sentence is symmetrical, but it does not, once again, go anywhere. The effect of rhythmic devices and of verbal repetition is to enact a circularity of sameness and repetition. 'Expectations' are fulfilled and yet somehow not fulfilled. Similarly, in passage E (above), the positioning of words, tense and sentence structure combine with 'cohesive' devices to reinforce further the deflation or reversal of expectations. In the first sentence, expectations of 'good weather' are set up, along with a 'romantic' picture of artists and bright colours. The reference to the war momument which 'glistened in the rain' tends to be read as 'whenever it rained'. The glistening seems lexically connected, too, with the bright colours. The sentence which follows, 'It was raining', deflates these expectations. We suddenly realise the artists and the good weather are absent.

Cohesive organisation in the opening paragraph may, then, have quite particular effects. On the one hand, exophoric references make us establish a familiar and stereo-typical world. On another level, the same familiarity is reinforced by repetition; the repetition works to make it all seem somehow *too* familiar.

This paragraph is 'deflationary', then, for a number of reasons. We expect repeated items to be further modified or qualified in some way. But they are not. Things are also 'deflationary' because the features bringing colour and life to the scene are characterised by their absence but are described almost as if they were present. The pattern is one of familiarity leading to over-familiarity and stereotype and of expectation leading to the frustration of expectation. And it is created in the very linguistic texture of the para-graph. And this is not to exclude the presence of semantic oppositions in the paragraph such as public garden (peace) v. *war* monument. One 'state' is quickly counteracted by its contrary.

Conclusion

The simplicity of the 'style' of this text does not point to a simple or straightforward interpretation. Complex effects – chief among these are a sense of expectation and 'deflation', emotional heightening and a *development* of the subjects' identity across the *process* of the text – are achieved using some very basic linguistic patterning.

Slight, but significant, shifts in awareness are also communicated by shifts among words or from one word to its lexical collocate or partner. In the case of something like 'cat', such shifts, though achieved by the simplest of means, cannot be without signifi-cance. In fact, we need to return here to questions raised in Section I such as: Is the cat the same as the 'kitty'? Why does the 'woman' undergo some metamorphosis in the course of the text from 'wife' to 'girl', and so on? And finally, we should remember that Hemingway's *neutral* style does not prevent authorial intrusion. Free indirect speech, again achieved by the simplest of means, allows an identification with a character to occur. It gives the subtlest of orientations to an otherwise indeterminate narrative.

I would argue that a dominant impression we are left with is that of the stereotyped nature of the relationship between the American wife and the American husband. The stereotypicality and familiarity of it all seems a basic part of Hemingway's purpose – particularly at the opening of the story. Within this pattern we are made, albeit only marginally, to identify with the needs of the wife. She is clearly searching for some means of escape from this routine scene. She seems to want a new identity. The hotel-keeper is ostensibly more sympathetic than her husband. The search for the kitty serves to rejuvenate her and to break the dull and repetitive frame in which she is trapped.

But what does the cat symbolise? How do we account for what the linguistic details of the text highlighted elsewhere suggest? That is, that the cat is not the same as the 'kitty' the wife is looking for. For, after all, if it is not what she is looking for, this may lead to a deflation of the wife's expectations. The linguistic texture of the story would lead us to conclude that the 'kitty' is not the same as the cat described at the end:

> In the doorway stood the maid. She held a big tortoise-shell cat pressed tight against her and swung down against her body.

I do not see a correlation here between 'cat' and 'kitty'. To me, this is a grotesque outcome to the kind of associations aroused in me by the word 'kitty'.

We must acknowledge, of course, that the wife's reaction is withheld from us and as a result an essentially indeterminate outcome to the narrative is preserved. But, recalling what we have analysed within the language of the story as a main pattern of frustration of expectation, it may not be too much of an assertion to say that an interpretation of the story in these terms is possible.

The hotel-keeper remains a hotel-keeper and is fixed within the strictly denotative role he is assigned by the linguistic representation 'the hotel-keeper'. If he doesn't supply the *right* cat, perhaps he is not quite a 'third party' but, like a 'model' hotel-keeper, simply attempting to placate the foibles of his hotel guests. Similarly, George remains George. Immovable, passive and the American husband. His wife's search hardly affects him.

In this situation the American wife evokes our sympathy (and the narrator's), but as the story progresses we are, as it were, moved towards a conclusion. As her desire for *a* cat becomes more and more indefinite, and as she becomes more desperate, we might conclude that the cat represents something in her experience which cannot be fulfilled – something which is present but is characterised here by its absence (like the artists and other 'features' of the opening paragraph). The cat begins by being something specific and ends up as a general symbol; simply

Cat in the Rain

It is neither definite nor indefinite. In fact, articleless singular headwords are unusual in modern English. One of the uses to which they are put is in captions to pictures or sculptures. Is Hemingway suggesting here that his story is analogous to the 'frozen action' of a picture, that is, activity within a frame which does not go anywhere? (See discussion by Widdowson (1975: 108–15) of a not unrelated feature of Roethke's poem 'Child on Top of a Greenhouse').

It might be ultimately that the indeterminacy I have felt in connection with the story stems not so much from the possibility of dual interpretation at the end, or from symbolic ambiguities surrounding 'cat', but from this intuition of expectations unfulfilled and leading only back to the same place.

As far as interpretation via linguistics is concerned, I would claim that the analysis undertaken appropriately substantiates my original intuitions and that I would want to use this analysis as the *basis* for any further work on the text. Certainly, it enables me to incline towards a particular interpretation in a relatively systematic and objective way. I use the word 'incline' advisedly and in recognition that interpretation is to a considerable extent an individual matter. But language is a shared property and should, therefore, when analysed, provide a common basis for the release of meanings. Whether this can be said of the analysis here of 'Cat in the Rain', I cannot be the judge.

References

Berry, M. (1975) *Introduction to Systemic Linguistics*. London: Batsford.

Leech, G. and Short, M. (1981) *Style in Fiction* (2nd edition 2007). Harlow: Longman.

Lodge, D. (1980) 'Analysis and interpretation of the realist text: a pluralistic approach to Ernest Hemingway's "Cat in the Rain" ', *Poetics Today* 1 (4): 5–22.

Pascal, R. (1977) *The Dual Voice*. Manchester: Manchester University Press.

Semino, E. and Short, M. (2004) *Corpus Stylistics: Speech, Writing and Thought Presentation in a Corpus of English Writing*. London: Routledge.

Semino, E., Short, M. and Culpeper, J. (1997) 'Using a corpus to test and refine a model of speech and thought presentation', *Poetics* 25: 17–43.

Short, M. (1996) *Exploring the Language of Poetry, Prose and Plays*. Harlow: Longman.

Sinclair, J.McH. (1972) *A Course in Spoken English: Grammar*. Oxford: Oxford University Press.

Toolan, M. (2001) *Narrative: A Critical Linguistic Introduction*. London: Routledge.

Widdowson, H.G. (1975) *Stylistics and the Teaching of Literature*. London: Longman.

Extracted from Ronald Carter (1982) 'Style and interpretation in Hemingway's "Cat in the Rain" ', in *Language and Literature*, London: Allen and Unwin, pp. 65–80.

Chapter 11

Changing the guard at Elsinore

WALTER NASH

Until the 1980s stylistic studies of dialogue, especially in dramatic texts, had been very limited. In the 1980s increased understanding of spoken interaction through the rapidly developing fields of discourse analysis and pragmatics supplied literary linguists with tools for the analysis of dialogue in fiction and in plays and in Chapter 8 of this volume Short illustrates the potential of this approach. In this paper, Walter Nash takes the opening scene to a seminal drama, Shakespeare's *Hamlet*, and uses a paraphrase of the discourse to illuminate and support the process of analysis. He shows how conversational patterns prefigure key themes in the play and that a micro-analysis of single components in the interaction between characters may have particu-lar relevance for our understanding of the macrotext of the whole play. The discussion of characters' speech acts, interpersonal strategies and actions is not a simply neutral account but is also linked here to the management of power relations and then, by extension, to a play not unconcerned with power plays.

For further reading in the analysis of the language of drama, see Culpeper *et al.* (1998) and in terms of language and characterization, Culpeper (2001).

A paraphrase

(A fortification. On a parapet, a sentry is keeping guard. His name is Frank. It is evidently a very cold night, or Frank is ill at ease, or both; as he paces back and forth he stamps, shivers, whistles under his breath. Presently another soldier, Bernie, is dimly seen on the stairs that climb to the parapet. As Frank comes towards him, he starts nervously.)

Bernie: Who's there?
Frank: (*startled and affronted.*) Eh? Oh no you don't! (*Then remembering the drill, issues the formal challenge.*) Halt! Who goes there?
Bernie: (*Trying to get the password right.*) Long live the king!
Frank: (*Uncertain.*) Bernie?

Bernie: Yes, it's me.

Frank: Here on the dot, aren't you?

Bernie: It's gone twelve. Time you were in bed.

Frank: I won't say no. It's freezing cold, and I've got the shakes.

Bernie: (*Intensely casual*) Anything to report?

Frank: No. Dead quiet.

Bernie: Off you go, then. If you run into Harry and Mark, tell them to get a move on, will you?

Frank: (*He has been moving away from Bernie, and now stands at the head of the parapet stair.*) Here they are now, I can hear them. (*As the newcomers emerge into view, he slips into his 'sentry' routine, forgetting, perhaps, that Bernie has now assumed the duty.*) Halt! Who goes there?

Harry: (*Who is not a soldier, but perceives the need to say something reassuring.*) We're on your side.

Mark: (*Who is, and who can therefore hastily produce a password not unlike the one already given by Bernie.*) Soldiers of the king.

Frank: (*Evidently satisfied with this response.*) Good-night, then.

Mark: (*A little surprised at this abrupt departure of the 'sentry' who has just challenged them.*) Oh! Cheerio, old son! Who's relieved you?

Frank: Bernie just took over from me. I'll say goodnight.

Mark: Hey there, Bernie!

Bernie: Over here. Say, is Harry with you?

Harry: (*Whimsical.*) Some of him is.

Bernie: Hello, Harry. Mark, I'm glad you're here.

Mark: (*With a stifled eagerness.*) Why – has – you know what – paid us a visit?

Bernie: (*Cautiously, watching Harry.*) Not that I know of.

This is how *Hamlet* opens; not in so many words, it is true, but in so many interactions or exchanges between professional soldiers who are frightened and excited and behave, on the whole, rather unprofessionally. The paraphrase of their conversation may reduce to modern banality the sharp impact of Shakespeare's dramatic language, but it has one advantage. The commonplace phrasing, unsanctified by time and literary reputation, presents a direct reading of motives, a reading here freely supported by the interpolation of explanatory directions. This means, of course, that the paraphrase is not simply a translation of the scene into modern colloquial English, but also an interpretation, or more precisely a close sequence of interpretations, from sentence to sentence, emphasis to emphasis, inflection to inflection. The paraphrase simply does what any producer of a play has to do. It reflects decisions about context and motive, which lead to decisions about language, about underlying meanings, about the stylistic cohesion of the scene. But any reader of a drama is a producer of the drama, for an audience of one. To read is to construct mentally an image of performance, and the mental image is reflected in paraphrase.

A commentary

To explain, and if need be justify, that mental image calls for a retracing, step by step, of the paths of meaning laid out in the original text. The first point for commentary is the obvious one, that Hamlet begins with an abortive exchange: a sentry is challenged by an intruder. Shakespeare put it thus:

> *Bernardo*: Who's there?
> *Francisco*: Nay, answer me; stand, and unfold yourself.

In the theatre, the onlooker must become instantly aware of the irregularity of Bernardo's behaviour. It is Francisco who is in charge, and who insists, correctively, on his authority; the actor playing him must surely stress the pronoun *me*. His first words are indignant and alarmed, but he then proceeds by the book, making the formal challenge his duty prescribes. In response, Bernardo produces what is evidently a password. Yet still there is a hint of abnormality in the conventional exchange:

> *Bernardo*: Long live the king!
> *Francisco*: Bernardo?
> *Bernardo*: He.

We have the impression that Francisco is not altogether certain of the newcomer's identity. It is in any case not the 'password' that reassures him; it is Bernardo's homely and laconic 'He' (= 'It's me'). It is a minor and possibly irrelevant detail, but it seems none the less that there is a momentary flaw in the formal exchange, a stutter, as it were, that is to be recalled a few lines further on, when the question of the correct password is again highlighted.

Francisco comments with surprise (or possibly gratitude, or even irony) on Bernardo's apparent punctuality:

> *Francisco*: You come most carefully upon your hour.

Sentries are not in the habit of arriving at their posts a moment earlier than the duty roster demands. Francisco's remark thus draws attention to a further oddity in Bernardo's conduct. He is a professional soldier, but tonight he is so inept that he challenges the man he is supposed to be relieving, gives a dubious password, and, most significantly, is nervously eager to come on duty. As to this matter, however, he is quick to disclaim punctuality, alleging that he is in fact *late:*

> *Bernardo*: 'Tis now struck twelve; get thee to bed, Francisco.

Late or early, Francisco is relieved to be relieved; so relieved, indeed that he openly confesses his relief:

> *Francisco*: For this relief, much thanks; 'tis bitter cold And I am sick at
> heart.

'I am sick at heart' has the ring of a significant announcement, though as yet the significance is obscure. Does he simply mean 'I am frozen to the marrow' (because of the 'bitter cold'), or is he complaining of something else, a psychic chill, a nameless glacial dread? Bernardo's next remark could be a response to the hidden implication, though on the face of it it seems non-commital:

Bernardo: Have you had quiet guard?

This may be the conventional inquiry, the customary speech act of the relieving sentry ('Everything OK?' 'Anything to report?'), or it may be taken as an oblique reference to something no one dares name on this dark night in this cold and lonely place. The words appear to carry a message beyond their commonplace significance, and Francisco's reply has the same air of coded cliché:

Francisco: Not a mouse stirring.

We are at this point no more than ten lines into the play, and its language is already touched by tremors of ambiguity and covert meaning. Bernardo's 'quiet' (in 'Have you had quiet guard') and Francisco's 'stirring' are suspect words, referring indirectly to some knowledge shared by the characters and as yet hidden from the audience.

These oblique references yield, for the moment, to the ordinary business of changing guard:

Bernardo: Well, good-night.
If you do meet Horatio and Marcellus,
The rivals of my watch, bid them make haste.

Either Bernardo is understandably anxious not to be left alone (it is, incidentally, a matter for puzzlement that Francisco has been allowed to stand solitary guard, without 'rivals'), or he is keen for some reason to have witnesses at hand. Francisco announces their advent:

Francisco: I think I hear them – Stand, ho! Who's there?

We are back to the business of challenging – and still it is a challenge from the wrong quarter, for Francisco has now been relieved and the sentinel's authority is properly invested in Bernardo. Once again, the military convention is violated, in a moment of excited apprehension. Horatio and Marcellus emerge from the darkness to reply to the challenge:

Horatio: Friends to this ground.
Marcellus: And liegemen to the Dane.

But what is Horatio doing, answering the challenge? As we are presently to learn, he is not a soldier, and his 'Friends to this ground' does not quite have the air of a soldierly response. It is apparently left to Marcellus, the professional, to redeem Horatio's civilian incompetence with a formula ('liegemen to the Dane') having the ring of a real pass-word and bearing, as it happens, some resemblance to the earlier 'Long live the king!' Francisco admits the incomers without further ado:

Francisco: Give you good-night.

Yet why should Francisco be so obviously satisfied with 'liegemen to the Dane' when earlier he has apparently been so cautious about 'long live the king'? Which is the correct password? Are there two passwords? Is the 'password' simply a brief expression of the appropriate sentiment, a variable form of loyal words? Surely not. A plausible explanation is that 'Long live the king!' is an approximation to the correct password, a fumbled attempt produced by Bernardo in his excitement. Given such a doubtful or approximate password, Francisco might well question the identity of the intruder; whereas, when the password convinces him, he has no more to say.

And now Marcellus is understandably a little surprised at being challenged by a man so obviously about to quit the scene:

> *Marcellus*:   O, farewell, honest soldier:
> Who hath reliev'd you?

Here is yet another piece of confusion. It is barely a moment since Bernardo has identified Marcellus as one of his 'rivals', and yet Marcellus apparently does not know the identity of the person he is about to join. Francisco obligingly reminds him:

> *Francisco*:   Bernardo has my place.
> Give you good-night.

That word 'place' is of some consequence. Earlier, *in* his 'place', Francisco has rightly insisted, 'Nay, answer *me*'; but it is not his 'place' to challenge Horatio and Marcellus, and he knows it. His exit speech serves merely to emphasize what we already know, that the usual drills are at sixes and sevens, and that nothing is being done properly or routinely on this strange night.

The subsequent exchanges between Marcellus, Bernardo and Horatio ask us to envisage a spacious darkness, an isolating expanse not easily represented on a small stage, Thus, the interlocutors are first within earshot, yet cannot see each other clearly:

> *Marcellus*:   Holla! Bernardo!
> *Bernardo*:   Say, What, is Horatio there?

Thus attention is drawn to Horatio, whose presence is evidently of some importance. He responds, speaking up on his own behalf:

> *Horatio*:   A piece of him.

The response is laconic and ironic, a humorous utterance that marks out the speaker as a different sort of animal from those around him. It is, to be sure, a very cold night, and people are behaving rather oddly, and Horatio may well be wondering why he is out at this hour with the superstitious soldiery when he might be tucked up in a warm place. Bernardo greets him and his companion:

> *Bernardo*:   Welcome, Horatio; welcome good Marcellus.

These 'welcome's seem a little out of the ordinary. Is 'welcome' a conventional salutation from one soldier on duty to another, or is Bernardo perhaps a little effusive, and do his words once again reveal an unwonted nervousness? Marcellus's next remark reads, indeed, like a response to some suppressed agitation in Bernardo's manner; or possibly Marcellus himself is so excited that he plunges straight into the matter that concerns him most, cutting short the exchange of civilities:

> *Marcellus*: What! has this thing appear'd again to-night?

And now we are very close – with 'this thing' – to discovering just what it is that has put these disciplined men into such disarray. Yet Bernardo still shies away from open discussion:

> *Bernardo*: I have seen nothing.

Taken at its face value, this is a baffling remark. Marcellus's question can be broadly supposed to mean 'have you – has Francisco – has *anybody* – seen "this thing" tonight?'; to which Bernardo replies, 'I have seen nothing.' But since it is not five minutes since he came on watch, who would expect him to have seen anything? Perhaps, then, we are to stress *I*, and paraphrase: 'I don't know about anyone else, but *I've* seen nothing.' Yet even this is a questionable assumption. We know that Bernardo has questioned Francisco about his 'quiet guard', and has received the assurance 'not a mouse stirring'. The stress on *I* would then be misleading, because it would imply that someone other than Bernardo might have seen *this thing* tonight – and Bernardo is aware that this is not the case. Whatever intonation or stress pattern we attribute to the utterance it remains a kind of lie, because it ostensibly allows Marcellus to draw the wrong inferences. This is obviously unsatisfactory; why would Shakespeare make a very minor character perpetrate such a stupid conversational cheat? One plausible conjecture is that Bernardo is passing a coded message, indicating his wariness of the outsider, Horatio. What is Horatio's attitude? The soldiers who keep the night watches on these grim, vast, dark battlements all know about 'this thing', whatever it is, but Horatio is not a soldier. He is a scholar, and as such may be inclined to pour rational scorn on the sentries' experience.

This is confirmed by Marcellus's next speech (not included in our paraphrase) and Horatio's subsequent comment:

> *Marcellus*: Horatio says 'tis but our fantasy,
> And will not let belief take hold of him
> Touching this dreaded sight, twice seen of us:
> Therefore have I entreated him along
> With us, to watch the minutes of this night;
> That, if again this apparition come,
> He may approve our eyes, and speak to it.
> *Horatio*: Tush, tush, 'twill not appear.

'This thing' is now 'this dreaded sight', 'this apparation' – in short, this ghost; and we may now fairly guess at the motive underlying Bernardo's 'I have seen nothing'. He is being cautious in the presence of the newcomer, the known sceptic, the educated fellow who has been brought along to bear corroborative witness, and, if necessary, to 'speak to' the phantom.

The speech of Marcellus quoted above is the real beginning of the play. From this point onwards, it is relevant to note, the dramatic discourse settles regularly into blank verse. In the speeches that precede it, from the first 'Who's there?' down to 'I have seen nothing', the prosodic impulse is sporadic, fragmented, as irregular as the exchanges themselves. The discourse is unsettled and holds no more than tenuously to predictable rules; people speak out of turn, with odd implications and unexpected responses. As a military exercise, this changing of the guard at Elsinore is a scrambling makeshift. It amounts to something not far short of panic, or at least close to the bounds of a controlled fear. It establishes, indeed, the mood of the play, which throughout is confused and full of apprehension.

An analysis

The structure of the discourse

Paraphrase and commentary are ways of *experiencing* literary discourse; and now comes the task of *analysing* the experience. The procedures supporting such an analysis can be freely drawn from sociolinguistics and pragmatics. These studies are conveniently oriented to the description of literary works in which dialogue figures prominently, and can often throw light on the dual function of such dialogue, on the one hand as a reflex of 'ordinary' conversation, and on the other as a literary artifice, an aesthetic structure with no more than superficial claims to naturalistic status.

The first task of the discourse analyst describing patterns of conversation is to determine their structure as a complex of exchanges minimally represented as I(nitiation) and R(esponse). In some descriptions (see, for example, Burton 1980; Carter and Burton 1982) the IR structure is related to a hierarchy in which the comprehensive unit is the *interaction*, comprising *transactions* between certain speakers on certain topics, realized in *exchanges* governing the phasing of the topic, the exchanges being worked out in *moves*, for example, opening moves, supporting moves, challenging moves, expounded by specific verbal *acts*, of eliciting, directing, informing, commenting, acknowledging and so forth. This hierarchical model echoes the taxonomy of forms propounded by systemic grammarians (Sentence–Clause–Group–Word–Morpheme); and has the same advantage of allowing access, for the purposes of 'coarse' or 'delicate' analysis, at different levels in the scheme.

A rigorous analysis of the first twenty-nine lines of *Hamlet* would thus account for the transaction structure, plot the exchanges and specify the component acts. Some of this activity, however, might well prove redundant. The necessary first step is to begin at the general level of the *transaction*, and to ask how many of these are involved in the represented interaction, i.e. in the passage beginning with 'Who's there?' and concluding in 'I have seen nothing'. It appears that there are two distinct transactions. The first reads thus:

Bernardo:	Who's there?	1
Francisco:	Nay, answer me; stand and unfold yourself.	2
Bernardo:	Long live the king!	3
Francisco:	Bernardo?	4
Bernardo:	He.	5

Francisco:	You come most carefully upon your hour.	6
Bernardo:	'Tis now struck twelve; get thee to bed, Francisco.	7
Francisco:	For this relief much thanks; 'tis bitter cold	8
	And I am sick at heart.	9
Bernardo:	Have you had quiet guard?	10
Francisco:	Not a mouse stirring.	11
Bernardo:	Well, good-night.	12
	If you do meet Horatio and Marcellus,	13
	The rivals of my watch, bid them make haste.	14
Francisco:	I think l hear them. . . .	15

And the second continues:

Francisco:	Stand, ho! Who's there?	15
Horatio:	Friends to this ground.	16
Marcellus	And liegemen to the Dane	17
Francisco:	Give you good-night.	18
Marcellus:	O, farewell, honest soldier:	19
	Who hath reliev'd you?	20
Francisco:	Bernardo has my place.	21
	Give-you good-night.	22
Marcellus:	Holla! Bernardo:	23
Bernardo:	Say,	24
	What, is Horatio there?	25
Horatio:	A piece of him.	26
Bernardo:	Welcome, Horatio; welcome good Marcellus.	27
Marcellus:	What! Has this thing appear'd again to-night?	28
Bernardo:	I have seen nothing.	29

Line 15 thus marks the closure of one set of exchanges and the transition to another set which is in some places quite closely mimetic of the first. The mimicry appears almost obviously in the parallel challenge routines of 2–3 and 15–17, but lines 2–7 and 15–22 are generally comparable. The utterances of 2–7 are concerned successively with challenging, with recognizing someone, with raising a query about the guard-changing routine, and with leavetaking. Lines 15–22 are correspondingly devoted to challenging, to recognition, to a question about the guard and to leavetaking. The verbal forms, however, are not directly correspondent. There are parallels, contrasts, comparables, thus:

Lines 2–7	*Lines 15–22*	
Stand, and unfold yourself.	Stand, ho! Who's there?	*Challenging*
Long live the king!	Friends to this ground.	*Identifying*
	And liegemen to the Dane	
Bernardo?	Give you good-night.	*Recognizing*
He.	O, farewell, honest soldier:	

You come most carefully upon your hour. 'Tis now struck twelve:	Who hath reliev'd you? Bernardo has my place	*Questioning, seeking to clarify situation*
Get thee to bed, Francisco.	Give you good-night.	*Leavetaking*

These topical *correspondences*, whether clear or muted, are perhaps not altogether surprising; the conventional conduct of the military occasion might be assumed to produce broadly similar speech acts. When the participants are briefly released from the dictates of convention and speak impulsively, as in lines 8–9 and 23–6, the parallels lapse. But only briefly; for in lines 10–11 and 28–9 we have what is clearly the most significant pair of correspondent exchanges:

Lines 10–11	*Lines 28–9*
Have you had quiet guard?	What! has this thing appear'd again to-night?
Not a mouse stirring.	I have seen nothing.

References

Burton, D. (1980) *Dialogue and Discourse: A Sociolinguistic Approach to Modern Drama Dialogue and Naturally Occurring Conversation*. London: Routledge.

Carter, R. and Burton, D. (eds) (1982) *Literary Text and Language Study*. London: Edward Arnold.

Culpeper, J. (2001) *Language and Characterisation: People in Plays and Other Texts*. London: Longman.

Culpeper, J., Short, M. and Verdonk, P. (eds) (1998) *Exploring the Language of Drama: From Text to Context*. London: Routledge.

Extracted from Walter Nash (1989) 'Changing the guard at Elsinore', in R. Carter and P. Simpson (eds) *Language, Discourse and Literature*, London: Unwin Hyman, pp. 23–41.

Chapter 12

But what *is* literature? Toward a descriptive definition of literature

WILLIE VAN PEER

In this chapter, Willie van Peer returns to a fundamental question for literary scholarship with a rational view of the parameters of literature. Drawing on insights from the field of pragmatics, as well as work across the social sciences, he makes a distinction between *text* and *discourse* that reframes the latter more restrictively than is typical in either critical theory or most approaches in linguistics. Although he argues for the inclusion of both social and psychological dimensions in the definition of literature, he returns constantly to an assertion of the importance of textuality and analytical empiricism, as a convincing rationale for stylistic exploration.

For further arguments for evidential and empirical approaches to literary scholarship, see Kreuz and MacNealy (1996), Ibsch *et al.* (2002), Miall (2006) and van Peer *et al.* (2007). See also, in this volume, Widdowson (chapter 4) and Cook (chapter 17).

THERE CAN BE LITTLE doubt that the definition of literature belongs to the most intricate epistemological problems of literary studies. Many scholars in the field seem to be content to bypass the issue as one not to be solved, or – as in the case of Eagleton (1983: 10) – to accept a verdict of aporia: 'anything can be literature', even if such statements lead to self-inflicted destruction: 'The final logical move in a process which began by recognizing that literature is an illusion is to recognize that literary theory is an illusion too' (Eagleton 1983: 204).

In this [chapter] I intend to leave aside such forms of naïve scepticism. Instead an effort at more rigorously outlining what is characteristic of the phenomenon called 'literature' will be presented. [. . .] Three categories will stand central to this enterprise: *language*, *text* and what will be termed *homiletical* forms of communication. [. . .] The result is a concept of literature which [. . .] may also serve as a descriptive basis for further study and deliberation in the theory of literature as a whole.

The first distinction drawn here is perhaps the least problematic one: literature is an art form which is dependent, like all art forms, on a specific medium. Without such a medium no artistic communication is possible. The concrete medium of literature is *language*. Without language there can be no literature. That is not to say that the use of language is a sufficient condition for the existence of literature. But it is a necessary one, in the same way as the human body is a necessary prerequisite for the art of dancing. Hence in the following considerations it will be assumed that literature is a *linguistic* form of art. This excludes some visual arts, such as the cinema, from our definition, even if they display similarities to certain literary characteristics. (Most films, for instance, present narratives which structurally resemble verbal stories; see also Chatman 1978). For reasons of space, I shall leave such matters out of consideration here, acknowledging that they need further attention, which would, however, distract from our present concerns. Literature, then, is to be defined as a form of art, the functioning of which is primarily dependent on the use of natural human language as its medium.

A second distinction relevant to a definition of literature is that between discourse and text. *Discourse* is understood here as the direct verbal interaction between participants. Discourse is the dominant mode in which we both produce and process language. One of its basic qualities is what has been termed its *impromptu* character by Enkvist (1988). The standard form of discourse is the one in which participants are in each other's physical presence, i.e. sharing the same *time/space* configuration. In this sense, it is not normally possible to become involved in a discourse with human beings who exist or have existed in other times – which does not mean that communication with them as such is excluded, only that such forms of communication are not *discourse* in the proper sense of the word. Similarly, until very recently in the history of mankind, it was not possible to engage in discourse with human beings not sharing the same space, this 'space' being limited in a physical sense by the range of the human voice and by the limits of auditory perception.

Discourse, as outlined here, may be distinguished from *text*. This concept, however, has proved rather resistant to adequate definition. Its treatment from the viewpoint of pragmatics, however, as developed in Ehlich (1984) and van Peer (1989), opens up new possibilities. Texts, in this view, emanate as a particular type of linguistic solution to a pertinent problem in the use of language, i.e. its *transient* character. Transcending the limits under which oral speech (as used in discourse) operates is precisely the aim for which texts have come into being. In other words, texts transcend the time and space barriers that discourse is subject to. Consequently, a distance between 'author' and recipient is introduced, a distance – in spatio/temporal terms – which may become considerable for some texts, e.g. the *Odyssey* or the epic of *Gilgamesh*. In contrast to the impromptu character of discourse, textual communication is usually *premeditated*. The major function of such linguistic constructions is to preserve and pass on knowledge and values judged relevant or important to the culture. Their number of recipients may thus be seen to be growing constantly over time. Note that these texts may be, and indeed often are, of an oral nature. Obvious examples that spring to mind are tales, myths, legends, epics, sagas, riddles, and many other types of text which lie at the heart of oral culture. The most fundamental characteristic of all texts (in contrast to discourse) is their capability of becoming detached from the utterance situation, their transference through time and space, and their subsequent re-introduction into a new utterance situation. [. . .]

As such, texts fulfil a major function in the development and constitution of *tradition*. They can do so because their form obeys principles of organization that differ markedly from those of discourse. This difference should be viewed as one of *degree*, though, and not as a watertight dichotomy. For instance, forms of discourse exist which are also partly premeditated and are thereby more easily amenable to de- and re-contextualization. One may think, for instance, of the ritual insults described by Labov (1972). In these, participants interact in the physical presence of each other and hence engage in discourse, while the structure of their verbal utterances enhances their partial repetition in other utterance situations. Such rituals can be said to be an inter-mediate form between discourse and text. Other examples of such intermediate forms are personal accounts or narratives, and proverbs.

The insight that textuality is a matter of degree, involving several criteria simul-taneously thus becomes unavoidable. In so far as a particular linguistic configuration develops more structural qualities that make it detachable from discourse praxis, it acquires extra textuality. Simultaneously, to the degree that more people and more generations of a society have frequent recourse to a text, the stronger its textuality will become. Thus it is possible to discern more *central* and more *peripheral* texts. A text such as the Bible, for instance, is so central to the culture of most western societies that its degree of textuality is several times higher than that of a ballad. The conclusion to be drawn is that textuality is partly a linguistic characteristic and partly the result of socio-cultural forces which provide the text its place and function within society as a whole.

So far, nothing has been said about *writing*. Although there can be few arguments against the existence of oral texts, there can also be little doubt that in present-day western societies the bulk of texts used in daily life exists in written or printed form. [. . . B]ecause of its material aspect, the written word may easily be separated from its utterance situation. A written text thus acquires, on top of the textuality it already possesses (by virtue of its being a 'text'), an autonomous character which makes it easier still to be detached from the spatio-temporal situation in which it originated. This further enhances its potential as a vehicle for preserving and passing on cultural tradi-tions. Besides 'thickening' the textuality of an utterance, writing also objectifies mean-ings to the extent that a new dimension may be added to its functioning, i.e. that of criticism. In the words of Goody (1977: 37) 'writing, and more specifically alphabetic literacy, made it possible to scrutinize discourse in a different kind of way by giving oral communication a semi-permanent form; this scrutiny favoured the increase in scope of critical activity, and hence of rationality, scepticism and logic' (see also Popper 1963: 148–52).

When we turn to the question which concerns us here, i.e. the definition of literature, it seems to be beyond doubt that, with regard to the distinction between text and discourse, literature belongs to the former category. Daily conversations are not remembered as literature, and this is not accidental: the phenomenon of literature consists of a body of *texts*. But, as has been pointed out before, although textual form may be stable over time, this is not by itself sufficient for the text's survival across different historical eras: the textuality of an utterance is thus not something which is solid for ever, but co-varies with historical and cultural evolution.

At first sight, this definition seems to create a problem concerning the position of the theatre. Are dramatic performances not a kind of discourse in the sense indicated above? If so, the relevance of the distinction seems to evaporate. The problem, however, is only an apparent one. Firstly, dramatic texts do correspond to the criteria for textuality established before. They are detached from the situation in which they were originally generated and are re-introduced time and again into new time/space constellations, as a consequence of which their number of recipients is growing constantly over time. Moreover, there is a considerable distance between recipients and author, who is often not involved in the performance. Acknowledging that – impromptu – elements of improvization may play a role in drama, it should be admitted that such improvization occurs only around a central textual core which as a rule is premeditated in its general structure and content. Finally, in so far as drama is judged as important by the community, it plays a distinctive role in the constitution of culture and the maintenance of its traditions. One must conclude that the dramatic genre is likewise composed of texts, which have, however, been conceived in such a way as to create the illusion of their being a kind of 'discourse' [. . .].

Having established the textual nature of literature, one must admit that this cannot be the end of the road, because there are various types of text which one would not, under normal circumstances, be prepared to categorize as 'literary': shopping lists, flight schedules, dictionaries or insurance policies will qualify as examples. The question is: why not? Apparently individuals have strong intuitions allowing a relatively straightforward categorization of texts into literature or non-literature; this has also been demonstrated empirically by Dimter (1981, 1985). What follows is an attempt to establish the basis upon which these intuitions rest. To this end, a further distinction, as developed by Ehlich and Rehbein (1980), is brought in. In their article, the authors point out the necessity of studying discourse as it is shaped by the needs and aims of social institutions. The role played by language within these institutions differs markedly. The military institution, for instance, uses language forms very different from those of the medical institution. Ehlich and Rehbein accordingly argue that a general theory of discourse will have to take institutional forces into account.

In the same article, they also address a specific problem posed by forms of discourse occurring outside institutional situations. Everyday conversations, story-telling in the pub, or talking about the weather at a bus stop all qualify as this type. Ehlich and Rehbein use the term *homiletical* discourse [in its original Greek sense, *homilētíkos*, meaning affable, social, relating to friendly companionship] for this type of discourse, and point out that its form and function differ categorically from those of *institutional* discourse. These kinds of homiletical discourse likewise belong, so their argument runs, to the study of discourse. The distinction between institutional and homiletical discourse presents a first general typological categorization in a theory of discourse.

This distinction with regard to discourse made by Ehlich and Rehbein (1980) may fruitfully – so I wish to propose – be expanded and applied to the textual dimension. First of all, it is easy to see how different types of text take their place in the concrete network of social institutions and are basically linguistic means by which these institutions operate. All forms of official documents and bureaucratic forms clearly fall within this category. The same holds for school-books; they are but part and parcel of the educational institution and rarely function outside its boundaries. Newspapers and magazines form an integral part of the institution of the press. And prayer books are instruments which religious institutions may employ in the social organization of their activities. In fact, an enormous number of texts are actually produced and used as an integral part of the way in which social institutions work. One may genuinely call these *institutional texts*. At the same time, however, a considerable number of texts escape such a categorization. A sonnet or a love song, a fairy tale or a novel, clearly do not rank as instruments used by particular social institutions. This has led some, perhaps also under the influence of so-called institutional aesthetics (see Dickie 1974, 1984), to believe that literature is an 'institution' too. Now it would be futile to deny the existence of social organizations aimed at the selection, production and distribution of literary texts. The presence of publishing houses, foundations, theatres, and regional or national bodies for funding and promoting literary activities in society are clear instances of these institutional anchorage points. However, it would at the same time be naïve to therefore conclude that literature is an institution in its own right. First of all, it remains vague what the central aims of such an institution would be. Notice that such vagueness in functionality does not present itself as a problem in other institutions; the military, the educational, the press, etc. all fulfil specifiable social aims within the structure of a society. No such clear function has been identified with respect to a 'literary' institution so far. Notice that to call literature an 'institution' and subsequently to define as the central function of this institution the distribution of literary texts comes close to being tautological. Certainly that is not the way in which the concept of institution is conventionally defined in sociology (see, for instance, Berger and Luckmann 1967, Laudis 1971, Schelsky 1973, Sullivan 1984). Second, the organizations named in this respect are merely responsible for the distribution of literature, and not for the various ways in which its private consumption takes place. As Geyer (1980) has shown, even under cultural policies of an extremely totalitarian state such as Nazi Germany, the institutional control over private reading failed, because of the essentially non-institutional character of the reading act. Finally, a good number of literary texts are produced and distributed without the help and outside the structural boundaries of the named organizations. This is so for the folk tale, the myth, the riddle, and for a good number of satires and songs, in fact for the whole realm of oral literature in society.

Rejecting the existence of a special 'institution' of literature does not, of course, solve the problem of how to account for the nature of non-institutional texts. It is in this respect that the concept of *homiletical* forms of communication is highly relevant. The suggestion I should like to advance is that texts designated as 'literary' are basically characterized by their homiletical nature. This demands a further specification of the nature of this concept. Let us first consider what must be *excluded* from it. Firstly, homiletical forms of communication refuse any direct contribution to labour. They are not geared toward division of labour or the execution of professional activities, nor toward the organization and control of these. Second, homiletical texts are not produced or read in order to fulfil tasks directly linked to the functioning of a particular institution. Third, they are not read to promote the accumulation of material wealth, benefit, or profit. Nor are they used to wield or exert power (although they may be used to legitimize or undermine prevailing power structures, as is the case with eulogy or invective). In sum, homiletical forms of communication display a degree of distance from everyday (economic and institutional) concerns. In this sense Kant (1952 [1790]: 42–4) heralds a fundamental characteristic of homiletical communication when he draws attention to the remoteness from external interest in dealing with works of art. This remoteness also forms the socio-cultural foundation of the literary theory of foregrounding (see van Peer 1990). It is also worth considering a way to describe homiletical types of text by means of a *positive* procedure. The main characteristic that may be discerned in this respect is their potential for providing *delight*. While institutional forms of communication take care of the practical needs and structural aspects of society and its institutions, their preservation and operation, homiletical texts offer a special provision for the experience of delight. This is not their only function, though. Perhaps as important is their potential for creating *group cohesion* and solidarity. A special bond is created between participants in acts of literary communication. [. . .]

Literary canons thus act as a cultural cement among individuals of a certain social group, often to the extent of excluding those not familiar with the canon from the circle of knowledgeable persons. Furthermore, homiletical texts are highly *reflective* forms of linguistic activity. Since they are not concerned with the immediate needs of daily life they generate a possibility for contemplating the general nature of things. Such reflective processes may be seen at work in the creation of a utopian vision or in the 'explanation' of a state of affairs by etiological stories. Or it may take the form of a critique of social structures, such as in satire.

These three characteristics, i.e. the reflective, socially cohesive, and delight inducing qualities of homiletical texts are perhaps the most important ones, although others may be added. One may see them at work in all literary works of art, be they Greek tragedies or Petrarch's sonnets, in the nineteenth century novel or in the heroic couplets of Pope, in Dante or in Cervantes, in Dostoevsky or in Tony Harrison's poetry. Oral forms of literature are no exception to this. Whether they be myths or fairy-tales, anecdotes, legends or nursery rhymes, they all manifest a reflective attitude toward reality; simultaneously they are powerful in creating group cohesion and a communality of feelings; and all of them are accompanied by (if not aimed at) some experience of delight.

It should be noted that some of these characteristics may also be found in text types that are not usually called literature. To cite one example only: philosophical or sociological treatises are also strongly reflective in kind, and tend to be outside the realm of immediate practical needs. Whereas these meet one requirement of homiletical texts, I propose to speak of 'literature' if and only if a text bears all of the characteristics named, while simultaneously not being bound by the aims and practices of a social institution. In the case of philosophical or sociological texts, the inducement of delight is hardly an aim in itself. Also they may actually work *against* the constitution of group cohesion. Moreover, they largely function within academic institutions geared toward the preservation of knowledge. In sum, then, the concept of literature is subject to relational constraints and must be viewed in terms of a continuum. Although in particular cases this may involve complex issues of categorization, literary texts are generally quite distinct from institutional types of texts. As homiletical texts, they aim at reflectivity, group cohesion, and the experience of delight. By fulfilling these functions cumulatively, they constitute different degrees of literariness. [. . .]

Previously the characteristics of homiletical texts have been defined in functional terms. Attention has been drawn to their reflective quality, their potential for consolidating group structure, and their provision of delight. However, in order for texts to fulfil such functions, they must possess certain formal qualities which allow them to do so. Because some forms facilitate the realization of a particular function more easily than others, while still others may actually impede it, it seems plausible that different text types will tend to develop different formal characteristics. [. . .]

When the formal make-up of homiletical texts is inspected the most salient quality one observes is the extra attention given to their linguistic structure (see also Jakobson 1960). This manifests itself in a great variety of devices, such as metrical structure and rhythmic variation, parallelism and juxtaposition, rhyme, assonance and alliteration, metaphor and ambiguity, paradox and irony, versification and sound symbolism, hyperbole and periphrasis, and many others laid down in traditional (and modern) inventories of rhetorical and poetic devices. The result is a general *elaboration of linguistic form*, unparalleled by other text types, except perhaps by those types which have their origin in religious institutions. In part these formal structures facilitate the provision of delight – in terms of an aesthetic response to them. Empirical validation of this claim has been provided with respect to one such formal device, i.e. metrical structure: in an experimental situation readers provided more positive ratings (bearing on aesthetic criteria) for a metrical than for an almost identical non-metrical variant of a text (see van Peer 1990).

Are definitional problems solved now? By no means. What shall we think, for instance, of a newspaper clipping being printed 'as if' it were a poem, in a volume of poetry, as mentioned by Culler (1975: 161). Or, to take another case: readers have been shown to give a similar amount and kind of attention to non-literary texts when an experimental situation induces them to do so (see Viehoff 1986). The examples are not fortuitous, as they have often been invoked in efforts at demonstrating the impossibility of establishing a watertight definition of what literature is. Can these issues be solved within the framework proposed here? It is my contention that this is possible by looking at the pragmatics of such instances. What is involved in the latter example is what could be called 'as if' behaviour. Readers are induced, indeed encouraged to consider a particular text 'as if' it were a poem, or a story. The mental activities of readers in such a situation are basically the same as in looking for figurative patterns in the shape of clouds. This projection of qualities on to objects belonging to a different sphere of reality is typically found in playful behaviour. Literature itself being a kind of game in its own right (see Huizinga 1955, Hutchinson 1983), it should surprise no one that readers will apply their knowledge of literature to non-literary texts when a situation compels them to do so. Thus there is nothing mysterious in the results of these experiments with regard to the *definition* of literature – which does not mean that they are useless; in fact they are particularly instructive in showing the kind of strategies readers bring to literary encounters.

The poet offering a newspaper clipping in a volume of poetry is likewise involved in a game; she or he invites the reader to consider the consequences of changing the conventions and knowledge by which we interpret the world. In this particular case the game is centred around conventional cultural knowledge and the influence of particular institutions constituting aesthetic artefacts. The attacks on this conventionality and on the institutional background of cultural symbols have their historical roots in the avant-garde movements that since the beginning of this century have attempted to change the funda-mentals of artistic communication and expression. These avant-garde movements may be interpreted as involved in a particular kind of cultural game (see Bürger 1984). And again the reader is lured into 'as if' behaviour. That she or he can do so quite successfully is a testimony only to the depth to which literary categories and their attributes have been internalized. That it cannot in any way undermine the validity of the definition pro-vided earlier, is witnessed by the fact that this kind of game-like behaviour is incidental only. Literature as a whole does not, will not, and cannot exist solely of newspaper clip-pings. It is only against the background of existing knowledge of literary characteristics that games of this type are possible.

The conclusion must therefore be that it is possible to come up with an objec-tive description of what literature is, i.e. a body of symbolic objects expressed in human language, possessing textual qualities of a non-institutional, homiletical kind. [. . .]

This [. . .] model of the literary object gives scope to the critical study of literature as a socio-cultural and historical phenomenon making use of language as its major medium of expression. First of all, it allows one to define a central domain, around which peripheral areas of varying 'literary' density exist, containing forms of both homiletical discourse and of institutional texts. Second, it demonstrates that literary texts are strongly linked to forms of human action [. . .]. What is sought and provided in the encounter with literary texts are – if my analysis holds – forms of reflectivity, feelings of togetherness, and the experience of delight. Although this might apply even to texts from outside the periphery, in general this is rare, for the simple reason that these texts have been devised to fulfil very different purposes. When therefore they do enter the realm of homiletical textuality and are treated as 'literary', this is often a construct of a social situation or of some kind of game that is being played, in which the activity of literary pattern recognition is projected on to texts which in themselves are alien to this aim. Since it is essentially a game which is at stake, it may, like all games, provide pleasure and insight, thereby corresponding closely to the central characteristics of homiletical texts. Finally, the model allows for social, cultural, and historical diversification. It is to be interpreted as a model of the way in which cultures employ texts of different types to realize certain individual and social functions.

Literature, in this view, is a complex symbolic form of acting socially, the theoretical foundations for its study having already been proclaimed by Pratt (1977). If the variety and complexity of such cultural artefacts baffle us, a retreat into relativism or scepticism is but the weakest theoretical position one can take. And as the history of scepticism shows, little progress is to be expected from such a stand. Whether, and how, adequate descriptive definitions of literature can be developed is an empirical question which must be investigated before one can foreclose its possibility.

References

Berger, P. and Luckmann, T. (1967) *The Social Construction of Reality*. London: Allen Lane.

Bürger, P. (1984) *Theory of the Avant-Garde*. Manchester: Manchester University Press.

Chatman, S. (1978) *Story and Discourse*. Ithaca, NY: Cornell University Press.

Culler, J. (1975) *Structuralist Poetics*. London: Routledge and Kegan Paul.

Dickie, G. (1974) *Art and Aesthetics*. Ithaca, NY: Cornell University Press.

Dickie, G. (1984) *The Art Circle: A Theory of Art*. New York: Haven.

Dimter, M. (1981) *Textklassenkonzepte heutiger Alltagssprache*. Tübingen: Niemeyer.

Dimter, M. (1985) 'On text classification', in T. van Dijk (ed.) *Discourse and Literature*, Amsterdam and Philadelphia: John Benjamins, pp. 215–30.

Eagleton, T. (1983) *Literary Theory: An Introduction*. Oxford: Basil Blackwell.

Ehlich, K. (1984) 'Zum Textbegriff', in A. Rothkegel and B. Sandig (eds) *Text – Textsorten – Semantik*, Hamburg: Buske, pp. 9–25.

Ehlich, K. and Rehbein, J. (1980) 'Sprache in Institutionen', in H.P. Athaus (ed.) *Lexicon der germanistischen Linguistik*, Tübingen: Niemeyer, pp. 338–45.

Enkvist, N.E. (1988) 'Styles as parameters in text strategy', in W. van Peer (ed.) *The Taming of the Text: Explorations in Language, Literature and Culture*, London: Routledge, pp. 125–51.

Geyer, H. (1980) *Popular Literature in the Third Reich*. Occasional Paper on General Theory, No. 60. Centre for Cultural Studies, University of Birmingham.

Goody, J. (1977) *The Domestication of the Savage Mind*. Cambridge: Cambridge University Press.

Huizinga, J. (1955) *Homo Ludens: A Study of the Play Element in Culture*. Boston: The Beacon Press.

Hutchinson, P. (1983) *Games Authors Play*. London: Methuen.

Ibsch, E., Schram, D.H. and Steen, G. (eds) (2002) *The Psychology and Sociology of Literature*. Amsterdam: John Benjamins.

Jakobson, R. (1960) 'Closing statement: linguistics and poetics', in T.A. Sebeok (ed.) *Style in Language*, Cambridge, MA: MIT Press, pp. 350–77.

Kant, I. (1952) *The Critique of Judgement* [original 1790]. Oxford: Oxford University Press.

Kreuz, R.J. and MacNealy, M.S. (eds) (1996) *Empirical Approaches to Literature and Aesthetics*. New York: Ablex.

Labov, W. (1972) 'Rules for ritual insults', in D. Sudnow (ed.) *Studies in Social Interaction*, New York: Free Press, pp. 120–69.

Laudis, J.R. (1971) *Sociology: Concepts and Characteristics*. Belmont, CA: Wadworth.

Miall, D. (2006) *Literary Reading: Empirical and Theoretical Studies*. New York: Peter Lang.

Popper, K. (1963) *Conjectures and Refutations*. London: Routledge.

Pratt, M.L. (1977) *Toward a Speech Act Theory of Literary Discourse*. Bloomington: Indiana University Press.

Schelsky, H. (ed.) (1973) *Zur Theorie der Institution*. Düsseldorf: Bertelsmann.

Sullivan, T.J. (1984) *Sociology: Concepts, Issues and Applications*. New York: Wiley.

van Peer, W. (1989) 'How to do things with texts: towards a pragmatic foundation for the teaching of texts', in M.H. Short (ed.) *Reading, Analysing and Teaching Literature*, London: Longman, pp. 263–93.

van Peer, W. (1990) 'The measurement of metre: its cognitive and affective functions', *Poetics* 19: 259–75.

van Peer, W., Hakemulder, J. and Zyngier, S. (2007) *Muses and Measures: Empirical Research Methods for the Humanities*. Cambridge: Cambridge Scholars Publications.

Viehoff, R. (1986) 'How to construct a literary poem?', *Poetics* 15: 287–306.

Extracted from Willie van Peer (1990) 'But what is literature?: toward a descriptive definition of literature', in R. Sell (ed.) *Literary Pragmatics*, London: Routledge, pp. 127–41.

Chapter 13

Deixis and the poetic persona

KEITH GREEN

In this article from 1992, Keith Green takes up a key notion in both linguistics and philosophy — deixis — and provides a model of deictic analysis that has since proven highly productive in stylistics. Green argues that deixis is continuous across all discourse, and that its use in lyric is a difference of degree not kind. He then sets out some of the characteristics of lyric poetry in general, arising from a close analysis of the deictics of a poem by the seventeenth-century poet Henry Vaughan.

The emphasis on deixis in literary texts developed after this article appeared, and deixis is now a key feature in stylistics. See, for example, Green's (1995) own edited collection, and also Duchan *et al.* (1995), Tsur (2003), McIntyre (2006) and Stockwell (2007), as well as chapter 16 in this volume by Werth.

[. . .]

What is deixis?

DEIXIS IS THE ENCODING in an utterance of the spatio-temporal context and subjective experience of the encoder. It is primarily linked with the *speech* or *discourse event*. It is the phenomenon whereby the tripartite relationship between the language system, the encoder's subjectivity and various contextual factors is foregrounded grammatically or lexically. For example, in Levinson's (1983) well-known deictic utterance, *Meet me here a week from now with a stick about this big*, there are certain words, such as *me, here, now* and *this*, which have part of their meaning which is context-sensitive. They also function from the perspective of the encoder or utterer and are thus significantly grammaticalised in the language. [. . .] Russell (1940) called deictics (or indexicals) *egocentric particulars*, and this is because there is a centre of orientation in deixis which is invariably egocentric. The *zero-point*, or *origo*, to use Bühler's (1934) terminology, is set by the encoder in relation to the spatio-temporal nature of the utterance. Any utterance relates both to the speaker's 'centre' and to the surrounding cognitive environment.

Deixis and use

One of the most important aspects of deixis is that it is invariably distinguished by its *use*. In order to clarify this, I should like to begin by making a distinction between deictic *terms* and deictic *elements*. A deictic term is part of a grammatically closed set which includes the personal and demonstrative pronouns, certain adverbials, definite referring expressions and the vocative particle [. . .]. A deictic element is not a term as such, but some part of the utterance which might be said to be deictic. In other words, there is a syntactic or semantic element which might function deictically. For instance, verbs are not normally deictic in themselves, except for those noted by Fillmore (1971), notably *come* and *go*, which encode movement towards and from the origo. Tense generally is a deictic element, however. The verb in a sentence such as *The sun shines brightly* is not deictic in the sense that the verb *to come* is, but is nevertheless deictic because it is part of a system which relates specific entities to reference points. But because it is deictic it is context-sensitive, and there are a number of ways of using the utterance *The sun shines brightly* and a number of contexts in which it might occur. There is no necessary link between tense and time; it is likely in this instance that the use of the present tense is not restricted to a particular time (which is the time of the utterance) but refers rather to a 'general' present. The progressive form would be a more likely occurrence if an immediate moment is being referred to. If I say one morning while looking out of my window, *The sky is blue*, then I am using this sentence deictically. If, however, I mean *The sky is blue* as a general statement – a proposition about a general state of affairs – then I do not use it deictically (I use it generically). Tense, therefore, can be deictic inasmuch as it can be used to encode specific temporal relations with respect to the encoder. [. . .] I must repeat, then, that deixis is distinguished by its use. [. . .]

The distinction between semantics and pragmatics

So far I have described a closed set of elements and terms which relate specific entities to a reference point – a set which is also determined by use and context. A central question noted by Levinson (1983) is whether the study of deixis belongs to the domain of pragmatics or semantics. This is a rather complex issue, but clearly there are elements of language, notably deictics, which are not accessible to a purely truth-conditional semantics. [. . .] If semantics is modified to take account of deixis, it becomes a context-conditional semantics, and the boundary between semantics and pragmatics becomes very blurred. [. . .] The core of such analysis is that sentences with deictic elements and terms encode propositions only by virtue of the specific contexts in which they occur. At this point the problem of context itself comes to the fore.

The problem of context

It is possible to see context functioning in three ways. By context I mean something wider than the co-text of any utterance:

1   Contexts are extralinguistic, but affect the range of possible meanings.
2   Contexts are actually brought about or changed by the utterance itself.
3   Contexts are in some way lexico-grammatically encoded in certain linguistic elements.

In (1) the implication is that the *situation of utterance*, which is extralinguistic, determines the potential meaning. Thus in my earlier example *The sky is blue*, only knowledge of the situation of the utterance will enable the decoder to interpret it as either deictic or generic. Point (3) states that certain linguistic elements encode contextual features. These, I suggest, are deictic elements and terms. I propose to reject (1) and fuse (2) and (3). I reject (1) because this cannot take account of the vast range of human communication which does not take place within the canonical situation of utterance – i.e. face-to-face. [. . .] Again, sentences only express propositions by virtue of specific contexts and a specific encoder within a deictic field. There is a reciprocity between linguistic elements and possible contexts, and those elements which enable this reciprocal relationship to proceed are deictic.

Indexical and symbolic

Just as the line between semantics and pragmatics is fuzzy, so is that between the *indexical* and *symbolic* meanings of deictic terms. The symbolic meaning of a deictic term is its meaning as it functions within the linguistic system. Thus *I* might be glossed as 'the person writing this sentence'; *you* as 'the addressee/participant in the discourse', and so on. I wish to be relatively uncontroversial about these definitions, although I realise the great philosophical problems involved in any description of *I* for instance. The indexical meaning is that which exists when we have ascribed referents to those discourse elements suggested by the symbolic meaning of a term. A very important point is that the symbolic meaning in part determines the range of indexical possibilities, thus accommodating my view of context outlined above. If I point to a particular item in a room and say 'that', we can say that the demonstrative encodes distance from the *origo*, whether actual or mental, and the coincidence of indexical and symbolic meaning is only possible when we know what object is being pointed to.

   In the discourse of the lyric poem it is unlikely that we can ascribe indexical meaning to symbolic elements of deictic terms. I suggest, however, that the indexical meaning is partly determined by the manifestation of symbolic meaning within certain contexts. Of course there are many discourses existing where we lack clear referents for indexical meanings. Within literary discourses it seems that lyric poetry is the genre least likely to assist us. In prose fiction, a more dialogic genre, various shifts of deictic centre occur (that is, from character to character) and we are more likely to see deictic terms verified intra-textually – for example, pronominal reference given a full cataphoric form.

   I want to try to clear away the distinction between two kinds of text, the 'literary' (or poetic) and the 'non-literary', as regards the function of context. Deixis is the most context-specific linguistic element, and it exists and occurs in the most situation-free as well as the most situation-bound utterances. Certain generic atomic propositions may have minimal deictic features, but most utterances contain them. Following Sperber and Wilson (1986), context can be seen as *the set of possibilities which exist in the universe of discourse and situation of utterance for the interpretation of that utterance*. If we reject the idea that context is situation (although I have accommodated the concept of situation in my definition of context) we can treat deixis in poetry not as a kind of 'pseudo-deixis', as some critics such as Culler (1974) have suggested, but simply as deixis framed by a particular genre. Context then becomes paradoxically more metacontextual (as in the work of Sperber and Wilson 1986) and encoded ('pointed to') by certain deictic elements.

The discourse of lyric poetry

I have so far discussed deixis *per se* and the functions of context. I must now attempt to define the discourse in which the deixis is to be found, for this is the pragmatic frame governing sense-making operations. There is a danger of treating a historical phenomenon (the lyric poem) as *sui generis*, and that may restrict any absolute definition of the kind of text I shall be examining. I make certain assumptions about the lyric poem, however:

1   It mobilises a monologic 'I' figure.
2   There will often be a dramatisation of situation.
3   Because of the absence of extralinguistic elements, actual situation and emotional situation will be compounded. For example, in Wordsworth's 'Nutting' (as is typical of many Romantic poems) a *situation* is being dramatised, but so too is the sensibility of Wordsworth in the dramatised situation. An *experiencing mode* and an *observing mode* are expressed simultaneously:

> . . . Then up I rose,
> And dragged to earth both branch and bough, with crash
> And merciless ravage; and the shady nook
> Of hazels, and the green and mossy bower,
> Deformed and sullied, patiently gave up
> Their quiet being: and unless I now
> Confound my present feelings with the past,
> Even then, when from the bower I turned away,
> Exulting, rich beyond the wealth of kings
> I felt a sense of pain when I beheld
> The silent trees and the intruding sky.

4   Referring expressions will be introduced on the basis of assumed knowledge on the part of the reader.
5   Spatial and temporal deixis will be used to orientate the reader to an assumed context.
6   The poem will assume an addressee and a decoder.

The lyric poem, then, is a particular kind of universe of discourse. The *environment* of the lyric poem must, in consequence, be matched up with the features we note in the analysis.

Deictic categories

The so-called 'traditional' categories of deixis are *time, place, person, social* and *discourse* (see Levinson 1983). I propose a new classification as follows:

1   reference
2   the *origo*
3   time and space
4   subjectivity

5   the text

6   syntax.

These categories have the advantage of including the more traditional elements while highlighting the egocentric nature of deixis (the *origo*) and giving prominence to the major deictic category, reference. Both *elements* and *terms* are also accommodated in this classification. I shall take these categories one at a time, and simply state what deictic terms or elements occur in them; but it must always be remembered that every item *depends on its use within certain contexts and under certain conditions*. As I have said, there can be no taxonomy of *use*. My explanations must necessarily be brief at this stage.

1   *Reference*: definite referring expressions; demonstrative determiners and pronouns; definite articles; pronominal expressions.

2   *The origo*: first and second person pronouns; vocatives; demonstrative adverbs; deixis encoding mental proximity/distance; honorifics. The second person is included here because it is a participant in the discourse, and is therefore more closely related to the origo.

3   *Time and space*: temporal adverbs; spatial adverbs; non-calendrical time-units (*today*, *next week*, etc.); tense; the concepts of *coding time*, *content time* and *receiving time* (and the analogous *coding place*, *content place*, and *receiving place*). Coding time is the time at which the utterance is 'transmitted'; content time is the time (or times) to which the utterance refers; and receiving time is the time when the utterance is received by the addressee or decoder. Many lyric poems dramatise coding time and content time as synchronous, as in the following lines from Donne's 'The Flea':

> Marke but this flea, and marke in this,
> How little that which thou deny'st me is;
> Mee it suck'd first, and now sucks thee.

4   *Subjectivity*: the complexities of modality, both epistemic and deontic. In particular there is a link between deixis and epistemic modality, for both encode the subjective experience of the encoder.

5   *The text*: all elements which orientate the text to itself for the reader/hearer; impure textual deixis is the phenomenon which falls between anaphora and discourse deixis. In the following lines from Larkin's 'The Winter Palace',

> Most people know more as they get older:
> I give all that the cold shoulder

the *that* refers not to a clear antecedent, as would be the case in anaphora, nor to a specific 'chunk' of discourse, as in discourse deixis. Rather it refers to the proposition implied in the opening line.

6   *Syntax*: certain syntactic forms have deictic function. Although there is no necessary correlation between syntactic form and function, it can be said, for instance, that the interrogative presupposes an addressee.

[. . .]

An analysis of Henry Vaughan's 'The Retreate'

[. . .] I want now to look at 'The Retreate' by Henry Vaughan and to examine a small number of its elements and terms in relation to the methodology already described. I have chosen Vaughan because there has already been some analysis of deixis in his poetry – notably by Roger Sell in his article 'The unstable discourse of Henry Vaughan' (1987). Vaughan is an interesting poet with regard to his use of deixis. His idiosyncratic usage is at once fascinating for analysis and a warning against making unwary generalisations about lyric poetry.

The Retreate

Happy those early dayes! when I
Shin'd in my Angell-infancy.
Before I understood this place
Appointed for my second race,
Or taught my soul to fancy ought
But a white, Celestiall thought,
When yet I had not walkt above
A mile, or two, from my first love,
And looking back (at that short space,)
Could see a glimpse of his bright-face;
When on some *gilded Cloud*, or *flowre*
My gazing soul would dwell an houre,
And in those weaker glories spy
Some shadows of eternity;
Before I taught my tongue to wound
My Conscience with a sinfull sound,
Or had the black art to dispence
A sev'rall sinne to ev'ry sence,
But felt through all this fleshly dresse
Bright *shootes* of everlastingnesse.
    O how I long to travell back
And tread again that ancient track!
That I might once more reach that plaine,
Where first I left my glorious traine,
From whence th'Inlightned spirit sees
That shady City of Palme trees;
But (ah!) my soul with too much stay
Is drunk, and staggers in the way.
Some men a forward motion love,
But I by backward steps would move,
And when this dust falls to the urn
In that state I came return.

The opening line features a definite referring expression with distal demonstrative *those*. (Demonstratives are described in terms of relative proximity to the encoder: *this* is proximal, *that* is distal. [. . .]) Most of the reference in the poem is made through the use of demonstratives, rather than the definite article. The initial clause, 'Happy those early days!', plunges us into the middle of a discourse, as much lyric poetry does. There is some syntactic ambiguity in the opening lines – we can read 'when I / Shin'd' as a separate clause or as a post-modifier to 'those early dayes'. Because of the exclamation mark, and despite the lower case 'w', I read the first clause as complete, thus giving it fuller deictic impact. Information after 'those early dayes' must lessen the deictic force of the utterance because it shifts our attention not to some presupposed referent seemingly outside the discourse (what 'early dayes'?) but to something qualified within the text itself.

I also assume that there is an ellipted main verb, the past tense copula *were*, but this is not immediately apparent on a first reading. 'Early' is deictic here, but only inasmuch as it sets up an opposition to a notional 'late'. 'Those early dayes' refers to a latent discourse referent. A demonstrative is used to refer to a temporal aspect. At this stage we do not know whether the 'dayes' are general (which would imply that the missing verb is *are*) or particular; but we get a clearer picture when we come to the second clause 'when I / Shin'd'. 'Shin'd' encodes past activity, but only in relation to the utterance's internal system of time referencing which has already been set up and controlled by the deictic references of earlier elements. This seems to happen retrospectively, for it is the simple past tense of 'shin'd' which enables us to read the deixis of 'those early dayes' in a particular way, in direct relation to 'shin'd'. The opening of a poem is obviously important because there is no previous discourse through which to interpret it except for the title, but this is not precise enough to enable us to assign the proper *indexical* meaning to the deictic elements and terms. But what are these 'early dayes' and who is the 'I' of the utterance? In discourse theory, if the conditions specified by any of the co-ordinates (speaker, place, audience, time, etc.) are altered, the contexts are altered. So how does the concept of context function here in relation to the deictic elements and terms which are clearly organising the poem's reference structure? The deictic elements and terms are constantly helping us to sort from possible contexts, helping us to move from *symbolic meaning* to some kind of *indexical meaning*. A powerful deictic centre is being mobilised without an immediate situation. The poem can be seen to embody a set of expectations or possible worlds. It will further *engage* in the set of those possible worlds and alter the context depending on the interaction of the conditions which specify the action of the discourse co-ordinates. In 'The Retreat,' deixis is often qualified by further deixis, and these elements are often 'personal'. When, later in the poem, reference is made to cultural and spatio-temporal elements, such qualification is missing. All the while, the deixis works to orientate our focus. In the early part of the poem there is ambiguity in the functioning of deictic expressions: an initial deictic term such as 'those early dayes' is supplemented with further deictic information 'when I / Shin'd.' This recurs in the expression 'this place / Appointed for my second race'. Thus Vaughan is assuming a certain amount of shared knowledge on the part of the reader; but because we cannot, naturally, see things from the perspective of his *origo*, he must also assist the reader in the assignment of *indexical* or *deictic* meanings.

In the latter part of the poem, however, referring expressions, though still mobilising the demonstrative, are not qualified with further deictic terms. They tend to suggest homophoric or anaphoric reference, although their function is not straightforward. 'That ancient track' (line 22) and 'that plaine' (line 23) are references to the earlier 'journey'. Although they are followed by two relative clauses (lines 24 and 25), they are not as closely linked syntactically as the earlier examples cited above. The subsequent information is in fact redundant with respect to deictic function. The expression 'That shady City of Palme trees' is more conventionally homophoric; but nevertheless it is metaphorically 'displaced' and encoded through the use of a distal demonstrative. The use of such demonstratives always implies a dual processing effort on the part of the known addressee. On the one hand, the demonstrative suggests that the element is known to us – that it is somewhere in the universe of discourse. On the other hand, the demonstrative does not merely give crude emphasis to a referent; it suggests that although the element is 'known' some extra processing effort must take place in order for it to be accessed. The final demonstrative uses – 'this dust' and 'that state (I came)' – reiterate the opposition between the proximal and distal perspectives of the speaker. 'This' is always something that, although proximal, the speaker of the poem wishes to move away from. This backward movement in both time and space is brought to a climax in the final line. Distal elements are huddled into a final phrase which includes the distal demonstrative 'this', the past tense verb 'came', and 'return', which is semantically opposed to 'came'.

As the poem progresses, we might assume that contextual or latent discourse referents are less likely to be introduced, for we read and interpret in the light of what has gone before – of previous elements in the utterance. This is partly evident in my initial example of the 'backward-looking' function of the deictic element 'shin'd' (line 2), but lyric poetry is also a genre where such referents are continually introduced. I have stressed that we construct a context from the deixis of the text (a context being the set of possibilities which exist in the universe of discourse and situation of utterance for the interpretation of the utterance); but the initial elements of the utterance must be more dense in terms of pragmatic activity. We cannot merely say the poem represents a kind of null context, where context is partly situation of utterance and partly based on previous elements in the discourse. Deictic expressions, certainly in the first part of the poem, are often qualified in a way so as to present the reader with further information; but that information often, too, comprises deictic elements or terms. My first example of this was the opening line. The following are the occurrences of deictic expressions qualified (post-modified) by a deictic element or term: 'those early dayes! when I shin'd', 'above a mile . . . from my first love', 'this place appointed for my second race', 'that plaine where first I left my glorious traine'. [The last two examples also contain a further qualification embedded in the first.]

[. . .]

Demonstrative reference is clearly an important aspect of the deixis of the poem: it encourages the reader to process the deictic meanings in a specific way. There are only three occurrences of the definite article: '*the* black art' (line 17), '*th*'Inlightned spirit' (line 25) and '*the* urn' (line 31). These uses are non-deictic. The article is unmarked as regards spatio-temporal relations; so the function of deictic reference is to set up a continual spatial, temporal and subjective opposition between proximal and distal relations. Temporal distance is encoded by the past tense, reflecting *content time*, which is separate from *coding time*. In the latter part of the poem a more general 'present' is implied, and this second content time is closer to the coding time.

Relevance, deixis and the poetic voice

So far I have been working 'backwards' from the specific deictic terms and elements of the poem to contextual possibilities and other pragmatic considerations. If we go one further stage in this direction we reach the metacontextual concept of *relevance*. Relevance can be seen as a concept governing interpretation (see Sperber and Wilson 1986). There is a context of relevance through which deixis is received, and we need to know to what extent analogy with other texts is pertinent. It should be possible to construct a pragmatic frame by which the deixis of lyric poetry in its various manifestations can be viewed.

What kind of speaker is presupposed to be uttering 'Happy those early dayes!'? The 'poetic voice' or 'persona' is a recognisable post-Renaissance phenomenon. As readers we expect such a persona to describe a scene, dramatise some situation, and express feelings. There is frequently a 'personal' element in poetry, but this element is couched within a highly formalised and conventional genre. This must affect and delimit the range of contextual possibilities and the frame of relevance.

[. . .]

Conclusion

I have stressed that I am taking a particular linguistic phenomenon, deixis, and examining its occurrences and behaviour in a specific genre. This leaves the possibility open of finding new insights into deixis *per se* as well as into its behaviour within a particular discourse. Because of this, I have not said that the analysis of deixis in the poetic text will necessarily be a useful *stylistic* procedure – giving greater insight into individual poems or poets. Most of the analysis of literary deixis has proceeded by using deixis as a kind of stylistic lever. I do not reject this out of hand; but it is not my primary purpose here; rather, it is to suggest a methodology which might enable us to gain insights into the functioning of the lyric poem *per se*, while always being mindful of the dangers of seeking generic overviews of historical phenomena. In 'The Retreate', a complex linguistic and pragmatic site is displayed, and it is deixis which largely holds this together, enabling frames of context to be created, and leading the reader around and into the work. It is the same – and we should not be surprised at this – in ordinary discourse.

We need to remember two fundamental points: language seems to be designed primarily for face-to-face interaction (that is, the canonical situation of utterance); and it is a capability of humans that they can mobilise discourse beyond this canonical situation and operate language free of contextual boundaries. It is the interrelationship of these points that enables the analysis of deixis in the genre of the lyric poem to proceed.

References

Bühler, K. (1934) *Sprachtheorie*. Jena: Fisher.

Culler, J. (1974) *Structuralist Poetics*. London: Routledge and Kegan Paul.

Duchan, J.F., Bruder, G.A. and Hewitt, L.E. (eds) (1995) *Deixis in Narrative: A Cognitive Science Perspective*. Hillsdale, NJ: Lawrence Erlbaum.

Fillmore, C. (1971) *Santa Cruz Lectures on Deixis*. Bloomington: Indiana University Linguistics Club.

Green, K. (ed.) (1995) *New Essays on Deixis*. Amsterdam: Rodopi.

Levinson, S.C. (1983) *Pragmatics*. Cambridge: Cambridge University Press.

McIntyre, D. (2006) *Point of View in Plays: A Cognitive Stylistic Approach to Viewpoint in Drama and other Text-Types*. Amsterdam/Philadelphia: John Benjamins.

Russell, B. (1940) *An Inquiry into Meaning and Truth*. London: Unwin.

Sell, R. (1987) 'The unstable discourse of Henry Vaughan', in A. Rudrum (ed.) *Essential Articles for the Study of Henry Vaughan*, New York: Archon, pp. 311–32.

Sperber, D. and Wilson, D. (1986) *Relevance: Communication and Cognition*. Oxford: Blackwell.

Stockwell, P. (2007) 'On teaching literature itself', in G. Watson and S. Zyngier (eds) *Literature and Stylistics for Language Learners*, London: Macmillan, pp. 15–24.

Tsur, R. (2003) 'Deixis and abstractions: adventures in space and time', in J. Gavins and G. Steen (eds) *Cognitive Poetics in Practice*, London: Routledge, pp. 41–54.

Extracted from Keith Green (1992) 'Deixis and the poetic persona', *Language and Literature* 1 (2): 121–34.

Chapter 14

Bakhtin, addressivity, and the poetics of objectivity

ALISON TATE

Much of modern stylistics sets itself up either in direct opposition or as an alternative to deconstructive views of language. Stylisticians have periodically revisited earlier work from central and eastern Europe for complementary approaches, and the work of Mikhail Bakhtin has been prominent especially for those stylisticians with a socio-linguistic or sociological training. In this chapter, originally delivered at a conference in the early 1990s, Alison Tate draws on this work to argue for an accommodation between individual uniqueness and social negotiation that is particularly important in theorising literary production and reading.

Introduction

W ALES (1988: 177) SUGGESTS that the impact of Bakhtin's ideas has 'yet to be fully felt in stylistics'; this article is intended as a contribution to the 'necessarily critical but constructive dialogue' which she sees as emerging. It concerns the term *dialogism* which is constantly recycled across Bakhtin's writings, identified with inton-ation in some of the earlier works, and with the stylistic and generic heteroglossia of language in his later books (see, for example, Bakhtin 1971, 1973, 1981, 1983). Some commentators feel this apparent movement from individual to social imports an irreconcilable ambiguity into the concept (see Segre 1985). In a recent collection of essays, for example, Hirschkop suggests that:

> a particularly significant focus of dispute has been and will be whether dialo-gism is a relation between individual utterances, and in that sense always in operation, or a more specifically historical phenomenon, depending on a con-frontation between social conventions of style or genre (Hirschkop 1989: 11).

Hirschkop's formulation of the conflict is revealing. It is between the idea of the utter-ance as representing 'unique experiential moments' and the 'varying styles of a language, the consistent patterns of usage which overlay a basic syntactic and grammatical structure' (p. 9) which 'would seem to negate this uniqueness of experience, and with it any possibility of maintaining a connection with value and intention' (p. 7). But there is only a problem, of course, if one considers the utterance as fundamentally individual (as 'unrepeatable performances, its entwinement with values wholly conditional on the recognition of the uniqueness of the utterance', creating 'something that had not been before, that is always new and nonreiterative' [Hirschkop 1989: 11]), and sociality as entering into language at some macrostructural level of stylistic or generic stratification.

I want here to trace a different conception of dialogism which assumes that the utterance is fundamentally social. This is an argument that takes its cue from another synonym for dialogism: the term *addressivity* which Bakhtin [1986: 95] uses in *Speech Genres and Other Late Essays*. What I want to show is that, apart from its role as ideational or extralinguistic reference, any mode of reference or way of presenting information about the world has implications, on the one hand, for the presentation of point of view and, on the other, for address, here loosely interpreted as reader positioning. I shall draw examples from early modernist poetry, a kind of poetry in which we also find great stress placed on the idea of the unique and unrepeatable utterance, and which seeks, in the name of presence and immediacy, to evade some of the discursive constraints of language, to get back to what William Carlos Williams called 'words washed clean' (1954: 163). The consideration of some of the problems associated with such poetry illuminates the tensions inherent in the idea of the unique utterance.

Reference and viewpoint

Problems of reference are a longstanding concern of linguistics; in a tradition dating back at least to Frege, reference-orientated treatments of naming have focused on the existential status of nouns and referring expressions. Proper names, articles, determiners, demonstratives and the like have been of interest for their truth values, or for their indications of uniqueness or definiteness (for example, Frege 1982; Hawkins 1978; Gazdar 1979; Werth 1984). Reference is a preoccupation of modernist poetry, too. Writers influenced by the poetics of objectivity were much concerned with the power of language to identify, name, and make valid statements about the existence of the phenomenal world. This is a poetry which had its own dream of extralinguistic reference in its appeal to the object, the fact or the thing: not surprisingly, it is also a heavily noun orientated or nominalist poetry (see Miles 1965). This is not a poetry, one might think, that is concerned with point of view or the presentation of person, rather aiming at the objectivity of a 'world seen without self'.

[. . .]

Strategies of reference

It is possible that the marked stress on concreteness and specific reference in imagist and objectivist poetry functions as a means to avoid stereotyped or conventional language usage. One thinks, for example, of Williams's campaign against vague generalizations in poetry, or Pound's abhorrence of abstractions (see, for example, Pound 1937: 51). But it is equally likely that concrete reference, in offering a way of referring without abstraction or classification, provides an escape from the imposition of a personal viewpoint on the world: it can be seen as a form of naming, a means to achieve the particularity of proper names, or the uniqueness and nonreiterability of the utterance. How does one achieve unique reference? William Carlos Williams is, of course, the poet who in *Paterson* proclaimed 'no ideas but in things' and who stressed above all the importance of achieving the particular. We might look at the strategies he uses to create the concrete image in that objectivist classic, 'The Red Wheelbarrow':

> *The Red Wheelbarrow*
>
> so much depends
> upon
>
> a red wheel
> barrow
>
> glazed with rain
> water
>
> beside the white
> chickens.
>   (Williams 1976: 57)

The poem points us towards a number of ways in which specification and uniqueness of reference might be achieved. Precision, for example, clearly is the greatest importance in achieving the concreteness of the image. In this poem the objects are precisely described and the relationship between them is carefully indicated. The colour specification is also careful: this is significant given that there are still arguments for the 'innocence' of sensory perception, and for colour as representing basic perceptual, rather than linguistic, categories. (Williams said: 'All I do is to try and understand something in its natural colours and shapes': quoted in Pound 1937: 69; see also Childs 1986: 48 on Pound's use of colour terms). Images are delineated: the line organization in the poem emphasizes the disjunction of the objects, functioning to isolate *chickens*, for instance, and, in the same instance, to separate the attribute *white* from its noun. Even here, however, one can note how easily 'naming' slips over into 'unnaming': for instance, the way that line division functions to separate compound nouns into their components in *wheel/barrow* and *rain/water*.

But is a non-subjective mode of unique reference really possible? It is noticeable how many problems surrounding reference are identified in the poetry. Marjorie Perloff (1981), for instance, characterizes it in terms of 'referential indeterminacy'; other commentators have remarked on problems centring on juxtaposition, and on metonymic and metaphorical confusions (see, for example Lodge 1977; Durant 1981). One of the paradoxes of imagist poetics is that a poetry ostensibly concerned with definition and specificity emerges as a discourse of mutability, paraphrase, redefinition, metaphorical respecification, and of metamorphosis.

It is possible to identify the process by which the simple metonymy of 'The Red Wheelbarrow' slides over into the multiple ambiguities of *The Cantos*. At the heart of it, one might suggest, are the coreferential problems involved in respecification of images: in juxtaposed structures our normal guides to interpretation are removed, there is no explicit indication as to whether coreference is intended or not. As Durant (1984: 158) shows, the problem can be seen to be of major importance in relation to another extract from *The Cantos*:

> Moon on the palm-leaf,
> confusion:
> Confusion, source of renewals;
> Yellow wing, pale in the moon shaft
> Green wing, pale in the moon shaft,
> Pomegranate, pale in the moon shaft
> White horn, pale in the moon shaft, and Titania
> By the drinking hole,
> steps, cut in the basalt.
> (Pound 1975: 100)

At the beginning of this extract there are examples of apposition which clearly demonstrate the metaphorical equating of entities: *Moon on the palm-leaf/confusion*. At the end, we have what is equally clearly the identification of discrete entities: *Titania, the drinking hole* and *steps*. In these latter lines what seems to be indicated is a visual frame; the implication is that the objects are present and available for description. From this assumption, for example, would follow the use of the definite article in *the drinking hole*; its use could be taken as an indication of shared knowledge. But what about the middle section of the extract? Parallels appear to exist for it to be interpreted in two ways: as a listing structure (*yellow wing . . . green wing . . . white horn*), or, alternatively, as the continuation of the metaphorical, appositional sequence beginning with *palm-leaf*. The problem can be seen to be one of scope. Even in the first three lines it is not clear whether the initial appositional series extends to equate *Moon on the palm-leaf/confusion/ source of renewals*, or whether the repetition of *confusion* acts as stage marker, giving us two series which may or not be equated through the common term. The extension of the initial appositional series could be held to end with the second line, or to extend as far as *pomegranate*.

Noun phrases which are paratactically juxtaposed can be taken as appositional, and thus coreferential, or alternatively as discrete items, as in a list. The one form of association can be taken as redefinition or metaphor, the other is metonymic: the presence or absence of coreferential identity is the basis of the contrast between metonymic and metaphorical relationships. We can see the potential confusion in such operations in one of Hulme's 'Images':

> The lark crawls on the cloud
> Like a flea on a white body.
> (Press 1969: 47)

This is ostensibly a simile, and reference in similes is usually considered non-referential (see DuBois 1980), that is, one should not be able to refer later to *the flea*; it has not become a discourse entity. However, the simultaneous operation of metaphorical transformation in the poem brings this non-referentiality into question: even in the first line of the couplet one already has a metaphorical confounding of lark and flea in the word *crawl*. The process is what Pound speaks of as *superpositions*, the gliding of one image over the other.

One can suggest reasons why many problems of modernist poetics seem to centre round co-reference: this is a poetry concerned with world reference and it makes little concession to discourse reference or 'information-packaging'. Coreferential identity has only a discourse status, the links indicated are purely textual, not those of the real world. DuBois (1980: 204) suggests the nature of the problem when he comments that 'this continuity of the real object with itself runs as a continuous thread in the real world, but in discourse the continuity can be expressed only intermittently, through phrases which appear at intervals in the narration'. If modernist conjuring with strategies of reference can be considered a means of evading the power of language to classify and abstract, the manipulation of coreference can be considered in a similar way. [. . .]

Reference and modes of address

Why should attempts to capture the concrete example, the unique utterance, result in readers' perceptions of ambiguity or obscurity? If modes of reference to extralinguistic reality have implications for the imposition of viewpoint in the text, they can also be regarded as reader oriented or associated with modes of address. Current accounts of textual structure suggest that the use of referring terms is governed by the assumptions of the speaker or writer about the reader/listener. Nouns and nominal reference, that is, not only function to delineate the writer's world view or to represent and classify a certain reality, the terms selected can also be considered to be influenced by the writer's assumptions about the reader's knowledge (see, for example, Clark and Marshall 1981; Givón 1983; Marslen-Wilson *et al.* 1982). Chafe (1976: 28) puts this in rather a different way: his main interest is 'in the ways in which a speaker accommodates his speech to temporary states of the addressee's mind' (see also Givón 1983; Brown and Yule 1983: 183–9).

These assumptions are marked in textual structure, in the way that reference terms are introduced into the discourse. Prince (1981: 233–7), for example, points out that what distinguishes between a reference to *he* and to *a guy I work with* is the different assumptions that the writer/speaker is making about the reader's knowledge. Considering the different ways in which introductory reference might be achieved, she suggests that terms such as *you, Noam Chomsky, a bus, the driver, a guy I work with*, or *one of these eggs* all reflect assumptions about the familiarity of their referents to the reader. Such forms are, moreover, consistent enough to be scaled along a dimension of 'assumed familiarity'.

One might, of course, question whether such scales apply to literary works; the practice of using *the* or *he* for example, at the opening of a narrative before the referent or name for the character is established is not uncommon, and this could be symptomatic of the rather different linguistic practices of narrative, poetry, or literary language more generally. Yet the general principle is argued by Ariel (1988: 68, 1989: 569): language basically provides speakers with a means to code the accessibility of the referent to the addressee, so that referring expressions function as guidelines for retrievals. Reference terms inevitably carry assumptions about the reader's or listener's knowledge; the key words in discourse oriented accounts of reference tend to be *accessibility, predictability, saliency,* and *retrievability* (see Prince 1981).

Make it new

Predictability, habituality, given information, assumptions about the reader? The emphasis in modernist poetry is on newness: Pound, for instance, insists that 'Literature is news that STAYS news' (1951: 29), it avoids 'ready-made conclusions and taking too much for granted' (see Pound 1937: 68). A writing practice which is vitally concerned with new information, one suspects, would have little time for *assumed familiarity* or, indeed, for any aspect of language which relates to presupposition or given information, whether implicated by reference terms or by topicalization or thematization. (A list of extracted rhemes, one might note, is strikingly reminiscent of some of the more fragmented imagist poems).

If clarity in writing was dear to Pound's heart, this was a very particular kind of clarity:

> . . . there are various kinds of clarity. There is the clarity of the request: Send me four pounds of ten-penny nails. And there is the syntactical simplicity of the request: Buy me the kind of Rembrandt I like. This latter is an utter cryptogram. It presupposes a more complex and intimate understanding of the speaker than most of us ever acquire of anyone. It has as many meanings, almost as there are persons who might speak it. To a stranger it conveys nothing at all.

> It is the almost constant labour of the prose artist to translate this latter kind of clarity into the former; to say 'Send me the kind of Rembrandt I like' in the terms of 'Send me four pounds of ten-penny nails' (Pound 1954: 50).

It is interesting to consider the differences between the two examples: they raise a number of issues about definiteness, specificity and point of view. They embody a comparison between a vague, diffuse, culturally connotative mode of reference, and what appears to be very much a Williams-type stress on the concrete and everyday object. On the one hand one has the 'high' cultural connotations of *the Rembrandt*, on the other, the prosaic reality of the *ten-penny nails:* the difference, perhaps, between art and life, or the aesthetic object and the functional object. *Four pounds of ten-penny nails* illustrates Pound's claims for a hard and direct poetry, the phrase is precise, quantified and costed; weight and quantity are specified. It is an impersonal phrase, which cannot be accused of 'emotional slither'; elsewhere Pound claims that 'numerals and words referring to human inventions have hard, cut-off meanings', that is, 'meanings which are more obtrusive than a word's associations' (1951: 37).

But there are more significant differences to be traced between the two requests. *Send me four pounds of ten-penny nails* has no apparent implications for the feelings or state of mind of either the writer or the recipient of the message; no presuppositions of shared knowledge appear to be involved. In contrast, *Buy me the kind of Rembrandt I like* embodies reciprocity – the recipient's perceptions of the writer's taste. It relies on the very 'second guessing' qualities that are characteristic of (if problematic for) theories of mutual knowledge.

If the request to *Send me the kind of Rembrandt I like* functions as a cryptogram, the crypto-qualities that Pound distinguishes are similar to those often associated with deictic reference, another area of linguistic functioning in which *I* is defined in relation to *you* and which is also susceptible to the comment that it has 'as many meanings almost as there are persons who might speak it . . . to a stranger it conveys nothing at all'. One finds a similar kind of reciprocity in address terms as well. Pound associates this indeterminacy quite explicitly with audience recognition and pre-knowledge: it 'presupposes a more complex and intimate understanding of the speaker than most of us ever acquire of anyone'.

The role of the reader

If modes of reference are implicated in conveying authorial viewpoint, and in creating the texture of the text via coreference and thematization, they have, then, at the same time, implications for the reader. Not only does a picture of the self or world of the author emerge – a particular discourse universe, system of classification, emphasis – but the assertions that make up this authorial self/world also carry assumptions and pre-sumptions about audience or reader.

One can describe the involvement of the reader in this process in two ways. One would be to consider readers as co-operative followers of instructions or communicative cues. Almost every aspect of the packaging of information in texts can be considered to offer guidance or instructions to the reader, on, for example, the relative importance of items of information, on how to relate items, equally on the continuing point or topic of interest to be followed through the text. Even in areas such as reference where the key relationships have always been considered as between signs and referents, questions of recipient design appear to be paramount. For the reader, making sense of the text involves following these instructions; if they are distorted or dislocated, then the text is regarded as incoherent, it does not *make sense*.

However, current theories of inferential understanding suggest a more fundamental reader involvement in the information structure of the text, and it seems worthwhile to briefly explore this idea. In suggesting a more critical role for the reader, it may begin to explain the extent to which readers of modernist poetry found the particular forms of textual disorientation they encountered radically disturbing and threatening.

Why should the disruption of reference be thought to be bound up with issues of the preconstructed or given information of the text? Various cognitive theories of linguistic understanding currently argue that understanding is an inferential, rather than a simple decoding process. The problem for such theories is not that readers use contextual knowledge to interpret the text, but to explain how they isolate the relevant contextual knowledge in specific instances, that is, to explain how, from the encyclo-paedic background knowledge that readers have to draw upon, they decide on the particular bridging inferences that should be brought to bear in specific instances. The problem is explored at length in Sperber and Wilson (1986). Blakemore (1989: 29) formulates the problem in the following way: given that natural language sentences do not express propositions, but simply provide linguistic blueprints for the construction of propositions, 'what we need is a theory which will explain how the hearer selects and uses the contextual information'.

One might suggest that the presuppositional or given/new structure of information in the text is bound up with this question in that it functions to indicate what knowledge is to be regarded as shared or mutual between writer and reader. It is not, it should be emphasized, that the information signalled as given is necessarily familiar to the reader.

Prince points out that only an 'omniscient observer' can claim to verify mutual knowledge, and to want to do so ignores what 'ordinary, non clairvoyant humans do when they interact verbally' (1981: 232). Speakers and writers need only presuppose common ground (see Brown and Yule 1983: 29; Stalnaker 1972: 321).

Information signalled as textually given may well be quite new to the reader; given information is context-creating as well as context activating. The point is that such information, presented as given, is intended to form part of the presupposed of the discourse, and thus the contextual field against which new information is to be interpreted. The information about assumed familiarity signalled by the information structure of the text is an important means of indicating precisely what contextual knowledge is to be drawn on by the reader. The reader, in turn, is constrained by his or her need to recognize the assumptions of shared knowledge made by the writer and embodied in the text in order to fill in the gaps and discontinuities of the text and make sense of it.

Interactionalist sociological theories have long suggested that reality is socially constructed, and taken the interaction as the site where such social meanings are negotiated (for example, Berger and Luckman 1966). In written language, whatever shared codes of genre or discourse may be operating, it is similarly the case that the co-text figures as the place of interaction, and of the negotiation of meaning. The co-text, or local discursive context, can function to signal or cue common ground in building up a delineation of relevant context, and thus the ground for, and the activation or limitation of contextual inference. The asymmetrical structuring of information in the text plays an important role in this process. What this implies for the reader is that understanding – making the kind of inferences intended by the writer – is at least in part achieved by assessing the meaning of the utterance in relation to the contextual horizon so far established as shared knowledge. In order to negotiate the discontinuities of the text, the reader has to put him or herself in the place of the writer and to adopt the world organization signalled by textual organization.

Michael Pecheux (1982: 76), via a different analysis, suggests a similar conclusion. Texts create 'a kind of complicity between the speaker and his addressee' as 'a condition of existence of a *meaning* for the sentence. The complicity in fact presupposes an identification with the speaker, in other words the possibility of thinking in his place'. The construction, like that of deictic person, is reciprocal or interactive, and one can argue that both deixis and the information-structure of the text function to create person, and structure address, because they conjure a preconstructed [notion] of the text which can be equated with the mutual knowledge necessary to ground interpretation. This, I suggest then, is the significance of the reciprocality that Pound objects to in language and the dilemma of an objectivist poetics. How can a writing practice reach out to reality when it is all the time enmeshed in textual constraints? How can it escape from self if even terms of reference have implications for both point of view and address. How can it escape from habitual contexts, if contextual assumptions are at the heart of linguistic understanding?

Conclusion

It seems to me that what the modernists were concerned to escape was a basic kind of textual addressivity in all cohesive text: the world creating, context creating power of text. Certainly, it appears that the difficulty of modernist poetry lies in the disruption of this aspect of textual functioning: the poetry can be taken as an object lesson as to what happens if one focuses on world reference to the exclusion of discourse reference, if one really attempts to get to 'words washed clean'. Correspondingly, the information packaging, or, more widely, the information structure, of the text merits investigation as an aspect of the dialogism of the text. For one thing, it would help to explain the importance of this area. [. . .] [Bakhtin identifies this importance as]:

> . . . an internal dialogism of the word [or text] . . . that penetrates its entire structure, all its semantic and expressive layers . . . which does not assume any external compositional forms of dialogue, that cannot be isolated as an independent act, separate from the word's ability to form a concept of the object (Bakhtin 1981: 279).

And returning, in conclusion, to the other interpretations of Bakhtinian dialogism, one might note that Hirschkop's conception of the dialogism of the utterance represents a similar move to that which can be traced within the poetics of objectivity. In both cases, one has a similar stress on the individuality, expressiveness and uniqueness of the utterance. For the poets, this is a resort to presence and immediacy as a way to escape poetic convention and the 'feudal masterbeats' of the past (see Williams 1954: 126). For the critic, it is the assumption that social aspects of language are a higher level reformulation of an asocial grammatical structure, or a purely expressive form. In each case there is a neglect of the ways in which utterances are fundamentally interactive and addressive.

References

Ariel, M. (1988) 'Referring and accessibility', *Journal of Linguistics* 24 (1): 65–87.

Ariel, M. (1989) 'Retrieving propositions from context: why and how', *Journal of Pragmatics* 12: 567–600.

Bakhtin, M.M. (1971) 'Discourse typology in prose', in L. Matejka and K. Pomorska (eds) *Readings in Russian Poetics*, Cambridge, MA: MIT Press, pp. 176–96.

Bakhtin, M.M. (1973) *Problems of Dostoevsky's Poetics* (trans. R.W. Rotsel). Ann Arbor: Ardis.

Bakhtin, M.M. (1981) *The Dialogic Imagination: Four Essays* (trans. M. Holquist and C. Emerson). Austin: University of Texas Press.

Bakhtin, M.M. (1983) 'Discourse in life and discourse in poetry', in *Bakhtin School Papers*, Oxford: RPT Publications, pp. 5–30.

Bakhtin, M.M. (1986) *Speech Genres and Other Late Essays* (trans. V.W. McGee). Austin: University of Texas Press.

Berger, P.L. and Luckman, T. (1966) *The Social Construction of Reality: A Treatise in the Sociology of Knowledge*. New York: Doubleday.

Blakemore, D. (1989) 'Linguistic form and pragmatic interpretation: the explicit and the implicit', in L. Hickey (ed.) *The Pragmatics of Style*, London: Routledge, pp. 24–38.

Brown, G. and Yule, G. (1983) *Discourse Analysis*. Cambridge: Cambridge University Press.

Chafe, W.C. (1976) 'Givenness, contrastiveness, definiteness, subjects, topics and point of view', in C.N. Li (ed.) *Subject and Topic*, New York: Academic Press, pp. 27–55.

Childs, J.S. (1986) *Modernist Form: Pound's Style in the Early Cantos*. London and Toronto: Associated University Press.

Clark, H.H. and Marshall, C.R. (1981) 'Definite reference and mutual knowledge', in A.K. Joshi, B.L. Webber and I.A. Sag (eds) *Elements of Discourse Understanding*, Cambridge: Cambridge University Press, pp. 10–63.

DuBois, J.W. (1980) 'Beyond definiteness: the trace of identity in discourse', in W.L. Chafe (ed.) *The Pear Stories*, Norwood, NJ: Ablex, pp. 203–74.

Durant, A. (1981) *Ezra Pound: Identity in Crisis*. Brighton: Harvester.

Durant, A. (1984) 'Pound, Modernism and literary criticism: a reply to Donald Davie', *Critical Quarterly* 28 (1–2): 154–66.

Frege, G. (1982) 'On sense and reference', in *Translations from the Philosophical Writings of Gottlob Frege*, Oxford: Blackwell, pp. 56–78.

Gazdar, G. (1979) *Pragmatics: Implicature, Presupposition and Logical Form*. New York: Academic Press.

Givón, T. (1983) *Topic Continuity in Discourse: A Quantitative Cross-language Study*. Amsterdam: John Benjamins.

Hawkins, J. (1978) *Definiteness and Indefiniteness*. London: Croom Helm.

Hirschkop, K. (1989) 'Introduction: Bakhtin and cultural theory', in K. Hirschkop and D. Shepherd (eds) *Bakhtin and Cultural Theory*, Manchester: Manchester University Press, pp. 1–38.

Lodge, D. (1977) *The Modes of Modern Writing: Metaphor, Metonymy and the Typology of Modern Literature*. London: Edward Arnold.

Marslen-Wilson, W., Levy, E. and Komisarjevsky, T.L. (1982) 'Producing interpretable discourse: the establishment and maintenance of reference', in R.J. Jarvella and W. Klein (eds) *Speech, Place and Action*, Chichester: Wiley pp. 339–78.

Miles, J. (1965) *The Continuity of Poetic Language: The Primary Language of Poetry 1540s–1940s*. New York: Octagon Books.

Pecheux, M. (1982) *Language, Semantics, and Ideology* (trans. H. Nagpal). London: Macmillan.

Perloff, M. (1981) *The Poetics of Indeterminacy: Rimband to Cage*. Princeton, NJ: Princeton University Press.

Pound, E. (1937) *Polite Essays*. London: Faber and Faber.

Pound, E. (1951) *The ABC of Reading*. London: Faber and Faber.

Pound, E. (1954) *Literary Essays of Ezra Pound*. London: Faber and Faber.

Pound, E. (1975) *The Cantos*. London: Faber and Faber.

Press, J. (1969) *A Map of Modern English Verse*. Oxford: Oxford University Press.

Prince, E.F. (1981) 'Towards a taxonomy of given-new information', in P. Cole (ed.) *Radical Pragmatics*, New York: Academic Press, pp. 223–55.

Segre, C. (1985) 'What Bakhtin left unsaid: the case of the Medieval romance', in K. Brownlee and M. Scordilis (eds) *Romance: Generic Transformation from Chrétien de Troyes to Cervantes*, Hanover, NH: Dartmouth College Press, pp. 23–46.

Sperber, D. and Wilson, D. (1986) *Relevance: Communication and Cognition*. Oxford: Blackwell.

Stalnaker, R.C. (1972) 'Pragmatics', in D. Davidson and G. Harman (eds) *Semantics of Natural Language*, Dordrecht: Reidel, pp. 380–97.

Wales, K. (1988) 'Back to the future: Bakhtin, stylistics and discourse', in W. van Peer (ed.) *The Taming of the Text: Explorations in Language, Literature and Culture*, London: Routledge, pp. 176–92.

Werth, P. (1984) *Focus, Coherence and Emphasis*. London: Croom Helm.

Williams, C.W. (1954) *Selected Essays*. New York: Random House.

Williams, C.W. (1976) *Selected Poems* (ed. C. Tomlinson). Harmondsworth: Penguin.

Extracted from Alison Tate (1994) 'Bakhtin, addressivity, and the poetics of objectivity', in R. Sell and P. Verdonk (eds) *Literature and the New Interdisciplinarity*, Amsterdam: Rodopi, pp. 135–50.

Chapter 15

Teach yourself 'rhetoric': an analysis of Philip Larkin's 'Church Going'

KATIE WALES

In recognising the roots of stylistics in classical rhetoric, Katie Wales reminds the reader that the discipline should not be absolutely formalist, and in fact stylistics has rarely focused on textuality to the exclusion of readerly affect and interpretation. Further, even though stylistics has often been portrayed as ahistoricist, in fact most stylistic work follows Wales' assertion here that literary production and intention are interesting factors of literary study but they are not the *only* things that can be interestingly considered. Stylisticians offer a corrective to this imbalance. Philip Larkin in particular, and like his near-contemporaries Sylvia Plath and Ted Hughes, has been especially poorly treated by literary critics and reviewers focusing on the claimed significances of biography over textuality. Wales' elegant account here serves to bring Larkin's poem back to the fore. For further stylistic analyses of modern poetry, see Jeffries (1993) and Verdonk (1993).

I T IS VERY EASY, for native speakers of English at least, to skip-read Larkin's poetry. The base of his poetic style appears to be common core English, and of his world of reference the common experiences of ordinary suburban men and women, albeit fixed in a period of time and place increasingly alien to the average high-tech student of the 1990s. Yet his poems do warrant rereading, and any methodical framework or scheme of analysis that encourages this can help readers towards a richer understanding and appreciation. A stylistic analysis can show how, even in Larkin's apparently 'plain'-style poems, interpretation is crucially dependent upon features of form: language is not simply a 'medium' for 'content', but a significant part of the whole experience we call literature. Moreover, such an approach, which highlights artefact and artifice, affective language and its effects, can help the reader to avoid the pitfalls of much Larkin criticism, which focuses over-simply on the 'producer' of meaning rather than the 'receiver', on Larkin the poet himself, his views and intentions.

Devices which stress artifice and effect were once the concern of traditional rhetoric, whence modern stylistics can trace its origins; but it is rhetoric in a wider sense which will form the analytical framework here. Following Leith and Myerson (1989) rhetoric is seen not as a static body of knowledge or 'rules' of design, but as a dynamic process in the transmission and interpretation of utterances between author and reader. It is viewed as an activity of perception and reception involving three main principles or 'foci': (1) address, (2) argument, and (3) play. Therefore 'all examples of language in use are Rhetorical in so far as they must carry the trace' of these elements (Leith and Myerson 1989: 114). One important consequence is that meaning in rhetorical discourses is not only referential but also comprises 'persuasive force and playful energy' (p. 235). Viewed broadly in this way, Larkin's poems are linguistically quite unordinary, highly rhetorical; and a good illustration of these principles is provided by 'Church Going' from *The Less Deceived* (1955) [see the poem at the end of this chapter]. As we shall see, however, it is not easy to isolate these elements in discussion, so subtly and so significantly are they interlinked.

'Address' supposes a 'speaker' and an 'addressee', the latter either explicitly addressed and therefore inscribed within the world of the text; or else existing outside it, implied or, again, directly addressed. Critical attention in the case of Larkin's poetry has most commonly focused on the speaker, who is usually assumed to represent the 'real' poet. I would prefer to talk about the 'persona(e)' in his poetry, from the Latin word for mask; and also to talk about the polyphony of 'voices', the variations of tone and tenor, often indeed within the same poem.

Right from the second word of 'Church Going' the reader is made aware of the dramatic mode of an 'I'-monologue, thrust into the middle of a first-person narrative, with the apparent 'historic' present tense of the informal and immediate account, firmly rooted in a specific situation:

> Once I am sure there's nothing going on
> I step inside, letting the door thud shut.

In the first two stanzas colloquial features of lexis ('some brass and stuff' (line 5); 'God knows how long' (line 8)) and syntax (ellipsis of conjunction in first line; absence of main verb in the 'listing' sentence, lines 3–8; contractions in *there's* (line 1) and *don't* (line 12)) suggest the voice and persona of an ordinary cycle-clip-wearing chap, not deeply affected by what he sees; and, to judge by the metaphors which occur quite frequently in these two stanzas, rather dismissive in his attitude (*'sprawlings* of flowers' (line 4); '. . . silence/Brewed . . .' (line 8); *'Hectoring* large-scale verses' (line 14); 'The echoes *snigger* briefly' (1. 16)). The physical and mental actions described which conclude the second stanza are in harmony, and epitomize the kind of agnostic persona presented so far:

> I sign the book, donate an Irish sixpence,
> Reflect the place was not worth stopping for.
>   (lines 17–18)

Yet is this all to the speaker? I frame this question with the same connective which frames the statement that begins the third stanza, so dramatically changing the tone:

> *Yet* stop I did: . . . (line 19)

There are hints already of another kind of attitude beneath the mask that seems to prevail in the first two stanzas, and with which the reader has been encouraged to identify. In line 7 the reader is confronted not only by a noun phrase striking in its conjunction of three adjectives ('tense, musty, unignorable'), but also by synaesthesia ('musty . . . silence') and the polysyllabic Latinate 'unignorable'. By such highlighting or foregrounding upon foregrounding 'unignorable' is certainly not ignorable. The mask has slipped to reveal a personality sensitive to his surroundings, who will take off the cycle-clips 'in awkward reverence' (line 9), who knows his 'pyx' (line 25) from his 'stuff' (line 5), and who is also sensitive to linguistic nuance, presuming his reader will appreciate the stylistic shift from colloquial to formal, not only within the stanza, but also within the phrase: what traditional rhetoricians termed *occupatio*. We can notice another example later in the poem:

'this accoutred frowsty barn' (line 53)

In the stanzas which follow the second, the overtly cynical, colloquial voice can still be heard in the projections of a negative future prospect for the church, in both its physical and spiritual dimensions. We can note, for example, further dismissive metaphors and striking neologistic compounds in stanza 5:

Some ruin-bibber, randy for antique,
Or *Christmas-addict*, counting on a whiff
Of gown-and-bands and organ-pipes and myrrh?
(lines 42–4)

This fifth stanza, linked by enjambment to the sixth, appears to confirm the cynical persona:

Or will he be my representative,
Bored, uninformed . . .
(lines 45–6)

But again, the connective *yet* qualifies, contradicts, concedes:

. . . knowing the ghostly silt
Dispersed, yet tending to this cross of ground
(lines 46–7)

Let us consider again line 19 that begins the third stanza, but in full: *Yet stop I did: in fact I often do*. It is not only the tone that changes here, but the whole mode of utterance of the poem so far. The narrative changes to reflective monologue, which is almost confessional; the historic present changes to the present of generalization; from simply 'listener' the reader is drawn into the poem as confidant(e). By the end of the stanza, moreover, the reader is more directly involved, jointly addressed, and implicated in the action, as the pronoun shift from *I* to 'inclusive' *we* confirms:

> Wondering what to look for; wondering, too, . . .
> What *we* shall turn them into, if *we* shall keep
> A few cathedrals chronically on show, . . .
> Shall *we* avoid them as unlucky places?
>
> (lines 21–7)

But the 'inclusive' *we* also has the resonance of the generic and universal: both speaker and reader are part of a collective voice of universal conscience for whom the speaker, in fact, acts as spokesman and 'representative' (line 45).

By the repetition of the verbs of speculation ('wonder') in the third stanza, and the succession of indirect and direct questions which continue into the fourth, fifth, and sixth stanzas, the essentially 'dialogic' nature of the apparent monologue is also revealed: the narrator's addressee is also himself. Such internal argument, but of a more pragmatic nature, is found already in the second stanza, in the form of free direct thought:

> Cleaned, or restored? Someone would know: I don't. (line 12)

But this 'bored, uninformed' persona, by letting his mind run more imaginatively and more philosophically as the poem progresses on a variety of projected speculations, expressed through a complex pattern of self-questioning, is eventually overcome, almost despite himself, by the serious-minded and respectful persona who has the last word in the final stanza.

In the dramatic interplay of the dual-voiced, split personalities, it is 'dialogue' in the Bakhtinian sense of 'dialectic' or 'internal polemic', that is a key structural device in the poem: 'address' inextricably involved with 'argument', the *inventio* of traditional rhetoric. From stanza 3 onwards the hypothetical possibilities of the future ('or . . . or') and the niggling doubts ('yet . . . but') are expressed in an appropriate syntax that is far from plain and simple, and which 'overflows' as it were the confines of the stanzas to suggest, sub-liminally, the power and seriousness of the argument. The blurring of the stanza divisions throughout the poem could almost be seen as a symbolic gesture, suggesting the rationality of prose as against the impressionism of poetry. In terms of syntactic complexity, indeed, the poem builds up to a powerful climax: stanzas 5 and 6 are linked by a sentence at least seven clauses long, followed by two more sentences, equally with at least seven clauses, which actually conclude the poem. Loosely constructed, in rhetorical terms, since they favour 'right-branching' structures dependent on a main clause, these sentences are yet highly indicative of an internal argument that is more and more qualifying, and yet also more and more positive, as the poem comes to an end. The conclusion in structure is a conclusion in argument, however vague and concessive it appears ('If only . . .' (line 63)). A sense of closure is anticipated by the last sentence of stanza 6, which links with stanza 7: in deictic terms it reintroduces the personal voice of the speaker, and brings him physically back to where he started:

> . . . For, though *I*'ve no idea
> What *this* accoutred frowsty barn is worth,
> It pleases *me* to stand in silence *here*;
>
> (lines 52–4)

So, as for the projected 'someone else' of the last stanza, there is again a 'gravitating to this ground', but with a new seriousness, and a sense of it as a *memento mori*. The word 'silence' in line 54 recalls the 'unignorable silence' of the first stanza, and the full sense of the adjective can now be appreciated. It can in no way be ignored any more than the questions of Faith it symbolizes.

All through the poem the reader is made aware of the physicality of the scene and of the church, and aware also of a transcendent dimension, reflecting both the abstractions of the narrator's train of thought and the supposed spirituality of the church as a symbol of the Christian faith. Many of the lexical items of the poem are strikingly grouped into two main lexical sets. One set, referring to concrete features, parts of a whole (metonyms), reveals the present and future condition of the church, as 'matting', 'seats', 'lectern', and 'roof' give way to 'Grass, weedy pavement, brambles, buttress, sky' (line 36). The other set suggests both perennial theological concerns ('power', 'superstition', 'belief', 'disbelief', 'marriage, and birth,/And death' (lines 50–1), 'destinies') and also individual impulses ('reverence', 'compulsions', 'hunger in himself'). Through the interweavings of the lexis, the physical and non-physical modes of existence are confirmed in their own 'dialectic'.

The final focus for consideration, the principle of 'play', actually heightens the dialogic mode of the poem, as it also heightens the reader's pleasure and stimulates rereadings. The *locus classicus* for double signification as well as semantic play is the pun, and there are some wonderfully subtle yet suggestive ones in 'Church Going'. From the very first line the reader is alerted to the 'echo' of phrase and title, and so is already made sensitive to the possibilities of a kind of distancing between word and referent that will eventually lead to an appreciation of the first line's irony, and of the title's multiple significance:

Once I am sure there's nothing *going on* (line 1).

On the level of 'plot', in the specific context of situation, this obviously refers to the church's lack of services on weekdays. We realize that the speaker's own visit has nothing to do with attending church regularly, the common meaning of 'churchgoing'. Moreover, by stanza 3, with the apparent conviction of lines like 'When churches fall completely out of use' (line 22), we can reread the verb phrase in line 1 in the more abstract sense of '(not) continuing into the future': cf. line 32 'Power of some sort or other will *go on*'; also line 35 'And what remains when disbelief *has gone*?' In the same way, a reading of the whole poem will draw the reader's attention back to the ironic ambiguity of ' "Here endeth" ' in line 15: the poem raises the possibility of the demise of the church as a whole, not only the end of the Lesson.

Aware of the temporal progression of beginning, growth, decay, and ending, which the poem raises as a theme, and alerted increasingly to irony and double meanings, the reader may also wish to go back to the first stanza and ponder again even the apparently 'ordinary'-sounding phrase 'Brewed God knows how long' (line 8). Given the situational context described, the colloquialism jars on the ears just as the cycle-clips jar visually: it is like swearing in front of the vicar, a social 'gaffe'. No blasphemy is really intended, although at one stage in its usage the phrase must have had more force. Etymologically, it reflects an age of belief precisely in the wisdom of God: God would know how long! And so its linguistic history nicely reflects in microcosm the ages of belief that the speaker is to project later in the poem: from 'belief' to 'superstition' and to 'disbelief' (stanza 4).

The play of etymological and current meanings continues in the third stanza, where here also play of form, through alliteration (and also assonance), provides foregrounding by sound-repetition against which the adverb *chronically*, rare in usage, is itself highlighted:

> . . . if we shall *k*eep
> A few *c*athedrals *ch*ronically on show,
> Their *p*archment, *p*late and *py*x in lo*ck*ed *c*ases,
> And let the *r*est *r*ent-free to *r*ain and sheep.
>   (lines 23–6)

Etymologically, 'chronically' (from 'chronical') would mean something like 'habitually', or 'over a long period of time'; but the dismissive tone conveyed by the alliterative context reinforces a pejorative sense associated with the current colloquial meaning of 'chronic', namely 'very bad', particularly associated with illness.

By the final stanza the dismissive, ironic voice has been displaced, but the etymological word-play remains: perfectly in keeping by this stage with the sensitive, intellectual persona, and perfectly in harmony also with the archaisms which themselves mirror the ancient tradition he is evoking (cf. *accoutred*, (line 53); *blent* (line 56)). Play of sound through repetition is also found, but no longer ironic:

> A *serious* house on *serious* earth it is . . .
> Are *recognized*, and *robed* as destinies.
> *S*ince *s*omeone will forever be *s*urprising
> A *h*unger in *h*imself to be more *serious*,
> And *gravitating* with it to this *ground*,
> Which, he once heard, was proper to *grow* wise in, . . .
>   (lines 55–62)

The polysyllable *gravitating* in one sense simply echoes the native *tending* in line 47:

> . . . yet *tending* to this cross of ground

reinforcing, however, more strongly the notion of being drawn by some strong impulse (not specified). Etymologically, like 'gravity', it derives from Latin *gravis* 'serious', the adjective that actually occurs three times in this stanza.

The play of form and meaning is what we have come to expect from and associate with poetry: we talk of the 'aesthetic function' of its language and the effect of pleasure on its readers. But, as Leith and Myerson conclude (1989: 243), verbal play can be 'more than just the acknowledgement of language's material properties'. So the word-play in 'Church Going' is self-reflexive in the deeper sense that it is itself part of the meaning of the poem, contributing to the ambiguities and conflicts of tone and theme, the complexities of address and argument. More generally, the suggestiveness of the language of the poem, which forces the reader to reassess the obvious interpretation of words, works almost unconsciously to reinforce the unsettling of fixed positions and stock attitudes, for which the poem overall is pleading.

Church Going

Once I am sure there's nothing going on
I step inside, letting the door thud shut.
Another church: matting, seats, and stone,
And little books; sprawlings of flowers, cut
5   For Sunday, brownish now; some brass and stuff
Up at the holy end; the small neat organ;
And a tense, musty, unignorable silence,
Brewed God knows how long. Hatless, I take off
My cycle-clips in awkward reverence,

10   Move forward, run my hand around the font.
From where I stand, the roof looks almost new —
Cleaned, or restored? Someone would know: I don't.
Mounting the lectern, I peruse a few
Hectoring large-scale verses, and pronounce
15   'Here endeth' much more loudly than I'd meant.
The echoes snigger briefly. Back at the door
I sign the book, donate an Irish sixpence,
Reflect the place was not worth stopping for.

Yet stop I did: in fact I often do,
20   And always end much at a loss like this,
Wondering what to look for; wondering, too,
When churches fall completely out of use
What we shall turn them into, if we shall keep
A few cathedrals chronically on show,
25   Their parchment, plate and pyx in locked cases,
And let the rest rent-free to rain and sheep.
Shall we avoid them as unlucky places?

Or, after dark, will dubious women come
To make their children touch a particular stone;
30   Pick simples for a cancer; or on some
Advised night see walking a dead one?
Power of some sort or other will go on
In games, in riddles, seemingly at random;
But superstition, like belief, must die,
35   And what remains when disbelief has gone?
Grass, weedy pavement, brambles, buttress, sky,

A shape less recognisable each week,
A purpose more obscure. I wonder who
Will be the last, the very last, to seek
40   This place for what it was; one of the crew
That tap and jot and know what rood-lofts were?
Some ruin-bibber, randy for antique,
Or Christmas-addict, counting on a whiff

Of gown-and-bands and organ-pipes and myrrh?
45   Or will he be my representative,

Bored, uninformed, knowing the ghostly silt
Dispersed, yet tending to this cross of ground
Through suburb scrub because it held unspilt
So long and equably what since is found
50   Only in separation – marriage, and birth,
And death, and thoughts of these – for which was built
This special shell? For, though I've no idea
What this accoutred frowsty barn is worth,
It pleases me to stand in silence here;

55   A serious house on serious earth it is,
In whose blent air all our compulsions meet,
Are recognised, and robed as destinies.
And that much never can be obsolete,
Since someone will forever be surprising
60   A hunger in himself to be more serious,
And gravitating with it to this ground,
Which, he once heard, was proper to grow wise in,
If only that so many dead lie round.

References

Jeffries, L. (1993) *The Language of Twentieth-Century Poetry*. Basingstoke: Palgrave Macmillan.
Larkin, Philip (1955) *The Less Deceived*. London: The Marvell Press.
Leith, D. and Myerson, G. (1989) *The Power of Address: Explorations in Rhetoric*. London: Routledge.
Verdonk, P. (ed.) (1993) *Twentieth-Century Poetry: From Text to Context*. London: Routledge.

Extracted from Katie Wales (1993) 'Teach yourself rhetoric: an analysis of Philip Larkin's "Church Going" ', in P. Verdonk (ed.) *Twentieth Century Poetry: From Text to Context*, London: Routledge, pp. 134–58.

Chapter 16

'World enough, and time': deictic space and the interpretation of prose

PAUL WERTH

Paul Werth begins this paper by setting out his text world theory, which was to be published as Werth (1999). The theory is a model of discourse processing that resolves the problem of contextual knowledge: Werth claims it is the text itself that determines those aspects of readerly knowledge that are drawn down for processing. Interestingly, although Werth (1999: 17) claimed that his framework could account for 'all the furniture of the earth and heavens', paraphrasing Bishop Berkeley's 1710 assertion of the existential primacy of mind, most of the examples for analysis that he used to develop text world theory were literary works, as in this chapter. Text world theory has recently become very influential in literary stylistics and cognitive poetics, and is being applied to text-types of all kinds, not exclusively literature. For further work, see Bridgeman (1998), Hidalgo Downing (2000), Stockwell (2002, 2008), Chilton (2004) and Gavins (2007), and chapter 25 in this volume.

[. . .]

DEICTIC INFORMATION, FRAME KNOWLEDGE and inferencing combine [. . .] to give the reader a very rich mental representation of the setting of a novel or story [. . .]. Together, they constitute what I call the world-building elements of the text. But this, in most cases, provides only the background to the story. The foreground consists of the descriptions and events which propel the story forward. I call this the function-advancing component, and it is made up of language denoting states, actions and processes. [. . .] Descriptions are state-propositions: they denote relatively permanent qualities. Actions and processes, on the other hand, always denote changes: movements, alterations, variations from one state to another. [. . .]

The author, of course, is a very important person in the process of creating a text world. But we should not forget that the author creates only a text; he/she will have a particular text world in mind, but there is no guarantee at all that the reader will manage to reproduce the same text world on reading that text. We cannot say that the author's text world is the definitive one, since, in fact, there is no such thing. We may say, therefore, that a text world does not come into being until each of the three elements – author, text and reader – are present. Since the interaction between an author, his text and reader X will be different from that between the author, his text and reader Y, a given text may correspond to many possible text worlds (though they may all be very close to one another). Furthermore, we may think of the text as providing the medium through which the author and the reader negotiate for a particular text world.

Let us now apply these ideas to a longer and more substantial text, the first chapter of E.M. Forster's *A Passage to India*:

> Except for the Marabar Caves – and they are twenty miles off – the city of Chandrapore presents nothing extraordinary. Edged rather than washed by the River Ganges, it trails for a couple of miles along the bank, scarcely distinguishable from the rubbish it deposits so freely. There are no bathing steps on the river front, as the Ganges happens not to be holy here; indeed, there is no river front, and bazaars shut out the wide and shifting panorama of the stream. The streets are mean, the temples ineffective, and though a few fine houses exist they are hidden away in gardens or down alleys whose filth deters all but the invited guest. Chandrapore was never large or beautiful, but two hundred years ago it lay on the road between Upper India, then imperial, and the sea, and the fine houses date from that period. The zest for decoration stopped in the eighteenth century, nor was it ever democratic. There is no painting and scarcely any carving in the bazaars. The very wood seems made of mud, the inhabitants of mud moving. So abased, so monotonous is everything that meets the eye, that when the Ganges comes down it might be expected to wash the excrescence back into the soil. Houses do fall, people are drowned and left rotting, but the general outline of the town persists, swelling here, shrinking there, like some low but indestructible form of life.
>
> Inland, the prospect alters. There is an oval Maidan, and a long sallow hospital. Houses belonging to Eurasians stand on the high ground by the railway station. Beyond the railway – which runs parallel to the river – the land sinks, then rises again rather steeply. On the second rise is laid out the little civil station, and viewed hence Chandrapore appears to be a totally different place. It is a city of gardens. It is no city, but a forest sparsely scattered with huts. It is a tropical pleasaunce washed by a noble river. The toddy palms and neem trees and mangoes and pepul that were hidden behind the bazaars now become visible and in their turn hide the bazaars. They rise from the gardens where ancient tanks nourish them, they burst out of stifling purlieus and unconsidered temples. Seeking light and air, and endowed with more strength than man or his works, they soar above the lower deposit to greet one another with branches and beckoning leaves, and to build a city for the birds. Especially after the rains do they screen what passes below, but at all times, even when scorched or leafless, they glorify the city to the English people who inhabit the rise, so that new-comers cannot believe it to be as meagre as it is described, and have to be driven down to acquire disillusionment. As for the civil station itself, it provokes no emotion. It charms not, neither does it repel. It is sensibly planned, with

a red-brick club on its brow, and farther back a grocer's and a cemetery, and the bungalows are disposed along roads that intersect at right angles. It has nothing hideous in it, and only the view is beautiful; it shares nothing with the city except the overarching sky.

The sky too has its changes, but they are less marked than those of the vegetation and the river. Clouds map it up at times, but it is normally a dome of blending tints, and the main tint blue. By day the blue will pale down into white where it touches the white of the land, after sunset it has a new circumference — orange, melting upwards into tenderest purple. But the core of blue persists, and so it is by night. Then the stars hang like lamps from the immense vault. The distance between the vault and them is as nothing to the distance behind them, and that further distance, though beyond colour, last freed itself from blue.

The sky settles everything — not only climates and seasons but when the earth shall be beautiful. By herself she can do little — only feeble outbursts of flowers. But when the sky chooses, glory can rain into the Chandrapore bazaars or a benediction pass from horizon to horizon. The sky can do this because it is so strong and so enormous. Strength comes from the sun, infused in it daily; size from the prostrate earth. No mountains infringe on the curve. League after league the earth lies flat, heaves a little, is flat again. Only in the south, where a group of fists and fingers are thrust up through the soil, is the endless expanse interrupted. These fists and fingers are the Marabar Hills, containing the extraordinary caves.

(Forster 1924/1984: 1–3)

We shall start by building up the basic details of the text world underlying [the] passage [. . .]. Remember that a text world is simply a representation of the cognitive space which the author and the reader are co-operating to form between them. For several reasons, this cognitive space is not a fixed, strictly-defined scene. First, no two readers bring exactly the same knowledge to bear in interpreting a text. Second, strictly speaking, even the same reader is in possession of a different body of knowledge on different occasions of reading the same text (since he/she will have done, experienced, learnt other things in the meantime) — and this applies to the author, too, of course, who we can think of as equivalent to a (somewhat privileged) reader. Third, the text itself is read through time, so it is accurate to think of the scene which it depicts as developing. When we also bring the function-advancing elements into the equation, which represent, for example, events, we can see that our representation must be thought of not as a picture or a photograph, but rather as a movie-film, made up of a large number of 'frames', succeeding each other in time.

Let us now go through [the] passage [. . .], picking out the deictic elements which build up the successive frames of this text world. We can at least tentatively take it paragraph by paragraph. Paragraph 1 is mainly in the simple present tense: the text is rather like a travel guide, describing a place as it is currently. The place, of course, is the city of Chandrapore. There are no real individualized characters, only generics (the invited guest, the inhabitants, people). There are plenty of objects, but they are all either parts of the city, associated with the city or located close to the city. In a word, they are all metonyms of the city: the Marabar Caves, the River Ganges, the rubbish, bazaars, the streets, the temples, a few fine houses, alleys, etc. In the middle of the paragraph, there is a short interlude in the simple past, providing a short history of Chandrapore, and using it to explain the few fine features of the place. This is a kind of flashback, but a participant-accessible one, since it is presented as a straightforward fact by the author, and the reader can simply accept it as factual.

Paragraph 2 is rather similar, simply in terms of the kind of deictic elements used. It is entirely in the guide-book present (with just one exception: 'were hidden'). The place has changed slightly, in the sense that the vantage-point (the camera-position, as it were) has moved back, so that we are given a different, and more inclusive, perspective of the scene, with the city and the river now just components of a larger view. Again, there are no real characters, only generic types (Eurasians, man, the English people, new-comers), while the objects are again metonyms of the place in general (Maidan, hospital, houses, railway, river, land, rise, civil station, gardens, etc.). Paragraph 2 also has a kind of insert in the middle, but it is not any kind of flashback; rather, it is a re-evaluation of the description in paragraph 1, as seen from the different viewpoint. We can regard it as an application of the new focus, rather than reflecting a temporary deictic change (which is what a flashback does).

Paragraph 3 continues the same process: the deictic viewpoint changes again, bringing the sky into focus. The previous focus is reduced to a very small part of the new one (the vegetation and the river). The tense used is entirely present simple (with one apparent exception: 'will pale down'), and the place is the sky. There are still no characters, and now not even any generics. Objects are again metonymic with the sky: clouds, stars, vault.

Paragraph 4 is different. Again with one apparent exception ('shall be beautiful'), the tense is simple present. The place now broadens to include everything which has been focused on before, but from an all-encompassing perspective. There are now some characters of a sort, though they are not human (but, as we shall see, they are given human, or super-human, attributes): the sky, the earth, the sun. Objects are again metonymic upon these (flowers, the Chandrapore bazaars, horizon, strength, size, the Marabar Hills, the caves).

Let us now look at the function-advancing part of the text. Paragraphs 1–3 are almost exclusively descriptive: thus, the function being advanced is that of scene description. This explains why there is so much metonymy, a common feature of descriptions; it also tells us not to expect too many events, and such events as there are will be subsidiary in some way (e.g. 'new-comers . . . have to be driven down', encoding not a single event, but a routine happening). Practically all the function-advancing expressions, then, will be shown by horizontal arrows, depicting steady states (qualities). A notable exception to this statement, at least on the face of it, is the insert in paragraph 2, which is full of very dynamic vocabulary ('rise', 'burst', 'seeking', 'soar', 'greet', 'beckoning', 'build', 'screen', 'glorify'). Note, however, that all this activity is metaphorical, a point which we shall return to.

Paragraph 4, on the other hand, the culmination of this first chapter, presents a rather more active face than has generally been the case up until now (with the exception of the insert in paragraph 2). Thus, apart from physical activity verbs ('do', 'rain', 'pass', 'infused', 'lies', 'heaves', 'thrust'), which are again metaphorical, we have mental and abstract activity verbs also: 'settles', 'chooses', 'infringe', 'interrupted'. However, 'containing' (in the last line of paragraph 4) is somewhat ambiguous in sense between a sort of activity (or process) – at any rate a dynamic use – and a stative verb denoting a steady state.

I shall now at this stage present a text worlds diagram for our observations so far, though at this point omitting the flashback in paragraph 1 and the metaphorical uses elsewhere. We will return to these subsequently, in our examination of the sub-world level. There are also other features which the reader will have spotted, such as the large number of negatives in paragraph 1. We shall have to see whether these too fall under the heading of sub-world accessibility. Figure 16.1 will be rather schematic – I shall in other words only include in it representative or general information.

Figure 16.1 should be interpreted like this: the scene is gradually described from a broadening perspective. The large squares represent separate, successive stages of this process. Since at each stage we are shown a wider vista, the later stages include the earlier ones, and are compared with them; the close detail of the earlier stages shrinks, as it were, to a more distant and simplified view (represented by a small square). The notation for this is meant to suggest the focusing of light rays by a lens – as in the viewfinder of a camera, for example.

As we shall shortly see, the notation for sub-worlds is rather similar: this is because there are important similarities between the concepts themselves. A focus, as we have seen, is a subsequent re-evaluation of a previous stage of text world, or part of it. A sub-world is a part of a text world which is outside the deictic definition which holds for that world. Both of them, then, are deictically distinct from their surrounding context: the focus because it is a return to an earlier viewpoint at a later stage, the sub-world because it is a departure to another viewpoint. An important difference, though, is that a focus is a concentrating of attention inwards, while a sub-world is an extension of view outwards. For this reason, the notation for the latter should be thought of as a cinematic projection (also, sub-worlds are shown with rounded corners). Let us look at a reasonably straight-forward sub-world first, the little history lesson in paragraph 1 (see Figure 16.2).

The large square in Figure 16.2 is meant to be the same as the leftmost square in Figure 16.1, but it is displayed even more selectively here. The flashback is triggered by way of an explanation for the existence of fine houses amidst so much squalor. The deictic alternation in this case is the time-frame, which is two hundred years earlier. The inference-box deduces this as referring to the eighteenth century, which picks up the mention of the declining zest for decoration.

We may now turn to the question of the large number of negatives and related expressions in paragraph 1. Here is a list of them:

(a)   straight negatives: 'nothing extraordinary', 'no bathing steps', 'not to be holy', 'no river front', 'never large or beautiful', 'nor was it ever democratic', 'no painting'

(b)   negative modification: 'scarcely distinguishable', 'scarcely any carving', 'the very wood'

(c)   words with negative meaning: 'trails', 'rubbish', 'shut out', 'mean', 'ineffective', 'hidden away', 'filth', 'deters', 'stopped', 'mud', 'abased', 'monotonous', 'excrescence', 'fall', 'drowned', 'left', 'rotting', 'persists', 'low'

(d)   concessives: 'except for the Marabar Caves – and *they* are twenty miles off', 'edged rather than washed', 'happens not to be holy', 'indeed', 'though a few fine houses exist', 'houses do fall, people are drowned, but . . .'

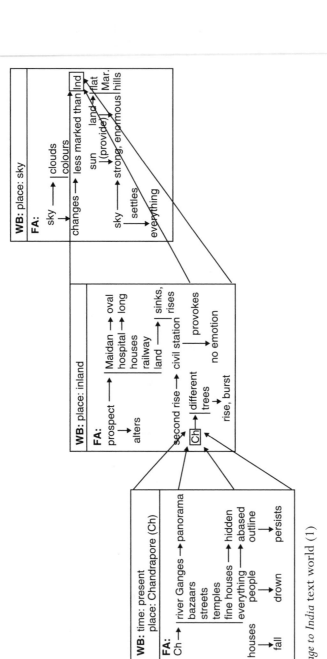

Figure 16.1 A Passage to India text world (1)

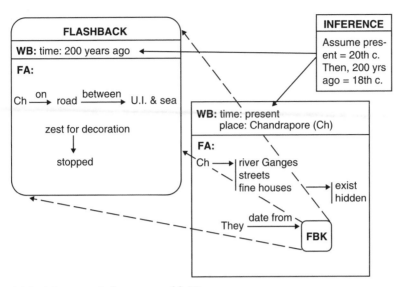

Figure 16.2 A Passage to India text world (2)

There are a number of questions which these expressions raise: first, what cumulative impression do they give? second, how does this actually work? third, how can we account for this? Opinions on the impression which this paragraph gives may very well vary, of course (see our previous discussion), but most readers are likely to agree that they carry away not only a picture of a dirty, squalid and totally unprepossessing place, but also that they share a sense of disappointment that such an exotic and promising location is so contrary to expectations.

Negatives and concessives work exactly in this way, in fact. Unlike positive sentences, negatives always operate in contrast to an expected state of affairs: expected in that it is normal or routine, or thought to be so. So, if you say 'John wasn't at Mary's party', this is in contrast to the previous idea or hope or expectation that John might have been at the party. If you say 'An aeroplane flew overhead', this is simply an observation; but if you say 'No aeroplane flew overhead', this must mean that you somehow expected one to. This happens throughout paragraph 1: 'There are no bathing steps on the river front'; the only reason for pointing this out is that in many other places along the Ganges, there are bathing steps. The same is true of words with negative meaning: you expect fine houses to be visible: these are hidden; you expect a river to flow, and wash its banks: this one merely trails along, and deposits rubbish freely. These expectations are cultural in nature: they come in fact from our knowledge-frames about India, rivers, cities, and so on. This is why the sentence 'There are no bathing steps on the river front' would be odd in a travel guide about Liverpool or New York (unless it were a guide written for Indians), while the sentence 'There are no ice-cream stalls on the river front', though perfectly true of Chandrapore, would nevertheless be extremely odd (yet for Liverpool or New York, perfectly normal).

Returning to the question of the effect all these negatives have, we can pick out one impression which will be important for our interpretation of the rest of the chapter, and indeed, for the whole novel, and that is the relative status and situation of the various groups of human beings in this place, as compared with the natural elements there. On the account of paragraph 1, human beings come out very poorly. The surroundings are squalid enough, and the inhabitants seem to be one with this degradation:

> The very wood seems made of mud, the inhabitants of mud moving. So abased, so monotonous is everything that meets the eye, that when the Ganges comes down, it might be expected to wash the excrescence back into the soil. Houses do fall, people are drowned and left rotting, but the general outline of the town persists, swelling here, shrinking there, like some low but indestructible form of life.
>
> (1984: 1)

They are equivalent, then, by the logic of this paragraph, to some lowly insect or microbe life-form.

Finally, how do we account for these phenomena in the model we have been using so far? Expectations, as we have seen, are part of the background of a text. The types we have looked at were cultural, and came from the frame-knowledge evoked by the entities and propositions in the text. Other kinds of expectations are built up out of personal experience of individuals and states of affairs: this also engenders frame-knowledge, but of a more personal type. Yet others come from what has actually been said and implied in the text itself: for example, if the text tells us that Bill, George and Susan are sitting on a couch talking about the World Series, we expect Bill, George and Susan to be present, even if they say nothing subsequently, until we are told otherwise. So, if the lights suddenly go out, and when they go on again, George says 'Susan's not here!' or 'Susan's gone!' or 'Where did Susan go?', this is because, like us, he expected her still to be there. To be brief, we can say that expectations form part of what is called the Common Ground of the discourse, the background knowledge necessary to understand not only the meaning of the words and sentences, but also the frames and inferences which they evoke. We can postulate, therefore, that negatives and concessives form sub-worlds also, since they constitute a departure from part of the deictic underlay of the discourse.

In order to account for this properly, we would have to show all the frame-knowledge which underlies the expectations in question. In fact, as has been my custom, I will be greatly selective in this explanation. However, there is an important point to be made first, and that is that there is more than one way of learning frame-knowledge. There are two, in fact. One is the usual way: by direct or indirect prior experience you acquire a set of facts, let us say, which are there in place when you happen to need them. So, for example, your knowledge about India might include images of people bathing in the Ganges, of richly carved decoration, of intricate buildings, and so on. The second way is by inference: because in some sense you know how negatives work, when you read 'There are no bathing steps on the river front', you immediately know that bathing steps would normally be expected, and you can add this deduced fact to your store. The result, of course, is identical.

In Figure 16.3, I shall assume prior knowledge, amassed in frames, and in contrast to which the negatives operate. Since frames encode all our general and personal knowledge, they may be expected to be very complicated affairs, overlapping and cross-referencing with each other in manifold ways. Some of these frames, furthermore, will not be based on straightforward classification (A is a B, A is part of B, A is a member of

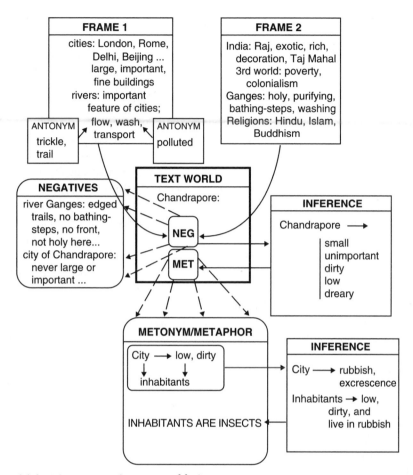

Figure 16.3 A Passage to India text world (3)

B), but rather on similarity, real or asserted (A is like B). This latter type is essentially how metaphor works. As usual, I shall not attempt to show anything like all this complexity in the diagram (see Figure 16.3), but will content myself with a rather schematic indication of the broad outlines.

Here is how Figure 16.3 should be read: the text world (still just the leftmost square in Figure 16.1) is shown with thicker lines. Around it are all the various types of knowledge with which we interpret the discourse in question: frames, containing general knowledge and connected information, including opposites (antonyms); inferences, or conclusions which can be deduced from other information which is present; and finally, the sub-worlds. The frames set up the complex network of expectations which we might hold about the set of topics under discussion; the text, by way of the negative sub-world, informs us where these expectations have been departed from. This leads us to draw a number of inferences about Chandrapore, and these inferences, via a conventional metonym ('a place is its inhabitants'), allow us to draw further inferences about the relationship between the city and its inhabitants. This then leads us to understand a metaphorical similarity between the inhabitants and the denizens of an organic heap of some kind.

I shall discuss one more point before drawing to a conclusion [see also Werth 1994]. We have seen that the inhabitants of Chandrapore – the native Indians – come out of this description very badly. What about the other human beings in the vicinity (the British colonialists, and their assistants, the mixed-race Eurasians)? And what about the natural elements in the scene? The answer is that the other humans fare even worse. The political power-relationships mimic the height above sea-level (let us say): the colonialist English are at the top, with people of mixed race (the Eurasians) in the middle, and the native Indians at the bottom of the power ladder. We also carry a strong cultural assumption that humankind is at the top of the ecological scale – so below the Indians would be the local flora and fauna. This is the very common metaphor POWER IS UP [see Lakoff and Johnson 1980, Lakoff and Turner 1989: 149]. However, this is not necessarily the pecking order from all points of view, as we are about to see.

In the first paragraph, the people of Chandrapore – that is, the native Indians – were characterized as mud moving, and the whole place was like some low but indestructible form of life. Compare this with the description of the Eurasians and the English in paragraph 2: the imagery describing their environment is predominantly geometrical and impersonal: oval, long, parallel, laid out, sensibly planned, disposed, intersect at right angles. The metaphor underlying these uses, I suggest, is GEOMETRICAL IS LIFELESS. The natives by contrast may be a low form of life, but they are a form of life. In stark opposition to 'man and his works', however – both native and colonialist – is the vegetation. This is almost violent in its mobility and vitality: the trees rise, burst out, they seek light and air, and are endowed with strength, they soar and greet and beckon and build, and they glorify the city. The most powerful movement that mankind can summon up, by contrast, is swelling and shrinking. We can nevertheless say that MOVEMENT IS LIFE – the vegetation (and by extension the land, as opposed to the people) is what is truly living in this landscape. There is also an irony in the reversed topography (see Figure 16.4).

The vegetation is depicted as having movement – but oddly enough, it has no colour, except by implication (we assume it to be green normally, and brown when scorched – but this is nowhere made explicit). It is the sky which is the repository of colour, which is presented as associated with divinity (see below), hence presumably is a transcendental property. So the colour-scale adds an extra level, and subsequently follows the vitality scale: the sky at the top (colours fully specified), next the vegetation (colours strongly implied), then the natives (mud-colour, presumably), and finally the colonialists. The last paragraph re-defines the power hierarchy ('The sky settles every-thing') into what in business circles is called a 'flat structure': the sky has all true power; everything else is intrinsically powerless, and only enabled by association with the sky (see below). Thus we can say that, locally in this novel, COLOUR IS VITALITY, and we

GROUP	POWER	TOPOGRAPHY	VITALITY
ENGLISH	TOP	SECOND (HIGHER) RISE	LEAST ANIMATE
EURASIANS	NEXT	FIRST (LOWER) RISE	NEXT LEAST ANIMATE
NATIVES	THIRD	GROUND LEVEL	MORE ANIMATE
VEGETATION	BOTTOM	IN THE GROUND	VERY ANIMATE

Figure 16.4 Power – vitality hierarchy

can draw further implications like EARTHLY POWER IS LIFELESS, EARTHLY POWER IS COLOURLESS.

The final two paragraphs of [the passage] reconcile the opposition in Figure 16.4 and at the same time render its earthly perspective obsolete: not only is the sky (which 'contains' Heaven, of course) described in terms of a temple ('dome of blending tints', 'stars hang like lamps from the immense vault'), and a kind of ultimate state of being, but it can also act divinely ('glory can rain', 'a benediction pass'). So, the land may be where the vegetation springs from, but it is the sky which is responsible for this ('By herself [the earth] can do little – only feeble outbursts of flowers'). Thus the vitality quotient – which, as we have seen, runs counter to both the topography and the political power – is actually in the gift of the sky. The sun infuses the earth with its power, and the vegetation reflects this directly. The native Indians, closer to the earth (even appearing to be made of it), benefit from some of this vitality, having at least life and movement, while the 'ruling classes', far away from the life-giving earth, lack vitality entirely. The sky, then, which is highest of all, restores the topographical metaphor: POWER IS UP, while at the same time 'explaining' the contrary direction of the vitality quotient. The colonialists are in a sense suspended between sky (strength) and land (size), thus partaking of neither. Figure 16.5 shows how these various metaphors combine to provide the underlying message – the sub-text – of this chapter.

This is the logic by which these metaphors work, yielding a rich interpretation of this prose passage:

> If power is up, then down is powerlessness; thus sky and sun are powerful, earth and things of the earth are powerless.
> If the sun is the father, then the father has power; if the earth is the mother, then the mother is powerless.

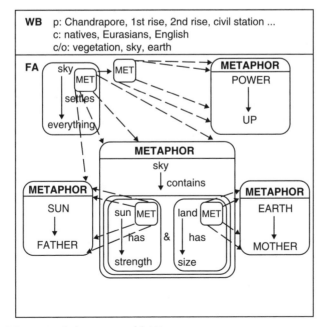

Figure 16.5 A Passage to India text world (4)

But the mother breeds life, so the earth breeds life.

Thus entities near the earth have life, entities away from the earth lack life.

The sun gives light and colour, and the sun is powerful, so light and colour are the signs of power.

So, entities close to the earth have life, but lack power; entities closer to the sky have power, but lack life. Only the vegetation bridges the gulf between high and low: it combines life and power into vitality.

These are the inferences which may be drawn from the metaphorical sub-worlds which we have postulated for paragraph 4. I have not shown them in a separate box this time because of their length: but the procedure is similar to the rather simpler one we explored in Figure 16.3. In Figure 16.3, inferences drawn from the negative sub-world led to a specific underlying metaphor for the paragraph; in Figure 16.5, inferences drawn from a number of conventional metaphorical and metonymic sub-worlds lead to the specific metaphors underlying paragraph 4.

References

Bridgeman, T. (1998) *Negotiating the New in the French Novel: Building Contexts for Fictional Worlds*. London: Routledge.

Chilton, P. (2004) *Analysing Political Discourse*. London: Routledge.

Forster, E.M. (1924/1984) *A Passage to India*. Harmondsworth: Penguin.

Gavins, J. (2007) *Text World Theory: An Introduction*. Edinburgh: Edinburgh University Press.

Hidalgo Downing, L. (2000) *Negation, Text Worlds and Discourse: The Pragmatics of Fiction*. Stanford, CA: Ablex.

Lakoff, G. and Johnson, M. (1980) *Metaphors We Live By*. Chicago: Chicago University Press.

Lakoff, G. and Turner, M. (1989) *More Than Cool Reason*. Chicago: Chicago University Press.

Stockwell, P. (2002) *Cognitive Poetics: An Introduction*. London: Routledge.

Stockwell, P. (2008) *Texture*. Edinburgh: Edinburgh University Press.

Werth, P.N. (1994) 'Extended metaphor: a text world account', *Language and Literature* 3 (2): 79–103.

Werth, P.N. (1999) *Text Worlds: Representing Conceptual Space in Discourse*. London: Longman.

Extracted from Paul Werth (1995) ' "World enough, and time": deictic space and the interpretation of prose', in P. Verdonk and J.-J. Weber (eds) *Twentieth-century Fiction: From Text to Context*, London: Routledge, pp. 181–205.

Chapter 17

Making the subtle difference: literature and non-literature in the classroom

GUY COOK

Stylistics holds most of its influence in and because of the language classroom. The practical outlook of most stylisticians arises from a long tradition of using literature in the context of language teaching, and innovations in such pedagogy in turn have generated a wealth of stylistic approaches and a rich set of analyses. The work done by students and new researchers in the field – perhaps more than in any other branch of literary study – are regarded as valuable contributions to the discipline. In this chapter, Guy Cook deploys a range of text-types, including literature, in order to make an argument about ideology and canonisation. In its interactive style, the chapter enacts its own discursive creativity. In drawing continuities between advertising and literary discourse, Cook argues for students thinking critically about canon and syllabus, and yet also argues for the value of literature and literary study.

Further work on the use of stylistics as pedagogy can be found in Brumfit and Carter (1986), Widdowson (1992), Carter and McRae (1996), Short (1996), Simpson (1997) and Watson and Zyngier (2007).

Language and influence

THERE IS IN BRITAIN a continuing undercurrent of disagreement about the teaching of literature, which surfaces from time to time in bitter and strongly-worded debate. The debate is between those who defend, as the only source of texts for literary study, that set of classics referred to as *the canon*, and those who argue that many of the texts in this canon are irrelevant to contemporary students, who should rather busy themselves with learning to cope with the vast array of genres in the modern world: including such *non-literary* discourse as information leaflets, news bulletins, newspapers and open ones whose values, though allowed to change, are repeatedly chosen and re-chosen by their populations, as the literary canon can be chosen and re-chosen by its readers. And, if the analogy holds, one might add that people are frequently fondest of their native country when they are away from it. Pursuing this analogy, what I am advocating is allowing the citizens of literature classes a trip abroad in the belief (perhaps mistaken) that most will return. What this means in practice is a syllabus which is a mixture: a mixture of canonised literary works with the non-literary or the sub-literary. There will inevitably be some intermarriages and offspring of mixed parenthood, some change of citizenship too – with some of which the teacher will inevitably disagree. But the overall situation is a good one: active, and stimulating the kind of atmosphere in which literature and literary appreciation can thrive.

The strategy of mixing the literary, the non-literary and the sub-literary has the advantage of deterring the idea implicit in many literature courses that literature is a use of language somehow unaffected by the staggering technological changes in the uses of language which have taken place this century. (The details and timing vary from place to place, but the technological revolution has affected almost all societies to a greater or lesser extent.) Just as the nature of language was fundamentally altered by the advent of writing and print, so over the last century or so our relationship to language has also changed under the impact of a series of new technologies (photograph, telephone, tape recorder, radio, film, television, video, computer) which, while not usurping (so far) the dominant use and status of print, have nevertheless altered the nature of our relationship to it. As literature is a discourse whose mode is writing or print (the very word derives from the Latin *littera*, a letter of the alphabet), this change cannot but affect our relationship to literature too. This has happened, I believe, in one of two ways.

Firstly (most obviously but ultimately least significantly) there are ways in which these technologies have usurped some of the uses of print. For a reason about which no satisfactory theory has ever been advanced, people seem universally to take delight in, or even need, the narration of fictional events (Beaugrande 1987). This need, fulfilled so often in print, has in many people's lives been taken over (in whole or part) by radio, television, video and film, in all of which media an extraordinary high proportion of time is given over to the depiction of fictional events. On one weekday evening selected at random, for example, I estimate 42% of all television broadcasting on the four British terrestrial channels between 5.30 pm and 1.00 am to be taken up by fiction.

Secondly, since the widespread availability of the computer, the nature of our experience of the written word is altered, not so much because new technologies replace the use of print but because they make its dissemination both easier and faster. (In this sense their effect on a literate culture is more comparable to the replacement of hand-writing by print than to the addition of writing to speech.) It is often forgotten, in the discussion of a 'computer culture', and the expression of fears for its detrimental effect on literacy, that the most widespread uses of computers involve writing.

Computers bring us more written language rather than less; but their effect on our experiences of those written words may nevertheless be large. Word processing a manuscript is a very different linguistic activity from writing it by hand or typing. The ease of correction and redrafting adduces quite different creative processes (not always with better results); electronic mail and computer networking, though written, encourage an on-line interactivity quite unlike that in a time-consuming exchange of letters; desk-top publishing, by making print runs both cheaper and faster, leads to an increase in numbers of publications (not necessarily a desirable outcome, as works of quality may become lost in an increase in quantity). These are changes in the *production* of writing. On the side of *reception*, the existence of the book as a physical object, so integral to many people's experience of literature, may be continuously eroded. Texts may be handled more and more on screen; the libraries of the future will allow the retrieval of reading matter on a screen as friendly to the eyes as a page of print.

What effect should this new environment have upon the teaching of literature? Clearly it should have some effect. The worst response possible would be to continue as though nothing had happened, as though books were a unique means of disseminating linguistic art. The increased quantity of print made possible by new technology entails a greater need for selectivity by the individual. One of the most important skills for the contemporary language and literature student is to know what *not* to read. In a chirographic culture only the most valued texts are copied; in a print culture the range widens (hence the novel, [. . . and also] the song and jingle, the romance and the soap opera. A further contradiction is that these newer, 'lower' genres are often recalled with more pleasure and accuracy than the supposedly 'higher' genres of the literary canon, while the attachment which this pleasure and knowledge would seem to indicate is simultaneously denied. The junior branches are viewed as lesser, trivial genres, something for the end of a hard day.

I am not suggesting that there is anything wrong with such double standards. On the contrary, single standards are perhaps both unusual and uninteresting. The conflict which arises when the two value systems are brought into contact is fertile and dynamic. Both Dr Jekyll and Mr Hyde as individuals are uninteresting – it is their irreconcilable but simultaneous presence within one body which intrigues. Students and teachers seem to alternate between one world of artistic values and another. Perhaps there is something to be gained from precipitating a clash. One way of doing this is to study works from the canon alongside texts from the technological profusion to which I have referred above.

Activities

The following are some suggestions for implementing the comparative study of literary and sub-literary or non-literary works. They all exploit a superficial similarity of form or content.

Activity 1

Choose an advertisement, a witty piece of graffiti, or a tabloid headline which compresses several meanings into a very few *words*. Consider it alongside a short poem on the students' syllabus which also generates more than one meaning. Ask them first to explain how the multiple meanings are achieved in both cases, and then ask why the literary example is generally considered more worthwhile.

One could take, for example, the two-page advertisement for Cinzano (Figure 17.1) which shows a sea urchin on the right-hand page, and a glass of Cinzano on the left-hand page, with the words over the sea urchin:

FOR A TASTE WITH
SPIKE YOU'LL PREFER
THE ONE ON THE LEFT
TO THE RIGHT ONE

Figure 17.1 Cinzano advertisement

and smaller letters under the glass of Cinzano. Consider how many meanings and how many different readings are packed into these twenty-four words. 'Spike' refers both to the spikes on the sea urchin and to the herbs and spices which sharpen the drink. 'The one on the left' refers to the glass of Cinzano but sets up the expectation that the phrase will be contrasted with the syntactically parallel phrase 'the one on the right'. The phrase actually used – 'the right one' – is thus foregrounded, a fact which helps draw attention to its double meaning. For 'the right one' (unlike 'the one on the right') can also mean 'the best one' or 'the correct one', and is indeed so used in the slogan describing Cinzano's main competitor Martini, which by analogy becomes equivalent to the sea urchin (an animal which, though painful to step on, is also positively associated with warm climates and holiday beaches). With all these multiple meanings set up, 'difference' in the smaller caption means all or any of the following: the difference between the sea urchin and Cinzano, the difference between Martini and Cinzano, the difference between the phrasing of 'the right one' and 'the one on the right', the difference between the right-hand and left-hand pages, the difference between a drink without herbs and spices, and one with them.

There are prosodic and phonological features of interest too. 'Spike' and 'spices' which are in this context both opposites and co-referential, are also very similar in spelling and sound, with only a 'subtle difference' between them. There is a fairly (though not exactly) regular rhythm, with most prosodic units being either iambs (an unstressed syllable followed by a stressed one) or anapests (two unstressed syllables followed by a stressed one). In the phrase 'the right one' two adjacent stresses bring emphasis at the end of the main slogan.

for a TASTE / with SPIKE /
you'll pre FER /
the ONE / on the LEFT /
to the RIGHT ONE /

If one reads the last line rhythmically as

our HERBS and SPIces
make the SUBtle DIFFerence

then both lines have so-called 'feminine' endings (i.e. unstressed syllables) in contrast with the 'masculine' endings (stressed syllables) of the larger slogan. This perhaps, together with the smaller print size on the left, iconically suggests the subtlety and delicacy of the Cinzano. The lay-out also plays a trick on our processing. The central position and larger size of the main slogan makes us read it first. We process the right page before the left page, reversing the usual order of reading. In advertising, right-hand pages are more expensive than left-hand pages as they are more likely to catch the eye of someone flicking through a magazine. What happens here, unusually, is that the product is pictured on the left page, presumably on the assumption that the words on the right-hand page, perceived first, will direct our attention towards it.

Students can be asked first to explain the word-play and the ways in which it exploits the linguistic system to create relevant multiple meanings. Secondly, they can be asked to evaluate the advertisement, to consider why it is not deemed 'equal' to poetry in its skill. Students may also wish to consider the interaction of pictures and words, the use and connotation of different typefaces and lay-outs. Though these are significant in many genres – such as advertisements – they are generally unimportant in literature.

The advertisement could then be contrasted with a short poem such as Blake's *The Sick Rose*, a favourite in poetry anthologies, and only ten words longer than the Cinzano ad.

The Sick Rose

O Rose thou art sick.
The invisible worm
That flies in the night
In the howling storm,

Has found out thy bed
Of crimson joy:
And his dark secret love
Does thy life destroy.

Here multiple meanings are generated not by technical word-play as in the ad, but by the potential for the description of the rose and the worm to be interpreted meta-phorically. Indeed, unless one reads this (somewhat absurdly) as a poem which is literally about a flower and a bug, it *must* be interpreted metaphorically. 'Bed', 'crimson joy' and 'dark secret love' may suggest analogies concerning (in) fidelity and sexuality, but it is the lack of precision as to what the infected rose symbolises which gives this image its power and potential to yield a vast variety of personal interpretations.

On a more technical level, it might be noted that this poem, like the Cinzano ad, mixes anapests and iambs.

o ROSE / thou art SICK. /
The inVIS / ible WORM /
That FLIES / in the NIGHT /
In the HOWL / ing STORM, /
Has FOUND / out thy BED /
of CRIM / son JOY: /
And his DARK / secret LOVE /
Does thy LIFE / des TROY. /

In both cases the use of words is skilful and meaning is compressed. What is it that makes the second seem to most people more serious, more moving, more profound?

Many teachers who have tried such an exercise encounter initial incomprehension or derision, but once (and if) the activity can be taken seriously, it will lead either to statements asserting the value and difference of literature (perhaps that literary texts demonstrate skill with language in the service of some larger or more serious goal), or to doubts about the judgements which the syllabus is handing down. In either case it will help students towards more independent and thoughtful judgement. If students feel this activity does not help them in their examinations, this may be true, but that is also an indictment of the examinations.

Activity 2

Identify a soap opera or film which is popular with a substantial proportion of the class. Choose a scene (and show it on video) in which the content is comparable with a scene from a play on their syllabus: an argument between mother and son for those studying *Hamlet*; a conspiracy to commit a crime for those studying *Macbeth*; accusation of adultery for those studying *Othello*. If there is time, transcribe the words from the soap opera and compare the language with a section of text from the play. Again, discuss why one is considered literary and the other is not. Discuss the degree to which they are dependent on images and acting, or can 'stand up' as written text.

There are some disadvantages of course. The search can be time-consuming for teachers (though it can also be an excuse to relax a little longer in front of the television) and the activity takes time away from the acquisition of the detailed knowledge of a set text demanded by examination syllabuses. 'Better' students may feel peeved that an advantage is being given to those with greater knowledge of popular culture. Yet again the activity may either highlight the virtues of the literary example, or stimulate a fundamental re-evaluation.

Activity 3

Contrast videos of a poetry reading with a stand-up comedy act or the performance of a solo singer-songwriter. They have a great deal in common (see Cook 1995). In both cases an individual stands on stage and delivers words which have been prepared in advance. In both cases, if the performance is successful, the audience approves of the soloist's skill with words and insights into life.

Activity 4

Take a passage from a 'lowbrow' successful novel and a 'highbrow' novel on the syllabus. Choose two passages which deal with comparable subject matters: a death, a wedding, a declaration of love, a funeral, a homecoming. Discuss why one work is elevated to the status of literature and the other – though perhaps 'gripping' and enjoyable – is not.

Consider for example these two passages, the first from Julie Burchill's best-selling novel *Ambition* (1990), the second from D.H. Lawrence's novel *The Rainbow* (1915).

> There were two people in the Regency four-poster that swamped the suite overlooking the Brighton seafront but only one of them was breathing; deeply and evenly, as she sipped flat Bollinger Brut and decided what to do next.
>
> Her name was Susan Street, and she was almost twenty-seven and almost beautiful with long dark hair, long pale legs and a short temper. Beside her lay a man who would never see fifty again and who now would never see sixty, either. He had been, until half an hour ago, the editor of the Sunday Best, a tabloid with teeth whose circulation was three million and rising. Unfortunately he would never see it reach four million, because his deputy editor Susan Street had just dispatched him to that big boardroom in the sky with a sexual performance of such singular virtuosity that his heart couldn't stand it.
>
> His heart, like everything else about him, was weak, she thought as she kissed his still-warm lips.
>
> *   *   *
>
> When Anna Brangwen heard the news, she pressed back her head and rolled her eyes, as if something were reaching forward to bite at her throat. She pressed back her head, her mind was driven back to sleep. Since she had married and become a mother, the girl she had been was forgotten. Now, the shock threatened to break in upon her and sweep away all her intervening life, make her as a girl of eighteen again, loving her father. So she pressed back, away from the shock, she clung to her present life.
>
> It was when they brought him to her house dead and in his wet clothes, his wet, sodden clothes, fully dressed as he came from market, yet all sodden and inert, that the shock really broke into her and she was terrified. A big, soaked, inert heap, he was, who had been to her the image of power and strong life.
>
> Almost in horror, she began to take the wet things from him, to pull off him the incongruous market-clothes of a well-to-do farmer. The children were sent away to the Vicarage, the dead body lay on the parlour floor, Anna quickly began to undress him, laid his fob and seals in a wet heap on the table. Her husband and the woman helped her. They cleared and washed the body, and laid it on the bed.

Both passages concern the reaction of a young woman to the sudden death of an older man. Both use comparable linguistic strategies, manipulating syntax to create rhetorical effect:

A big, soaked, inert heap, he was, who had been to her the image of power and strong life.

Beside her lay a man who would never see fifty again, and who now would never see sixty, either.

Yet one is instantly perceived as light-hearted and without pretensions to literariness, the other as (at least attempting to be) profound. Is this only because the dead man in one is the woman's adoptive father, and in the other a casual lover, or is it signalled stylistically by choice of language or semantically by choice of detail? Is levity necessarily non-literary? How exactly does Burchill signal that the death is to be taken lightly, while Lawrence identifies it as a matter for reflection and grief?

Conclusion

It is questions and activities like these which, I believe, help students to appreciate that literature (if not specific literary works) is something special, subtly different from the clever manipulation of language for non-literary purposes. Going outside the canon may lead students actively to confirm and create their own judgements of excellence in the present, rather than passively receiving the judgements of others from the past. It is a cause for optimism when these judgements confirm our own, and the power of literature to transcend generational difference.

References

Beaugrande, R. de (1987) 'Schemas for literary communication', in L. Halasz (ed.) *Literary Discourse: Aspects of Cognitive and Social Psychological Approaches*, Berlin: de Gruyter, pp. 49–100.

Brumfit, C. and Carter, R. (1986) *Literature and Language Teaching*. Oxford: Oxford University Press.

Burchill, J. (1990) *Ambition*. London: Corgi.

Carter, R. and McRae, J. (1996) *Language, Literature and the Learner: Creative Classroom Practice*. London: Longman.

Cook, G. (1995) 'Language play in English', in J. Maybin and N. Mercer (eds) *Using English: From Conversation to Canon*, London: Routledge, pp. 198–227.

Lawrence, D.H. (1915) *The Rainbow*. London: Methuen.

Short, M. (1996) *Exploring the Language of Poems, Plays and Prose*. London: Longman.

Simpson, P. (1997) *Stylistics: A Resource Book for Students*. London: Routledge.

Watson, G. and Zyngier, S. (eds) (2007) *Literature and Stylistics for Language Learners: Theory and Practice*. Basingstoke: Palgrave Macmillan.

Widdowson, H. (1992) *Practical Stylistics*. London: Longman.

Extracted from Guy Cook (1996) 'Making the subtle difference; literature and non-literature in the classroom', in R. Carter and J. McRae (eds) *Language, Literature and the Learner: Creative Classroom Practice*, London: Routledge, pp. 151–66.

PART THREE

New directions

Educating the reader: narrative technique and evaluation in Charlotte Perkins Gilman's *Herland*

JEAN JACQUES WEBER

This chapter is a good example of how a detailed microanalysis of only a few stylistic features can illuminate large issues of narrative technique. Focusing on terms with an evaluative flavour, Weber shows, with particular reference to notions of gender, how the text encourages the reader to be drawn into a particular ideology and perspective. The author, Charlotte Perkins Gilman, accomplishes this very subtly, leaving the stylistic technique mostly below the level of readerly consciousness. Weber's analysis itself is deceptively simple, but it serves to bring to awareness the stylistic texture of the novel with a wealth of clear evidence.

*H*ERLAND IS AN EARLY feminist utopia written by Charlotte Perkins Gilman in 1915. Though it may seem dated in some of its late-Victorian attitudes, towards sex in particular, it is still full of stimulating ideas that can challenge even the modern reader. In fact, many recent critics have insisted on the book's power to shake the reader out of her, or mostly his, unquestioned, naturalized assumptions about women and men. For instance, Burton [1985: 93] points out that feminist utopias such as *Herland* 'forbid a passive reading, and demand, in their various ways, that the reader participate, think, work at her or his reading and understanding'. Ferns [1998: 31] contrasts *Herland* with earlier utopias written by men and similarly claims that it 'encourages what most utopian fictions prior to it seek to suppress: an active participation on the part of the reader'. Here is a final quote from another contemporary critic, again insisting on the active role demanded of the reader of *Herland*:

> The alert contemporary reader is already familiar with the information, which the women want to elicit from their male visitors and so has privileged access to the resisting text. The men themselves are the uncharted territory which gets mapped and plotted: in this novel the colonizers are colonized, the explorers explored. . . . It is the ironic process of discovery and filling, the parodic moment of American colonial history, which the

novel itself 'fills in' for its readers, and the readers fill in for the novel. Part
of the novel's didactic purpose then is to challenge the boundaries between
what is given and what is withheld in order to allow the reader to be active
in the construction of the women's texts, which remain of the novel, part of
its range, but not *within* the novel, not part of its text.

[Bennett 1998: 48]

What I should like to investigate in this paper is exactly how Gilman succeeds in
actively involving the reader. As Bennett points out, the exploration of Herland *by* three
men turns into an exploration *of* the men and their attitudes towards women. This in
turn becomes, at least by implication, an exploration of the reader's assumptions. And to
close the circle of exploration, we can return to the text and analyse what it is about
Gilman's narrative technique that allows her to challenge the reader in this way.

Herland is the story of three American men who hope to discover the 'strange and
terrible Woman Land' [p. 2; quotations are from the 1997 edition of Gilman's novel].
The three are clearly differentiated in their attitudes towards life in general, and women
in particular: Van, the narrator, is a sociologist with, he claims, a scientific approach to
life; Terry is the experienced womanizer with a 'practical' attitude towards life, ready to
exploit and use women for his own purposes; and Jeff is the chivalrous, gentle and
romantic Southerner who idealizes women. In a first encounter upon their arrival in
Herland, they get to know three Herland women, Ellador, Alima and Celis, and eventually will fall in love with them and marry them. But before this, they go through a
number of adventures: they are taken 'prisoner' and held in a kind of fortress, and after
a futile attempt at escape, they are taught the language and history of Herland. They find
out that Herlanders are indeed a new race of women who can reproduce through
parthenogenesis (virgin birth capacity) and whose lives are centred around this experience of motherhood. They are amazed at how these mothers have constantly 'striven for
conscious improvement' (p. 78) in every area of their lives: their religion is a religion of
progress, and the sole aim of their system of education is to 'allow the richest, freest
growth' (p. 102) for the children. During their discussions with the Herland women,
the men gradually reveal – willy-nilly – the deficiencies of their (our) own world and
become more and more aware of the positive achievements of Herland.

The triple wedding between the three American men and the three Herland
women brings out their completely different views of sex and love. Indeed, for the last
2,000 years, these women have had no notion of sex, nor do they know anything about
marriage and married life. In his utter frustration, Terry tries to rape his 'wife' Alima,
but he is overpowered and finally expelled. Ellador and Van leave with Terry, with
Ellador due to report back to the Herlanders on the outside world, while Jeff and his by
now pregnant Celis stay on in Herland.

A major theme of the book is defeated expectation. What the three men find in
Herland goes against all their expectations:

And we had been cocksure as to the inevitable limitations, the faults and
vices, of a lot of women. We had expected them to be given over to what
we called 'feminine vanity' – 'frills and furbelows', and we found they had
evolved a costume more perfect than the Chinese dress, richly beautiful
when so desired, always useful, of unfailing dignity and good taste.

We had expected a dull submissive monotony, and found a daring social inventiveness far beyond our own, and a mechanical and scientific development fully equal to ours.

We had expected pettiness, and found a social consciousness besides which our nations looked like quarreling children – feebleminded ones at that.

We had expected jealousy, and found a broad sisterly affection, a fair-minded intelligence, to which we could produce no parallel.

We had expected hysteria, and found a standard of health and vigor, a calmness of temper, to which the habit of profanity, for instance, was impossible to explain – we tried it.

[Gilman 1997: 81]

But the male characters' expectations are not the only ones to be defeated in *Herland*. In this chapter I focus on how the reader's expectations – both generic and 'evaluative' – are defeated. As far as generic expectations are concerned, the reader might well have expected a feminist utopia to be told from a female point of view, whereas in Gilman's text we actually have a male narrator, Van. What makes *Herland* nonetheless a feminist utopia is the fact that the male narrator's patriarchal assumptions are deconstructed, thus eroding his traditional male narrative authority, until the power to name and construct reality passes into the hands of the Herland women. This is very different from Gilman's famous short story 'The Yellow Wallpaper' where, despite its female narrator, the power to construct reality remains in the hands of her cold, sane and rational husband-doctor, who by contrast defines his wife as irrational, mentally sick and in need of a particular medical treatment – a diagnosis that the wife explicitly accepts even while struggling against it. In *Herland*, on the other hand, the relation between what is normal and what is abnormal has been inverted by the end of the book. Even though we are in the presence of a male narrator, he gradually learns to accept the Herlanders' world as the norm, while seeing his/our world more and more as a negative deviation from it:

We had quite easily come to accept the Herland life as normal, because it was normal – none of us make any outcry over mere health and peace and happy industry. And the abnormal, to which we are all so sadly well acclimated, she [Ellador] had never seen.

[Gilman 1997: 136]

Another expectation that many readers may have held, at least in the initial stages of their reading, is that, in the contrast between Herland and our world, the Herland women would be evaluated positively, whereas the men (especially Terry) and their world would be evaluated negatively. But again, our expectations are defeated at least to some extent. In the brief analysis below, we shall see that in fact the Herlanders as well as Terry are evaluated both positively and negatively. The evaluative devices that I have looked at are the following:

Main evaluative devices in *Herland*:

1.   explicit evaluation
     a.   evaluative adverbs and adjectives
     b.   evaluative comments

2.   implicit evaluation
    a.   metaphor
    b.   other lexical innovations

The main distinction is between explicit and implicit evaluative devices, the difference being that in the latter the evaluative element is not directly inscribed in the text,
but has to be inferred and (re)constructed by the reader [see Calvo and Weber 1998:
130–4 for more on this distinction]. First I focus on evaluative adverbs and adjectives, of
which Gilman makes frequent use in her descriptions of the characters' verbal, and
other, behaviour. In order to keep the analysis manageable, I ignore Van and Jeff, and
only concentrate on what we might expect to be the two extremes of Gilman's evaluative continuum in *Herland*, namely Terry at one end and the Herlanders at the other. As
expected, Terry is indeed associated with a large number of negative dimensions of
behaviour:

- *negative behaviour or attitude:* bitterly, dryly, grim(ly) (both adverb and adjective
  forms occur), rudely, savagely, sourly, angry, critical, immensely disgusted, irritable, jealous, severe.
- *sense of superiority (often in connection with irony or sarcasm):* grandly, incredulous(ly),
  mightily, triumphantly, that funny half-blustering air of his, contemptuous,
  defiant, masterful, patronizing, suave.
- *lack of restraint:* he quite desperately longed to see her, madly in love, who fretted
  sharply in his restraint, in desperate impatience.
- *lack of honesty or intention to deceive:* most winningly, his brilliant ingratiating smile.
- *lack of intelligence:* fondly imagining.

The Herlanders, on the other hand, tend to be associated with the positive end of
these and other behavioural dimensions:

- *positive behaviour or gentleness:* apologetically, civilly, courteously, gently, kind(ly),
  polite(ly), sweet(ly).
- *good humour:* delightedly, gaily, laughingly, merrily, smiling(ly), contented,
  mischievous.
- *sense of restraint or emotional balance:* calm(ly), patient(ly), smoothly and evenly, the
  evenest tempers, restrained, serene.
- *sense of morality or honesty:* frank(ly), honestly, frank and innocent, sincere.
- *intelligence or desire for knowledge:* farsightedly, eager(ly), subtly, intelligent, deeply
  wise.
- *courage or strength:* daringly, decidedly, solidly, steadily, assured and determined,
  brave and noble, powerful, sturdy, wholly unafraid.
- *feelings or sensitivity:* wistfully, deeply, reverently tender, a deep, tender reverence.

So far, the distribution of explicit evaluative devices conforms to the reader's
expectations, but this is by no means the whole story. Interestingly, Terry is also
attributed evaluative devices, which situate him on the positive side of many of the above
dimensions:

- *positive behaviour:* (Terry) finished politely, made a polite speech.
- *good humour:* he added cheerfully, he pleasantly inquired, when specially mischievous.
- *restraint:* Terry patiently explained, he cried softly in restrained enthusiasm.
- *honesty:* he honestly believed.
- *intelligence:* said Terry sagely, he was considerably wiser.
- *courage or strength:* He was a man's man, very much so, generous and brave and clever.
- *feelings or sensitivity:* Terry was keenly mortified.

Moreover, the Herland women are also given negative evaluative devices stressing in particular their emotional coldness: *grave, grim, severe(ly), stern, unsmiling.* Sometimes, though, when a negatively evaluated adverb or adjective is used of the Herlanders, its effect is toned down by being combined with a more positively evaluated one:

Zava, observing Terry with her *grave sweet* smile

She explained to me, with *sweet seriousness*

strength was of small avail against those *grim, quiet* women

one or two more *strong grave* women followed

Moadine, *grave and strong*, as sadly patient as a mother.

We can conclude that, just as with Terry, the evaluation of the Herland women is both positive and negative. Though presented in a basically positive way, the Herland world is perhaps a bit too serious, too bland. For Terry, it is like 'perpetual Sunday school' (p. 99), and Van calls the Herland view of love and sex 'rather . . . prosaic' (p. 138). Even Ellador, a Herlander herself, is aware of this when she says: 'I can see how monotonous our quiet life must seem to you, how much more stirring yours must be' (p. 135).

This blandness and monotony of Herland life is further emphasized by an implicitly evaluative metaphor, which is repeated a couple of times in the text, in which Herlanders are compared to ants or bees:

'Go to the ant, thou sluggard – and learn something', he [Jeff] said triumph-antly. 'Don't they cooperate pretty well? You can't beat it. This place is just like an enormous anthill – you know an anthill is nothing but a nursery. And how about bees? Don't they manage to cooperate and love one another?' (p. 67)

'You're talking nonsense – masculine nonsense', the peaceful Jeff replied. He was certainly a warm defender of Herland. 'Ants don't raise their myriads by a struggle, do they? Or the bees?' (p. 99)

Note, however, that in both contexts the metaphor is not wholly negative, unlike in Huxley's anti-utopia *Brave New World*, where the Brave New World citizens are also compared to ants, aphids and maggots. [There, the metaphors are wholly and consistently negative: 'The approaches to the monorail station were black with the ant-like pullulation of lower-caste activity' (Huxley 1966: 65); 'Like maggots they had swarmed defilingly over the mystery of Linda's death. Maggots again, but larger, full grown, they now crawled across his grief and his repentance' (Huxley 1966: 165)]. The Biblical quotation in the first *Herland* extract above ('Go to the ant thou sluggard') emphasizes the positive implications of the image. Moreover, in each case the speaker is Jeff, who is in fact the staunchest advocate and admirer of Herland among the three men, as the narrator himself points out (in the second extract above: 'He was certainly a warm defender of Herland'). The evaluative implication of this metaphor is therefore somewhat ambiguous: whereas it may have been seen in a rather positive light by Gilman herself and many of her contemporary readers, it will probably be interpreted in a more negative way by late twentieth century (or early twenty first century) readers – unless, perhaps, they are devout Christians.

Other evaluations of Herland characters are equally ambivalent. To give just one more example, Gough [1998] discusses Ellador's reaction to Van's sexual advances in the following scene:

> She was impressed visibly. She trembled in my arms, as I held her close, kissing her hungrily. But there rose in her eyes that look I knew so well, that remote clear look as if she had gone far away even though I held her beautiful body so close, and was now on some snowy mountain regarding me from a distance. (p. 138)

and she comments on the ambivalence of Ellador's stance: 'is she admirably detached and objective or cold and unemotional?' [Gough 1998: 139–40].

In the face of such ambivalent evaluations of Herland and its inhabitants, the reader is left free to make up her or his own mind. However, the reader who takes a more negative perspective is brought up short, because his perspective then comes close to Terry's views, which are more and more discredited and ridiculed within the novel. Even his best friends, Jeff and Van, gradually turn against Terry and reject his totally inadequate attitudes towards women. Here is a sample of Van's negatively evaluative comments about Terry:

> It was really unpleasant sometimes to see the notions he had. (p. 9)

> I hated to admit to myself how much Terry had sunk in my esteem. (p. 74)

> But when all that is said, it doesn't excuse him. I hadn't realized to the full Terry's character – I couldn't, being a man. (p. 130)

But again, as we almost expect by now from Gilman, there is also a reverse side to the presentation of Terry. Van's negatively evaluative comments are balanced by positively evaluative comments such as the following:

> I always liked Terry. (p. 9)

> Terry, at his worst, in a black fury for which, as a man, I must have some sympathy. (p. 123)

'After all, Alima was his wife, you know', I urged, feeling at the moment a sudden burst of sympathy for poor Terry. For a man of his temperament – and habits – it must have been an unbearable situation. (p. 139)

Even Ellador, towards the end of the book, learns to empathize, at least to some extent, with Terry:

'And I begin to see – a little – how Terry was so driven to crime'. (p. 139)

Thus even Terry is not evaluated wholly negatively, mostly because of the friendship between Van and Terry, which has only gradually been weakened. An open-minded evaluative stance similar to Van's would also seem to be the normal position to take up for the (male) reader of *Herland*; he might well adopt the perspective of Van who learns to appreciate more and more both Herland in general and Ellador in particular, as can be seen from the following comments, in each of which the key-word is *grow* or *growth*:

There was *growing* in our minds, at least in Jeff's and mine, a keen appreciation of the advantages of this strange country and its management. (p. 77)

I think it was only as I *grew* to love Ellador more than I believed anyone could love anybody, as I *grew* faintly to appreciate her inner attitude and state of mind. (p. 109)

I can see clearly and speak calmly about this now, writing after a lapse of years, years full of *growth* and education. (p. 121)

So we *grew* together in friendship and happiness, Ellador and I. (p. 130; author's italics)

Female readers might perhaps tend to identify more directly with the Herland women's position, so that their process of reading the male narrator's text becomes a process of reading between the lines, of seeing through the language, of noticing and deconstructing the androcentric assumptions, norms and values underlying what Van says. But since Van himself is involved in a process of growing, since he becomes more and more aware of the gaps in his own text and of the untenability of his male-dominated world's assumptions, there is no fundamental difference any longer. The text moves from initial divergence of world-views to final convergence, which makes possible the happy-end between Ellador and Van. Moreover, it is not just Van who moves towards the Herlanders' position, but there is a similar movement on Ellador's part towards Van's position, as we have seen for instance in Ellador's expression of sympathy for Terry quoted above. Thus both Ellador and Van are involved in a process of ideological growth, and the reader, whether she or he identifies more with the Herlanders or with Van, cannot help being involved in a similar process of questioning and learning. As Gough [1995: 204] puts it, 'the text enacts a mothering process upon its implied reader, who must "grow" ideologically in the same way that Jeff, and particularly Van, as narrator, "grow".'

In the final part of this chapter, I should like to consider briefly why Gilman may have opted for this particular didactic technique. Her ultimate aim would seem to be a reconceptualization of our cognitive schemata or mental models, especially concerning the nature of love and the roles of women and men. She wants us to change our notions of what is essentially feminine and what is merely male-constructed, as Van does in the following extracts:

> Here you have human beings, unquestionably, but what we were slow in understanding was how these ultra-women, inheriting only from women, had eliminated not only certain masculine characteristics, which of course we did not look for, but so much of what we had always thought essentially feminine. (p. 57)

> These women, whose essential distinction of motherhood was the dominant note of their whole culture, were strikingly deficient in what we call 'femininity'. This led me very promptly to the conviction that those 'feminine charms' we are so fond of are not feminine at all, but mere reflected masculinity – developed to please us because they had to please us, and in no way essential to the real fulfilment of their great process. (pp. 58–9)

Gilman wants us to step out of fixed gender roles, as defined by our society, and to see femininity as well as masculinity as ideological constructs. She makes us aware of this by contrasting the Herland schemata of men and women with our own:

> When we say men, man, manly, manhood, and all the other masculine derivatives, we have in the background of our minds a huge vague crowded picture of the world and all its activities. To grow up and 'be a man', to 'act like a man' – the meaning and connotation is wide indeed. That vast background is full of marching columns of men, of changing lines of men, of long processions of men; of men steering their ships into new seas, exploring unknown mountains, breaking horses, herding cattle, ploughing and sowing and reaping, toiling at the forge and furnace, digging in the mine, building roads and bridges and high cathedrals, managing great businesses, teaching in all the colleges, preaching in all the churches; of men everywhere, doing everything – 'the world.'
> And when we say women, we think female – the sex.
> But to these women, in the unbroken sweep of this two-thousand-year-old feminine civilization, the word woman called up all that big background, so far as they had gone in social development; and the word man meant to them only male – the sex. (p. 137; author's italics)

One important way in which Gilman strengthens the effect upon her reader is through the use of lexical innovations, which frequently include an evaluative element. Deirdre Burton [1985] has written a paper on 'linguistic innovation in feminist utopian fiction' (including *Herland*), but disappointingly she only comments on Gilman's frequent use of inverted commas to 'make strange' certain words and concepts. However, Gilman does introduce a large number of lexical innovations in *Herland*. These include:

struggling manfully, but held secure most womanfully (p. 23),

It's better than we'd have been likely to get in a man-country (p. 28),

these ultra-women, inheriting only from men (p. 57),

No pentagonal bodyguard now! (p. 74),

As I've said, I had never cared very much for women, nor they for me – not Terry-fashion (p. 90),

We have our woman-ways and they have their man-ways and their both-ways (p. 97),

We do things from our mothers – not for them (p. 112),

I will give two illustrations, one away up, the other away down (p. 123),

How could we be aloner? (p. 125),

we get tired of our ultra-maleness and turn gladly to the ultra-femaleness (p. 129),

she deliberately gave me a little too much of her society – always de-feminized, as it were (p. 130),

He professed great scorn of the penalty and the trial, as well as all the other characteristics of 'this miserable half-country' (p. 134),

as for Jeff, he was so thoroughly Herlandized (p. 135),

These were women one had to love 'up', very high up, instead of down (p. 141).

You may already have spotted the expression 'ultra-women' in one of the quotations above, but perhaps more interesting examples of lexical innovation from an ideological and evaluative point of view are 'womanfully' and 'loving up':

> We were borne inside, struggling manfully, but held secure most woman-fully, in spite of our best endeavors. (p. 21)

> These were women one had to love 'up', very high up, instead of down. They were not pets. They were not servants. They were not timid, inexperienced, weak. (p. 141)

While both coinages challenge the masculine preconception of women as weak and easily frightened, the latter also reminds us that even love includes a vertical dimension of power. Terry's view of love is obviously 'loving down', with the male in control, which can turn nasty as in his attempt to master and rape Alima. Their relationship founders on a conflict of attitudes, a mismatch of love schemata, whereas Ellador and Van manage to bridge these differences in their respective world-views, and thus achieve a more fulfilling, and positively evaluated, relationship of 'loving up'.

Our study of Charlotte Perkins Gilman's narrative technique in *Herland* has shown how the author skillfully defeats her reader's expectations. In particular, by present-ing balanced views of both the male chauvinist individual and the utopian female community and by avoiding any kind of black and white stereotyping, she unsettles the reader's 'evaluative' expectations. The resulting evaluative ambivalence of the text puts the reader in a position of potential ideological growth, similar to the male narrator's and his female partner's. In the process of constructing their own evaluations of Herland and the Herlanders, many readers, again like Van, are forced as it were into questioning or revising some of their deeply rooted views about the sexes and their relations. It is this highly effective narrative and evaluative technique which makes *Herland* an extremely rewarding reading experience and ensures its lasting appeal.

References

Bennett, B. (1998) 'Pockets of resistance: some notes towards an exploration of gender and genre boundaries in *Herland*', in V. Gough and J. Rudd (eds) *A Very Different Story: Studies on the Fiction of Charlotte Perkins Gilman*, Liverpool: Liverpool University Press, pp. 38–53.

Burton, D. (1985) 'Linguistic innovation in feminist utopian fiction', *Ilha do Desterro: A Journal of Language and Literature* 14: 82–106.

Calvo, C. and Weber, J.J. (1998) *The Literature Workbook*. London: Routledge.

Ferns, C. (1998) 'Rewriting male myths: *Herland* and the utopian tradition', in V. Gough and J. Rudd (eds) *A Very Different Story: Studies on the Fiction of Charlotte Perkins Gilman*, Liverpool: Liverpool University Press, pp. 24–37.

Gilman, C.P. (1997) *Herland* (ed. Anne J. Lane). London: The Women's Press [original 1915].

Gough, V. (1995) 'Lesbians and virgins: the new motherhood in *Herland*', in D. Seed (ed.) *Anticipations: Essays in Early Science Fiction and its Precursors*, Liverpool: Liverpool University Press, pp. 195–215.

Gough, V. (1998) ' "In the twinkling of an eye": Gilman's utopian imagination', in V. Gough and J. Rudd (eds) *A Very Different Story: Studies on the Fiction of Charlotte Perkins Gilman*, Liverpool: Liverpool University Press, pp. 129–43.

Huxley, A. (1966) *Brave New World*. Harmondsworth: Penguin [original 1932].

Extracted from Jean Jacques Weber (2000) 'Educating the reader: narrative technique and evaluation in Charlotte Perkins Gilman's *Herland*', in T. Bex, M. Burke and P. Stockwell (eds) *Contextualized Stylistics*, Amsterdam: Rodopi, pp. 181–94.

Chapter 19

Satirical humour and cultural context: with a note on the curious case of Father Todd Unctuous

PAUL SIMPSON

For most of its history, stylistics has featured 'odd' or 'deviant' language use as a key focus of exploration. Even while the discipline was accumulating other tools to allow the investigation of more subtly discoursal features, stylisticians have remained interested in stylistic deviance. This is often because the literary use of odd language provides an insight into the workings of everyday language, by exaggerating or illuminating some of the general properties of natural language. Of course, the stylistic analysis also provides an opportunity for engaging very precisely with the literary text itself, with key perennial issues of defamiliarisation and literariness, and with social and ideological effects on readers. In this chapter by Paul Simpson, a discourse stylistic approach is taken to a popular television comedy script. Simpson gets at the heart of the humour in his literary text, but he does it with a systematic stylistic analysis, and he does not neglect the important social and ideological dimensions of his discussion, at the same time making connections to continuities in literary history and culture.

For more on the ideology of satirical language, see Simpson (2003), and, for ideological effects, Simpson (1993) and Toolan (1990 and 1992).

Introduction

THIS [. . .] CHAPTER EXAMINES comic discourse from a contextualized-stylistic perspective. More specifically, it sketches a general model for the study of satirical humour before offering a short analysis of certain patterns of dialogue in a television situation-comedy. It is hoped that the analysis, which refers specifically to comic dialogue in an Irish context, will feed directly into larger issues to do with culturally-situated aspects of verbal humour. The paper also assesses the manner by which discoursal and generic properties of comic discourse resurface across time, and asks if it *is* feasible to talk of diachronic, culture-specific verbal humour. Another aim is to develop the notion of satirical discourse beyond that conventionally classified as 'literary'. To this end, the principal satirical material analysed will be taken from the television series

Father Ted, a popular sitcom, which has been screened extensively in both Britain and Ireland.

Background to the present study

Although this short study is focused principally on localized features of dialogue in the context of Irish humour, it is underpinned theoretically by a broader-based analytic model [presented in full in Simpson 2003]. [. . .] [This] operates from the premise that satirical discourse comprises at least four basic components. [. . .] The four components are: *setting, method, uptake* and *target* [. . .u]nder the rather improbable acronym 'SMUT'. Into the four components have been factored some concepts and categories from the 'General Theory of Verbal Humour' (GTVH), which is a contemporary model of humorous discourse drawn mainly from research in psychology and cognitive linguistics [see Raskin 1985, Attardo 1997 and Veatch 1998]. In particular, [SMUT] subsumes the GTVH's three key stages for the production of a comic text, which are: *setup, incongruity* (or *script opposition*) and *resolution* [Attardo 1997: 396]. The additional criteria present in the SMUT model are there to highlight the special nature of satire when compared to humorous discourse generally.

The first of the four categories is *setting*. This is intended to tally with Nash's [1985: 9–10] observation that any 'act' of humour requires as its initial, principal reference a *genus*, which is 'a derivation in culture, institutions, attitudes, beliefs'. [. . .] Setting therefore is essentially a *non*-linguistic component covering the preparatory preconditions necessary for the construction of satirical discourse. Such preconditions take as given the fact that satire is ultimately an ironic, non-literal reading of a text (and not a heavily cued reading as many other text types are) and in consequence is perpetually prone to failure or misfire. Thus, the preparation of a satirical text requires the satirist to calculate, *a priori*, the potential knowledge base of the reader, viewer or listener (or, to coin a term, the 'satiree').

This translates into inferences not only about the satiree's cultural and encyclopaedic knowledge, but, in the case of contemporary political satire, about their knowledge of contemporary events and current affairs as well. For instance, when its source material is a topical news item, a satirical text works within a highly restricted cognitive backdrop, with preparatory preconditions requiring some assessment of how much recent news coverage can be assumed to be known to potential satirees. This is one index of the 'shelf-life' of contemporary political satire: as its target fades from collective memory, the satirical text, in direct proportion, becomes progressively more opaque.

Method, the second of the SMUT model's four components, is a linguistic stage proper. This category corresponds to Nash's [1985: 9–10] general observation that humour requires both 'a locus in language' and a 'characteristic design, presentation, or verbal packaging'. In keeping with the GTVH, this is a temporally ordered, two-stage process with the *setup* phase (normally) preceding the *incongruity* phase. The setup lays the groundwork by establishing an accessible, neutral context which is congruent with the experience of the receiver of the text [Attardo 1997: 411]. Although not funny *per se*, the setup is a necessary preliminary to the incongruity. The concept of incongruity is based on the notion of 'script opposition' but has been expanded outwards by humorologists to account for a host of potential cognitive-psycholinguistic oppositions. Semino [1997: 137] (whose work on text worlds in poetry complements that on the GTVH in several respects) notes the humorous potential of this device when she remarks that jokes commonly 'achieve their effect by leading interpreters to activate a particular script and then forcing them to switch to another, often leading to absurdity'. This setup-to-incongruity transition is most apparent in formulaic jokes comprising a triad of scenarios in which the violation occurs on the third scenario (that is, of the 'An Englishman, a Scotsman and an Irishman walked into a pub . . .' variety).

[. . .]

The third of the SMUT model's four components is *uptake*. Like the setting stage, this category is drawn largely from concepts in linguistic pragmatics and is meant, particularly, to echo Austin's concept of 'uptake'. In Austin's [1962: 116] framework, uptake encompasses the understanding of the illocutionary force and content of the utterance by its addressee, and the perlocutionary effects on the addressee brought about by means of uttering the sentence, such effects being special to the circumstances of the utterance. The concept of perlocution in satirical discourse relies heavily on inferencing by the satiree; an inferencing which requires the resolution of the incongruity created in the method stage along with an identification of the satirical *target* (see below). Humorologists working within the GTVH model have suggested that satisfactory resolution of incongruity requires the deployment of a 'local logic mechanism' [Attardo and Raskin 1991: 303, Ziv 1984: 90]. This mechanism functions by conserving in 'working memory' the multiple scripts projected by the incongruity for the period of time necessary for the research of a cognitive rule capable of solving the incongruity [Attardo 1997: 412]. Interestingly, Attardo also adds (p. 409) that incongruities are least likely to be resolved definitively in 'absurd humour', suggesting, in effect, that absurdism is fundamentally the most open-ended of all forms of humorous discourse.

[. . .]

The last of the four categories is *target*. What arguably separates out parody from satire is the latter's perceived 'object of attack'. As Dane has remarked, 'satire refers to things; parody to words. The target and referent of satire is a system of content. . . . that of parody is a system of expression' [Dane 1980: 145]. This distinction between satire and parody is not straightforward, as Dane later observes, and in certain discourse contexts the two areas may fuse and overlap. [. . .] It is worth noting that Dane, although working in a markedly different scholarly framework, coins the term 'gentle satire' to cover the sorts of texts that parallel the category defined here. He suggests that 'gentle satire' occupies one extreme of a continuum at the opposite pole of which sits 'invective, polemic' [Dane 1980: 152].

By way of conclusion to this section, it is important to reinforce the point that a single satirical text may realize multiple targets. Thus, discussing a text in terms of its perceived target is largely a question of balance and emphasis; the principal impetus may be from one subtype but that can be expanded outwards to cover the other three. Furthermore, all categories of target can expanded upwards to critique the ideological practices of elite groups, dominant institutions or powerful individuals. Whereas, for instance, Alexander Pope's 1735 attack on Timon and his tasteless villa (in 'Epistle to Burlington') may start on the personal plane, it can easily be 'upgraded', as it were, to cover the arrogance and folly of *nouveau riche* sections of eighteenth century society. This is not to suggest that the satirist's own ideological standpoint is necessarily a radical or progressive one; in fact, according to Dunne [1994: 149–50], there is little evidence that satirists are motivated by any clearly articulated political principles, or by any consistent political ideology. However, this point (and the other issues raised in this conclusion) are from an area of investigation that is beyond the scope of this chapter and so they must be dealt with elsewhere. The next task in the present study will be to look more closely at certain aspects of verbal humour in their cultural context.

Verbal humour and textual satire: *Father Ted*

Father Ted currently ranks as one of the most popular sitcoms in British television history. The principal characters featured in the series are three Irish priests, and their house-keeper, who inhabit a parochial house set on the fictitious Craggy Island. The original idea for the series was taken initially by its two writers, Arthur Linehan and Graham Mathews, to RTE (the Republic of Ireland's terrestrial TV station). RTE turned it down, allegedly on the grounds that the material it contained was too sensitive. It was then offered to Hatrick Productions who went on to produce all three series and a Christmas special for British TV's Channel Four. The first series very quickly achieved so-called 'cult status', and having proved hugely popular in Britain, was then sold on to RTE whereupon it became, in 1997, the most watched television programme in the Republic of Ireland. Aside from its less than prescient business acumen, RTE's nervousness about taking on the production initially was understandable. For a start, the launch of the series coincided with a period in Ireland when the institution of the Catholic Church was in turmoil, and when, for the first time in its history, it experienced a marked shortfall in new recruits to its seminaries [see Ryan 1997]. Moreover, the three priests who inhabit Craggy Island are strident satirical caricatures indeed: Father Jack (played by actor Frank Kelly) is a decrepit, foul-mouthed alcoholic; Father Dougie (Ardal O'Hanlon) is a ludicrously asinine novice whose ignorance of matters spiritual beggars belief; and the eponymous Father Ted (the late Dermot Morgan) is an ambitious schemer whose mysterious financial past has brought about his exile to Craggy Island. Ardal O'Hanlon, who like Dermot Morgan began his career as a stand up comic, has remarked of this characterization that:

> there are only three types of people in the world. The old drunk letch, the young naive innocent and the shifty cagey wannabe. *Father Ted* discovered that and so did Shakespeare.
>
> [O'Hanlon 1998: 83]

And finally, Mrs Doyle (played by actress Pauline McLynn) is an absurdly selfless and devoted housekeeper who possesses a frenzied sense of loyalty to the trio of inept clerics.

The world of *Father Ted* is indeed a bizarre one, as would any world be if it were inhabited almost exclusively by objectionable clerics. Furthermore, the actual location for 'Craggy Island', where most of the outdoor action is shot, is Ennistymon in County Clare which, with its striking limestone scree slopes and cliffs, creates a spartan and often alienating backdrop to the plot lines of various episodes. The dynamics of this sitcom undeniably offer ample opportunity to pillory the Catholic church relentlessly. Yet, while it is true that the image of the clergy does not emerge positively from *Father Ted*, one would nonetheless be hard pushed to call the production 'hard-hitting' by any stretch of the imagination. For one thing, the few secular denizens who also inhabit this curious clerical world fare no better than the priests. However, it is arguably certain

aspects of the discoursal construction of the programme that are primarily responsible
for its sometime oblique satirical thrust. A more detailed explanation of this hypothesis
will be presented later in the discussion.

Before that, and to give a flavour of the discourse universe that is *Father Ted*, I propose to examine a short sequence of dialogue which featured in the one-off Christmas
Special first screened in 1997. In this episode, Father Ted has just learned that he is about
to receive the 'priest of the year' award (a meaningless achievement by any stretch of
the imagination, but one which means all to the ambitious Ted). The scene is the sitting
room of Craggy Island parochial house, where much of the indoor action tends to be
shot. After a knock at the door, a stranger is shown in by Mrs Doyle. Perhaps inevitably,
the visitor turns out to be a priest. The new priest, played by the actor Gerard MacSorley,
speaks with a marked Northern Irish accent which is somewhat in contrast to the
Southern Irish English spoken by all the other characters present. The new priest
appears to know Ted intimately: his embraces, slaps on back, pretend shadow boxing
and remarks to the effect that Ted hasn't changed a bit after all these years are clearly the
actions of someone who considers Ted an old and close friend. So intimate is the new
priest's behaviour that Ted feels too embarrassed to ask him to identify himself. After a
failed attempt to get the stranger to write his name in the parish visitors' book, and
when Mrs Doyle has just asked to be introduced to the 'new Father', Ted finds himself
'interactively cornered', so to speak. It is this impasse which triggers the following
quickfire sequence of dialogue:

Mrs Doyle: [To Ted] Father . . . aren't ye goin' to introduce me to the new Father?
Ted: [Squirming] Oh, right . . . right. [7 second pause] Actually, I'll tell you
what. See if you can guess!
Mrs Doyle: [Puzzled] Guess?
Ted: C'mon! Have a go!
Mrs Doyle: God, Father, sure it could be anythin'.
Ted: [Through gritted teeth] Still, though, give it a try.
Mrs Doyle: [Resigned. 11 second pause while she thinks and then, confidently,
proclaims] Fr Andy Riley?
New Priest: No. [Laughs]
Mrs Doyle: [More quickly] Fr Desmond Coyle?
New Priest: No.
Mrs Doyle: [More quickly again] Fr George Burke?
New Priest: No.
Mrs Doyle: Fr David Nicholson?
New Priest: No.
Mrs Doyle: Fr Declan Lynch?
New Priest: No. [Smiling] I'll give you a clue.
Mrs Doyle: [Suddenly vociferous, and wagging her finger] NO CLUES!
[With renewed vigour] Fr Ken Sweeney?
New Priest: Nope.
Mrs Doyle: Fr Neil Hannon?
New Priest: [Shakes head]
Mrs Doyle: Fr Keith Cullen?
New Priest: [Shakes head]

Mrs Doyle:	Fr Kieran Donnelly?
New Priest:	No.
Mrs Doyle:	Fr Mick McEvoy?
New Priest:	No.
	[A slow dissolve out of shot into a black screen, then a fade in again to suggest the passage of time. Other characters present now appear to be falling asleep]
Mrs Doyle:	[rapidly now] Fr Henry Bigbiggy?
New Priest:	No.
Mrs Doyle:	Fr Hank Tree?
New Priest:	No.
Mrs Doyle:	Fr Hiroshima Twinkie?
New Priest:	No.
Mrs Doyle:	Fr Stig Bubblecart?
New Priest:	No.
Mrs Doyle:	Fr Johnnie Hellsapoppin?
New Priest:	No.
Mrs Doyle:	Fr Luke Duke?
New Priest:	No.
Mrs Doyle:	Fr Biggy Furry?
New Priest:	No.
Mrs Doyle:	Fr Chewy Lewy?
New Priest:	No.
Mrs Doyle:	Fr Hairy Cakelineham?
New Priest:	No.
Mrs Doyle:	Fr Reboola Conundrum?
New Priest:	No.
Mrs Doyle:	Fr Peewee Stairmaster?
New Priest:	No.
Mrs Doyle:	Fr Jemima Rakhtoum?
New Priest:	No.
Mrs Doyle:	Fr Spodo Komodo?
New Priest:	No.
Mrs Doyle:	Fr Todd Unctuous?
New Priest:	[Suddenly elated] YES! WELL DONE!
	[12 seconds of Mrs Doyle beaming amid audience applause and laughter]
Ted:	[Incredulous] Is that it? Father Todd Unctuous?

We never know for sure if Todd Unctuous is the new priest's name. As it happens, his arrival on Craggy Island marks the first stage of his nefarious scheme to steal Ted's 'priest of the year' trophy. Unctuous, it seems, is a priest unnaturally obsessed with awards; later in the episode, after he is unmasked as a thief, he attributes the origins of his covetous obsession to 'backhanders' at Holy Communion and christenings. Thereafter, he confesses, he became ever more fixated on the ultimate prize: the 'priest of the year' award.

All this matters relatively little in the context of *Father Ted*. What does matter is the delight taken in stretching to their limit the structures and boundaries of social interaction. The axiom 'dialogue for dialogue's sake' is apposite here, just as it is in much of

Father Ted. In this episode, Mrs Doyle, after some initial reticence, is prompted to guess the name of a complete stranger. Assiduous in every respect, she attempts to guess *both* first name and last name, and decorously, always prefixes this pair of names with the title 'Father'. Mrs Doyle's task is nigh on impossible by any reasonable measurement, and the implications and ramifications of her extended name-search will be discussed a little later in this section. For the moment, it is necessary to say something about the discourse structure of this conversation in more rigorously linguistic terms.

Drawing on the categories and notation developed in Francis and Hunston's [1992] model of discourse structure, Mrs Doyle's name-search exhibits a symmetrical pattern of *eliciting* exchanges. Subsequent to the organizational exchanges which prompt it, a regular discoursal structure is initiated with Mrs Doyle's first question to Unctuous. The contiguous exchanges which flow from this are all two-part structures exhibiting the elements of structure *Initiation* (I) and *Response* (R). The discourse moves which fill I and R are respectively, *eliciting moves* (from Mrs Doyle) and *informing moves* (from Unctuous). Each of the move elements is realized by a single discourse *act*. The eliciting moves all contain a *neutral proposal* which seeks polarity information, thereby requiring the addressee to make a decision between 'yes' and 'no'. In all but one of the informing move slots, a *reject* is offered. This is realized by 'no' or its variants (notice Unctuous's shaking of the head in places) and its function is to reject the underlying presuppositions in a previous eliciting move. The pattern, of course, breaks down in that last startling exchange where the eliciting move from Mrs Doyle receives an informing move containing a polarity-endorsing act known as a *confirm* [Francis and Hunston 1992: 131].

To highlight the regularity of the whole pattern, [it is possible] to render down further the structural units in this sequence of exchanges into a *schematic structure* [see Eggins 1994: 34]. Within systemic-functional linguistics, this form of idealization of data has proved a useful method for exploring the generic properties of certain discursive practices; as in, for example, Ventola's [1987] study of the generic proprieties of service encounters. Although this type of abstraction is difficult in conversational interaction where there are looser constraints on what units follow what, it is still possible, in a highly rigid discourse pattern like Mrs Doyle's name-search, to filter out the raw elements of schematic structure. First of all [using Eggins' (1994) notation], this two-part structure comprises an **A** element (realized by the eliciting moves) and a **B** element (the informing moves). Stage **A** obviously precedes stage **B** in a fixed order, thus: **A^B**. Moreover, as the sequence as a whole is recursive, this will be signalled by a preposed, right-angled arrow in the following schematic structure formula:

↵{**A^B**}

This schematic structure is intended to tease out only the most core of the structural features of this series of exchanges. There will be good reason to return to it shortly, but before that some comment needs to made about Mrs Doyle's search in terms of the SMUT model outlined earlier. First of all, it would fair to say that this type of exuberant play on the routines of social interaction is typical of much dialogue in *Father Ted*. Although the programme's satirical targets are multiple, much of its emphasis is *meta-discoursal*. This greater focus on textual (rather than personal, experiential or episodic) targets does not exactly let the clergy off the hook, but it does have a deflective function and, as Dane [1980: 152] suggests, some forms of 'gentle satire' (for which the present text is strong candidate) are actually 'affirmative'. Standing in marked contrast to this, argues Dane, is the negative and subversive satirical subgenre 'invective', in which 'the individual's behaviour is stressed over his societal role and the ideals of that role'. It is true that the actions of the priests in *Father Ted* are highly questionable, but their impact is often parried by the focus on the comic excesses of the dialogue. To put it another way, were the focus of attack personal in the first instance, then greatly increased would be the discoursal proximity of the programme as a whole to vitriol or invective. This brings us to the question of satirical method. As mentioned earlier, Mrs Doyle's bizarre interactive routine is activated by the opposition between possible and impossible. What is more, she sets about her task with gusto. The fact that the names offered after the fade out sequence are markedly outlandish, while those of the preceding half would not have passed muster in any Irish telephone directory, suggest that she has trawled deep and wide for her suggestions. And the *coup de grâce* to all this is, of course, that she succeeds!

In terms of some of the issues developed [above], the type of incongruity that this impossible–possible opposition engenders makes it difficult to reach a resolution; and the lower the degree of 'resolvability', the greater the degree of absurdism. In fact, the interactive world of *Father Ted* in general seems to tread a fine line between, on the one hand, full-blown absurdism, and on the other, a slightly out-of-kilter surrealism. I have suggested elsewhere [Simpson 1998] that an index of 'classic' absurdism is the way characters in a represented world are never surprised by the improbable or unexpected. A formula for this might be that characters in an unbelievable world act believably, so to speak, whereas in the context of the surreal, characters in a believable world act unbelievably. One of the enigmas of *Father Ted* is that it seems to straddle the two domains: characters may question initially the oddity of certain situations, but they quickly acquiesce and comply. For instance, Mrs Doyle is puzzled at first but follows Ted's lead anyway, while Ted's incredulity at the end of the name-search gives way to his acceptance that Unctuous is indeed the new priest's name.

Linguistic humour: culturally situated?

This short concluding section attempts to situate the analysis of *Father Ted* within a wider discourse context before discussing some of the theoretical issues attendant on the contextualized-stylistic study of verbal humour. As a first step towards this, I propose to consider briefly a further sequence of dialogue which is taken from Irish comic writer Flann O'Brien's novel *The Third Policeman* (1974). The centrality of comic dialogue in O'Brien's work as a whole has been well documented, and its place in this particular novel often singled out for particular attention [see Clissmann 1975: 163]. In this passage, the unnamed first person narrator is quizzed by a grotesque and intimidating police sergeant. In spite of having been told quite clearly that his interlocutor has no name, the sergeant initiates the following series of exchanges:

> Then he [the Sergeant] spoke.
> 'Are you completely doubtless that you are nameless?', he asked.
> 'Positively certain.'
> 'Would it be Mick Barry?
> 'No.'
> 'Charlemagne O'Keeffe?'

'No.'
'Sir Justin Spens?'
'Not that.'
'Kimberly?'
'No.'
'Bernard Fann?'
'No.'
'Joseph Poe or Nolan?'
'No.'
'One of the Garvins or the Moynihans?'
'Not them.'
'Rosencranz O'Dowd?'
'No.'
'Would it be O'Benson?'
'Not O'Benson.'
'The Quigleys, the Mulrooneys or the Hounimen?'

[O'Brien 1974: 87–8]

Readers may have already registered the discoursal connections between this segment of dialogue, which continues in this manner for a further 32 lines before the
sergeant gives up, and Mrs Doyle's name search. I have noted in an earlier stylistic commentary on *The Third Policeman* (predating the *Father Ted* series) that much of the dialogue
of the novel is comprised of recursive strings of exchanges which are often triggered in
the opening phase of interaction and which have no obvious end-points [Simpson 1997].
Looking again at this dialogue in the light of the schematic structure potential proposed
for the *Father Ted* sequence, the ⌐$\{A^\wedge B\}$ formula is very much in evidence here also.
This formula represents coding at the broadest and most abstract level, so there will of
course be obvious differences between the two texts in terms of characterization, period
and genre. Moreover, the outcome of the two name searches is not the same: Mrs Doyle
is successful, the Sergeant is not. These differences apart, these two sequences nonetheless exhibit remarkably strong convergence in terms of their underlying schematic
structure. As to whether Linehan and Mathews consciously drew upon the O'Brien
material or whether they unconsciously replicated the formula, we will never know. The
point at issue is that the same form of metatextual verbal humour resurfaces and is indeed
congruent with a new discourse context created some thirty years later; the discoursal
formula is therefore both resurgent within a culture and across time. It is interesting to
note that much of what is said about Flann O'Brien's brand of verbal humour can readily
be applied to Linehan and Mathews' sitcom. For example, critics have said of the former
that it borders on the edge of nonsense and is tinged with the grotesque, and that it
displays enough playfulness to keep it from crossing over into absurdity and enough
inconsistency to prevent it from becoming fantasy [see Tigges 1998, and Nilsen 1996].
All of these points are as apposite to *Father Ted* as they are to O'Brien's work.

It may even be possible to look further back for diachronic evidence that the verbal
pattern discussed here has an even longer tradition in Irish humour. The *Ulster Saga* is a
collection of Celtic tales that were originally written in the eighth century and which
have survived through extant manuscripts compiled in the twelfth century. While the
absence of direct speech representation in the tales themselves makes parallels with the

present data difficult to draw, there is nonetheless a clear emphasis in the tales and in the scholarly literature surrounding them of the comic potential of verbal 'flyting'. These linguistic duels often occur in the initial stages of interaction and involve lengthy interrogation by a speaker about the other interlocutor's identity and capacities. For example, Mandel [1982: 44] notes that the trickster Bricriu, a particularly mischievous figure in the Irish tales, employs 'verbal battle' instead of 'real battles, which he avoids like the plague'. Mandel's conclusions suggest that elements of metatextual satire were developing in this early period of Irish literary history:

> The verbal exchanges within early [Irish Gaelic] myths and tales, the flytings with warlike and magical power that were in the arsenal of the trickster, became transformed into satire.
>
> [Mandel 1982: 47]

Another major tale in the Saga, the *Táin Bó Cúailgne* (The Cattle Raid of Cooley) suggests additional parallels with the *Father Ted* passage examined here. One feature of Mrs Doyle's questions is that they comprise names which gradually progress from the commonplace to the abstruse. Kelleher [1972] has noted that a common stylistic element in the *Táin* is the use of a litany, which develops from the mundane to the almost farcical. For instance, Cú Chulainn's daily activities begin with leaps and rope-walking – unremarkable preparation for a warrior prince. However, this litany develops into what Kelleher calls a 'spoof list' which culminates in the seemingly impossible feat (translated here from Old Irish) of 'climbing a javelin with the stretching of the body on its point, with the demeanour of a noble warrior'.

[. . .]

[A final] question which needs to be addressed is how the formal properties of textually-oriented satire can be accommodated within functional models of genre [such as Eggins' (1994)]. This study has been operating on the assumption that satire is *not* a genre of discourse; but a discursive practice that does things *to* genres of discourse. That is to say, satire has the capacity to consume, assimilate or recontextualize other discourse genres. In an observation that tallies with the diachronic perspective taken in this section, Threadgold [1989: 114] remarks that generic repetition over time brings about 'a recontextualizing and resemanticizing which produces "degenerescence" and generic change'. The notion of 'degenerescence' and its relationship to satirical discourse is one of a number of topics that undoubtedly merit further study. [. . .].

References

Attardo, S. (1997) 'The semantic foundations of cognitive theories of humor', *Humor* 10 (4): 395–420.

Attardo, S. and Raskin, V. (1991) 'Script theory revis(it)ed: joke similarity and a joke representation model', *Humor* 4: 293–347.

Austin, J.L. (1962) *How to Do Things with Words*. Oxford: Clarendon Press.

Clissmann, A. (1975) *Flann O'Brien: A Critical Introduction to His Writings*. Dublin: Gill and Macmillan.

Dane, J. (1980) 'Parody and satire: a theoretical model', *Genre* 13: 145–59.

Dunne, G. (1994) *Satire: A Critical Reintroduction*. Lexington: University Press of Kentucky.

Eggins, S. (1994) *An Introduction to Systemic Functional Linguistics*. London: Pinter.

Francis, G. and Hunston, S. (1992) 'Analysing everyday conversation', in M. Coulthard (ed.) *Advances in Spoken Discourse Analysis*, London: Routledge, pp. 123–61.

Kelleher, J.V. (1972) 'Humor in the Ulster Saga', in H. Levin (ed.) *Veins of Humor*, Cambridge, MA: Harvard University Press, pp. 35–56.

Mandel, S. (1982) 'The laughter of Nordic and Celtic-Irish tricksters', *Fabula* 23 (1/2): 35–47.

Nash, W. (1985) *The Language of Humour*. London: Longman.

Nilsen, D.F. (1996) *Humor in Irish Literature: A Reference Guide*. Westport, CT: Greenwood.

O'Brien, F. (1974) *The Third Policeman* [original 1967, Dalkey Press]. London: Picador.

O'Hanlon, A. (1998) 'Divine comedy: interview with Ardal O'Hanlon', *New Woman* (January): 82–5.

Raskin, V. (1985) *Semantic Mechanisms of Humor*. Dordrecht: Reidel.

Ryan, J. (1997) 'Brothers in brown', *The Big Issue* 83: 6.

Semino, S. (1997) *Language and World Creation in Poems and Other Texts*. Harlow: Longman.

Simpson, P. (1993) *Language, Ideology and Point of View*. London: Routledge.

Simpson, P. (1997) 'The interactive world of *The Third Policeman*', in A. Clune and T. Hurson (eds) *Conjuring Complexities: Essays on Flann O'Brien*, Belfast: Institute of Irish Studies, pp. 73–81.

Simpson, P. (1998) 'Odd talk: studying discourses of incongruity', in J. Culpeper, M. Short and P. Verdonk (eds) *Exploring the Language of Drama: From Text to Context*, London: Routledge, pp. 34–53.

Simpson, P. (2003) *The Discourse of Satire: A Stylistic Model of Satirical Humour*. Amsterdam: Benjamins.

Threadgold, T. (1989) 'Talking about genre: ideologies and incompatible discourses', *Cultural Studies* 3 (1): 101–27.

Tigges, W. (1988) *An Anatomy of Literary Nonsense*. Amsterdam: Rodopi.

Toolan, M. (1990) *The Stylistics of Fiction*. London: Routledge.

Toolan, N. (ed.) (1992) *Language, Text and Context*. London: Routledge.

Veatch, T. (1998) 'A theory of humor', *Humor* 11 (2): 161–215.

Ventola, E. (1987) *The Structure of Social Interaction: A Systemic Approach to the Semiotics of Service Encounters*. London: Pinter.

Ziv, A. (1984) *Personality and Sense of Humor*. New York: Springer-Verlag.

Extracted from Paul Simpson (2000) 'Satirical humour and cultural context: with a note on the curious case of Father Todd Unctuous', in T. Bex, M. Burke and P. Stockwell (eds) *Contextualized Stylistics*, Amsterdam: Rodopi, pp. 243–66.

Chapter 20

(Sur)real stylistics: from text to contextualizing

PETER STOCKWELL

It is possible to produce a linguistic analysis even of texts that are at first glance meaningless, obscure or extremely difficult: as long as those texts draw on resources of language, their obscurity is explainable in structural terms. However, for an analysis to become stylistic as well as linguistic, the issues of effectiveness and meaningfulness need to be incorporated. In this sense, stylistics is not decontextualised, though it often aims for a more even-handed interest in forms of context other than the simply historical. Peter Stockwell makes this point at the beginning of this chapter, before describing the exploratory process by which he draws on insights from lexical semantics to understand a surrealist text that defies an easy resolution.

The chapter is taken from a collection of papers (Bex *et al.* 2000) that explores the nature of stylistics as a contextualised and contextualising activity, based on principles set out in Peter Verdonk's series, *From Text to Context*: Verdonk (1993), Verdonk and Weber (1995) and Culpeper *et al.* (1998).

[. . .]

A variety of contexts

I T I S S I M P L I S T I C and easy to equate context with history. In my recent critical reading into the literature of surrealism, for example, almost all of the studies have concerned themselves with historical matters. Surrealism is often described as a narrative with sources, influences and parent-figures in late nineteenth century French Symbolism, early century Fauvism, and First World War Dadaism [see, for example, Gascoyne 1936, Balakian 1967, Rubin 1968, Tashjian 1975 and Short 1980]. There are often chronologies of key events in the history of surrealism [Rubin 1968: 197–216] and the critical material is loaded with names and places and dates and times all associated with the period of production of surrealist texts. All of these studies privilege the historical description of the inter-war years with surrealism as the focus. When the literary output of surrealism (in the form of actual poetic texts) is described, the discussion tends to relate the specific text to the general historical context: surrealist literature as a response to the militaristic logic of the war, as being in alliance with communism, as a movement developing alongside cubism, futurism, or early psychoanalysis.

The only other type of context represented as having any importance is the biographical context. Studies describe the backgrounds, conversations and lives of the surrealist writers and artists [Read 1936, Motherwell 1951, Waldberg 1965, Balakian 1970], either recounted first-hand in the form of memoirs, journals or diaries, or as studies in the historical reconstruction of a life-story. Perhaps inevitably, given the nature of this documentary evidence, biography is presented chronologically and as an aspect of history. Where related contexts are mentioned, such as the psychology, philosophy, and artistic sense of the surrealist writers, these are subsumed into more general historical factors. Aspects of the writers' lives are selected for recounting, for example, only when they seem to have a relevance to the broader historical narrative.

There are all sorts of different relevant contexts embedded in this general historicism, which are obscured by the overall view. Of most interest for me are the various *linguistic* contexts surrounding surrealism. Surrealist writing and speech (at staged events such as meetings and exhibitions, early versions of performance art) involve a range of techniques. The surrealist principle of 'objective chance' led to the use of collage, where two or more disconnected elements were brought together in a shocking and unexpected juxtaposition. In poetry this produced 'automatic writing', in which the writer would try to set sentences down with as little rational thought as possible. Sometimes this was genuinely random, as in the surrealist practice of writing 'chain-poems' involving different people composing a line each, or in the game 'the exquisite corpse' in which a piece of paper is passed around and each new writer adds a word, phrase or sentence while only seeing the last contribution (an early composition produced the game's name). Sometimes the irrationality was a little more studied and deliberate:

> There would be a verb, a subject, a complement, adverbs, and everything perfectly correct, as such, words; but meaning in these sentences was a thing I had to avoid. . . . The verb was meant to be an abstract word acting on a subject that is a material object, in this way the verb would make the sentence look abstract. The construction was very painful in a way, because the minute I *did* think of a verb to add to the subject, I would very often see a meaning and immediately I saw a meaning I would cross out a verb and change it, until, working for quite a number of hours, the text finally read without any echo of the physical world.
> (Marcel Duchamp, quoted in Schwarz 1969: 457)

[. . .]

In the literary criticism of surrealism (as in that of most genres and works) a whole range of contexts are subsumed within the historical overview. Biographical, cultural, linguistic, artistic, purposive, receptive, idiosyncratic and pedagogic contexts are all considered (if at all) as parts of the historical reconstruction of the text's meaning. It seems to me that a receptive approach is particularly illuminating with surrealism, for example, since the techniques of surrealism have been used throughout the century for all sorts of non-revolutionary purposes, and readers' reactions to surrealist texts vary enormously. What a stylistic exploration can achieve is a constant refocusing on the various forms of context. The pragmatic technique of working back and forth from text to linguistics serves to create a process of contextualizing, in order to avoid the trap of text-context binarism. I will illustrate this in the rest of this paper.

A whole-context example

Here is a poem by Hugh Sykes Davies, of the London Surrealist Group, originally published in *London Bulletin* (No. 2) in May 1938:

Poem

It doesn't look like a finger it looks like a feather of broken glass
It doesn't look like something to eat it looks like something eaten
It doesn't look like an empty chair it looks like an old woman searching in a heap
    of stones
It doesn't look like a heap of stones it looks like an estuary where the drifting filth
    is swept to and fro on the tide
It doesn't look like a finger it looks like a feather with broken teeth
The spaces between the stones are made of stone
It doesn't look like a revolver it looks like a convolvulus
It doesn't look like a living convolvulus it looks like a dead one
KEEP YOUR FILTHY HANDS OFF MY FRIENDS
USE THEM ON YOUR BITCHES OR
YOURSELVES BUT KEEP THEM OFF MY FRIENDS
The faces between the stones are made of bone
It doesn't look like an eye it looks like a bowl of rotten fruit
It doesn't look like my mother in the garden it looks like my father when he came
    up from the sea covered with shells and tangle
It doesn't look like a feather it looks like a finger with broken wings
It doesn't look like the old woman's mouth it looks like a handful of broken
    feathers or a revolver buried in cinders
The faces beneath the stones are made of stone
It doesn't look like a broken cup it looks like a cut lip
It doesn't look like yours it looks like mine
BUT IT IS YOURS NOW
SOON IT WILL LOOK LIKE YOURS
AND ANYTHING YOU SEE WILL BE USED
AGAINST YOU

(in Germain 1978: 104–5)

The initial reaction of most readers I have ever discussed this poem with is one of confusion. The fact that it has no title, other than a baldly descriptive one, to offer a contextualizing meaning often prompts them to the usual literary critical default strategy: tell me when it was written and who Hugh Sykes Davies was. However, it takes quite a lot of historical and biographical context to make that sort of sense out of the poem (as will emerge below), and there is another ideological context (of surrealism), which produces an interpretation at odds with a purely historically-founded relevance. Instead, [. . .] I am going to blend a basically stylistic analysis with a consideration of various contexts.

Surrealism and lexical semantics

The most obvious form that the poem presents (apart from being set out conventionally like a poem) is the syntactic arrangement of the first few lines: 'It doesn't look like x, it looks like y.' This arrangement is composed of a negated assertion, followed by an assertion framed positively. Unlike my prototypical form two lines above, the poem does not separate the two clauses with a comma; in fact there are no punctuation marks used in the poem at all. This syntactic parallelism of negation and assertion is most often generally used by a speaker grasping to pin down a definition of something that is difficult to describe, and which has no precise lexical item to refer to 'it'. The repetition of the indeterminate 'it' throughout the poem reinforces this perception.

In general usage, the elements in each clause are usually semantically linked: for example, 'It's not a tree, it's a bush', 'It doesn't look like a boat, it looks like a motorbike with water-jets', and so on. In these examples, the two elements share some features in common (trees and bushes are both general terms for plant-types, have leaves and branches, grow in soil, are common garden sights) but, crucially, have one or a few features of difference that make the utterance meaningful and purposive (bushes are usually smaller and more compact than trees). The purpose of the utterance is to represent a refinement of precision in definition.

A closely related set of semantic relations in general usage takes the form: 'It's not a computer strictly, more a complex adding machine', or, 'He's a farmer, or more exactly, a stockman', or, 'It's not exactly raining, more drizzling.' In all of the forms mentioned so far, there is an aspect of *synonymy* of various types. While absolute synonymy of different lexical items is very rare (if not impossible), it is possible to speak of *cognitive synonymy*, which can be defined:

> x is a cognitive synonym of y if (i) x and y are syntactically identical, and (ii) any grammatical declarative sentence s containing x has equivalent truth-conditions to another sentence s^1, which is identical to s except that x is replaced by y.
>
> (Cruse 1986: 88)

The syntactic form used in the poem sets up a negation, followed by an assertion, which looks at first as if the two elements are being presented as opposites (*cognitive antonyms*). However (as my own examples above illustrate) the two terms are more usually in a relation of *plesionymy*.

> Plesionyms are distinguished from cognitive synonyms by the fact that they yield sentences with different truth-conditions: two sentences which differ only in respect of plesionyms in parallel syntactic positions are not mutually entailing. . . . There is always one member of a plesionymous pair which it

is possible to assert, without paradox, while simultaneously denying the other member.

(Cruse 1986: 285)

The examples Cruse then goes on to cite begin to look very like those above: 'It wasn't foggy last Friday – just misty', 'It wasn't a tap I heard – more of a rap', 'He was not murdered – he was legally executed.' The point is that the syntactic arrangement presented initially by the poem is apparently the same used in general to present the semantic relation of plesionymy. This goes some way to explaining my initial intuition that the poem frames itself as an act of definition and refinement.

However, the poem is problematic at this point, since the two elements in each of the first few lines of the poem are not in a clear plesionymic relation with each other. The poem uses the customary syntactic form of the plesionym, but presents elements that are semantically incompatible, or at least not easily compatible. The nature of the incompatibility varies: shift of material, species and manufacture (finger – feather of broken glass); shift of the direction of the verb (eat – eaten); shift from object to action (empty chair – old woman searching); and so on. In each case, the semantic distance can be said to increase. Despite the syntactic presentation, the semantic relation between the two elements seems to move towards non-synonymy.

> The line between plesionymy and cognitive synonymy can be drawn with some precision. However, the limits of plesionymy in the opposite direction along the scale of synonymity are more difficult to specify; as the semantic distance between lexical items increases, plesionymy shades imperceptibly into non-synonymy.
>
> (Cruse 1986: 286)

In fact, the first few lines of the poem appear to be similar to the 'odd' examples which Cruse then goes on to give to illustrate the area in which plesionymy 'shades imperceptibly' into non-synonymy:

> ? My father's a policeman – or, more exactly, a butcher.
> ? Our dog – or, more exactly, our cat – died yesterday.

Where these two examples are close to non-synonymy, I would put the lines from the poem firmly into the shady area closer to plesionymy.

The important thing in the poem is that there is the form of plesionymy but the actual denial of it. However, in setting up this apparent form, the poem disposes the reader to make an identification of sorts between the uneasily compatible elements. The selection of elements, by their semantic distance from each other, works with the opposite force to disrupt any readerly attempt at identification. In the reader's world, there is little common identifiable semantic ground between what empty chairs look like and how old women searching in heaps of stones might appear. Nevertheless, it is very difficult for readers to abandon a text as absolutely incomprehensible; we all prefer to *make sense* of things.

At this point Cruse's work on lexical semantics runs out of usefulness: deviant combinations (very like those that appear in the poem) are simply labelled as 'odd' and used to circumscribe the definitions of semantic well-formedness. What any given readers make of the plesionymic forms of the poem is likely to form a range of idiosyncratic interpretations. However, there are some cognitive constraints on these interpretations, such that most readers with whom I have discussed the poem tend to grapple with similar features in the first line, for example. The syntactic form and the non-use of a comma encourage a readerly construction of identity across the elements, and the blend between plesionymy and non-synonymy can only lead such an interpretation into unreality. That is, whatever 'it' is, it is almost impossible to settle on a referent in our real world that both 'doesn't look like a finger' in a specific way worth mentioning, and also 'looks like a feather of broken glass'. On the way to this realization – which is compounded by the repetition of the strategy in succeeding lines – the reader struggling for meaning inevitably passes through a range of idiosyncratic resonances. Some of these that I have recorded in discussion with readers include noticing that fingers and feathers can be seen to operate as digits, and an identification of humans and birds is made. Of course, the 'feather' is not literal here but is a metaphorical figuring of a sliver of broken glass, and readers have said that this places images of cut and bleeding fingers into their minds, or fingers that are broken, or broken wings on birds with dead glassy eyes, and other resonant images.

Further lines increase the difficulty of such interpretations. While there are conceivably some conceptual similarities between fingers and feathers, the points of contact between 'an empty chair' and 'an old woman searching in a heap of stones' is less direct. One reading connected the empty chair with an absent husband or son, and a desperate search for the missing person or his grave. Similarly encouraged by the syntactic parallelism in succeeding sentences, readers often generalize the strategy across lines, and this is supported by the repetition of phrases across lines in the poem. So, for example, the grave which is the 'heap of stones' turns out to be the watery grave of one killed at sea, swept into the filthy estuary and echoed later in the image of 'my father when he came up from the sea covered with shells and tangle'.

Dissonant semantic relations begin to find their way into phrases as well. Again, 'it doesn't look like a finger', but now 'it looks like a feather with broken teeth'. Here the figurative feather of the first line has entered the unreal world of reference, but is further given teeth, which have been broken. Cruse (1986: 106) calls lexical items which create such dissonance *xenonyms*; where such odd or incompatible lexical semantic relations are arranged across and between sentences we might call the overall effect *cognitive xenonymy*. In order to negotiate these effects, readers have to hold several possible rich interpretative paths at once. None of my readers were ever assertive enough to say, 'This means x.' Most of their readings presented several different possibilities and they refused to settle on any one of them.

Having reached this point stylistically we can approach it through the historical context. Surrealism came late to Britain and the English language. The magazine, *transition*, published from Paris in English, welcomed surrealism in April 1927. The third edition in June of that year contained poetry by Kurt Schwitters ('Blue is the colour of thy yellow hair / Red is the whirl of thy green wheels'). Notices of surrealist activity appeared in the early 1930s in *The Spectator*, *New Statesman and Nation*, and *The Criterion*. However, the central core of the 'London Surrealist Group' did not form until the mid-1930s around David Gascoyne, Roland Penrose and Hugh Sykes Davies.

The semantic arrangement that Hugh Sykes Davies employs involves the dissonant combination of elements that are conceptually dissimilar in our familiar real world. This is an advanced form of one of the earliest of surrealist techniques, usually called 'collage', since in painting it involved gluing scraps from disparate sources onto a canvas. Collage was used widely both in (the precursor movement) Dada and in early surrealism. It was originally devised as a means of closing the gap between art and reality by borrowing objects themselves. Artists such as Braque, Picasso and, most successfully, Schwitters put metro tickets, newspaper cuttings, concert programmes and other *objets trouvés* into their paintings. Like such 'found objects' in sculpture, collage resists the glorification of the artist.

The most (in)famous example of the 'ready-made' found object was the urinal that Marcel Duchamp produced at an exhibition of 1917, signed 'R. Mutt' and entitled 'Fountain'. He defended this object to the selection committee of the exhibition:

> Whether Mr. Mutt with his own hands made the fountain or not has no importance. He CHOSE it. He took an ordinary article of life, placed it so that its usual significance disappeared under the new title and point of view – created a new thought for that object.
>
> (trans. in Short 1980: 25)

The collage technique in poetry manifests itself in the strangeness and difficulty of juxtapositions that resist literal interpretation. Most readers try to make sense of phrases such as 'see the pulse of summer in the ice' (Dylan Thomas), 'blue bugs in liquid silk' (Philip O'Connor), 'The worlds are breaking in my head' (David Gascoyne), and 'With the forks of flowers I eat the meat of morning' (Charles Henri Ford) by attempting to apply a metaphorical interpretation. However, subsequent sentences often disrupt any line of coherence that the reader might establish. With the collage technique, there can be little appeal to authorial intention: the last of the examples, by Ford, is the first line of a chainpoem blindly written by nine authors.

In surrealist thinking, the best image or phrase involved the greatest possible semantic distance between elements, the most extreme xenonym, in other words.

> The image is a pure creation of the spirit. It cannot be born of a comparison but of the bringing together of two realities, which are more or less remote. The more distant and just the relationship of these conjoined realities, the stronger the image – the more emotive power and poetic reality it will have.
>
> (Pierre Reverdy, in Waldberg 1965: 22)

Hugh Sykes Davies' technique can be seen as a complex development of this basic compositional device. For the surrealists, such cognitive disruptions provided an opportunity for the reader to enter into a creative relationship with the surrealist text, allowing access to a reality undistorted by bourgeois rationalism or authority. The strategy is a dialectical one, as Herbert Read (in the introduction to *Surrealism* in 1936) states:

> In dialectical terms we claim that there is a continual state of opposition and interaction between the world of objective fact – the sensational and social world of active and economic existence – and the world of subjective

fantasy. This opposition creates a state of disquietude, a lack of spiritual equilibrium, which it is the business of the artist to resolve. He resolves the contradictions by creating a synthesis, a work of art which combines elements from both these worlds, eliminates others, but which for the moment gives us a qualitatively new experience.

(Read, quoted in Germain 1978: 25–6)

Collage and 'automatism' (unplanned and undrafted unconscious writing) produced artistic works based on chance rather than conscious manipulation. Chance ambiguities, puns, coincidences, improbabilities, slips of the tongue and other random accidents were seized on by surrealists as having a reality of their own. Duchamp's painting of a moustache on the Mona Lisa was entitled 'LHOOQ', which, pronounced in French, happens to sound like '*Elle a chaud au cul*' (loosely translated, 'she has a hot arse'). Roger Vitrac vandalized public notices to generate multiple possibilities: '*Défense de fumer les fusées des femmes*' (Don't smoke/light the rockets/groupings/musical scale of women). The ravings of lunatics were reprinted. All of these were demonstrations of the 'objective chance' in collocations of words.

> Automatic writing is no more than the re-introduction of objective chance into language, whereas objective chance is the automatic writing of fate in seemingly raw facts.
>
> (Carrouges 1968: 272)

As an example, the artist Victor Brauner was hit in the eye and blinded in 1938 by a glass thrown by the Spanish surrealist Oscar Dominguez. Years previously in 1931, Brauner had painted a self-portrait with one eye crushed and his face bloody. In 1932, another self-portrait showed him with his eye pierced by a sharp instrument with the letter 'D' on the handle. The surrealist notion of objective chance ideologizes all such material, conceptual and linguistic congruences.

In the Hugh Sykes Davies poem, there are multiple seemingly significant patterns and parallelisms at several different levels of linguistic organization. One of the organizing principles of xenonymic elements seems to be simply phonological coincidence, linking 'finger – feather', 'revolver – convolvulus', 'spaces – faces', 'stones – bone', and the velar and labial plosives and liquid sound repetition in 'It doesn't look like a broken cup it looks like a cut lip'. Repetition of sounds and particular words across the poem give the illusion of a tight cohesive structure. There are several related semantic fields across the poem: 'eaten', 'broken teeth', 'rotten fruit', 'old woman's mouth', 'broken cup', 'cut lip'; and 'estuary', 'the tide', 'the sea', 'shells and tangle'. These lend a sense of cohesion, but without much real coherence. Nevertheless, it is difficult to avoid the habit of trying to link up all the connections and see significance in them.

The poem seems centrally to be concerned with specification and categorization. Yet there are several points at which it seems to disrupt the whole principle of categorization. In the spaces between the lines 'It doesn't look like x it looks like y', are the lines:

> The spaces between the stones are made of stone. . . .
> The faces between the stones are made of bone. . . .
> The faces beneath the stones are made of stone.

The first of these can easily be interpreted as calling into question the idea of separate categories: if even the space beyond the boundary of the stone is itself stone, then the notion of the boundary loses all meaning. The second of the lines invokes skeletal images (and reminded one reader of the heap of stones she read as a grave). The last of these lines seems to have resonances of carved effigies, or petrified people (in both senses), or is a play on 'stony-faced'. By this point towards the end of the poem, the paranoid world of the poem has become so firmly established that definite reference can be made to 'the faces' and 'the stones'. Similarly, phrases which began as suggested similes have by the end become definite references ('the old woman's mouth') or have appeared as real elements in the newly-constructed world ('broken feathers', 'a revolver').

Even the apparently determined assertions of identity in the attempts at definition are subject to embedded qualification. Most lines are subordinated to the verb of appearance ('looks like'), which introduces doubt in what you are able to see and whether you can trust what you see. These also render the definitions as similes and negated similes. Unlike a metaphor, the last thing 'it' can *be* if it only looks 'like' a 'feather of broken glass' is a feather of broken glass. The non-simile assertions of the three 'spaces and stone' lines extracted above are made to seem even more definite and literal by this contrast.

The binaries of negation and assertion, 'living' and 'dead', 'mother' and 'father', and 'yours' and 'mine' are paralleled by the collage of register. Twice the register of definition is interrupted by what seems like another 'voice', graphologically indicated by capitalization and a variation in syntactic form. The first of these, with the imperative, the evaluative adjective 'FILTHY', the reference to self and the abuse-term 'BITCHES', makes the capitalization appear to represent angry shouting. The final section of the poem cohesively takes up the last 'negation-assertion' pattern, and ends with the warning: 'AND ANYTHING YOU SEE WILL BE USED AGAINST YOU'. This alludes, of course, to the old police caution on arrest ('anything you say may be used against you') but the change of verbal modality alters it from a caution to a threat, and the involuntary nature of the word 'see' (as opposed to voluntarily 'watching' or 'looking') makes real the final sense of paranoia that has been accumulating throughout the poem.

Reading reception and cognition

Within surrealist ideology, the technique of juxtaposing contraries and xenonyms will dispose the reader to dialectical overload. The notions of automatic writing and objective chance were later developed into Salvador Dali's theory of the 'paranoiac-critical method'. This was propounded by Dali and translated into English by David Gascoyne shortly before Hugh Sykes Davies wrote his poem.

> Paranoiac-critical activity organises and objectivises in an exclusivist manner the limitless and unknown possibilities of the systematic associations of subjective and objective phenomena, which appear to us as irrational solicitations, exclusively in favour of the obsessive idea. By this method paranoiac-critical activity discovers new and objective 'significances' in the irrational; it makes the world of delirium pass tangibly onto the plane of reality.
>
> (Dali 1936: 17)

In this surrealist view, the surrealist object (whether a sculpture, painting or poem) is a concretized and *realized* dream-image. The surrealist image is literal and has to be taken seriously. Furthermore, the experience of reading surrealistically effects the disposition of the reader to escape the confines of rationality, civilized order, repression and the fetters of institutions and authorities. The process of reading surrealism is claimed to be as creative and liberating as the production of automatic writing, hallucination or dream.

[. . .]

The discussion integrated and contextualized

In the discussion above I have not been very disciplined in the traditional sense. I have wandered around from critical theory to linguistic theory, included lexical semantics, a note on some bits of phonology and graphology, some cognitive linguistics, and skipped from history to sociology to reception theory along the way. However, it seems to me that this is the only thing to do if I am not simply to treat literature as data, nor to produce too partial a reading of a poem, nor to invalidate the interpretations of real readers, nor to produce an 'explanation' that explains nothing but its own terminology, nor to miss out on the myriad branching possibilities that readings of surrealism offer.

Together with Verdonk and Weber (1995: 2), I prefer to see this 'creative inter-action between writer, text, reader and context' as integrated analysis, working from text to context, back to text, back to context, in order to understand both textuality and contextualizing processes (for in the end they are the same thing), in order to enrich in this sort of analytical reading, out loud on paper, the resonances of the literature. The approach is not simply a matter of the freeplay of meaning. Of all literature, even surrealist texts are not indeterminate, but can be seen to generate a range of different though related interpretations. I have not been the only reader here; my practice has tried to be reader-informed and inter-subjective. The discussion is open to all con-textualizations, but is constrained by the actuality of the text and by our current best understanding of linguistics and cognition.

Placing a surrealist text – and particularly this Hugh Sykes Davies poem – in the middle of this discussion is not entirely coincidental, of course. To this extent, chance may well be objective, as the surrealists supposed:

> It is the avowed aim of the surrealist movement to reduce and finally to dispose altogether of the flagrant contradictions that exist between dream and waking life, the 'unreal' and the 'real', the unconscious and the con-scious, and thus to make of what has hitherto been regarded as the special domain of poets, the acknowledged common property of all. So far as the surrealists themselves are either writers or painters, it is also at the same time their aim to extend indefinitely the limits of 'literature' and 'art' by continually tending to do away with the barrier that separates the contents of the printed page or of the picture-frame from the world of real life and of action.
>
> (Gascoyne 1936: x)

The surrealist technique was the dialectical route of passing beyond false binary opposi-tions of life and art, reality and dream, or even text and context. The disciplined act of contextualizing, explicit, aware, scientific, receptive, and moving between text and context, is the future ground of real stylistics.

References

Balakian, A. (1967) *Literary Origins of Surrealism: A New Mysticism in French Poetry*. London: London University Press.

Balakian, A. (1970) *Surrealism: The Road to the Absolute* (revised edition) [original 1959]. London: George Allen and Unwin.

Bex, T., Burke, M. and Stockwell, P. (eds) (2000) *Contextualised Stylistics*. Amsterdam: Rodopi.

Carrouges, M. (1968) 'Le hasard objectif', in F. Alquié (ed.) *Le Surréalisme*, Paris: Mouton, pp. 269–78.

Cruse, D. (1986) *Lexical Semantics*. Cambridge: Cambridge University Press.

Culpeper, J., Short, M. and Verdonk, P. (eds) (1998) *Exploring the Language of Drama: From Text to Context*. London: Routledge.

Dali, S. (1936) *Conquest of the Irrational* (trans. D. Gascoyne). London/Paris: Julien Levy.

Gascoyne, D. (1936) *A Short Survey of Surrealism*. London: Cobden-Sanderson (reprinted 1970, London: Frank Cass).

Germain, E.B. (ed.) (1978) *Surrealist Poetry in English*. Harmondsworth: Penguin.

Motherwell, R. (1951) *The Dada Painters and Poets*. New York: Wittenborn Schulz.

Read, H. (ed.) (1936) *Surrealism*. London: Faber and Faber.

Rubin, W.S. (1968) *Dada, Surrealism, and Their Heritage* (exhibition catalogue). New York: Museum of Modern Art.

Schwarz, A. (1969) *The Complete Works of Marcel Duchamp*. New York: Harry M. Abrams.

Short, R. (1980) *Dada and Surrealism*. London: Laurence King.

Tashjian, D. (1975) *Skyscraper Primitives: Dada and the American Avant-Garde 1910–1925*. Middle-town, CT: Wesleyan University Press.

Verdonk, P. (ed.) (1993) *Twentieth Century Poetry: From Text to Context*. London: Routledge.

Verdonk, P. and Weber, J.-J. (eds) (1995) *Twentieth Century Fiction: From Text to Context*. London: Routledge.

Waldberg, P. (1965) *Surrealism*. London: Thames and Hudson.

Extracted from Peter Stockwell (2000) '(Sur)real stylistics: from text to contextualizing', in T. Bex, M. Burke and P. Stockwell (eds) *Contextualized Stylistics*, Amsterdam: Rodopi, pp. 15–38.

Chapter 21

Feeling moved by metaphor

RAYMOND W. GIBBS JR

Raymond Gibbs is a psychologist rather than a stylistician, but this chapter reflects the increasing interest each field has in the other's work. Psychologists and cognitive scientists have become interested in the affective values that readers attach during literary reading, and stylistics has been able to expand its repertoire of analytical tools in the form of *cognitive poetics*. Here, Gibbs demonstrates the continuities between the ways that people express their emotional lives through both creative and conventional metaphor and the use of metaphorical expression in poetic texts.

For more on the intersections between cognition, psychology and literary linguistics, see Emmott (1997), Semino and Culpeper (2002), Stockwell (2002, 2008), Gavins and Steen (2003) and Bortolussi and Dixon (2003).

Metaphor and poetry

METAPHOR HAS A SPECIAL ability to evoke deep emotional responses and elevate the human spirit. A wonderful example of this is provided by the American poet Allen Ginsberg, who was most famous for his work in the 1950s and 60s as part of the 'beat' movement in American poetry and literature. In the 1960s, Ginsberg recounted his most powerful aesthetic experience in reading poetry. When he was a student back in the 1940s, Ginsberg was lying in bed in his New York apartment on a hot summer afternoon reading the work of William Blake. At one point. Ginsberg reports that he suddenly just knew that it was the voice of Blake himself coming to him across the vault of time. The Blake poem Ginsberg was reading is titled 'Ah Sunflower' (Blake 1982).

> Ah, Sunflower, weary of time,
> Who countest the steps of the sun,
> Seeking after that sweet golden clime
> Where the traveller's journey is done;

Where the youth pined away with desire,
   And the pale virgin shrouded in snow,
Arise from their graves and aspire
   Where my Sunflower wishes to go!

Ginsberg described his immediate experience after reading this poem in the following way: 'The peculiar quality of the voice was something unforgettable because it was like God had a human voice, with all the infinite tenderness and mortal gravity of a living Creator speaking to his son' (Ginsberg 1966: 38). Ginsberg had this immediate, deep understanding that he was the sunflower, and that bright sunlight day on the grimy rooftops of New York outside his window was the 'sweet golden clime' itself. Ginsberg said: 'My body suddenly felt light, and a sense of cosmic consciousness, vibrations, understanding, awe, and wonder and surprise . . . Kind of like the top of my head coming off, letting in the rest of the universe connected to my own brain' (Ginsberg 1966: 40).

Ginsberg's poetic experience was not centred on metaphor alone, but Blake's metaphors took centre stage in Ginsberg's emotional, aesthetic response to 'Ah Sunflower!'. In essence, Ginsberg's account of being moved by metaphor is beautifully captured by an aphorism created by another great American poet, Wallace Stevens: 'Reality is a cliché from which we escape by metaphor' (Stevens 1954). Ginsberg was clearly transformed when reading Blake, almost as if he was escaping from clichéd reality.

My experience as a metaphor (and poetry) enthusiast mirrors in smaller ways the kinds of emotional transformations that Ginsberg felt. I believe, following Stevens, that metaphor can move us to consider ideas that seemingly depart from aspects of our everyday reality. Yet I have also come to believe, paradoxically, from years of research in the field of experimental psycholinguistics that Stevens' expressed belief about metaphor as an escape from reality is quite wrong. There is sufficient evidence to conclude that people's ordinary understanding of many aspects of everyday language is itself constituted by metaphorical schemes of thought (Gibbs 1994). These metaphorical concepts explain why we create and indulge in language that is seen by many as clichéd, conventional, or idiomatic. In this way, metaphor reflects important aspects of mundane reality and is not merely an escape from ordinary thought and reality. Our use of metaphor does not signify an unworldly transcendence from ordinary language, thought, or reality. Instead, what is most clichéd and conventional about reality are those aspects of experience that are primarily constituted by metaphorical thought.

But how do we describe our felt experiences of being moved by metaphor? If metaphor is really a fundamental part of everyday cognition, what makes it appear as a special type of language that emotionally moves us in the ways it often does? I argue in this [chapter] that metaphor is fundamental to our cognitive understanding of emotions and that our emotional experiences are inherently structured by metaphor. Moreover, we respond aesthetically and emotionally to metaphor as a felt sense of embodied movement. This sensation of the body in action has both depth and texture. I describe linguistic analyses in support of these ideas and present some preliminary empirical evidence that suggests the importance of embodied movement in our appreciation of poetic metaphor.

[. . .]

The importance of emotional movement

What does it mean to say that reading or hearing metaphor 'moves' us in some way? Why do we talk about emotional reactions in terms of 'being moved'? The word emotion is derived from the Latin *e* (out) and *movere* (to move). The emphasis on movement in emotion is a recurrent theme. Arnold and Gasson (1954: 294) suggest 'that an emotion or an affect can be considered as the felt tendency toward an object judged suitable, or away from an object judged unsuitable, reinforced by specific bodily changes according to the type of emotion'. Adler (1931: 42) defined emotions as 'psychological movement forms, limited in time'. Having an emotion may clearly involve some sense of bodily movement.

Most cognitive theories admit that an important body component in the emotion process is the readiness to take action (Lazarus 1991, Oatley 1992). This readiness to act is closer to a corporeal, felt urge to do something – approach someone, strike something or someone, touch something, run away from something or someone, etc. Emotion is not identical to simple action like kicking, embracing, running etc., but reflects a change in postural attitude, or an affective sense of such action (Sheets-Johnstone 1999).

One early study surveyed people about their sense of movement when thinking of different emotion terms (Manaster, Cleland and Brooks 1978). Participants rated their felt movement (i.e., either toward others or away from others) for 140 emotion terms. The results showed that there were a group of 20 emotions words which tend to move people toward others (e.g., *love*, *jolly*, *affectionate*, *sexy*, *confident*, *sentimental*), and another group of 20 emotion words that moved people away from others (e.g., *hate*, *humiliated*, *sulky*, *bitter*, *guilty*, *aggravated*). Findings such as these support the idea that the primary feeling of having an emotional experience is that of being moved. Each emotion reflects different, sometimes subtle, bodily movements. We may at times experience some emotion as passively being moved rather than as moving ourselves.

In cases when we do not move our bodies, we feel our emotions as if something within us has moved (De Rivera 1977). The experience of embodied movement is especially salient when we are emotionally engaged in the world, whether or not we are self-consciously aware of that engagement. The fundamental relation between embodied action and emotion is captured by the idea that to 'be moved' refers to feeling as if one is in a different position in regard to one's situation. Emotional experience involves our perceptible sense of meaningful change in a situation and in ourselves under some circumstance. Emotions arise as we become displaced and dislocated to another position in adaptive response to some situation. We cannot experience emotions without some sense of movement, distance, and depth.

For instance, when people feel joy, they have re-positioned themselves as being *on top of the world*, or when they feel emotionally troubled, then they experience a burden *on one's shoulders*, when there is a downward turn of the body as the head drops and the person slouches. Feeling superior to another makes us feel as if we are *looking down* on that person, or that they are *beneath us*. Feeling admiration for another makes us *look up* at that person. When I feel overwhelmed, the world seems too close, suffocating me. Being in love suggests a closeness or proximity to our loved one, while hatred repositions us away from others. When I feel lonely, I experience my body as separated from others. When undergoing an emotional experience, we feel as if we are in the grasp of an emotion that we are being swept away by its hold and force. Cognitive linguistic studies on the metaphorical nature of emotion talk illustrate the importance of movement in people's emotional experiences. For instance, Kövecses (2000a, 2000b) provides numerous examples of how emotions are understood as forces that appear to change people's embodied positionings. Consider some of these conceptual metaphors, and relevant linguistic examples, that are specific instantiations of the generic-level EMOTION IS FORCE metaphor:

EMOTION IS AN OPPONENT
He was *seized* by emotion.
He was *struggling* with his emotions.
I was *gripped* by emotion.
She was *overcome* by emotion.

EMOTION IS A WILD ANIMAL
His emotions *ran away with* him.
She kept her emotions *in check*.
He couldn't *hold back* his feelings.

EMOTION IS A SOCIAL FORCE
He was *driven by* fear.
His whole life was *governed by* passion.
He was *ruled by* anger.

EMOTION IS A NATURAL FORCE
I was *swept off my feet*.
I was *overwhelmed* by her love.

EMOTION IS A MENTAL FORCE
Our emotions often *fool* us.
His emotions *deceived* him.
She was *misled by* her emotions.

EMOTION IS INSANITY
She was *beside herself with* emotion.

EMOTION IS PHYSICAL AGITATION
The speech *stirred* everyone's feelings.
I am all *shook up*.
He was slightly *ruffled by* what he heard.
The children were *disturbed by* what they saw.

EMOTION IS A PHYSICAL FORCE
When I found out, it *hit me hard*.
That was *a terrible blow*.
She *knocked me off my feet*.
They *gravitated toward each other* immediately.

I was *magnetically drawn to* her.
I am *attracted to* her.
That *repels* me.

These different conceptual metaphors together paint a picture of the most pervasive folk theory of the emotion process in English (Kövecses 2000b): (1) cause of emotion – force tendency of the cause of emotion – (2) self has emotion – force tendency of emotion – (3) self's force tendency – emotion's force tendency – (4) resultant effect. This schema reflects our basic understanding of emotions as different physical/embodied forces interacting with one other.

Our way of characterizing the felt dimension of emotional experience is in terms of 'affective space', or the space we move through as we experience distinct emotions. This idea of affective space is nicely illustrated by considering how we hesitate in advancing when worried, gently blossom when in love, distinctly loiter about when sad or depressed, or suddenly burst forward when feeling outraged. Affective space has a sensuous feel to it, a texture that makes it neither purely mental, nor reducible to the physiological body.

[. . .]

Moving through affective space has a textured, palpably felt dimension, just in the way that we can feel different textures of substances we touch with our skin. Physical substances we touch have a depth to them, and this is precisely why our emotions are also experienced at different levels of depth. The language people use to talk about the nuances of their emotions reveals important aspects of the textured, in-depth feel of different emotions. Consider some of the felt textures associated with different emotions (Cataldi 1996). For example, when feeling very frightened, we feel our bodies to be frozen solid, almost petrified, we radiate with love or bask in pride, or drown in sorrow, or effervescently bubble over in happiness, or blissfully walk on air in joy, or wallow in self-pity, or cautiously tread on pins and needles when feeling apprehensive. We feel steamy when lustful, we feel dry, stifled, and stale when bored. Yet being serene feels smooth, while gratitude has a plush, or lavish feel. When we are simply worn out, we may feel affectively stuck in some situations, as when we are in a pinch or a jam.

[. . .]

Most generally, each emotion is distinguishable by skin-deep textures that are felt when we move through affective space. Furthermore, the greater the emotional extreme, the more depth we feel in our textured experiences. For example, an irritable situation may feel sticky to us, which in turn requires that we handle this with a gentle touch or special handling. Other times, the heat of an emotion leaves us feeling burned. Unemotional persons are rigid, or stiff. Cruel individuals are hardened, calloused, or cold-blooded.

An emotion may have distinctive kinetic forms that are dynamically congruent with it, but these forms are not identical with the emotion. We may distinguish between an emotion, in terms of its affective feel and any postural attitudes it exhibits, and the actual kinetic form that manifests the emotion. People may corporeally experience an emotion, even though the actual body movement does not occur. Thus, people may inhibit the movement associated with an emotion if necessary. We may learn to mentally simulate our actions – move quickly, move our arms around, get red in the face, and so on, without physically engaging in these actions. In this way, emotions are kinaesthetic or potentially kinaesthetic, and what is kinetic may be affective or potentially affective (Cataldi 1996, Sheets-Johnstone 1999).

[. . .]

Studies on movement and poetic metaphor

Recent empirical studies support the claim that people experience felt movement when using and reading metaphors in discourse. The first project along this line examined the embodied metaphors six women employed in their narratives about their experiences with cancer (Gibbs and Franks 2002). Six women in recovery from different forms of cancer were interviewed and asked to talk about their learning that they had cancer, their treatment and subsequent recovery. These interviews lasted from 20–35 minutes. Overall, the women produced 796 individual linguistic metaphors (an average of 132 metaphors per person). These diverse linguistic metaphors were structured by just 22 conceptual metaphors, such as CANCER IS AN OBSTACLE ON LIFE'S JOURNEY and EMOTIONAL EFFECT IS PHYSICAL IMPACT. 77% of the women's metaphorical language reflected embodied metaphors in the sense that the source domains (e.g., obstacles on life's journey) involved some aspect of recurring sensori-motor experience. For example, the women employed language like *to get through, to get over* something, and talked of *to move into a new space*. One woman commented that *having cancer was like walking off the face of the earth*. A different woman described her cancer experience in the following manner: *When people say that the world is round it is a lie. It's flat and I know what the edge looks like*. Another woman noted that *cancer is something that pulls you back to the core of life itself*, and another said that *cancer forced me to begin stripping away a lot of things that don't matter*. Finally, one woman talked of her experiences in particularly poetic terms when she personified cancer as a dance partner: *I felt like my spirit was able to sing again and that I had taken off the cloak of disease – that I had been carrying this cloak of disease for about six months and that in dancing I had taken it off and my spirit was singing again*. Note the skin-like quality of the emotional experience mentioned here as the woman soon learned to take off *the cloak of disease*.

These brief examples illustrate the power of embodied metaphor in women's understanding of their cancer experiences. Most notably, these instances show the primacy of the body in movement through affective space in people's descriptions of their emotions. A separate analysis revealed, in fact, that 82% of the language these women used to talk about emotions involved embodied movement as a textured experience. These findings provide support for the claim that our emotions are often experienced, even if metaphorically, in terms of the body in action.

A different empirical project examined people's emotional reactions to poetic metaphors (both literary and non-literary) (Gibbs 1999). My interest here was to see whether people responded emotionally to poetic metaphors in terms of a felt sense of embodied movement that has both texture and depth. Reading metaphors in poetry often generates a cerebral satisfaction. But reading poetic metaphor also creates a bodily reaction that feels deeply aesthetic. A.E. Houseman illustrated the physicality of poetry with power and humour in the following passage (Houseman 1981: 123):

Poetry indeed seems to me more physical than intellectual. A year or two

ago I received from America, in common with others, a request that I would
define poetry. I replied that I could no more define poetry than a terrier
could define a rat but that I thought we both recognize the object by the
symptoms which it provokes in us . . . Experience has taught me, when I am
shaving in the morning, to keep watch over my thoughts, because if a line of
poetry strays into my memory, my skin bristles so that the razor ceases to
act. This particular symptom is accompanied by a shiver down the spine.
There is another which consists in a constriction of the throat, and precipita-
tion of water to the eyes. And there is a third which I can only describe by
borrowing a phrase from one of Keats' last letters, where he says, speaking
of Fanny Brawne, 'everything that reminds me of her goes through me like a
spear.' The seat of this sensation is in the pit of the stomach.

Houseman's statement nicely illustrates the power of poetry to move us as readers, and
this felt sense of movement is quite visceral, and not purely intellectual. I have recently
begun a research project examining college students' felt sense of emotional movement
when reading poetic metaphors. Students were presented with mixed lists of metaphors
(both literary and non-literary – taken from Katz, Paivio, Marschark and Clark 1988),
and non-metaphorical paraphrases of these statements. Presented below are examples of
these stimuli.

Literary Metaphors

> Man is a *leaf in the garden of God.*
> The soul is *a rope that binds heaven and earth.*
> Clouds are *weavers of the sky.*
> Water is *the blood of soft snows.*
> Love is *the star guiding every wandering ship.*
> Hope is *a green log on the fire.*
> Man is *the wandering outlaw of his own dark mind.*

Non-Literary Metaphors

> The creative mind is *a kettle on the stove.*
> Dictionaries are *microscopes of words.*
> Ritual is *the prison of individuality.*
> Conscience is *a thorn in the mind.*
> Beggars are *the tapeworms of the city.*
> A liar's tongue is *a spear of distrust.*
> Television is *the aspirin for boredom.*

Literary Paraphrases

> Man is *a small part of God's creation.*
> The soul *connects the physical to the spiritual.*
> Clouds *embellish the appearance of the sky.*
> Water is *the essence of soft snows.*
> Love *gives direction to one's life.*

Non-Literary Paraphrases

> The creative mind is full of ideas.
> Dictionaries tell you what words exactly mean.
> Conscience can distress the mind.
> Beggars are the plight of the city.
> A liar's words cannot be trusted.
> Television alleviates boredom

Students were presented with a booklet containing 24 statements (6 literary meta-phors, 6 non-literary metaphors, 6 literary paraphrases, and 6 non-literary paraphrases). An individual student only received either a metaphor or its specific paraphrase. Across the entire experiment, equal numbers of participants saw all the metaphors and para-phrases. In the experiment, a statement (either metaphor or paraphrase) was presented at the top of each page. Participants were instructed to closely read the statement and to then provide ratings for the following claims. First, students were asked to rate, on a 7-point scale, whether *You feel some emotional reaction to the statement*. Following this, students rated whether *You feel some strong sense of your emotional body* in each of the following ways: (a) moving toward someone or something, (b) moving away from someone or something, (c) expanding (i.e., growing larger or outward), and (d) con-tracting (i.e., growing smaller or inward). Again, students gave their ratings on a 7-point scale. Next, participants were asked whether *You feel an emotional texture* along the dimensions of (a) smoothness – roughness, (b) cold – hot, and (c) superficial – depth. Once more, students gave their ratings to each question along 7-point scales. Finally, participants were asked whether *You feel differently about the main topic of the statement having read the statement*. These ratings were also given on a 7-point scale.

My interest was to see if there were differences in the ratings for the two kinds of metaphors, and between the metaphors and paraphrases. Preliminary data analysis revealed that there were few differences overall in people's felt emotional reactions to the two types of metaphors. This finding is not too surprising given that the non-literary metaphors seem particularly apt and reasonably poetic, even if they originated in non-literary sources (e.g., newspapers, magazines, and essays). Both kinds of metaphor were equated in terms of their comprehensibility and imageability (as determined by the ratings provided by Katz et al. (1988).

But there were important differences in the ratings for the metaphors and the paraphrases. These differences are best captured by a series of correlations on students' ratings for the different questions. Overall, for both literary and non-literary metaphors, not for their respective paraphrases, there were significant positive correlations between

a)   emotional reaction and movement toward topic
b)   emotional reaction and felt bodily expansion
c)   emotional reaction and felt texture of depth
d)   movement toward a topic and felt texture of depth
e)   a topic and felt texture of smoothness
f)   movement away from a topic and felt texture of roughness.

These correlation patterns suggest that people appear to experience a greater sense of emotional movement that has both texture and depth when reading the two kinds of metaphors than they did when reading non-metaphorical paraphrases.

Consider just a few instances of these findings by reading several metaphor–paraphrase pairs. When people read *Dew is the last gold of perished stars* and *Dew is the last product of dead stars*, they experienced more felt bodily heat for the metaphor and more felt texture of depth for the metaphor than for the paraphrase. Similarly, when reading the metaphor–paraphrase pair *Water is the blood of soft snows* and *Water is the essence of soft snows*, people felt the same overall emotional reaction for both statements, but much more felt bodily heat for the metaphor, more felt texture of depth for the metaphor, and felt more differently about the topic (i.e., water) for the metaphor than for the paraphrase. For the pair *Thunderclouds are wild horses galloping across the sky* and *Thunderclouds move loudly across the sky*, people experienced more movement toward topic (i.e., thunderclouds) for the metaphor and more felt texture of depth for the metaphor than for the paraphrase. Finally, when reading the statements *The creative mind is a kettle on the stove* and *The creative mind is full of ideas*, people experienced much more emotional reaction to the metaphor, more felt bodily expansiveness for the metaphor, more felt texture of depth for the metaphor, and felt more differently about the topic having read the metaphor than when they saw the paraphrase.

In general, although these data are preliminary, they support the claim that people feel more subjective emotional movement reading poetic metaphors than they did reading non-metaphorical paraphrases of these statements. Future research will be directed to extending these findings by altering participants more explicitly to their felt embodied experiences of movement, depth, and texture, before offering their ratings to different metaphors and paraphrases.

Conclusion

My long-term interest as a psychologist and metaphor scholar is to explore the embodied foundation of human thought and language. Recognizing how our linguistic and non-linguistic symbols are grounded demands that we explicitly explore the connections between meaningful patterns of language use and recurring patterns of embodied experience in people's everyday lives. My work thus far suggests that emotion is conceived of, and experienced in terms of embodied movement through affective space in dimensions that are textured and have depth. Furthermore, our experiences of understanding and appreciating metaphoric talk and literature involves the felt sensations of being 'moved' which are neither purely mental nor physiological but some interaction of the two. We may actually move our bodies at times when experiencing different emotions (e.g., our facial displays, our gestures, our entire bodies). Yet even when our bodies are still, we may nonetheless experience simulated action as an essential part of the emotional process. This felt sense of movement is readily experienced when we encounter metaphorical language (or art).

References

Adler, A. (1931) *What Life Should Mean to You*. New York: Blue Ribbon Books.
Arnold, M. and Gasson, J. (1954) *The Human Person*. New York: Ronald Books.

Blake, W. (1982) *The Complete Poetry and Prose of William Blake* (ed. D. Erdman). Berkeley: University of California Press.

Bortolussi, M. and Dixon, P. (2003) *Psychonarratology*. Cambridge: Cambridge University Press.

Cataldi, S. (1996) *Emotion, Depth, and Flesh*. Albany: State University of New York Press.

De Rivera, J. (1977) *A Structural Theory of the Emotions*. New York: International Universities Press.

Emmott, C. (1997) *Narrative Comprehension*. Oxford: Clarendon Press.

Gavins, J. and Steen, G. (eds) (2003) *Cognitive Poetics in Practice*. London: Routledge.

Gibbs Jr, R.W. (1994) *The Poetics of Mind: Figurative Thought, Language, and Understanding*. New York: Cambridge University Press.

Gibbs Jr, R.W. (1999) *Intentions in the Experience of Meaning*. Cambridge: Cambridge University Press.

Gibbs Jr, R.W. and Franks, H. (2002) 'Embodied metaphor in women's narratives about their experiences with cancer', *Health Conununication* 14 (2): 139–65.

Ginsberg, A. (1966) 'The art of poetry VIII: interview with Allen Ginsberg', *Paris Review* 37: 13–55.

Houseman, A.E. (1933) *The Name and Nature of Poetry* [original lecture 1933]. New York: Macmillan.

Katz, A., Paivio, A., Marschark, M. and Clark, J. (1988) 'Norms for 204 literary and 260 nonliterary metaphors on 10 psychological dimensions', *Metaphor and Symbolic Activity* 3: 191–214.

Kövecscs, Z. (2000a) *Metaphor and Emotion*. New York: Cambridge University Press.

Kövecscs, Z. (2000b) 'Force and emotion', in L. Albertazzi (ed.) *Meaning and Cognition*, Amsterdam: Benjamins, pp. 145–68.

Lazarus, R. (1991) *Emotion and Adaptation*. New York: Oxford University Press.

Manaster, G., Cleland, C. and Brooks, J. (1978) 'Emotions as movement in relation to others', *Journal of Individual Psychology* 34: 244–53.

Oatley, K. (1992) *The Best Laid Schemes: The Psychology of Emotion*. New York: Cambridge University Press.

Semino, E. and Culpeper, J. (eds) (2002) *Cognitive Stylistics*. Amsterdam: Benjamins.

Sheets-Johnstone, M. (1999) *The Primacy of Movement*. Amsterdam: Benjamins.

Stevens, W. (1954) *The Collected Poems of Wallace Stevens*. New York: Vintage.

Stockwell, P. (2002) *Cognitive Poetics*. London: Routledge.

Stockwell, P. (2008) *Texture*. Edinburgh: Edinburgh University Press.

Extracted from Raymond W. Gibbs (2002) 'Feeling moved by metaphor', in S. Csábi and J. Zerkowitz (eds) *Textual Secrets: The Message of the Medium*, Budapest: Eotvos Lorand University, pp. 13–28.

Chapter 22

Point of view in drama: a socio-pragmatic analysis of Dennis Potter's *Brimstone and Treacle*

DAN McINTYRE

In spite of its success with poetry and prose texts, stylistics has only recently discovered adequate models for the analysis of drama. In the past, there have been too many factors to take into account, which meant that stylisticians often had to ignore performance in favour of playtext, or treat the script as an idealisation of a performance when drawing on pragmatic and sociolinguistic frameworks of language use in context. Dan McIntyre here returns to useful work on point of view in order to present a rigorous analysis of Dennis Potter's play. Of course, this also leads the discussion into a stylistic engagement with the notion of character, which is another area in which stylistic attention has recently produced useful work.

McIntyre's (2006) book develops the themes of this chapter. For more on the stylistics of drama, see Short (1996), Culpeper *et al.* (1998) and the chapters on drama in Lambrou and Stockwell (2007). See also this volume, chapters 9, 11 and 19.

Introduction

I**N THIS ARTICLE I** suggest that applying theories of point of view to written dramatic texts can be profitable for understanding characterisation, and also that studying viewpoint in drama might lead to a greater appreciation of how point of view is conveyed linguistically in texts. I demonstrate this through a socio-pragmatic analysis of Dennis Potter's play *Brimstone and Treacle*, showing how the viewpoints of the characters in the text are manifested linguistically, and how the linguistic indicators of point of view in drama go beyond those associated with narrative fiction.

[. . .]

Chatman's approach to point of view

Chatman's work on point of view (1978, 1986, 1990) provides a useful starting point for an analysis of viewpoint in drama, primarily because he develops his model through an analysis of both prose fiction and film. It is thus one of the few theories of point of view to take account of drama as well as prose, albeit drama on screen. (Of course, the differences between drama on stage and screen are significant, but for my purposes, the fact that point of view had been studied in relation to drama at all was helpful.)

Chatman (1990: 143) proposes that it is necessary to make a terminological distinction within prose fiction between the point of view of the narrator and the point of view of the character. He suggests the term *slant* to refer to attitudes expressed by the narrator, and *filter* to refer to the mental activity of the characters (see Sasaki 1994, for a synopsis and application of Chatman's approach to a short story by D.H. Lawrence).

Chatman's distinction allows for the possibility of examining point of view as filtered through particular characters, and in non-narrative drama it seems likely that this will be the most prevalent form of viewpoint expression. Nevertheless, slant can still be an issue in drama and is expressed most obviously through stage directions. Not all stage directions will indicate point of view, but some will contribute to the manifestation of viewpoint, as in the following example from Howard Brenton's [1982] play, *Hitler Dances*:

> **Linda** (*very angry stamping her foot*) Stupid! *Stupid*! I think that's jus' *stupid*. War is *stupid*.
>
> (Brenton 1982: 9)

In the above example, the stage directions preceding Linda's speech contribute to the characterisation of Linda at that particular moment in the play, by emphasising her point of view of events. However, since the stage directions do not come from the character, they cannot be seen as filtered point of view; rather they are an instance of *slanted* point of view. The propositional content of Linda's speech, and its graphological characteristics (i.e. the italicisation) also contribute to our understanding of the character of Linda, demonstrating how both filtered and slanted point of view can often go hand in hand to work as a tool for characterisation. Any model of point of view in drama, then, must also take slant into consideration, and I demonstrate this in my analysis [. . .].

Subsumed under the *filter* category, I also find it useful to add two point of view categories suggested by Chatman in his earlier work (1978). These are the categories of *perceptual* and *conceptual* point of view, *perceptual* relating to sight, and *conceptual* relating to cognition.

Perceptual point of view is a literal viewpoint; i.e. exactly that which a character physically sees. Wales (2001: 306) notes that this refers to an 'angle of vision'. In drama, characters' perceptual viewpoints can be important contributions to their characterisation. Weingarten (1984) discusses one such example in his analysis of Antonio Buero Vallejo's *La Fundacion*, a play about five political prisoners being held in a death cell, one of whom has been so completely broken by torture and his subsequent betrayal of his comrades that he has convinced himself that the prison is actually a research laboratory, and that he and his fellow prisoners are research workers. Weingarten's discussion focuses on how the playwright limits the perceptual point of view within the play to that of the deluded prisoner, Tomás, to such an extent that when the curtain rises, the audience sees not a prison cell, but a well furnished dormitory room, reflecting Tomás' perception of his surroundings.

A character's *conceptual* point of view, on the other hand, has no relation to what he or she physically sees, but is rather a manifestation of his or her ideology, attitudes, way of thinking etc., as this extract from *All Quiet On The Western Front* shows:

> The front is a cage in which we must await fearfully whatever may happen. We lie under the network of arching shells and live in a suspense of uncertainty.
>
> (Remarque 1987: 70)

Here the protagonist, a young German soldier in the First World War, explains his notion of the trench warfare and front line fighting in which he is engaged. Note that there is no mention of what he physically sees, no verbs of perception related to sight, only a manifestation of his attitude to the subject. This is apparent through his use of the adverb of manner 'fearfully', and in the negative connotations of the word 'cage' which he uses to describe the front metaphorically. A cage is often used to keep an animal against its will, and it is this definition which seems most likely and allows us to interpret the above extract most clearly. The use of metaphor also suggests that what is being described is something which cannot be explained in purely literal terms (note the narrator's second metaphor, that he lives in 'a suspense of uncertainty'), which in turn suggests that we are not dealing with physical perception.

We can see how conceptual viewpoint can be conveyed in drama if we consider the following brief extract from Dennis Potter's play [*Brimstone and Treacle*], where one character's point of view is filtered through another:

> [CONTEXT: Mr Bates is trying to explain to his wife, Amy, that their daughter, Patricia, is permanently brain-damaged and will not recover.]

> **[71] Bates** Patricia is gone from us, Amy. She has gone forever. You must accept it.
>
> (Potter 1978: 3)

Here, information about Amy Bates is filtered through Bates' own speech, namely the presupposition that she does not accept that Patricia 'is gone'. So in addition to Bates' own point of view of the situation (that it is a hopeless case) we also know something about his wife's conceptual viewpoint.

Conceptual point of view, in Chatman's terms, is a wider category of figurative viewpoint than Fowler's (1986) notion of *ideological* point of view. Ideological point of view deals with socio-political beliefs whereas Chatman's category is used to describe our numerous figurative conceptions and judgements of the world, and our way of conceptualising the world and our position within it. Conceptual point of view would appear to incorporate ideological viewpoint. I therefore adopt the term *conceptual point of view* in my analyses.

In my analysis I concentrate mainly on those points of view filtered through the characters; it is likely that filtered viewpoint is the most prominent point of view type in non-narrative drama. However, I also take into consideration slanted point of view, since this too can affect characterisation, as we have already seen. In addition I consider both conceptual and perceptual point of view, in order to take into account the variety of means by which viewpoint can be expressed in drama, and the effects on characterisation that this has.

Linguistic indicators of point of view

[. . .]

Short (1996) discusses point of view at the micro-level by considering those elements of a text which indicate viewpoint. Short collates these into a checklist of linguistic indicators of point of view in prose fiction. I find this approach useful since it allows us to start with the text itself, rather than trying to impose the pre-defined, large-scale categories suggested by, for example, Uspensky (1973) and Fowler (1986). This is of particular importance when attempting to study point of view in drama, since it is by no means clear that Fowler's categories will work on dramatic texts (certainly, the categories he uses to describe different types of narrators are unlikely to fit, since these have been developed exclusively through the analysis of prose texts). There is also the problem that Fowler's categories do not allow for cases where point of view continually shifts within a text.

Short (1996) explains that the following will indicate viewpoint in prose fiction texts: (i) schema-oriented language, (ii) value-laden expressions, (iii) given versus new information, (iv) verbs and adverbs of perception, cognition and factivity, (v) deixis, and (vi) event-coding. These are explained with examples from both prose fiction and drama in McIntyre (1999), but a short example here, from *Richard III* [I.ii.94], will show how Short's categories might usefully be employed in the study of drama. The following is an example of value-laden expressions indicating viewpoint:

[CONTEXT: Lady Anne, widow of Edward, Prince of Wales, is responding to Richard's assertion that he did not kill her husband.]

Anne In thy *foul* throat thou liest: Queen Margaret saw thy *murd'rous* falchion smoking in his blood[.]

(Shakespeare 1993, my italics)

The italicised words in the above example are instances of what Short refers to as value-laden language. Language that is value-laden expresses something about the speaker's attitude to that which is described or perceived. Value-laden language will thus reveal something about a dramatic character's conceptual point of view. In the above example, this would be that Lady Anne believes that Richard did actually kill her husband (implicated by the value-laden adjective 'murd'rous'), and that he is a repugnant character (implicated by the negative connotations of the adjective 'foul'). There are, of course, other viewpoint indicators in this extract. For example, the term 'smoking' is, in this instance, a value-laden metaphor charged with negative connotations.

[. . .]

An analysis of point of view in *Brimstone and Treacle*

Like many of Dennis Potter's works, *Brimstone and Treacle* is a deeply disturbing play with a strong element of black humour. It concerns a typically suburban couple, Tom and Amy Bates, and their struggle to care for their daughter Pattie, the victim of a road accident which has left her paralysed and in a near vegetative state. The tension in the household is almost tangible. Mr Bates is angry, disturbed and resigned to the fact that his daughter will never recover. Mrs Bates is deeply sad yet utterly convinced that Pattie will get better, that her constant prayers will be answered. Both are exhausted though with the pressure of caring for their now mentally handicapped child, and the strain is beginning to affect their own relationship.

Then one night a character called Martin arrives at the Bates' house claiming to be an old friend of Pattie's. Martin explains that he had been in love with Pattie and had asked her to marry him. Pattie, however, had been unsure and had asked Martin for a period of separation in order for her to make a decision. Martin agreed and went to America to work, where he subsequently lost contact with her.

Martin, unsurprisingly, is not all that he seems. He is, or at least believes himself to be, a demon of sorts. Mr Bates immediately makes apparent his mistrust of the seemingly too-good-to-be-true visitor, though Mrs Bates is touched by Martin's apparent devotion to their daughter. Martin asks to stay the night in order to ease their burden of caring. Mrs Bates is thrilled at the prospect and, reluctantly, Mr Bates agrees. Martin appears to be the perfect guest, and even offers to look after Pattie the following day so that Mrs Bates is able to go out. Once she has gone though, Martin's true character is revealed and he rapes the helpless Pattie. Mr and Mrs Bates return to find Martin preparing dinner. Mrs Bates is overcome with emotion and thanks God for sending Martin to them. She also notices that Pattie seems suddenly more alert.

Martin agrees to stay longer, despite Bates' misgivings. That night, when the couple have gone to bed, Martin attempts to rape Pattie a second time. This time though, she screams, awakening Mr and Mrs Bates. In a panic, Martin rushes out, leaving the Bates' to comfort their daughter. Pattie then speaks and asks what has happened. Mr and Mrs Bates sob with relief. It appears that Martin's sexual assault has somehow 'cured' their daughter. Pattie then remembers the events and screams out as the lights go down and the play ends.

The play is undoubtedly controversial in the issues it raises. Potter, however, saw it as a religious drama parodying 'particular forms of faith' and suspected that had Martin been characterised as an angel, the play would not have met with so much disapproval (Potter 1978: iv). In the extracts quoted, stage directions are indicated by italic type.

[What follows is] an analysis of filtered and slanted conceptual and perceptual points of view in *Brimstone and Treacle*. Limitations of space necessarily mean that this analysis cannot extend to the whole play, and so I have chosen representative sections to illustrate the points I am making. In the course of my analysis I also relate my findings with regard to viewpoint to the play as a whole, and consider the dramatic consequences of the exhibition of particular points of view. I begin by considering evaluative lexis as an indicator of point of view in the text.

Using Short's (1996) checklist of linguistic indicators of point of view, it is also relatively straightforward to spot examples of the expression of viewpoint, as can be seen in the following example:

[CONTEXT: Bates has become angry at what he sees as societal problems in England. Encouraged by Martin, he begins a tirade of abuse.]

[211] **Bates** There'll always be an England. Ha! Not with the buses stinking of curry and half the cities full of coloured men, there won't!

[212] **Martin** Deport them, that's what I say. Every nation has a right to defend its own culture. That's always been so. England for the English, I say. It's only a slogan, of course, but slogans are the salt of action. They quicken the mind and sharpen the resolve.

Bates looks at him with a new respect.

(Potter 1978: 31)

The negative connotations of the participle 'stinking' in turn 211 suggest Bates' opinion of what he is talking about is also negative. This is further confirmed by the logical presupposition inherent in the utterance. Bates begins the turn with a declarative ('There'll always be an England') and then imposes a condition (that this will not be so if the buses 'stink' of curry and the cities are filled with coloured people). The progressive participle 'stinking' suggests that this particular action is ongoing, with the consequent logical implication that there will not 'always be an England'. And Bates' discriminatory attitude suggests that, to him, this is something to be regretted. In addition to the negatively-charged lexis in Bates' turn, we can also note the hyperbole in what he says. Van Dijk (1991: 192), in his discussion of what he terms 'semantic strategies' in racist language notes that hyperbole is a common feature of this type of discourse. In this example we also find slanted point of view, exhibited in the stage direction. This also suggests that Bates is respectful of Martin's point of view, the consequence of this being that Bates implicates himself with the same point of view. The conceptual point of view he is exhibiting, then, is one of racist intolerance.

We can also notice the presence in this example of what Fowler (1986) calls 'generic sentences', which can indicate point of view. These are 'generalized propositions' (Fowler 1986: 167), such as Martin's statement in turn 212 that slogans 'quicken the mind and sharpen the resolve'. Arguably, this further reveals Martin's particular ideology and contributes to our construction of his character. Turning again to van Dijk's (1991) work on racist language, we can also note that Martin adopts the semantic strategy of 'mitigation and excuse' (van Dijk 1991: 190), justifying his explicitly racist outburst by his explanation that 'every nation has a right to defend its own culture'. Following this, we find negatively-charged lexis coming from Martin in turn 289:

[289] **Martin** Camps. Any camps for the time being. Oh, think of it! Hundreds of people. No, thousands of people. Hundreds of thousands. Millions. Rounded up from their stinking slums and overcrowded ghettos. Driven into big holding camps, men, women, piccaninnies. Oh, you'll hear de calypso then all right. You'll hear de darkies sing! You'll see England like it used to be again, clean and white. They won't want to go – dey won't want to, massa! – So we'll have to push them and prod them and hunt them down. They'll *fight*, so we shall have to shoot them and C. S. gas them and smash down their doors. Eh? Eh? Put barbed wire round them. Searchlights on the corners. Eh?

He is rocking with glee.

Think of all the *hate* they'll feel! Think of all the hate we'll feel when *they* start killing us back. Think of all the violence! Think of the pain and the de-gred-at-ion and in the end, in the end, the riots and the shooting and the black corpses and the swastikas and the . . .

(Potter 1978: 33)

Here again we can notice evaluative lexis ('stinking slums', piccaninnies', 'darkies', 'ghettos') and also a number of terms with negative connotations – for example, 'rounded up', 'barbed wire' and 'searchlights'. There is also a conventionalised association in the line, 'You'll hear de darkies sing', arising from the non-standard definite article, suggesting that at this point Martin affects a stereotypical Black English accent. This too has consequences both in terms of the viewpoint Martin is expressing and his perception of the relationship between himself and Mr Bates. Martin's adoption of a stereotypical Black English/Caribbean vernacular (also suggested by the hyphenation in 'de-gred-at-ion') is an instance of metaphorical code-switching (Blom and Gumperz 1972). This type of code-switching is characterised by the use of non-standard language to signal an in-group relationship between conversational participants. As Blom and Gumperz (1972: 425) say, 'this may, depending on the circumstances, add a special social meaning of confidentiality or privateness to the conversation'. Martin's motivation for doing this is likely to be a desire to foster a close relationship between himself and Mr Bates, in order to ingratiate himself with the family and thereby create the opportunity to assault Pattie. The success of this strategy depends largely on Martin establishing common ground and consensus between the conceptual viewpoints that he and Mr Bates express, the results of which can be seen towards the end of the play.

This, the implied excitement through the use of exclamation marks, and the slanted point of view in the stage directions telling us that Martin is 'rocking with glee', all combine to convey the impression that Martin is enjoying his 'vision'. It may, of course, be the case that this is not Martin's actual viewpoint, but one that is affected for strategic reasons. It is possible that Martin's hysteria is brought on in part by what he perceives to be the success of his own strategy. This interpretation is supported by the fact that in turn 291, when Bates interrupts him to shout, 'No! Stop it!', Martin is able to immediately break off from his tirade to ask, 'No?'. If turn 289 represented his actual conceptual viewpoint, we would perhaps expect him to go on defending it, even after Bates' interruption. Further support for this interpretation can be found in the fact that Martin does not attempt to mollify what he is saying through the use of particular semantic strategies, such as those discussed by van Dijk (1991: 180–98). Nevertheless, the conceptual point of view expressed is, of course, inherently racist, and the fact that it may not be entirely genuine would suggest that Martin is deliberately trying to provoke a reaction from Bates. In this case, the metaphorical code-switching may be seen as a contributory factor in this attempt, Martin guessing that Bates will reject the closeness between participants that such a strategy assumes.

The use of evaluative lexis to express a particular viewpoint, such as can be seen in the above extracts from *Brimstone and Treacle*, is generally what we might expect to find in conversation. Of more interest, perhaps, are those elements of the text which require more explanation than lexical features alone can provide, which I discuss next.

[. . .]

If we now move on to consider in more detail how the Bates' express their *conceptual* points of view with regard to their daughter's vegetative condition, it becomes clear their notion of what it is to be co-operative in a conversational exchange highlights some of the problems with [the classic] Gricean theory [of the co-operative principle: Grice 1975]. In the following extracts, Mr and Mrs Bates are debating the severity of Pattie's condition:

[30] **Mrs Bates** (*to Mr Bates*) Oh, please. It upsets Pattie when you raise your voice.

[31] **Bates** (*quieter*) Don't be foolish. Don't say things like that. How – how can she tell when . . . (*But his voice trails off as Pattie turns her head and seems to look at him.*)

[32] **Mrs Bates** She knows what goes on. I keep trying to tell you.

[33] **Bates** (*staring at her, frightened*) Of course she doesn't –

[34] **Mrs Bates** She knows when you are angry. And she knows when I am sad.

[35] **Bates** (*hiss*) That's not possible –

[36] **Pattie** Mmmm mmmmm kh.

[37] **Mrs Bates** Listen to her then. She's trying to talk. She is, Tom. I don't care what you say.

Bates stares at her, then twists his head away.

[38] **Pattie** Ooo oooh!

[39] **Bates** But that's – terrible. What you are saying is – horrible. If she responds to our moods and therefore in some sense understands – God above, is it possible that she c . . . comprehends more than she can communicate – ?

[40] **Mrs Bates** Yes, I'm sure of it.

[41] **Pattie** Yaaa!

Pause.

[42] **Bates** (*whisper*) That is too much to bear. (*Loudly*) Horrible. Horrible. Horrible!

[43] **Mrs Bates** No, Tom. It's a sign of improvement. It shows that things are going on inside her. The doctors don't know everything. They're not right all the time. She's getting better!

(Potter 1978: 2)

Fourteen of Mrs Bates' utterances are declaratives. All contain factive verbs in the present simple tense, suggesting that the statements she makes are 'eternal' truths. We can also note, then, that all the above turns comply within the Maxim of Quality ['be truthful'] as Mrs Bates understands it. Mrs Bates cannot possibly be certain that Pattie comprehends her own situation, yet her constant use of factive present simple verbs suggests that this is indeed what she genuinely believes to be the truth. This is an important issue for the analysis of point of view; characters adhering strictly to the Maxim of Quality can be said to be expressing an explicit *conceptual* viewpoint. However, this does highlight one of the inherent problems with Gricean theory, namely that Grice does not take into account the fact that different speakers may have different notions about co-operation within a conversational exchange. In Gricean terms, Mrs Bates is being maximally co-operative since she is complying with the Maxim of Quality. How-ever, Mr Bates has an entirely different notion of what it is to do this. This is expressed in turn 35 when he says, 'That's not possible'; in Bates' view, by saying this, he is comply-ing with the Maxim of Quality, despite the fact that this viewpoint is the direct opposite of what Mrs Bates has just suggested. Bates uses exactly the same strategies as his wife for expressing viewpoint. Turns 31, 33 and 35, for example, all comply with the Maxim of Quality as Bates understands it; they are expressions of what he believes to be the actual situation. He is, then, expressing his point of view in the same way as Mrs Bates does in turns 30, 32, 34, 37 and 43. His statement to Mrs Bates, 'Don't be so foolish', implies that he believes her *conceptual* point of view to be 'foolish', which in turn indicates that he rejects the notion of Pattie's point of view being the same. He confirms this in turn 33 by stating what he actually believes. Again, the declarative structure and the present simple factive verb (the anaphoric reference to *know* in turn 32) suggest that this is the 'truth' as he believes it. And the fact that it is not possible for him to say for certain that Pattie does not comprehend the world around her, leads us to also conclude that he is making an assumption of her *conceptual* point of view. Mr Bates is also expressing his *conceptual* point of view by stating that of another character.

We can also note, then, that being conversationally co-operative does not always result in a harmonious exchange. The important issue for our purposes is that an adherence to the Maxim of Quality can be seen as indicative of a character's *conceptual* point of view, with regard to what they believe to be the truth. This is an issue which relates to work that has been carried out within sociology on the subject of differing notions of reality. Harris (1984: 18), in a paper exploring the use of questions as controlling devices in magistrates' courts, explains that speakers can begin an inter-action from 'radically different perspectives of reality'. Her data focuses on interactions between magistrates and defendants, concerning the payment of fines, and she notes that the different perspectives from which the interactants start might be characterised as 'two separate paradigms of reality which all too often are in contradiction' (1984: 19). Archer (2002) adopts the term 'reality paradigms', and applies the notion in a socio-pragmatic analysis of the Salem witchcraft trials, noting that '(1) interlocutors operate out of and filter information about their world[s] through particularised "perspectives of reality", and that (2) these "perspectives" can and do clash' (Archer 2002: 20). It appears that this is very much what the characters of Mr and Mrs Bates do in *Brimstone and Treacle*. Mr Bates refuses to believe that Pattie will recover, whereas Mrs Bates is firmly convinced that this is the case. The reality paradigms within which they operate, then, are 'does not believe' and 'believes', respectively. And this, obviously, has ramifications for what these characters take to be the truth. It seems to be the case that whenever characters' reality paradigms clash, we encounter dramatic discord (as in turns 30 to 43 above). Similarly, when characters' reality paradigms correspond with each other, then we see dramatic harmony, as in Bates' and Martin's turns below:

[CONTEXT: Bates has just told several jokes at the expense of the Irish.]

[264] **Martin** Mind you, the Irish are beyond a joke. Have a drop more. And you, Mumsy.
[265] **Bates** Thank you.
[266] **Mrs Bates** I feel a bit squiffy already! (*But she tosses it back again.*)

[267] **Bates** I agree with you there, Martin. A quarrelsome lot of thick drunks. There's far too many of 'em over here in the land they're supposed to hate. Ship them back, I say, and the sooner the better. Bombs and all.

[268] **Martin** Them, and the blacks.

[269] **Bates** *Especially* the blacks. Send them back to their own countries.

(Potter 1978: 32)

It is at this point in the play that Bates begins to accept Martin, having previously been wary of his presence. It appears that this is due in part to the fact that both he and Martin are expressing conceptual viewpoints which are roughly the same. In effect they are both operating within the same reality paradigm that might be characterised as 'ethnic minorities are a social problem'. Although it may seem rather obvious that Martin and Bates hold this view, the significance lies with the fact that this shared reality paradigm allows the two characters to establish common ground. It is significant, too, that this consensus occurs in Act Four, towards the end of the play, as this corresponds, albeit ironically, with the Aristotelian notion of resolution following complication in terms of plot structure.

[. . .]

References

Archer, D.E. (2002) 'Can innocent people be guilty? A sociopragmatic analysis of examination transcripts from the Salem witchcraft trials', *Journal of Historical Pragmatics* 3 (1): 1–31.

Blom, J.-P. and Gumperz, J.J. (1972) 'Social meaning in linguistic structures: code-switching in Norway', in J.J. Gumperz and D. Hymes (eds) *Directions in Sociolinguistics: The Ethnography of Communication*, Oxford: Basil Blackwell, pp. 407–34.

Brenton, H. (1982) *Hitler Dances*. London: Methuen.

Chatman, S. (1978) *Story and Discourse: Narrative Structure in Fiction and Film*. Ithaca, NY: Cornell University Press.

Chatman, S. (1986) 'Characters and narrators: filter, center, slant, and interest-focus', *Poetics Today* 7 (2): 189–204.

Chatman, S. (1990) *Coming to Terms: The Rhetoric of Narrative in Fiction and Film*. Ithaca, NY: Cornell University Press.

Culpeper, J., Short, M. and Verdonk, P. (eds) (1998) *Exploring the Language of Drama: From Text to Context*. London: Routledge.

Fowler, R. (1986) *Linguistic Criticism*. Oxford: Oxford University Press.

Grice, H.P. (1975) 'Logic and conversation', in P. Cole and J.L. Morgan (eds) *Syntax and Semantics 3: Speech Acts*, New York: Academic, pp. 41–58.

Harris, S. (1984) 'Questions as a mode of control in magistrates' courts', *International Journal of the Sociology of Language* 49: 5–27.

Lambrou, M. and Stockwell, P. (eds) (2007) *Contemporary Stylistics*. London: Continuum.

McIntyre, D. (1999) 'Towards a systematic description and explanation of point of view in dramatic texts, with special reference to Dennis Potter's *Brimstone and Treacle*', unpublished MA dissertation, Lancaster University.

McIntyre, D. (2006) *Point of View in Plays*. Amsterdam: John Benjamins.

Potter, D. (1978) *Brimstone and Treacle: Theatre Script with Introduction*. London: Eyre Methuen.

Remarque, E.M. (1987) [1929] *All Quiet on the Western Front*. London: Pan.

Sasaki, T. (1994) 'Towards a systematic description of narrative "point of view": an examination of Chatman's theory with an analysis of *The Blind Man* by D. H. Lawrence', *Language and Literature* 3 (2): 125–38.

Shakespeare, W. (1993) [1623] *Richard III*. Ware: Wordsworth.

Short, M. (1996) *Exploring the Language of Poems, Plays and Prose*. London: Longman.

Uspensky, B. (1973) *A Poetics of Composition*. Berkeley: University of California Press.

Van Dijk, T. (1991) *Racism and the Press*. London: Routledge.

Wales, K. (2001) *A Dictionary of Stylistics* (2nd edition). London: Longman.

Weingarten, B.E. (1984) 'Dramatic point of view and Antonio Buero Vallejo's *La Fundacion*', *Hispanic Journal* 5 (2): 145–53.

Extracted from Dan McIntyre (2004) 'Point of view in drama: a socio-pragmatic analysis of Dennis Potter's *Brimstone and Treacle*', *Language and Literature* 13 (2): 139–60.

Chapter 23

Conrad in the computer: examples of quantitative stylistic methods

MICHAEL STUBBS

The use of computers and the new research opportunities offered by large databases of language are revolutionising applied linguistics in the same way that the invention of the portable tape-recorder did in previous decades. Many stylisticians have been instrumental in developing these new technologies to produce a sophisticated *corpus stylistics*. It is interesting that such paradigm-turns in the field continue to generate new answers to similar questions that were posed for stylisticians in the early days of the discipline, concerning interpretation, the status of analysis and the nature of textual evidence. In this chapter, Michael Stubbs uses the occasion of an analysis of Conrad's *Heart of Darkness* as an opportunity for addressing those issues afresh. For further work in the field, see Adolphs (2006), Semino and Short (2004), Sinclair (2004) and Hoover *et al.* (2008).

T HIS ARTICLE APPLIES QUANTITATIVE methods of text and corpus analysis to a stylistic interpretation of Joseph Conrad's *Heart of Darkness*. I will try to bear in mind two criteria for computer-assisted methods which were set out very clearly by Kenny (1992): they must provide results which would be impossible to obtain without a computer, and they must be respected as an original scholarly contribution within literary studies. In the early 1990s, Kenny could find only a 'sadly small' number of studies which contain 'solid results obtained by techniques for which the computer is indispensable'.

Stylistics has long led an uneasy half-life, never fully accepted, for many related reasons, by either linguists or literary critics. Linguists are often sceptical of stylistics because they are less interested in explaining particular individual texts than in developing general theories, and there is no convincing theory of text-types within which a theory of literary texts might be situated. However, individual texts can be explained only against a background of what is normal and expected in general language use, and this is precisely the comparative information that quantitative corpus data can provide. An understanding of the background of the usual and everyday – what happens millions of times – is necessary in order to understand the unique. Literary scholars are often sceptical about reductionist claims that statistics can define a literary style or contribute to a literary interpretation. Further, even if stylistic analyses of poems are accepted as complementing other methods of close reading, these methods seem unworkable for novels. However, individual hermeneutic methods also simplify, and quantification can make more explicit the evidence on which interpretations are based. Sometimes it is useful to reduce huge amounts of information to simple summaries ('All Jane Austen's novels are social satires about courtship and marriage'), but sometimes detailed statistics are required to reveal 'hitherto inaccessible regions of the language [which] defy the most accurate memory and the finest powers of discrimination' (Burrows 1987: 3).

In a notorious attack on quantitative procedures, which has never been fully answered, Fish (1996) accuses stylistics of being 'circular' and 'arbitrary', of relying on selective attention to data, and of being caught in a logical dilemma. Either we select a few linguistic features, which we know how to describe, and ignore the rest; or we select features which we already know are important, describe them, and then claim they are important. Since a comprehensive description is impossible, and since there is no way to attach definitive meanings to specific formal features, stylisticians are apparently caught in a logical fork (which I will call the Fish Fork). Yet even if quantification only confirms what we already know, this is no bad thing. Indeed, in developing a new method, it is perhaps better not to find anything too new, but to confirm findings from many years of traditional study, since this gives confidence that the method can be relied on. I will return below to a very simple response to the Fish Fork: namely that it applies to any study of anything.

[. . .]

I will certainly not argue that a purely automatic stylistic analysis is possible. The linguist selects which features to study, the corpus linguist is restricted to features which the software can find, and these features still require a literary interpretation. However, since authors express their ideas through language, software can identify textual features which are of literary significance, including features which critics seem not to have noticed. In addition, as Sinclair (1975) argues, there is a serious gap in linguistic theories if they cannot explain the language of those texts which have the highest literary and cultural prestige.

[. . .]

Joseph Conrad's *Heart of Darkness* is a very short novel, of less than 40,000 words. It was published in 1899 in magazine instalments, then in 1902 in book form. [. . .] A hundred years after its publication, it is still possibly 'the most commonly prescribed novel in . . . literature courses . . . in American universities' (Achebe 1988). [. . .] Yet, despite extensive critical discussion, there is surprisingly little work on the book's linguistic style. [. . .]

The narrative of *Heart of Darkness* is embedded in different frames:

1. The book starts with an unnamed narrator on a boat on the Thames.
2. Marlow becomes the narrator, and talks about the Thames in Roman times.
3. Marlow tells of his visit to a European city.
4. Marlow tells the story which takes up most of the book: he travels up a river in Africa in search of an ivory trader called Kurtz. He finds him, but Kurtz dies on the trip back down river.
5. Marlow tells of his visit to Kurtz's fiancée back in the European city.
6. [There is nothing corresponding to frame 2, but some vocabulary from frame 2 is repeated in frame 7.]
7. The book ends with a paragraph from the unnamed narrator back on the Thames.

Marlow's boat trip turns into his obsession with Kurtz, a trader who has been stealing ivory from the inhabitants of the region. He has apparently gone mad, is worshipped as a god by the native population, seems to have an African mistress, and may have been implicated in cannibalism.

[. . .]

Given the extensive criticism of the book, we cannot approach it as naive readers (though the software can). There is considerable consensus among critics about major leitmotifs and themes, including the hypocrisy of the colonizers, and breakdown as a symbol of the unreliability of progress and civilization. Marlow's boat keeps breaking down, the colonial outposts are littered with *decaying machinery* (p. 22), Kurtz has a mental breakdown, and there are breakdowns in communication: people speak different languages, Marlow tells a lie about Kurtz to Kurtz's fiancée, and amongst the most frequent content words in the book is the lemma *SILENCE* <freq 37> [angled brackets denote frequencies]. Other major themes are conveyed by repeated lexical contrasts, especially light and dark, restraint and frenzy, appearance and, reality. There are frequent references to dreams (p. 48), nightmares (p. 100), trances (p. 56), phantoms and apparitions (pp. 85, 87, 105, 110) and visions (p. 105), and Marlow has trouble maintaining *contact with reality* (pp. 19, 54). Critics point out that Conrad uses these contrasts to question whether 'heart of darkness' refers to 'darkest Africa', as the stereotype has it, or rather to the immorality of the white colonialists. In fashionable modern terminology, Conrad deconstructs the often taken-for-granted oppositions, white–black and good–bad. For readers around 1900, there would have been intertextual references to the books *Through the Dark Continent* and *In Darkest Africa*, published in 1878 and 1890 respectively, by Henry Morton Stanley (the Stanley who 'found' David Livingstone). The frequent contrasts of light and dark may also have recalled Genesis 1:1 to 1:5.

[. . .]

Vague impressions and unreliable knowledge

A further major theme of the book is Marlow's unreliable and distorted knowledge. Marlow himself never quite understands (and readers never quite find out) what *monstrous passions* (p. 95) and *vile desires* (p. 105) Kurtz has indulged. Conrad writes that an unnamed narrator says that Marlow says that an unnamed Russian says that Kurtz has talked to him: but we never discover what Kurtz has said. At the end of a series of story-tellers who quote story-tellers, nothing reliable remains. Kurtz dies uttering the words *The horror! The horror!* but we never find out what that refers to: perhaps that Kurtz is now horrified by what he himself has done? [. . .]

The unnamed narrator in the outside frame comments ironically that *we knew we were fated [. . .] to hear about one of Marlow's inconclusive experiences* (p. 10). Leavis (1962: 180) thought that Conrad simply didn't know what he wanted to say. [. . .] However, Watt (1988) argues that lack of clarity is part of the point of this impressionist and early modernist story. He points out that mist or haze is a persistent image, and words from this lexical field are frequent in the book (in total almost 150, well over one per page on average):

- blurred 2, dark/ly/ness 52, dusk 7, fog 9, gloom/y 14, haze 2, mist/misty 7, murky 2, shadow/s/y 21, shade 8, shape/s/d 13, smoke 10, vapour 1

Marlow is frequently looking into a fog, uncertain of what he is seeing. Things are constantly *in a muddle* and *chaos* (p. 26). Unexplained things happen: a man hangs himself for no apparent reason (p. 21). As he approaches Kurtz, Marlow is confused by signs and symbols that he cannot decode: a faded message on a board which is difficult to *decipher* (he cannot read its *illegible signature* at all, p. 53); a book with strange writing in the margins which he thinks is *cipher* (it turns out to be Russian, pp. 54, 78); round carved balls on posts (which turn out to be *symbolic*: when he looks at them more carefully through a telescope, he sees that they are human skulls, pp. 75, 82); and a figure dressed as a harlequin (p. 75), who is *improbable, inexplicable, and altogether bewildering* (p. 78). Literary critics tend to identify a few content words, such as *fog* and *mist*, *vague* <5> and *indistinct* <4>:

- I saw <u>vague</u> forms of men
- Marlow ceased, and sat apart, <u>indistinct</u> and silent

However, they tend to ignore the many grammatical words denoting vagueness and uncertainty. The word *something* occurs over 50 times, in expressions such as:

- I don't know – <u>something</u> not quite right
- reminded me of <u>something</u> I had seen – <u>something</u> funny

There are over 200 occurrences of *something, somebody, sometimes, somewhere, somehow* and *some*, plus around 100 occurrences of *like* (as preposition), plus over 25 occurrences of *kind of* and *sort of*, all often collocated with other expressions of vagueness:

- the <u>outlines</u> of <u>some sort of</u> building
- seemed somehow to throw <u>a kind of</u> light
- I <u>thought</u> I could see <u>a kind of</u> motion
- <u>indistinct</u>, <u>like a vapour</u> exhaled by the earth . . . <u>misty</u> and silent

If we add all this to occurrences of *seemed* <ca 50>, words expressing vagueness are very frequent <ca 385>: well over three per page. Here are simple comparative frequency statistics for vague words, normalized to occurrences per 1000 running words.

HEART = Heart of Darkness.
FICTION = a corpus of fictional texts of over 710,000 words. [. . .]
WRITTEN = the one-million-word written component of the BNC [British National Corpus] sampler.

	(1) HEART	(2) FICTION	(3) WRITTEN
some	2.6	1.5	1.5
something	1.3	1.0	0.4
somebody	0.2	0.1	0.05
sometimes	0.6	0.2	0.2
somewhere	0.2	0.2	0.03
somehow	0.2	0.1	0.04

Frequencies are consistently higher in HEART than in FICTION, and higher in FICTION than in WRITTEN.

Some (very) simple frequency data

Textual frequency is not the same as salience, and does not necessarily correspond to what readers notice and remember in a text. This is one clear limitation on studies which look only at the words on the page, and I will show below that word-frequency lists have other severe limitations.

Neverthless, there must be some relation, even if indirect, between frequent vocabulary and content, and frequency lists are one essential starting point for a systematic textual analysis. A list of the most frequent lexical words (i.e. excluding very high frequency grammatical words) in *Heart of Darkness* does not initially look very promising:

- said 131, like 122, man 111, Kurtz 100, see 92, know 87, time 77, seemed 69, made 65, river 65, came 63, little 62, looked 56, men 51, Mr 51, long 50

Using 'keywords' software (Scott 1997), we can also check which words are both frequent in *Heart of Darkness* and also significantly more frequent than in a reference corpus (again the 'imaginative prose' [fiction] corpus defined above). These are all the content words among the top 50 keywords, which both occur 20 times or more in the novel and are also significantly more frequent than in the reference corpus (listed in descending frequency in the novel):

- Kurtz 100, seemed 69, river 65, station 48, great 46, manager 42, earth 39, ivory 31, pilgrims 31, darkness 25, bank 25, forest 23, wilderness 22, Kurtz's 21, cried 20

Frequent nouns may indicate superficial topics in a text (*Kurtz, river*), but not its underlying themes: this is not a book 'about' a river. Verbs are often a better candidate for stylistically relevant words. So, we can also use software to lemmatize the text and list the top 10 verb lemmas:

- SAY, SEE, LOOK, KNOW, COME, MAKE, SEEM, HEAR, TAKE, THINK

Now, the most frequent word-form of all (*said*) and the most frequent verb lemma (SAY) are of course very frequent in fiction in general, and the mental verbs (*see, know, looked*, etc.) are also usually frequent in fictional texts (for quantitative data, see Stubbs and Barth 2003). However, other words are of more interest: many occurrences of *like* <ca 100> and of *looked* <ca 25> are in vague expressions such as 'x was like y' and 'x looked like y' or 'it looked as though'. This implies that we must look not just at individual words, but at their recurrent phraseology: see below.

Although such lists might seem to offer only the crudest kind of content summary, note for the present that SEEM is among the top words in all three lists, and that several words in the lists concern uncertainty, perception and knowledge. This statement clearly involves a subjective interpretation of potential literary significance, but the statement is based on objective textual features.

Word distribution and text structure

The first reason why counting individual words is certainly not sufficient is that the interesting content words are not (by definition) evenly distributed across the text, but are clustered at different places. For example, some words (e.g. *Buddha*) occur only in the opening and closing narrative frames (pp. 10, 111) and are thus used to mark text structure. The book starts on the Thames, describes a journey up the River Congo (unnamed), and ends back on the Thames. At the beginning and the end we have:

- the Thames . . . a <u>waterway leading to the uttermost ends of the earth</u> (pp. 5–6) . . . <u>Marlow sat</u> cross-legged . . . he had the pose of a <u>Buddha</u> . . . we felt <u>meditative</u> (pp. 6, 10).
- <u>Marlow</u> . . . <u>sat</u> apart . . . in the pose of a <u>meditating Buddha</u> (p. 111) . . . the tranquil <u>waterway leading to the uttermost ends of the earth</u> (p. 111, last sentence).

At the beginning, Marlow visits a city like a *whited sepulchre* (p. 14). He enters offices, past *high houses* in a *narrow and deserted street*, through *doors standing ponderously ajar*. In the offices a *door open[s]* (p. 14). At the end, back in the *sepulchral city* (p. 102), he visits Kurtz's Intended through a *ponderous door, between tall houses* in a street as quiet as *a cemetery*. In the Intended's house is a piano like a *sarcophagus*. A *high door open[s]* and the Intended comes in (p. 105). This verbal trick is also used to express Marlow's similarities to Kurtz: both are described as a *voice* (pp. 39, 67, 69, 86) and as an *idol* (pp. 6, 84).

Such distributional facts, which start to say something about the structure of the whole text, can be tracked with a simple program. For example, the words *heart, dark* and *darkness* occur throughout the book, but increase in frequency at the very end when the story almost becomes *too dark – too dark altogether* (p. 111). Similarly, the lemmas DREAM <15> and NIGHTMARE <6> are very differently distributed. DREAM occurs twice at the very beginning, then several times in a cluster, when Marlow is *trying to tell* his dream (p. 39), then fairly regularly throughout the rest of the story. NIGHT-MARE occurs once at the beginning, where there are *hints for nightmares* (p. 21), and then in a cluster towards the end (ca p. 95), all in collocations with *Kurtz*. In terms of word distribution, Marlow's dream turns into a nightmare.

The verb lemma KNOW is frequent <122>, and fairly evenly distributed throughout the text. Many instances are negative, either grammatically (*I don't know*, *he did not know*) or by implication (*he wanted to know*, *if only he had known*). This is a novel about the fallibility and distortions of human knowledge. Right at the end, there is a cluster of positive examples: Kurtz's Intended repeats over and over that

- I alone <u>know</u> how to mourn for him . . . I am proud to <u>know</u> I understood him better than any one . . . You have heard him! You <u>know</u>! . . . You <u>know</u> what . . .

The irony is of course that she knows nothing of what Kurtz has done. (On how patterns of lexico-grammar can express the 'fallibility of human knowledge', see also Hardy and Durian 2000.) These examples show how the distribution of individual words can be studied, but require (as Fish 1996 would doubtless point out) that the analyst knows beforehand which words might be of interest.

Text and inter-text

The second reason why studying only individual words in the text is inadequate is that any text makes references to other texts. Allusions to the Aeneid, to the figures of the Fates in Greek mythology, to Dante's depiction of hell, and to the Faust legend are discussed in detail by Lothe (2000, 2001). [. . .]

The frequent references to fools <*fool, foolish* 18> and to madness and insanity <*mad, madness, insanity* 11> can also be taken as allusions to the Ship of Fools, the medieval satire on vices and follies. [. . .] As critics have pointed out (e.g. Dorall 1988, LaBrasca 1988), the themes of carnival, insanity and the ship of fools are perhaps even more evident in *Apocalypse Now*, Coppola's film adaptation of Conrad's book.

Quotes and near-quotes from specific texts can quickly be identified by computer-assisted searches. The phrase *whited sepulchre* (p. 14), with two later references to the *sepulchral city*, is from Matthew 23:27. Other Biblical references were probably more obvious to readers around 1900. In the opening and closing paragraphs (pp. 5–6 and 111) of the book, we have the phrase

- waterway leading to the <u>uttermost</u> ends of the earth

The word *uttermost* is not frequent in general English (or in Conrad's other writings), but it is frequent <29> in the King James translation of the Bible, sometimes in the phrase *uttermost part(s)* of the earth <5>. The phrase *the ends of the earth* is also frequent <30> in the Bible. [. . .]

There are lexical allusions to Dickens's *Tale of Two Cities* (the knitters of black wool recall the women knitting at the foot of the guillotine), and to Jules Verne's *Voyage au Centre de la Terre* (Marlow sets off as if on a journey to *the centre of the earth* (p. 18); he is a *wanderer on a prehistoric earth*, as though the earth was *an unknown planet* (p. 51)). Cannibalism and atavism (the fear that 'civilized' humans could revert to a more primitive type) were something of an obsession in Victorian Britain, and crop up in various pseudo-anthropological books of the time and in novels such as R.L. Stevenson's *The Strange Case of Dr Jekyll and Mr Hyde* (1886), H.G. Wells's *The Time Machine* (1895), Bram Stoker's *Dracula* (1897) and Conan Doyle's *The Hound of the Baskervilles* (1902), all published within a few years of *Heart of Darkness* (Griffith 1995, Breuer 1999). Inter-textuality, by definition, implies that a text can be read at different levels. The women knitting black wool can be taken as merely a realist detail, but also as a reference to the Greek Fates and/or a reference to Dickens's women under the guillotine. The forest can be taken as merely an African forest and/or a reference to all the forests in which characters in folk-tales get lost.

Collocations: words and words

The third reason why individual words can only be a starting point is that collocations create connotations. For example, *grass* <freq 18> is usually associated with death, decay and desolation: it sprouts through the stones in the *city of the dead* (p. 14), and through the bones of a dead man (p. 13); old machinery is abandoned in it (p. 22). Here are selected examples (emphasis added):

ast to meet my predecessor, the	grass	growing through his ribs was
enetian blinds, a dead silence,	grass	sprouting between the stones,
upon a boiler wallowing in the	grass,	then found a path leading up
er the empty land, through long	grass,	through burnt grass, through
ically childish in the ruins of	grass	walls. Day after day, with th
layer of silver – over the rank	grass,	over the mud, upon the wall
as though he had been a wisp of	grass,	and I saw the body roll over
mit was half buried in the high	grass;	the large holes in the peake
all fours – I've got him.' The	grass	was wet with dew. I strode ra

The words GLITTER <14>, GLEAM <8>, GLISTEN <3> and GLINT <2> connote things which are ominous and dangerous: GLITTER collocates with *dark*, *sombre*, *gloom*, and the *infernal stream*; GLEAM collocates with *blood* and *fire*; people's eyes *glitter*, *glisten* and *gleam*; arrows *glint* when they are being shot at Marlow (p. 65). Some such associations are signalled explicitly in the text. In Brussels, Marlow looks at the coloured patches on a map of colonial countries (p. 14). Later, he meets the Russian harlequin figure whose clothes are covered with coloured patches (p. 75), and Marlow says:

- His aspect reminded me of something I had seen – something funny I had seen somewhere.

The connotations of individual words can be inferred from their recurrent collo-cates, but only if we know in advance which words to look at (the Fish critique again). However, software can identify clusters of words which co-collocate across the text, by recording the collocates of each word in the text within a given span, and then summing the collocates for each node-word. (On this technique, see Phillips 1985.) For example, 10 high frequency words (*the*, *of*, *and*, *to*, *a*, *in*, *that*, *is*, *was*, *it*) were deleted from the text, and collocates of all other words were recorded in a span of 10. One example of a collocational cluster which the software then identified is: *gloom*, *brooding*, *still/stillness*, *reaches* (in the sense of *the upper reaches of the Thames*), plus more marginal collocates: *sombre*, *death*, *black*, *silence*, *mysterious*.

Phraseology: words and grammar

A fourth limitation on looking at individual words is that words occur in recurrent lexico-grammatical patterns. Critics have complained that the book is repetitive: 'a bombardment of emotive words, and other forms of verbal trickery' (Achebe 1988). However, *Heart of Darkness* is not very repetitive in the sense of using the same words from a small vocabulary over and over again. We can check how many different words Conrad uses as a proportion of the total running words (that is, the type-token ratio of the text). Over the first 2,000 words, this ratio rises a little more slowly than *Middlemarch* by George Eliot, a little faster than *Oliver Twist* by Charles Dickens, and considerably faster than *Death in the Afternoon* by Ernest Hemingway, who is almost stereotypically a writer who (deliberately) uses a small vocabulary. These comparative figures are provided by Youmans (1990). So *Heart of Darkness* is well within the norms of English fiction, and this does not explain complaints about repetitiveness.

The impression of repetitiveness arises rather from Conrad's use of particular grammatical patterns, including long strings of adjectives and nouns:

- the air was warm, thick, heavy, sluggish (p. 48)
- joy, fear, sorrow, devotion, valour, rage – who can tell? (p. 52)
- was it superstition, disgust, patience, fear [. . .]? (p. 60)

He also repeatedly uses nominal groups consisting of an abstract noun (usually two abstract nouns) plus an adjective with a negative prefix:

the aspect	of an	unknown	planet
the darkness	of an	impenetrable	night
the extremity	of an	impotent	despair
the heart	of an	impenetrable	darkness
the sea	of	inexorable	time
the shape	of an	unrestful and noisy	dream
the stillness	of an	implacable	force
the test	of an	inexorable physical	necessity

When Leavis (1962) famously complains about Conrad's repetitive style, he gives the individual words *inscrutable*, *inconceivable* and *unspeakable*, but seems to miss the grammatical generalization that Conrad uses a large number of words with negative prefixes <ca 200>: two per page on average. The following are the most frequent:

- impossible/ity 12, uneasy/iness 8, unexpected/ness 7, impenetrable 6, inconceivable/ly 6, incredible 5, indistinct/ly 5, intolerable/ly 5, unknown 5, incomprehensible 4, inscrutable 4, unearthly 4, unsound 4

In addition to these 200 or so words (mainly adjectives), a further 50 end in *-less* (e.g. *colourless*, *heartless*), and there are a further 500 occurrences of *no*, *not*, *never*, *nothing*, *nobody* and *nowhere*, plus a further 50 occurrences of *without*. The total frequency of these negatives is over 800: around one in every 50 words of running text.

On interpreting patterns

Now, the difficulty, to which Fish (1996) correctly points, is to say what this pattern means. A plausible interpretation is based on presuppositions. A negative statement usually implies that a positive was expected, and many examples emphasize how alien Africa is when contrasted with things back home. If Marlow says the African coast is *featureless* (p. 19) and *formless* (p. 20), this is because we do not expect coasts to be like this. If he says *there were no villages* (p. 58) along the river, then this is because we expect villages along rivers. If the river flows by *without a murmur* (p. 38), then this is because we expect a river to make some sound. If he says that *nothing happened* (pp. 20, 111), then this is because we expect something to happen. This theme is sometimes explicit: the earth is *unearthly*, as opposed to what we are *accustomed to look upon* (p. 51); and Marlow fails to recognize the skulls on the stakes because he *had expected to see a knob of wood* (p. 82). (EXPECT <17>)

Watt argues that 'there are no negatives in nature, but only in the human consciousness' (1960: 259). Tabata (1995: 102), quoting Watt, argues that negatives signal subjectivity, and shows that Dickens's first-person narratives have many more negatives than his third-person narratives. Werth (1995) argues that the negatives in the opening of E.M. Forster's *Passage to India* signal unexpected aspects of the scene. Hidalgo Downing, quoting Werth, discusses the pragmatic function of negatives in implying more than is literally said (2000: 217): they deny expectations and challenge background propositions (2000: 223), they are a way of questioning reality and are therefore an alienation device (2000: 219, 222). Many of her comments apply to *Heart of Darkness*, where the frequent negatives represent a world which is strange, foreign, alien, contrary to cultural expectations, and *impenetrable to human thought* (p. 79). They construct a contrast between the supposedly civilized world which Marlow has left and the supposedly primitive world which he encounters. In 'An Outpost of Progress' (1898), a short story which is a precursor to *Heart of Darkness*, Conrad writes of the *vast and dark country* where the story takes place as *the negation of the habitual* and *the affirmation of the unusual*.

[. . .]

More on phraseology: recurrent word sequences

A fifth limitation of looking at individual words is that words occur in recurrent two-, three-, four- and five-word lexico-grammatical patterns which pervade the text. The top two-word sequence is of course a pair of grammatical words, *of the* <241>, which might seem of little interest, though a concordance shows that around half of the occurrences are followed by a place term: *of the forest(s)* <9>; *of the land* <9>; *of the river* <7>; *of the earth* <6>; *of the wilderness* <5>; *of the world* <5>; *of the stream* <4>; etc. This is three to four times higher than in a large corpus of general English.

The top two-word sequence which contains a content word is *seemed to* <46>: it occurs every couple of pages on average. Now *seemed* has risen right to the top of a frequency list.

	(1) HEART	(2) FICTION	(3) WRITTEN
seemed to	1.2	0.4	0.09

The top four-word sequences relate to the central themes of geographical and psychological space, appearance and reality, and Marlow's uncertainty about everything. The complete list of four-word sequences which occur more than five times each is

it seemed to me	7
as far as I	6
as though I had	6
with an air of	6
the depths of the	6

The first four concern uncertainty and the fifth is a place expression. We can also identify more abstract phrasal frames. These sequences each occur individually more than once, and differ in only one word from other sequences:

the bottom	of the	
the depths	of the	
the edge	of the	
the face	of the	
the middle	of the	
the midst	of the	
the recesses	of the	
the rest	of the	<total freq 26>
as though I	had	
as though he	had	
as though it	had	
as though they	had	<total freq 15>
I don't know how		
I don't know I		
I don't know what		
I don't know why		<total freq 10>

These phrasal patterns both contribute to the feeling that the text is very repetitive, and also convey major themes in the text, such as Marlow's uncertainty about appearance and reality, and places, geographical and psychological. These themes are conveyed not only by words from specific lexical fields (e.g. 'fog' and 'dreams'), plus individual vague words, but also by these recurrent phrases. The observation that *Heart of Darkness* contains many negatives and many occurrences of as if and as though has been made by literary critics (Senn 1980, Stampfl 1991). I am claiming not that quantitative corpus methods produce entirely new insights into the text, but that they describe more accurately the range of lexico-grammatical patterns which Conrad uses.

[. . .]

Conclusions

An unsolved problem for stylistics is how close attention to a text can be reconciled with an understanding of its cultural and historical background. My discussion assumes that a literary text is not a self-contained autonomous object. First, all texts consist of fragments of other texts: they make references to text-types (e.g. black comedy), to other stories (e.g. the Faust legend) and to individual texts (e.g. the Bible). Second, there are no clear boundaries between a literary text and general language use. Since a text is a selection from the potential of the language, we require hermeneutic methods which identify observable evidence of meaning in the form of inter-textual relations between texts and corpora. Comparative corpus methods now allow us to study how far texts consist of recurrent phrasal patterns which are widespread in the language as a whole. In some ways, the language of *Heart of Darkness* deviates from the norm of everyday language use, but many recurrent phrases in the book are significant because they exploit the routine phraseology of the language.

An overall discourse schema in the book is Europe and Africa, the River Thames and the River Congo, light and dark, all with the much commented ambiguity between these poles:

- 'And this [= the Thames] also', said Marlow suddenly, 'has been one of the *dark* places of the earth', (p. 7)

These themes are conveyed partly by recurrent phrasal schemas which position characters and readers – depending on who they are – in the centre, on the brink, over the edge, or beyond the pale. These phrases can be used concretely and literally, but they constantly evolve – in texts and over time – into abstract and metaphorical uses, and this seems to be a linguistic universal. Does this help to explain why the book is so popular? It not only fits into widely popular text-types (e.g. adventure story) and contains repeated images from folk tales (e.g. dark forests and devils dancing by firelight) but also uses a highly frequent phraseology which reflects social obsessions and stereotypes of civilized and primitive, home and abroad, us and them, centre and periphery.

My argument might now seem to be impaled on the Fish Fork. If I had discovered that this phraseology was more frequent in *Heart of Darkness* than in general English, then I would have argued that it is interesting for *this* reason, but since I have discovered that it is a pervasive feature of general English, then I have argued that it is interesting for *that* reason. However, as I have noted above, I think there is a very simple response to the Fish Fork: it applies to any study of anything. Pure induction will never get you from empirical observations to interesting generalizations. You have to know where to look for interesting things. As Grice (1989: 173) puts it: 'you cannot ask [. . .] what something is unless (in a sense) you already know what it is'. However, this is true only 'in a sense', since the aim is to say systematically and explicitly what something is: and that is where empirical, observational analysis can contribute. It is not possible (or desirable) to avoid subjectivity, but observational data can provide more systematic evidence for unavoidable subjective interpretation.

The computer does not provide a single method of text analysis, but offers a range of exploratory techniques for investigating features of texts and corpora. The findings of corpus stylistics (comparative frequencies, distributions and the like) sometimes document more systematically what literary critics already know (and therefore add to methods of close reading), but they can also reveal otherwise invisible features of long texts. The phraseology which I have described is a formal, observable, objective feature of the book. It is only one feature, and it is open to different interpretations, but it was not created by my analysis.

References

Achebe, C. (1988) 'An image of Africa: racism in Conrad's *Heart of Darkness*', in R. Kimbrough (ed.) *Joseph Conrad: Heart of Darkness*, New York: Norton, pp. 251–62.

Adolphs, S. (2006) *Introducing Electronic Text Analysis. A Practical Guide for Language and Literary Studies*. London: Routledge.

Breuer, H. (1999) 'Atavismus bei Joseph Conrad, Bram Stoker und Eugene O'Neill', *Anglia* 117 (3): 368–94.

Burrows, J.F. (1987) *Computation into Criticism*. Oxford: Clarendon.

Dorall, E.N. (1988) 'Conrad and Coppola: different centres of darkness', in R. Kimbrough (ed.) *Joseph Conrad: Heart of Darkness*, New York: Norton, pp. 301–11.

Fish, S.E. (1996) 'What is stylistics and why are they saying such terrible things about it?', in J.J. Weber (ed.) *The Stylistics Reader*, London: Arnold, pp. 94–116 [original 1973].

Grice, H.P. (1989) 'Postwar Oxford philosophy', in *Studies in the Way of Words*, Cambridge, MA: Harvard University Press, pp. 171–80 [original 1958].

Griffith, J.W. (1995) *Joseph Conrad and the Anthropological Dilemma*. Oxford: Clarendon.

Hardy, D. and Durian, D. (2000) 'The stylistics of syntactic complements: grammar and seeing in Flannery O'Connor's fiction', *Style* 34: 92–116.

Hidalgo Downing, L. (2000) 'Negation in discourse: a text world approach to Joseph Heller's *Catch-22*', *Language and Literature* 9 (3): 215–39.

Hoover, D., Culpeper, J. and Louw, W. (eds) (2008) *Approaches to Corpus Stylistics*. London: Routledge.

Kenny, A. (1992) 'Computers and the humanities', Ninth British Library Research Lecture.

LaBrasca, R. (1988) 'Two visions of "The Horror!" ', in R. Kimbrough (ed.) *Joseph Conrad: Heart of Darkness*, New York: Norton, pp. 288–93.

Leavis, F.R. (1962) *The Great Tradition*. London: Chatto & Windus.

Lothe, J. (2000) *Narrative in Fiction and Film*. Oxford: Oxford University Press.

Lothe, J. (2001) 'Cumulative intertextuality in *Heart of Darkness*', in G. Fincham and A. de Lange (eds) *Conrad at the Millennium*, New York: Columbia University Press, pp. 177–96.

Phillips, M.K. (1985) *Aspects of Text Structure*. Amsterdam: North Holland.

Scott, M. (1997) *WordSmith Tools* (Software). Oxford: Oxford University Press.

Semino, E. and Short, M. (2004) *Corpus Stylistics. Speech, Writing and Thought Presentation in a Corpus of English Writing*. London: Routledge.

Senn, W. (1980) *Conrad's Narrative Voice*. Bern: Francke.

Sinclair, J.M. (1975) 'The linguistic basis of style', in H. Ringbom (ed.) *Style and Text*, Stockholm: Sprakforlaget Skriptov AB & Abo Akademi, pp. 75–89.

Sinclair, J.M. (2004) *Trust the Text. Language, Corpus and Discourse*. London: Routledge.

Stampfl, B. (1991) 'Marlow's rhetoric of (self-)deception in *Heart of Darkness*', *Modern Fiction Studies* 37: 183–96.

Stubbs, M. and Barth, I. (2003) 'Using recurrent phrases as text-type discriminators', *Functions of Language* 10 (1): 65–108.

Tabata, T. (1995) 'Narrative style and the frequencies of very common words', *English Corpus Linguistics* 2: 91–109.

Watt, I. (1960) 'The first paragraph of *The Ambassadors*: an explication', *Essays in Criticism* 10: 250–74.

Watt, I. (1988) 'Impressionism and symbolism in *Heart of Darkness*', in R. Kimbrough (ed.) *Joseph Conrad: Heart of Darkness*, New York: Norton, pp. 311–36.

Werth, P. (1995) 'World enough and time', in P. Verdonk and J.J. Weber (eds) *Twentieth Century Fiction*, London: Routledge, pp. 181–205.

Youmans, G. (1990) 'Measuring lexical style and competence: the type-token vocabulary curve', *Style* 24 (4): 584–99.

Extracted from Michael Stubbs (2005) 'Conrad in the computer: examples of quantitative stylistic methods', *Language and Literature* 14 (1): 5–24.

Chapter 24

'Split selves' in fiction and in medical 'life stories': cognitive linguistic theory and narrative practice

CATHERINE EMMOTT

Alongside the sort of corpus stylistics exemplified in the previous chapter, in recent years the field has been revolutionised by drawing on work in cognitive science, in the form of *cognitive poetics*. Catherine Emmott's chapter here presents the notion of 'split-selves', and demonstrates its pervasiveness and importance in literary narrative. Though her work draws on cognitive psychology in order to explore interesting literary and stylistic avenues, Emmott illustrates again in return the value of stylistics in presenting linguistic detail for psychologists and cognitive scientists.

This chapter develops Emmott's (1992, 1997) own earlier work, which was also used by Stockwell (2000, 2002). For further work in cognitive poetics, see Semino and Culpeper (2002) and Gavins and Steen (2003).

[. . .]

T HE 'SPLIT SELF' IS a pervasive theme in narrative texts. There are, of course, well-known examples such as Robert Louis Stevenson's (1995 [1886]) classic *The Strange Case of Dr Jekyll and Mr Hyde* and [numerous] modern science fiction stories [. . .]. In such texts [. . .], the split provides a key contribution to the plot of the story. Beyond this, the theme can be found in a wide range of fictional and non-fictional narratives, since it commonly occurs at times of personal crisis [. . .]. More generally, this theme reflects the sense of fragmentation of identity in postmodern society. The split might also be seen as inherent in the narrative form, since first-person narratives generally invoke a current self reporting on a past self and since breaks in narrative chronology (such as flashbacks) provide the means of juxtaposing different versions of an individual at different points in time.

In this [chapter], I explore the 'split self' phenomenon in a variety of narratives, including fictional texts and non-fictional medical 'life stories'.

The complex, multi-faceted self

[. . .]

The Cartesian dualism of mind and body has been heavily debated by philosophers for centuries and has recently been challenged by some neurologists (some of whom argue that the mind is simply a creation of the physical brain (Gazzaniga 1998)). Whether or not mental and physical dualism is an accurate physical and psychological description, there is nevertheless a 'folk notion' that we are 'inside' our bodies, hence mind-body 'split self' metaphors are common in narratives, often accompanied by the container metaphors identified by cognitive linguists. So, in Doris Lessing's (1972) *Four-Gated City*, for example, the narrator observes that:

> *Jack of ten years* ago and *Jack now* were not the same person . . . It was probable that some time while he had been ill the old Jack had simply died, or gone away, and this new person *had walked in and taken possession*. (Lessing 1972: 419–20)

This example shows a third person's perception of another's changing personality [. . .]. The notion of a new person taking possession of a body can also be used to express self-alienation. In John Braine's (1959) *Room At The Top*, the I-narrator, Joe Lampton, describes his own revulsion with the new version of himself as follows:

> I hated Joe Lampton, but he looked and sounded very sure of himself *sitting at my desk in my skin* . . . (Braine 1959: 219)

Over a stretch of narrative, Joe signals his feelings and emphasises the split by his choice of referring expressions. He uses third person tags with his own direct speech when he is making glib, heartless comments. So on hearing of Alice's death, his reaction is: ' "I expected it", Joe Lampton said soberly, "She drove like a maniac. It doesn't make it any the less tragic though." ' (p. 219). However, when Joe reacts with horror at the precise details of her death, the 'I' form is used in the speech tags: ' "Jesus Christ", I said "Jesus Christ" ' (p. 219). As in the classic 'Jekyll and Hyde' story, good and bad alternate, but here they do so in a single body.

[. . . N]on-fictional 'paralysis narratives' also make use of the 'folk notion' of a mind–body split to highlight the importance of lost bodily functions and to explore whether loss of movement leads to a corresponding loss of self. This depends on the nature of the individual injury and the personal philosophy of the writer. McCrum (1998) says that 'We live in our bodies' (p. 50, repeated on p. 149), with the very negative conclusion that 'The body fails; you fail' (p. 149) and that such bodily failure 'threatens *the flimsy edifice* that we call "the self"' ' (p. 50). It seems that in McCrum's view the individual is 'in' the body but nevertheless inextricably linked with the fate of the body. Reeve (1998) attempts to use the metaphor in a religious sense to see the spiritual dimension, but finds it difficult to match this view with the magnitude of the experiential loss of bodily contact (e.g. in considering his relations with his children and the loss of his previous sporting lifestyle):

> The sensory deprivation hurts the most . . . The physical world is still very

meaningful to me; I have not been able to detach myself from it and live entirely in my mind. While I believe it's true that we are not our bodies, that *our bodies are like houses we live in* while we're here on earth, that concept is more of an intellectual construct than a philosophy I can live by on a daily basis. (Reeve 1998: 274)

Not surprisingly, these 'paralysis narratives' often view the building metaphor as a prison rather than a house (e.g. McCrum 1998: 3 and 15). In Bauby's (1998) book, the repeated use of the prison metaphor is particularly appropriate because his condition is termed 'locked-in syndrome'. The title of his book, *The Diving-Bell and the Butterfly*, reflects this, since the 'diving-bell' is seen to hold his body prisoner (p. 11) and he is caught in an 'imprisoning cocoon' (p. 48) that encloses his mind, but from which he is sometimes able to escape 'like a butterfly' by the power of his imagination (p. 13). The metaphor is also used in an extended way throughout Bauby's narrative. For example, he describes his left eye as 'the only window to my cell' (p. 61), he views the news that he will be able to use a wheelchair as a 'life-sentence' (p. 17), wonders whether 'the cosmos contain[s] keys for opening up [his] cocoon' (p. 139) and whether he can 'buy [his] freedom back' (p. 139). The use of a particular metaphor is not always consistent though, since in Bauby's case it is sometimes the body that is the prisoner (in the 'diving-bell' example above) but sometimes the mind that is imprisoned in the body (p. 12). McCrum's use of the metaphor also varies, with the prison sometimes being the body (p. 3), sometimes ill-health (p. 15), sometimes the hospital/home (p. 108, p. 216) and sometimes misery (p. 133). It might, therefore, be better to regard these prison metaphors as simply expressing the emotional feeling of frustration rather than provid-ing a well-worked out scheme of the narrator's view of mind–body relations. To provide an overall picture, the metaphors have to be seen in conjunction with the more explicit statements in these narratives about the nature of the loss and the effect on the sense of self.

[. . .]

Social roles and imaginary selves

As many social theorists have observed, we see different aspects of the self in different social situations as we adopt different social roles in our professional and family lives (James 1910, Billington *et al.* 1998: 49–52, Bosma and Kunnen 2001). In fictional nar-ratives, characters sometimes go as far as to apply different names to different aspects of their personality, as perceived by and/or presented to others around them. In Lessing's (1972) *The Four-Gated City*, Martha creates a persona for herself whom she calls 'Matty', representing the non-conformist aspects of her personality. Similarly, in Sue Townsends (1989) *Rebuilding Coventry*, the character called Coventry has a counterpart called Lauren, who is trapped within her and signifies her rebellion against the constraints of family life:

Lauren is quarrelling non-stop with Coventry. They are both worn out . . .
Lauren has been screaming 'Let me out'. (Townsend 1989: 52)

Coventry begins not only to imagine Lauren, but to act out this identity and other

named identities too. Eventually, a single name becomes an inappropriate way of designating her, all the underlined female names in the main paragraph below co-referring to
her past identities, and the name Suzanne Lowe referring to her new identity which is
spatially separated in the aeroplane. By contrast, the 'my' in 'my children' either has to
be interpreted as conflating all these identities or must be assumed to designate either
the most recent identity, Suzanne Lowe, or her original identity, Coventry Lambert:

> I remember looking out of the little window and seeing the airport lights in
> the far distance. Somewhere, down there, were my children, preparing to
> go home. And down there with them, now left behind, were *Miss Coventry
> Lambert*, my parents' daughter; *Mrs Derek Dakin*, my husband's wife; *Margaret
> Dakin*, my son's invention; *Lauren McSkye*, Bradford Keynes's student; and
> *Jaffa*, Dodo's friend.
> 'Where are we going?' asked *Suzanne Lowe*. (Townsend 1989: 150)

The identities in the above quotation are linked to how the character is perceived and
perceives herself within specific social sub-groups and/or at different stages in the
narrative. By contrast, in Lessing's *The Four-Gated City*, Martha's sense of different
identities is more fluid, with Martha describing herself, using the container metaphors
that cognitive linguists have drawn our attention to, as sometimes giving 'house-room'
to 'Matty' (p. 15) and, conversely, Martha is sometimes 'shut inside' Matty, having
'walked in' and 'intruded' (p. 15).

In the non-fictional 'paralysis narratives', social roles are inextricably linked with
the different views of the 'self' before and after the stroke/accident [. . .]. The paralysis
of the body immediately disconnects the victim from the normal social appointments
and obligations [. . .]. The social roles discussed so far [. . .] may be partly forced on
individuals by current circumstances, but different versions of the self are also created
in the imagination in line with fears, hopes, predictions, etc. about the future (Fiske and
Taylor 1991, Weber 2000). The ability of the human mind to reflect on possible
alternative selves is particularly important in narrative texts since these 'imagined
selves' can motivate action, add to suspense and encourage strong empathy. So, for
example, when Simpson [1988] breaks his leg on the mountain, his first thought is 'I'm
dead' (p. 64). This is a prediction about a possible future self that highlights the severity
of the accident. In Labov's (1972) narrative framework, this mention of the worst
possible outcome adds to the narrative climax by showing the potential danger that the
protagonist faces. The ability of the human mind to create 'imagined selves' also means
that even a protagonist/narrator who is incapable of action can live a fantasy life. Bauby
[1998], for example, although almost entirely unable to move, imagines himself, with
deep irony, to be 'the greatest director of all time' (p. 37), a chef preparing a banquet
(pp. 44–5), a visitor to Hong Kong (pp. 111–12) and a Formula 1 racing driver (p. 125).

The changing self

On a moment-by-moment basis the human self changes so that, in certain respects, a
new version of the self is formed with every narrative action. For this reason, some
linguists suggest that readers of narratives need to create mental representations of char-
acters/individuals that are constantly updated (Brown and Yule 1983, Emmott 1997,

Culpeper 2001). Although there are constant minor changes in personality, individuals themselves nevertheless recognise the factors that remain constant and generally perceive a continuing self-identity. Memory is thought to have an important role in this respect, as does our ability to create coherent 'narratives' of our lives (e.g. Gazzaniga 1998, Bosma and Kunnen 2001).

In extreme circumstances, though, the continuity can break down. Lessing's character Matty in *A Proper Marriage* (1966, a novel in the same series as *The Four-Gated City*) experiences a rapid alternation between different selves during the pain of childbirth, caused by the fact that the cycles of pain and painlessness are so all-encompassing and so radically different experientially that she cannot even recall what the previous state felt like:

> . . . the condition of painlessness seemed as impossible as the pain had seemed only a few moments before. They were *two states of being*, utterly disconnected, without a bridge . . . *There were two Marthas*, and there was nothing to bridge them. (Lessing 1966: 163–4).

This moment-by-moment fluctuation of self during waves of pain lasting for several hours is rather different from the splitting into a 'before' and 'after' state following a major life-event (presumably, a rather different 'split-self' metaphor could be used to represent a character before and after childbirth). The physical and psychological trauma of a paralysing stroke/accident leads to much questioning of self-identity in the 'paralysis narratives', often by means of the notion of 'split selves'. McCrum, for example, frequently refers to his 'old self' or his 'lost self' in contrast to his 'new life' (McCrum 1998: 151 and 128). Bauby [1998], who can no longer speak, is dependent on his old friends to transmit an image of his past self to others ('Henceforth my life is divided between those who knew me before and all the others', p. 94). These 'split self' metaphors are re-enforced by other comments on self-identity. Everyday questions and comments suddenly acquire a deeper philosophical meaning for the stroke/accident victim. Bauby is asked on the telephone 'Are you there . . .?' and he tells the reader that at times he does not know anymore (p. 49). Likewise, the paramedics who discover McCrum after his stroke ask 'Who are you?' (p. 15) and he uses the question 'Who am I?' to structure his narrative, introducing sections of autobiographical background (pp. 23–4) and philosophical comment (pp. 190 and 215).

Although the 'split self' metaphor often sets the agenda for discussing identity, there is frequently an assertion of continuity in spite of the trauma. Sometimes, the concentration on particular social roles can provide some sense of self-identity even in the face of significant loss. Bauby, for example, spends Father's Day with his son and comments that 'a rough sketch, a shadow, a tiny fragment of a dad is still a dad' (p. 78). Reeve chooses the title *Still Me* for his book, partly providing a pun on his paralysed state, but also echoing his wife's assertion that 'You're still you' (p. 32), a comment which he repeats and uses to structure his narrative (pp. 54 and 94). McCrum's assessment of his situation is somewhat ambivalent. He says that 'At one obvious level I have changed significantly; at another I feel myself to be just that: myself' (p. 106). Indeed, in certain respects McCrum's stroke gives him a clearer perspective on his life and his convalescence period enables him to be 'alone with a rather interesting person, someone I had never spent much time alone with: myself' (p. 55). Nevertheless, the image of fragmentation still persists:

> The conundrum of stroke recovery is that while one's conscious efforts are devoted to recovering *one's lost self*, the cruel fact is that *this former self* is *irretrievably shattered into a thousand pieces*, and try as one may to *glue those bits together again*, the reconstituted version of the old self will never be better than *a cracked, imperfect assembly*, a constant mockery of one's former, successful individuality. (McCrum 1998: 151)

Generally, in these 'paralysis narratives', the question of self-identity hinges on the individual's own subjective value judgement of whether the important aspects of life remain. Furthermore, the use of the 'split self' metaphor is complicated by the fact that it may frequently be the victim's 'life' or 'world' that is described as split, rather than the self itself:

> On the evening of my collapse, I'd done something that I now think of as typical of *my 'old' life*. (McCrum 1998: 8)

> . . . how ruthlessly I had been *disconnected from the world* of appointments and obligations (McCrum 1998: 11)

> I have indeed begun *a new life*, and that life is here, in this bed, that wheel-chair and those corridors. Nowhere else. (Bauby 1998: 137)

These life/world splits may sometimes reinforce the notion of the 'split self' (e.g. McCrum 1998: 208). Conversely, on other occasions, life/world splits may allow a means of commenting on the changes in everyday circumstances (such as loss of independence and professional status, restrictions on 'taken for granted' domestic routines, and the physical confinement of a hospital bed, whilst not necessarily suggesting a break in identity).

Narrative juxtaposition

In the previous section, individuals perceived themselves to be 'split' (or considered this to be a possibility) because of a transitory sense of experiential discontinuity or because of a traumatic life change. Even where change is very gradual and not viewed as a challenge to self-identity by the individual concerned, the act of narration itself may set descriptions of different versions of an individual alongside each other and thereby provide a third person narrator and/or the reader with a salient contrast, as in the example below:

> I have an old sepia photograph of Da as a young boy, standing by a birdtable with my grandmother beside him. *She is beautiful and dressed in elegant twenties-style clothing.* It is an image I can never reconcile with *the frail hypochondriac old woman* I met on a few occasions in my later years. (Simpson 1994: 16)

In everyday life, the photograph image and the image locked in Simpson's memory are in quite distinct physical domains, but the written narrative mode allows juxtaposition of the two descriptions in the same medium of the text (see Fauconnier 1994 for a mental space analysis of this type of example, also Semino 1997: 104–7 for a stylistic discussion of a character stepping across such boundaries in a postmodern poem).

In narrative text, not only are descriptions juxtaposed, but it is possible to juxtapose different versions of characters who are performing actions in past and present contexts. In previous work (e.g. Emmott 1992, 1997) I have termed these 'narrative enactors'. Since switches between spatio-temporal contexts can be unclearly signalled and sometimes overtly ambiguous, it is possible not only for different enactors to be juxtaposed but for a reader to be temporarily unsure about which enactor is intended, sometimes for stylistic effect. In Emmott (1997: 187), for example, I discuss one case in Lelands (1983: 40) 'In a suburban sitting-room' where there is a scene shift between:

> *Last sentence of scene (i):* a mother shouting at her little girl Emma that her father would be furious when he arrives home and sees the mess she has created by her painting, and

> *First sentence of scene (ii):* unattributed direct speech 'Why have I got to come home to this mess every day?' addressed to Emma as she is painting.

The obvious inference is that the father is, later in the day, arriving home and chastising the child. However, as we read on it becomes clear that this is in fact an adult version of Emma, still painting but now attracting the wrath of her husband not her father. Until this point neither the adult Emma or her future husband have been mentioned at all in the story. If the reader initially erroneously sees the second scene as describing the child Emma (and it is difficult to see what other option there is for a reader in this particular case), it is then necessary for the reader to 'repair' his/her mental model of the scene and replace the child enactor with the adult enactor. This has the neat effect of providing us with an infantilised first view of the adult Emma and highlighting the extent to which, at different stages in her life, she has continued to paint and has been subject to the censure of her male relatives. Generally, 'enactors' provide a view of different versions of a character for the reader (either for contrast or ironic comparison), but the character him/herself may have no sense of being 'split'.

The double/multiple selves of the first-person narrator

As has been frequently observed by narratologists (e.g. Genette 1980, Bal 1997) first person narration intertwines different voices of an individual, since most first person narration involves a narrating self (self1) looking back in time at events involving an earlier version of the self (self2). This is very obvious in the 'paralysis narratives', particularly when the narrators describe the occurrence of their illness/injury. Reeve1, for example, has no memory for the events immediately preceding his accident, so has to rely on others to provide the information to enable him to describe what happened to Reeve2 (hence, the use of distancing phrases such as 'Later . . . I was told' (Reeve 1998: 18), 'Witnesses said' (p. 19), 'Apparently' (p. 19) that are scattered at intervals through this part of his narrative). McCrum1 remembers some of the events of his stroke, but supplements the thoughts of the barely conscious McCrum2 (e.g. 'I was oblivious to this cerebral drama', p. 4; 'in retrospect, I realise', p. 5; 'With what I now see must have been an extraordinary effort', p. 12; 'Weeks later I discovered . . .', p. 14). Sometimes the naïve voice of the past self is clear, so it is presumably McCrum2 who thinks, during his stroke, 'Whatever it was would pass' (p. 9). Nevertheless, the narrating self has knowledge of how events will develop (Bauby1's voice recalls the 'last' (p. 127, p. 128, p. 131) events of his former life, including his 'final' (p. 131) meal) and technical knowledge of the illness/injury that is only gained through post-illness/injury explanations and reading of the medical textbooks (e.g. McCrum 1998: Chapter 2).

These narratives are double-voiced (Bakhtin 1973) and, in the paragraph above, I have used binary notation (e.g. McCrum1, McCrum2) to represent the present and past selves of the narrator. However, when a first-person narrator remembers his previous act of remembering, there may be multiple selves which necessitate a more complex notation system. In the 'paralysis narratives' the narrator (self1) frequently looks back at his convalescence, recalling how his convalescent self (self2) thought of himself either at the moment of his stroke (self3) or before his stroke (the 'former/old/lost self' discussed earlier, self4). So in the following example, McCrum1 [. . .] is narrating, McCrum2 is at home convalescing after his stay in hospital and McCrum2 is reliving the events experienced by McCrum3 as McCrum3 regained consciousness after his stroke (the episodic memories of McCrum2 being prompted by the return to the same location):

> Even now, completing this chapter as the second anniversary of my stroke approaches, I (self1) can see that, much as I might hope to relegate this personal catastrophe to a file labelled 1995–96, in truth its effects will be with me (self1) for much longer . . . At first I (self2) was glad to be home . . . then *I* (self2) found myself reliving my first day again and again, *I* (self2) could not walk up the stairs without seeing *my naked body* (self3) curled foetally on the mezzanine. I (self2) could not lie in bed and escape retracing *my* (self3) confused journeys across the map of the ceiling that long ago Saturday. Whenever *I* (self2) stood on the front step, *I* (self2) saw my helpless body (self3) being stretchered out by the paramedics in the summer evening light. (McCrum 1998: 216–17)

'Special effects' in narrative and non-narrative

Although written narrative can always juxtapose descriptions of different versions of an individual, it is only when the normal physical laws are overridden (as in Science Fiction and Fantasy genres and in imaginary sub-worlds in other works) that an individual can actually exist in duplicate in the same physical space. Time-travel stories provide a means of achieving this (e.g. Ryder [2003]). In J.K. Rowling's (1999) *Harry Potter and the Prisoner of Azkaban*, for example, moving the hourglass back by three hours allows the current versions of Harry and Hermione (Harry1 and Hermione1) to step back into an earlier spatio-temporal context and view the past versions of themselves (Harry2 and Hermione2). Linguistically, there is potential for ambiguity since the same names and pronouns (e.g. 'Harry', 'he') denote earlier and later versions of the characters and indeed, even 'we' is used in direct speech to describe both their current and past selves.

So, for example, Harry says to Hermione 'Are you telling me . . . that we're here in this cupboard and we're out there, too?' (Rowling 1999: 289). There is, nevertheless, little confusion since Harry and Hermione are identifiable as the main observers (until the final climax of the episode), watching and listening to Harry2 and Hermione2 in 'replayed' events that the reader will recognise as having previously occurred. So in sentences like 'We just heard ourselves leaving' (p. 290), 'We'll see us' (p. 290) and 'Harry heard his own voice' (p. 291), the referring expressions in agent position can be assumed to denote the 'current' versions of the characters. Sometimes spatial information in the post-modifier of the name clarifies which version of the character is intended (e.g. 'The Hermione in the pumpkin patch', p. 292; 'The Harry and Hermione hidden in the trees', p. 292), assuming the reader is keeping track of which version of the character is in which part of the location.

The time travel episode here serves various plot functions. As in many such stories, Harry1 and Hermione1 are able to change the course of events in the past, hence changing the 'present' for themselves when they return to it. Also the episode allows Harry1 to understand his past, since he realises that Harry2 must have previously seen him, mistaking Harry1 for his father ('he had seen *himself*, p. 300 (Rowling's italics)). Although Harry1 and Harry2 are inherently different (by three hours and by the knowledge difference of those three hours), the duplicates in the story are more important for their role in the action than as a means of exploring the nature of the self. Some time-travel stories may explore the different selves in more detail. Stephen Fry's *Making History* (1996), for example, explores cultural differences by showing the puzzlement of a British character, Michael Young, who, having changed history, wakes up to find that he has suddenly become an American, Mikey (Michael D. Young). Nevertheless, plot factors appear to be most crucial even in this story since Fry's novel is primarily about repeated attempts to change the course of history in order to avoid the holocaust or, in other possible changed worlds, similar acts of genocide.

[. . .]

Overall, therefore, 'special effects' involving duplicates may [. . .] create striking effects and, in the case of time-travel stories, may contribute significantly to the plot of a story, but they do not necessarily have the objective of providing a comment on the nature of the human self. In the case of visual special effects, it is perhaps inappropriate to use the term 'split self' since often a duplicate may, arguably, have no real 'self'.

[. . .]

Conclusion

In this [chapter], I have attempted to produce a preliminary framework for categorising 'split selves' in narrative [. . .]. 'Split self' phenomena are so pervasive and complex that undoubtedly there is much more analysis work that needs to be done before any conclusions can be drawn about the use of these metaphors in specific genres such as medical 'life stories', and across a range of other genres. More work also needs to be done both in terms of assessing how current theoretical frameworks, such as cognitive linguistics and social psychology, can be applied to narrative analysis and in terms of building new frameworks, such as mental modelling approaches to the dynamic representation of characters in extended texts. In developing new techniques for analysis, it seems useful to apply an eclectic approach, drawing on currently fashionable theories such as cognitive linguistics, but also recognising the value of more familiar approaches in stylistics and narratology that may provide more sophisticated methods of handling extended texts. Stylisticians may find cognitive linguistics a useful addition to their 'toolbox', but, conversely, cognitive linguists may also have much to learn from stylisticians about how to handle extended narratives.

References

Bakhtin, M.M. (1973) *Problems of Dostoyevsky's Poetics* (trans. R.W. Rotsel). New York: Ardis [original 1929].

Bal, M. (1997) *Narratology: Introduction to the Theory of Narrative* (2nd edition). Toronto: University of Toronto Press.

Bauby, J.-D. (1998) *The Diving-Bell and the Butterfly* (trans. J. Legatt). London: First Estate [original 1997].

Billington, R., Hockey, J. and Strawbridge, S. (1998) *Exploring Self and Society*. Basingstoke: Macmillan.

Bosma, H.A. and Kunnen, E.S. (eds) (2001) *Identity and Emotion: Development through Self-Organisation*. Cambridge: Cambridge University Press.

Braine, J. (1959) *Room at the Top*. Harmondsworth: Penguin.

Brown, G. and Yule, G. (1983) *Discourse Analysis*. Cambridge: Cambridge University Press.

Culpeper, J. (2001) *Language and Characterisation: People in Plays and Other Texts*. London: Longman.

Emmott, C. (1992) 'Splitting the referent: an introduction to narrative enactors', in M. Davies and L.J. Ravelli (eds) *Advances in Systemic Linguistics: Recent Theory and Practice*, London: Pinter, pp. 221–8.

Emmott, C. (1997) *Narrative Comprehension: A Discourse Perspective*. Oxford: Clarendon Press.

Fauconnier, G. (1994) *Mental Spaces*. Cambridge: Cambridge University Press [original 1985].

Fiske, S.T. and Taylor, S.E. (1991) *Social Cognition*. Mountain View, CA: McGraw Hill.

Fry, S. (1996) *Making History*. London: Arrow.

Gavins, J. and Steen, G. (eds) (2003) *Cognitive Poetics in Practice*. London: Routledge.

Gazzaniga, M.S. (1998) *The Mind's Past*. Berkeley: University of California Press.

Genette, G. (1980) *Narrative Discourse*. Oxford: Basil Blackwell.

James, W. (1910) *Psychology: The Briefer Course*. New York: Holt.

Labov, W. (1972) *Language and the Inner City*. Philadelphia: University of Pennsylvania Press.

Leland, J. (1983) 'In a suburban sitting-room', in *The Last Sandcastle*, Dublin: The O'Brien Press, pp. 38–69.

Lessing, D. (1966) *A Proper Marriage* (Book Two of the *Children of Violence* series). London: Grafton Books.

Lessing, D. (1972) *The Four-Gated City* (Book Five of the *Children of Violence* series). London: Grafton Books.

McCrum, R. (1998) *My Year Off: Rediscovering Life after a Stroke*. London: Picador.

Reeve, C. (1998) *Still Me*. London: Arrow.

Rowling, J.K. (1999) *Harry Potter and the Prisoner of Azkaban*. London: Bloomsbury.

Ryder, M.E. (2003) 'I met myself coming and going: co(?)-referential noun phrases and point of view in time travel stories', *Language and Literature* 12 (3): 213–32.

Semino, E. (1997) *Language and World Creation in Poems and Other Texts*. London: Longman.

Semino, E. and Culpeper, J. (eds) (2002) *Cognitive Stylistics*. Amsterdam: John Benjamins.

Simpson, J. (1988) *Touching the Void*. London: Pan.

Simpson, J. (1994) *This Game of Ghosts*. London: Vintage.

Stevenson, R.L. (1995) 'The strange case of Dr Jekyll and Mr Hyde', in *Markheim, Jekyll And The Merry Men: Shorter Scottish Fiction*, Edinburgh: Canongate, pp. 229–94 [original 1886].

Stockwell, P. (2000) *The Poetics of Science Fiction*. London: Longman.

Stockwell, P. (2002) *Cognitive Poetics*. London: Routledge.

Townsend, S. (1989) *Rebuilding Coventry*. London: Methuen Mandarin.

Weber, R.J. (2000) *The Created Self: Reinventing Body, Persona and Spirit*. New York: W.W. Norton & Co.

Extracted from Catherine Emmott (2002) ' "Split selves" in fiction and in medical "life stories": cognitive linguistic theory and narrative practice', in E. Semino and J. Culpeper (eds) *Cognitive Stylistics,* Amsterdam: Benjamins, pp. 153–81.

Chapter 25

'Too much blague?': an exploration of the text worlds of Donald Barthelme's *Snow White*

JOANNA GAVINS

One of the most influential approaches in recent years has been that of *text world theory*. This framework has been particularly attractive for stylisticians because it offers a means of discussing contextualised and cognitive understanding without ignoring the linguistic texture of the literary work. In this chapter, Joanna Gavins explores the text worlds of an Absurdist text, in order to demonstrate its textual and cognitive mechanics. In this approach, author and reader are inherent parts of the model, encompassing areas of literary study traditionally neglected by stylistic text analysis.

For more on text world theory, see Werth (1999), Hidalgo Downing (2000), Gavins (2007) and chapter 16 in this volume.

Introduction

THE NOTION THAT HUMAN beings process and understand discourse, both factual and fictional, by constructing mental representations in their minds is now a common one in cognitive theory. These mental representations have been variously called 'mental models' in cognitive psychology (e.g. Johnson-Laird 1983), 'mental spaces' in cognitive linguistics (e.g. Fauconnier 1994) and, more recently, 'narrative worlds' in cognitive psychology (e.g. Gerrig 1993) and 'text worlds' in cognitive poetics (e.g. Werth 1999). In these last two areas of study, the text-as-world metaphor has most frequently been employed to describe the readerly sensation of being 'immersed' in a particular fiction, in which the characters, scenery and unfolding plotlines are constructed in as complex and richly-detailed a manner as those we encounter daily in the real world.

This chapter takes a somewhat more eccentric text as its main subject for analysis, with the aim of broadening our understanding of literary worlds in all their diversity. Donald Barthelme's (1996) *Snow White*, originally published in 1967, transposes the eponymous heroine of the classic fairy-tale to contemporary downtown New York, where she shares her life with her seven diminutive companions. As we shall see, however, this modified location is not the only deviation *Snow White* makes from preceding versions of the tale and Barthelme's retelling is by no means straightforward. This chapter employs Text World Theory (see Werth 1994, 1995a, 1995b, and 1999; Hidalgo Downing 2000; Gavins 2000 and 2001) as a means of exploring the precise nature of the fictional worlds created by his absurd adaptation. The basic mechanics of this approach to cognitive poetic analysis are outlined briefly in the following section of this chapter.

Text World Theory

Text World Theory provides a methodological framework through which both factual and fictional discourses may be systematically examined in their entirety: from the pragmatic circumstances surrounding their genesis, through to the conceptual consequences of specific language choices. A typical Text World Theory analysis normally begins by separating a given discourse into three interconnecting levels. The first of these, the *discourse world*, contains two or more participants engaged in a language event. [. . . T]heir discourse world will be governed by certain tacit discourse principles, according to which the participants both expect and agree to perform coherent and co-operative communication. Furthermore, Text World Theory recognises that the personal 'baggage' each participant brings with them to the language event, in the form of their memories, intentions, knowledge and motivations, has the potential to affect the process of joint negotiation at the core of the discourse world.

As the language event progresses, each participant constructs a mental representation, or *text world*, by which they are able to process and understand the discourse at hand. This world forms the next level of a Text World Theory analysis. The precise structure and contents of the text world are dictated both by linguistic indicators contained within the discourse and by further inferences drawn from the participants' background knowledge and experience. This way, though many different participants may be basing their mental representations on the same linguistic information, each of their individual text worlds will be unique to its creator. In general, however, all text worlds are made up of a combination of *world-building elements* and *function-advancing propositions*. [. . .]

Once the text world is constructed and developing, countless other worlds which depart from the parameters of the initial text world may also be created. These departures form the final layer of Text World Theory and are called 'sub-worlds' in Werth's (1999) original framework. They may be created either by the discourse participants, in which case they can be described as *participant-accessible*, or by characters in the text world, in which case they can be described as *character-accessible*. In my own Text World Theory model, which differs slightly from Werth's, these departures are simply new worlds that can be divided into two distinct categories (see Gavins 2001). The first of these is the category of *world-switches*. Should the central focus of the discourse be switched, for example to a different place, a new world corresponding with that scene is created. Flashing backwards or forwards in time has a similar effect. Instances of direct speech and direct thought also cause world-switches, since they alter the temporal parameters of the text world by introducing present-tense discourse into a past-tense narrative.

Other new worlds, known as *modal worlds*, may also be created as the result of modalisation in discourse (see Simpson 1993 for a useful overview of modal systems). Deontic modality, for example, expresses the degree of obligation attached to the performance of a particular action and includes modal auxiliaries such as 'may', 'should', 'must', and so on. Consider the following sentences: 'You should *go straight to the police*', 'You may *have another biscuit*', 'I must *take this suit to the cleaner's*'. The action being modalised in each of these examples (shown in italics) can be seen to set up an unfulfilled future situation that is separate from its originating text world. Similarly, boulomaic modality expresses the desires of a speaker or writer and stipulates the conditions by which those desires can be satisfied. Once again, consider the following examples: 'I hope that *you're happy*', 'I wish *I had a car like that*', 'She wants *to be left alone*'. [. . .]

Epistemic modality, in all its linguistic forms, also creates new modal worlds in the minds of the discourse participants. [. . .] For example, varying degrees of epistemic remoteness may be expressed through epistemic modal auxiliaries such as 'could' and 'might', as well as through modal lexical verbs such as 'think', 'suppose' and 'believe'. The epistemic modal system also includes a sub-system of 'perception' modality. [. . . Examples] include such [. . .] constructions as 'it is clear that', 'it is apparent that' [. . .] 'clearly', 'apparently' and 'obviously'. Once again, the use of these linguistic expressions results in the formation of a new, epistemically remote modal world in the minds of the discourse participants.

Similarly remote worlds can also be formed without the presence of epistemic modal auxiliaries or lexical verbs. Conditional constructions, for example, [. . . h]ypotheticals, [. . .] instances of indirect thought and indirect speech, [. . . and] focalised narratives can also be seen to be modal-world forming, since they filter both world-building and function-advancing elements through the unverifiable perspective of one or more characters.

Each of the three levels of Text World Theory are discussed in further detail in the following section of this chapter, which begins the exploration of the text worlds of *Snow White*.

Snow White: a Text World Theory analysis

The first thing to note about the discourse world which surrounds a reading of Barthelme's *Snow White* is how the reader's background knowledge is immediately brought into play in the discourse process on contact with the novel's title. The majority of contemporary western readers will recognise the proper name it contains, which subsequently activates a store of cultural knowledge, most probably formed as a result of recurrent lifelong contact with both traditional and contemporary versions of a popular fairy-tale. [. . .] The first paragraphs of the text, however, are unlikely to match most people's 'Snow White' prototype exactly:

> **SHE** is a tall dark beauty containing a great many beauty spots: one above the breast, one above the belly, one above the knee, one above the ankle, one above the buttock, one on the back of the neck. All of these areas are on the left side, more or less in a row, as you go up and down:

-
-
-
-
-
-

The hair is black as ebony, the skin is white as snow.

(Barthelme 1996: 9)

As well as containing some unconventional graphology, this introduction lacks the 'Once upon a time' opening typical of many fairy tales, beginning instead with a description of an unnamed female. Many readers will nevertheless be able to repair the passage's central reference chain, linking the third person reference that opens Barthelme's novel with the character of Snow White, perhaps aided in part by the direct borrowing of the Brothers Grimm's more familiar description of her: 'The hair is black as ebony, the skin is white as snow'.

This correlation aside, however, little else in the text which follows bears such a direct resemblance to any previous version of the Snow White story. For instance, seven men are mentioned on the page which follows that quoted above. The reader may infer from their number that these characters fill the traditional roles of the seven dwarves. The men's names, however, are given, not as Sleepy, Happy, Dopey, Sneezy, Bashful, Grumpy and Doc, but as Bill, Kevin, Edward, Hubert, Henry, Clem and Dan. A further departure from tradition can be identified in the temporal setting of Barthelme's text. Although not explicitly mentioned, a contemporary backdrop can, once again, be inferred from certain culture-specific references. There is mention, for example, of a 'shower room' (Barthelme 1996: 10), a 'typewriter' (p. 15), 'Chairman Mao' (p. 22), 'Mars Bars' (p. 27) and 'Charlton Heston' (p. 27). [. . .]

The majority of critics writing on *Snow White* (e.g. Ditsky 1975, Coutrier and Durand 1982, Morace 1984, Trachtenberg 1990) devote at least part of their attention to certain linguistic incongruities also contained within Barthelme's text. Particularly helpful is an early stylistic analysis by McNall (1975), the main focus of which lies in the identifiable patterns of lexical repetition in Barthelme's text. However, McNall also makes some mention of the characters' actions in the novel, or, rather, the lack of them. She comments that

> the speakers in *Snow White* are engaged characteristically in plans, medita-
> tions, speeches, sermons, fantasies . . . commonly they fail to bring these
> off. The plans do not materialize, the meditations do not lead to realiza-
> tions, the speeches and sermons do not convince, and fantasies are, after all,
> fantasies.

(McNall 1975: 85–6)

McNall also notes that removing the novel's 'description assertions', which she defines as 'a sentence with the copula for main verb' (McNall 1975: 82), would remove the greater part of the text. The vast majority of the remaining narrative is made up of primarily mental and/or emotional activity. However, this observation remains rela-tively underdeveloped in McNall's essay and thus provides a useful starting point for a Text World Theory analysis of *Snow White*.

McNall's comments on the peculiarity of action in Barthelme's text are drawn, in particular, from her examination of the following episode and its numerous consequences:

> SNOW WHITE let down her hair black as ebony from the window. It was Monday. The hair flew out of the window. 'I could fly a kite with this hair it is so long. The wind would carry the kite up into the blue, and there would be the red of the kite against the blue of the blue, together with my hair black as ebony, floating there. That seems desirable. This motif, the long hair streaming from the high window, is a very ancient one I believe, found in many cultures, in various forms. Now I recapitulate it, for the astonishment of the vulgar and the refreshment of my venereal life.'
>
> (Barthelme 1996: 86)

In Text World Theory's terms, perhaps the most remarkable thing about this passage [. . .] is the minimal world-building information it contains. The character of Snow White is apparently the only entity present, at a window nominated by a definite article, yet otherwise indistinct. Perhaps even more strangely, the reader is told the precise day on which the incident takes place, but not the date or the hour. The only physical action in the passage takes place in its first sentence, as its function-advancing proposition tells us that 'Snow White let down her hair'. The entire remainder of the episode is devoted to Snow White's speech about her motivations for, and feelings about, her behaviour.

The structure of the passage can be translated into a text world diagram (see Figure 25.1), which makes evident the imbalance between the detail contained in the episode's initial text world, in which Snow White lets down her hair, and that contained in the world-switch created by her direct speech. The originating text world is shown to the left of the diagram and is divided into separate world-building (WB) and function-advancing (FA) sections. The function-advancing section can be seen to contain only one function-advancing proposition ('Snow White let down her hair'). This is set against a minimalistic background, constructed according to the sparse world-building information provided. This information is separated in the diagram into *time* (t), *location* (l), and *characters* (c).

The new world which then splits off from the initial text world is shown originating from direct speech (DS) in the diagram. This world contains not only Snow White's direct assertion of her reasons for her actions ('for the astonishment of the vulgar and the refreshment of my venereal life'), but also three further embedded modal worlds. The first of these is epistemic in nature and results from Snow White's construction of a hypothetical situation in which she flies a kite in her hair. The origins of this world are shown in the diagram as a HYP world embedded within the speech world. The second modal world, also epistemic, occurs as a result of the perception modality contained in her comment that such an event would '*seem* desirable'. This is shown in the diagram as the uppermost epistemic world (EPS) branching off from the speech world. The latter part of the same sentence, of course, consists of a boulomaic modal adjective, which creates a further embedded boulomaic modal world (BOUL). A final epistemic world is then constructed around Snow White's comments on the cultural significance of what she has done, as she states that she *believes* the hair 'motif' to be 'a very ancient one'. The

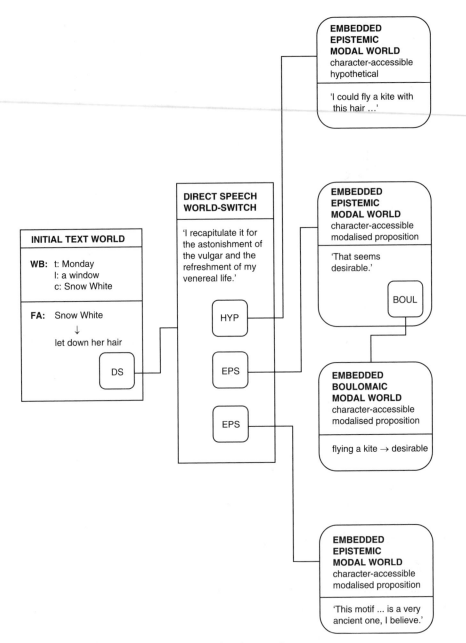

Figure 25.1 Embedded worlds in Snow White's speech

motif is also, of course, one which belongs in an entirely different fairy tale, namely that of Rapunzel.

The letting down of Snow White's hair, which occurs about half-way through *Snow White*, is followed by a number of episodes headed 'Reaction to the hair'. The following is a reproduction of one of them, in full:

> *Reaction to the hair:* 'Well, that certainly is a lot of hair hanging there,' Bill reflected. 'And it seems to be hanging from our windows too. I mean, those

windows where the hair is hanging are in our house, surely? Now who amongst us has that much hair, black as ebony? I am only pretending to ask myself this question. The disgraceful answer is already known to me, as is the significance of this act, this hanging, as well as the sexual meaning of the hair itself, on which Wurst has written. I don't mean that he has written *on* the hair, but rather about it, from prehistory to the present time. There can be only one answer. It is Snow White. It is Snow White who has taken this step, the meaning of which is clear to all of us. All seven of us know what this means. It means that she is nothing else but a goddamn degenerate! is one way of looking at it, at this complex and difficult question. It means that the "not-with" is experienced as more pressing, more real, than the "being-with". It means she seeks a new lover. *Quelle tragédie!* But the essential loneliness of the person must also be considered. Each of us is like a tiny single hair, hurled into the world among billions and billions of other hairs, of various colours and lengths. And if God does exist, then we are in even graver shape than we had supposed. In that case, each of us is like a tiny mote of pointlessness, whirling in the midst of a dreadful free even greater pointlessness, unless there is intelligent life on other planets, that is to say, life even more intelligent than us, life that has thought up some point for this great enterprise, life. That is possible. That is something we do not know, thank God. But in the meantime, here is the hair, with its multiple meanings. What am I to do about it?'

(Barthelme 1996: 98–9)

The structure of this passage can be seen to be greatly similar to that which caused it and is illustrated in Figure 25.2. Where Snow White's reflections on her hair took up five sentences, Bill manages to extend his to a total of twenty-three. Furthermore, Bill takes no physical action, apart from the speech itself, during the entire episode. The world-building elements of his text world are also even more minimalistic than those which defined Snow White's surroundings in the earlier passage. Since his remarks are directed at Snow White's hair, however, we can assume fairly safely that he is positioned within roughly the same spatial and temporal parameters as she was: below a window in their house, on a Monday.

Once again, far greater detail goes into the construction of the world of Bill's speech than that of his immediate location. Once again, the direct speech world-switch is followed by a further four embedded modal worlds. The first is created as a result of Bill's somewhat reluctant epistemic commitment to location of the window from which the hair is hanging, as he relegates his assertion, 'those windows where the hair is hanging are in our house', to a question: 'surely?' This qualification positions the information contained within Bill's initial statement at a greater epistemic distance, both from Bill and the reader, in an embedded epistemic modal world. A second modal world, also epistemic in nature, is then created as Bill goes on to speculate about the existence of God, in the conditional construction beginning 'And if God does exist . . .'. This initial clause, of course, sets up a remote world in which the second clause of the conditional is the case ('we are in even graver shape than we had supposed . . . each of us is like a tiny mote of pointlessness, whirling in the midst of a dreadful free even greater pointlessness'). A similar construction forms the next remote world to be

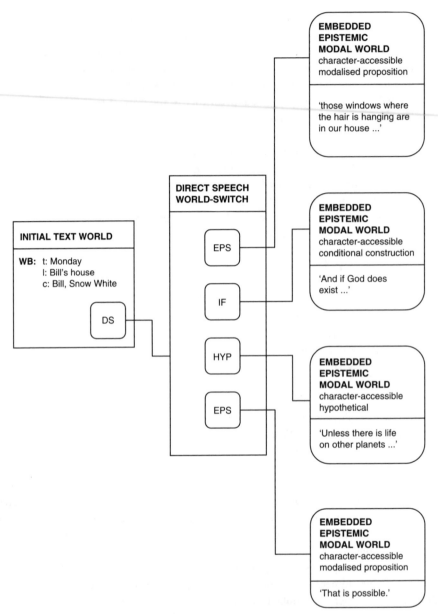

Figure 25.2 Embedded worlds in Bill's 'Reaction to the hair' speech

embedded in Bill's monologue, as he pursues a further hypothetical, 'unless there is life on other planets'. A final world is then created as Bill adds a modalised comment, expressing his opinion on the likelihood of the hypothetical situation he has constructed: 'That is possible'. The same state of affairs (life on another planet) is then recreated in a completely separate epistemic modal world, according to the speaker's altered epistemic commitment to it.

An emphasis on the speech and thoughts of the characters, rather than on their actions or their surroundings, is typical of each of the 'Reaction to the hair' episodes.

However, this feature is by no means confined to these sections of the novel alone. Throughout *Snow White*, as McNall points out, 'any act is given far less prominence than its problematical motives, and/or the problematical reactions to it' (McNall 1975: 83). Scattered amongst the 'Reaction to the hair' sections of *Snow White* are a number of episodes headed 'Lack of Reaction to the hair'. Despite the suggestions of differing action-content made explicit in their titles, however, the text world structures of both the 'Reaction' and 'Lack of Reaction' episodes are practically identical. In one of these episodes, for example, Dan (another dwarf) gives a speech to an unspecified audience in unspecified surroundings. The text world which corresponds to this section of the novel does at least contain one physical action, as Dan pulls up boxes for his audience to sit on. Once again, though, a speech world dominates the episode as Dan muses, ironically, over the topic of 'linguistic stuffing' for a total of three pages, creating numerous embedded modal worlds as he goes, making this one of the longest sections in the entire novel.

Indeed, the vast majority of the text of *Snow White* is made up of its characters' verbal and mental contemplations. Almost the entire first half of the novel is devoted to the dwarves' speculations about what might be bothering the apparently depressed and dissatisfied Snow White, interspersed by her own commentary on the situation. Snow White seems to have taken to writing poetry and also throwing tantrums, although the dwarves' main concern is her recent loss of sexual appetite. The action the dwarves take in an attempt to reawaken her interest in them, however, is limited to a single (and perhaps unsurprisingly unsuccessful) decision to purchase a fancy new shower curtain.

A distinct pattern of text world structures can thus be seen to emerge as the narrative of *Snow White* unfolds. Furthermore, the prominence of speech worlds throughout the text means that, for much of the discourse process, the reader must rely on the characters to provide the world-building and function-advancing information necessary to construct a coherent mental representation of the novel. On occasion, this proves to be a reasonably straightforward exercise, particularly when the characters make direct reference to their surroundings. At other times, the reader may have to work slightly harder to make inferences that will enhance the detail of their text world of *Snow White*. The inference made about Bill's proximity to Snow White during his 'Reaction to the hair' speech, discussed earlier, is one such example. A great deal of the time, however, the characters offer practically no help in the construction of the reader's text world and can even be seen to be actively complicating the process.

In the following extract, Bill is defending himself in court, where he stands charged with having delusions of grandeur. This has led Bill, the judge explains, to throw a six pack of beer through the windscreen of a car belonging to two complete strangers, named Fondue and Maeght:

> 'You cherished for those two, Fondue and Maeght, a hate.' 'More of a miff, your worship.' 'Of what standing, in the time dimension, is this miff?' 'Matter of let's see sixteen years I would say.' 'The miff had its genesis in mentionment to you by them of the great black horse.' 'That is correct.' 'How old were you exactly. At that time.' 'Twelve years.' 'Something said to you about a horse sixteen years ago triggered, then, the hurlment.' 'That

is correct.' 'Let us make sure we understand the circumstances of the hurlment. Can you disbosom yourself very briefly of the event seen from your point of view.'

(Barthelme 1996: 165)

Bill's explanation of events is far from brief, however, and offers no clarification of either the significance of the black horse or the reasons behind his violent outburst at Fondue and Maeght, who remain similarly vague figures throughout the scene. Instead, the judge and Bill continue their exchange of bizarre neologisms (e.g. 'hurlment', 'disbosom', 'sensorium', 'cutaneous injurement', 'scoutmysteries', 'self-gratulation') for a further four pages, in a highly infelicitous conversation without apparent aim or conclusion (see Gavins 2000, and Simpson 1997 and 2000, for discussion of similar linguistic incongruities in other Absurdist texts).

Bill and the judge are not alone in their linguistic eccentricity. The other characters, too, have a persistent habit of coining peculiar or meaningless words and phrases. At one point, for example, Snow White exclaims, 'I am tired of being just a horsewife!', a term which is subsequently adopted by all the other characters in the text. Snow White's initial play on words, then, rapidly becomes a social institution, one which Edward (another dwarf) even goes to the extent of defending passionately in a lengthy sermon. Such appropriations, however, do little to aid the efficiency of the reading process, with the majority of the characters' coinages remaining obscure and unexplained following their initial use. Faced with such impenetrable communication between the characters, the reader might reasonably expect clearer direction from Snow White's implied authorial voice. As we have already seen, however, the prominence of speech worlds in the majority of the novel's episodes means that the reader has very little contact with this omniscient textual entity. More often than not, the information he provides about the text world that contains Snow White and her companions is so scant that the reader must rely entirely on the references those characters make to their surroundings in order to form any coherent mental representation of them.

[. . .]

Despite sporadic instances of cooperative communication, then, the senselessness of these repeated episodes may undermine the trust of many readers in the reliability of the authorial voice. Further processing problems may also arise from the following textual interruption:

QUESTIONS:
1. Do you like the story so far? Yes ( ) No ( )
2. Does Snow White resemble the Snow White you remember? Yes ( ) No ( )
3. Have you understood, in reading to this point, that Paul is the prince-figure? Yes ( ) No ( )
4. That Jane is the wicked stepmother-figure? Yes ( ) No ( )
5. In the further development of the story, would you like more emotion ( ) or less emotion ( )?
6. Is there too much *blague* in the narration? ( ) Not enough *blague*? ( )
7. Do you feel that the creation of new modes of hysteria is a viable undertaking of the artist of today? Yes ( ) No ( )

8.   Would you like a war? Yes ( ) No ( )
9.   Has the work, for you, a metaphysical dimension? Yes ( ) No ( )
10. What is it (twenty-five words or less)?_____
11. Are the seven men, in your view, adequately characterized as individuals?
     Yes ( ) No ( )
12. Do you feel that the Author's Guild has been sufficiently vigorous in repre-
     senting writers before Congress in matters pertaining to copyright legisla-
     tion? Yes ( ) No ( )
13. Holding in mind all works of fiction since the War, in all languages, how
     would you rate the present work, on a scale of one to ten, so far? (Please
     circle your answer)
     1 2 3 4 5 6 7 8 9 10
14. Do you stand up when you read? ( ) Lie down? ( ) Sit? ( )
15. In your opinion, should human beings have more shoulders? ( ) Two sets of
     shoulders? ( ) Three? ( )

                                                    (Barthelme 1996: 88–9)

This questionnaire appears about half-way through *Snow White*, at the close of Part One of the text. Questions 3 and 4 may aid certain inferences already in process, confirming that Paul is intended to fill the traditional role of Prince Charming and that another character, Jane, is the wicked stepmother. This information aside, however, the majority of the questionnaire is, at worst, nonsensical ('Is there too much *blague* in the narration?') or, at best, unrelated to the main narrative [. . .]. Those questions that do relate to the reading of *Snow White* do so by foregrounding the fictionality of the text. When question 13 asks, 'how would you rate the present work, on a scale of one to ten', for example, emphasis is placed on the discourse world relationship between the reader and author. The author's potential ability, yet ultimate failure, to create rounded, believable characters and a coherent plot structure are thus also brought to the reader's attention.

Conclusions

The Text World Theory analysis of *Snow White* presented in this chapter has shown how Barthelme's readers are provided with only minimal world-building information on which to base their mental representations of the text. Furthermore, very little physical action takes place in any of the worlds created during the course of the novel and the greater part of the function-advancing in *Snow White* takes place within speech-initiated world-switches and embedded epistemic modal worlds. Our comprehension of the text is then further complicated by the fact that a great deal of what the characters say and think is, at best, long-winded and irrelevant rambling and, at worst, utterly nonsensical. No additional guidance is offered by the authorial voice in the novel, which often adopts the same senseless discourse itself and provides only minimal insight into the characters' feelings and motivations. It would seem, then, that the challenging nature of this text is due mainly to the uncooperative behaviour of the reader's co-participant in the discourse world. The author of *Snow White* can be seen to reject persistently his obliga-tions to communicate clearly and efficiently, as he creates both a troublesome textual counterpart for himself and numerous other text world entities with similarly uncooperative tendencies.

The central question that Barthelme's novel raises for cognitive poetics, then, is whether such troublesome discourse-world relationships create insurmountable problems in the processing of literary texts. It is certainly possible that the bizarre text worlds of *Snow White* might prove so taxing to some readers that they will be led to abandon their reading of the novel entirely. For many others, though, the demanding nature of the worlds described above will be the novel's central attraction [. . .]. Indeed, the canonical status granted many similarly 'difficult' texts would suggest that these kinds of text worlds are highly prized in our society. It is also possible that for many readers the complex and chaotic structure of the novel may actually form the basis of an interpretation of its meaning. Despite the unruly behaviour of the author, his textual counterpart and his characters, a reading of *Snow White* as a cooperative text is still possible through the metaphorical mapping of its structural absurdity onto the day to day experience of human existence.

References

Barthelme, D. (1996) *Snow White*. New York: Simon Schuster [original 1967].

Coutrier, M. and Durand, R. (1982) *Donald Barthelme*. London: Methuen.

Ditsky, J.M. (1975) ' "With ingenuity and hard work, distracted": the narrative style of Donald Barthelme', *Style* 9: 388–400.

Fauconnier, G. (1994) *Mental Spaces: Aspects of Meaning Construction in Natural Language*. Cambridge: Cambridge University Press.

Gavins, J. (2000) 'Absurd tricks with bicycle frames in the text world of *The Third Policeman*', *Nottingham Linguistic Circular* 15: 17–33.

Gavins, J. (2001) 'Text World Theory: A Critical Exposition and Development in Relation to Absurd Prose Fiction', PhD thesis, Sheffield Hallam University.

Gavins, J. (2007) *Text World Theory: An Introduction*. Edinburgh: Edinburgh University Press.

Gerrig, R. (1993) *Experiencing Narrative Worlds: On the Psychological Activities of Reading*. New Haven: Yale University Press.

Hidalgo Downing, L. (2000) *Negation, Text Worlds and Discourse: The Pragmatics of Fiction*. Stanford, CA: Ablex.

Johnson-Laird, P.N. (1983) *Mental Models*. Cambridge: Cambridge University Press.

McNall, S.A. (1975) ' "But why am I troubling myself about cans?": style, reaction, and lack of reaction in Barthelme's *Snow White*', *Language and Style* 8: 81–94.

Morace, R.A. (1984) 'Donald Barthelme's *Snow White*: the novel, the critics and the culture', *Critique* 26: 1–10.

Simpson, P. (1993) *Language, Ideology and Point of View*. London: Routledge.

Simpson, P. (1997) 'The interactive world of *The Third Policeman*', in A. Clune and T. Hurson (eds) *Conjuring Complexities: Essays on Flann O'Brien*, Belfast: Institute of Irish Studies, pp. 73–81.

Simpson, P. (2000) 'Satirical humour and cultural context: with a note on the curious case of Father Todd Unctuous', in T. Bex, M. Burke and P. Stockwell (eds) *Contextualized Stylistics*, Amsterdam: Rodopi, pp. 243–66.

Trachtenberg, S. (1990) *Understanding Donald Barthelme*. Columbia: University of South Carolina Press.

Werth, P. (1994) 'Extended metaphor: a text world account', *Language and Literature* 3: 79–103.

Werth, P. (1995a) 'How to build a world (in a lot less than six days and using only what's in your head)', in K. Green (ed.) *New Essays on Deixis: Discourse, Narrative, Literature*, Amsterdam: Rodopi, pp. 49–80.

Werth, P. (1995b) ' "World enough and time": deictic space and the interpretation of prose', in P. Verdonk and J.J. Weber (eds) *Twentieth-Century Fiction: From Text to Context*, London: Routledge, pp. 181–205.

Werth, P. (1999) *Text Worlds: Representing Conceptual Space in Discourse*. London: Longman.

Extracted from Joanna Gavins (2003) 'Too much blague? An exploration of the text worlds of Donald Barthelme's *Snow White*', in J. Gavins and G. Steen (eds) *Cognitive Poetics in Practice*, London: Routledge, pp. 129–44.

Chapter 26

A cognitive stylistic approach to mind style in narrative fiction

ELENA SEMINO

In this chapter, Elena Semino develops Fowler's (1996) notion of *mind style* in order to contrast it with the notion of ideological point of view, drawing a more delicate distinction than Fowler that allows her to focus on individual rather than social consciousness. She draws on conceptual metaphor and blending theory from cognitive linguistics, and in so doing produces a detailed analysis of the deviant criminal mind in John Fowles's *The Collector* (1998).

The stylistics of viewpoint and consciousness continues to be a major theme in the field. For further work see Semino (1997), Palmer (2004), Zunshine (2006) and McIntyre (2006).

Introduction

[. . .]

I N *LINGUISTIC CRITICISM,* FOWLER (1996) explicitly presents the notion of 'mind style' as equivalent to those of 'world view' and of 'point of view on the ideological plane':

> Discussing this phenomenon in literary fictions, I have called it *mind style*: the world-view of an author, or a narrator, or a character, constituted by the ideational structure of the text. From now on I shall prefer this term to the cumbersome 'point of view on the ideological plane' [. . .]: the notions are equivalent.
>
> (Fowler 1996: 214)

The potential application of three different terms to a very broad and general phenomenon, however, seems to me unsatisfactory. In addition, the definitions provided by Fowler himself appear to convey different slants depending on which term he is using at the time. [. . .]

My own proposal is to build on Semino and Swindlehurst (1996) in order to arrive at a clearer and more helpful use of existing terminology. I will use 'world view' as the most general term, referring to the overall view of 'reality' or of the 'text actual world' (Ryan 1991) conveyed by the language of a text (or part of a text). And I will use the terms 'ideological point of view' and 'mind style' to capture different *aspects* of the world views projected by texts.

The notion of 'ideological point of view' is most apt to capture those aspects of world views that are social, cultural, religious or political in origin, and which an individual is likely to share with others belonging to similar social, cultural, religious or political groups. These include, for example, beliefs concerning the place of humans in the universe or the nature of justice, as well as moral judgements, attitudes towards different social or ethnic groups, and so on. [. . .]

The notion of 'mind style' on the other hand, is most apt to capture those aspects of world views that are primarily personal and cognitive in origin, and which are either peculiar to a particular individual, or common to people who have the same cognitive characteristics (for example as a result of a similar mental illness or of a shared stage of cognitive development, as in the case of young children). These aspects include an individual's characteristic cognitive habits, abilities and limitations, and any beliefs and values that may arise from them.

[. . .]

The present chapter is therefore part of an emerging cognitive stylistic tradition in the analysis of mind style. Although the notion of mind style can be applied to authors, narrators and characters, I will follow Bockting in relating mind style specifically to characterisation, both in third-person and first-person narration (see also Culpeper 2001: 288–9). I will also be concerned with mind styles that involve cognitive problems, including, in the case of Clegg in *The Collector*, mental illness of some sort. While, as Leech and Short (1981) have shown, mind styles can be seen to vary on a scale from 'normality' to 'deviance', the notion is most useful where narratives involve the foregrounding of linguistic patterns that suggest some salient cognitive habit or deficit.

[. . .]

The mind style of Frederick Clegg in John Fowles's *The Collector*

The Collector, John Fowles's first and widely acclaimed novel, was first published in 1963. It provides a chillingly realistic account of how Frederick Clegg, a clerk with a passion for collecting butterflies, kidnaps art student Miranda Grey, and keeps her captive in the cellar of a secluded Sussex cottage until she dies of pneumonia two months later. The novel is divided into four parts, with the two main characters alternating in the role of first-person narrator. Part 1 is Clegg's account of events up to the point when Miranda falls ill. Part 2 consists of the diary kept by Miranda during her captivity, and provides her version of events, and of her previous life, up to her fatal illness. Parts 3 and 4 are both told by Clegg. In part 3 he narrates Miranda's death and his actions in its immediate aftermath. In part 4 he begins to tell of his post-Miranda life, ending on a disturbing account of how he is now closely watching another young woman, much like he did Miranda at the beginning of the novel.

[. . .]

The [literary] criticism of the novel has focused on a number of central themes. These include the class contrast between Clegg and Miranda, the way in which the two characters can be seen to symbolise a wider struggle between a creative and educated elite and the philistine and uneducated masses, and the significance of intertextual references to Shakespeare's *The Tempest* (Clegg tells Miranda that he is called Ferdinand, but she refers to him as 'Caliban'). As far as Clegg in particular is concerned, he has been variously described by literary critics as a prototypically weak man, a victim of circumstances, a psychopath and a schizophrenic (Wolfe 1976, Olshen 1978, Conradi 1982, Salami 1992). His difficulties with class differences and sex are discussed at length, and reference is often made to the fact that Clegg frequently uses metaphorical expressions where Miranda and various other people and events are described in terms of butterflies and butterfly collecting. However, no systematic investigation has been made of the linguistic construction of Clegg's personality and world view, and, in particular, no theoretically informed account has been proposed of how Clegg's use of butterfly metaphors relates to his mind style and his actions.

[. . . A] number of salient aspects of Clegg's world view can be captured by the notion of ideological point of view, notably the bulk of his opinions and attitudes towards sex, gender and class. [. . .] On the other hand, the frequency and nature of his reliance on butterfly metaphors, especially in relation to Miranda, is a peculiar feature of his mind style. This combines with various aspects of Clegg's ideological point of view to produce a realistic impression of what is a rather unrealistic case of mental insanity: although Fowles's novel was partly inspired by a real kidnapping (Olshen 1978: 15–16), Clegg is very different from real-life psychopaths, who, unlike him, normally carry out violent physical assaults on their victims, often of a sexual nature. The rest of this [chapter] will focus on how the use of butterfly metaphors contributes to the linguistic projection of Clegg's criminal and disturbed mind.

Clegg's mind style and cognitive metaphor theory

[. . .]

From the very beginning of his narrative, it is obvious that Clegg metaphorically constructs Miranda as a butterfly. The extracts below are taken from the first two paragraphs of the novel:

(1)   When I had a free moment from the files and ledgers I stood by the window and used to look down over the road over the frosting and sometimes I'd see her. In the evening I marked it in my observations diary, at first with X, and then when I knew her name with M. (p. 9)

(2)   I watched the back of her head and her hair in a long pigtail. It was very pale, silky, like burnet cocoons. (p. 9)

(3)   Seeing her always made me feel like I was catching a rarity, heart-in-mouth, as they say. A Pale Clouded Yellow, for instance. I always thought of her like that, I mean words like elusive and sporadic, and very refined – not like the other ones, even the pretty ones. More for the real connoisseur. (p. 9)

As the first extract shows, seeing Miranda triggers in Clegg the same behaviour as seeing butterflies: he records each sighting in his entomological 'observations diary'. In the second extract, a description of her hair involves a simile drawing from what I will call his BUTTERFLY source domain ('like burnet cocoons'). The third extract includes a series of metaphorical expressions that realise a set of correspondences between the BUTTERFLY source domain and his domain of experience relating to Miranda – his MIRANDA target domain: Miranda corresponds to a rare butterfly (a 'Pale Clouded Yellow'); seeing her corresponds to catching a rare butterfly; and the difficulty of seeing Miranda is positively constructed by applying to her lexical items that are used in entomology guides to describe butterflies (e.g. 'elusive', 'sporadic'). Further metaphorical expressions through-out Clegg's narrative express parallels between unexpectedly sighting Miranda and unexpectedly sighting a butterfly (p. 26), between kidnapping Miranda and catching a rare butterfly (p. 31), between trying to deal with Miranda's pleas for freedom and catching a butterfly without a net (p. 40), between his emotional reaction to Miranda's beauty and his emotional reaction to a butterfly's beauty (p. 80), and between Miranda's attempt at seduction and a caterpillar trying to rush its development into a butterfly (p. 95).

The frequency and elaboration of metaphorical expressions drawing from the source domain of butterflies suggests that a systematic set of correspondences between the BUTTERFLY domain and the MIRANDA domain is part of Clegg's conceptual structure. Because the relevant metaphorical expressions do not relate to a conventional pattern in English, the corresponding conceptual mapping is idiosyncratic rather than con-ventional, and therefore a feature of Clegg's mind style. The fact that Clegg constructs Miranda and his relationship with her in terms of his experience as a butterfly collector is entirely consistent with the view of metaphor proposed by cognitive metaphor theory [see Lakoff and Johnson 1980, Lakoff and Turner 1989]. On the one hand, Clegg's BUTTERFLY domain (or, in schema theory terms, his BUTTERFLY schema [Cook 1994]) is highly elaborated, and has positive emotional associations. Clegg is therefore overlexical-ised in the semantic field of lepidoptery. On the other hand, because of his moral views and his lack of experience, his schemata relating to women and relationships with them are limited, and carry negative emotional associations. He therefore constructs his relationship with the woman of his dreams in terms of what he knows best: collecting butterflies. It is significant that in the third extract above Clegg himself points out that the correspondence between Miranda and a rare butterfly is more than simply a matter of linguistic expression: 'I always *thought* of her like that' (p. 9, my emphasis).

The title of the novel itself metaphorically refers to Clegg as 'The Collector', a description that is used by Miranda in her own diary. Clegg never explicitly uses this phrase in his own narrative, but his use of the BUTTERFLY source domain always casts him in the role of butterfly collector and Miranda in the role of butterfly. The extract below relates to a conversation between Clegg and Miranda during her captivity.

(4) After, she was always telling me what a bad thing I did and how I ought to realize it more. I can only say that evening I was very happy, as I said above, [. . .]. My feelings were very happy because my intentions were of the best. It was what she never understood.

To sum up, that night was the best thing I ever did in my life (bar winning the pools in the first place). It was like catching the Mazarine Blue again or a Queen of Spain Fritillary. I mean it was like something you do only once in a lifetime and then again often not;

something you dream about more than you ever expect to see come
true, in fact. (p. 31)

It is clear from this example, and from the first extract above, that the BUTTERFLY
metaphor does not simply affect Clegg's language and thoughts, but also guides his
actions. The difference between extracts (1) and (4), however, is that the wealth
provided by his pools win has triggered a crucial change in the correspondences
between the BUTTERFLY source domain and the MIRANDA target domain. While before his
win *catching* a butterfly was mapped on *seeing* Miranda, after his win *catching* a butterfly
is mapped on *catching* Miranda.

It is the fact that Clegg *acts* on his idiosyncratic BUTTERFLY metaphor that has
criminal and disastrous consequences. More specifically, his crucial failing, and a sign of
some kind of mental illness, is not so much the fact that he adopts an unconventional
metaphor in his language and thought, but the fact that he maps an insect onto a human
being, and proceeds to act on the basis of this mapping. His aims in capturing Miranda
are also parallel to his aims in collecting butterflies. Although he is attracted to her, he
shuns any sexual relations: all he wants is to have control over and unlimited access to
Miranda, so that he can watch her at leisure, and occasionally take photographs of her:
'What she never understood was that with me it was having. Having her was enough.
Nothing needed doing. I just wanted to have her, and safe at last' (p. 95). In addition, it is
obvious from extract (4), and many other places in Clegg's narrative, that the BUTTERFLY
metaphor also guides and/or reflects his moral attitude and his emotional reactions. He
does not feel guilty for kidnapping Miranda; rather, he feels elated, as he would after the
capture of a butterfly.

The connection between Miranda and butterflies in Clegg's mind is not just a
metaphorical one. In his dreams, for example, Miranda is described as always 'loving me
and my collection' (p. 10), and he only manages to hold the floor in his conversations
with Miranda when he talks about butterflies. On the other hand, expressions drawing
from the BUTTERFLY source domain are not exclusive to Miranda as target domain. He
expresses his disgust with a prostitute with whom he had an unsuccessful sexual
encounter by describing her as a 'specimen you would turn away from, out collecting'
(pp. 14–15). He compares 'classy newspapers' and art galleries to 'the cabinets of
foreign species in the Entomology Room at the Natural History Museum, you could see
they were beautiful but you didn't know them' (p. 19). At the end of the novel, he
expresses his gloomy view of the human condition by drawing from the more general
domain of insects: 'I think we are just insects, we live a bit and then die and that's the
lot' (p. 277).

These examples suggest that Clegg's schemata to do with insects, and butterflies in
particular, are frequently applied as metaphorical source domains to construct a range of
experiences. The BUTTERFLY domain, in particular, has high 'multivalency' (Goatly 1977:
258–9) or a very wide 'scope' (Kövecses 2000), due to its salience, its high level of
elaboration and its positive emotional associations.

As far as conceptual structure is concerned, therefore, Clegg's mind style is
characterised by a systematic mapping between the BUTTERFLY domain and the
MIRANDA domain, or possibly the domain of women in general. This mapping includes
correspondences between behaviour and properties appropriate to butterflies, and
behaviour and properties relating to women. In addition, Clegg has a more general

cognitive tendency to conceive of his experiences in terms of butterflies and butterfly collecting. Other lepidopterists may share the contents of his BUTTERFLY schema, and possibly the tendency to make frequent recourse to it, but the way in which Clegg applies the BUTTERFLY domain to Miranda is peculiar to him and an expression of perversion and mental illness. Cognitive metaphor theory is useful in relating linguistic patterns to thought and actions, and in explaining why the implausible story of an insane lepidopterist who collects women without even wishing to touch them is generally described as 'realistic' by the critics (e.g. Wolfe 1976, Conradi 1982).

Clegg's mind style and Blending theory

Up to the point of Miranda's kidnapping, the BUTTERFLY metaphor functions as a fairly successful tool for Clegg's thoughts and actions. After the capture, however, the clashes in some of the correspondences that make up the mapping become more evident, and the instantiations of the BUTTERFLY metaphors tend to express situations of impasse and conflict.

The extract below is taken from the end of a conversation where Miranda has been trying to persuade Clegg to free her, promising that, if he does, she will not denounce his crime, but rather grow to admire him and see him as often as he likes. Clegg's usual difficulties in talking to Miranda are particularly acute in this case. He awkwardly says that he has to leave and quickly makes for the door. Miranda makes a final plea.

(5)   'Please,' she said. Very gently and nicely. It was difficult to resist.
        It was like not having a net and catching a specimen you wanted in
        your first and second fingers (I was always very clever at that), coming
        up slowly behind and you had it, but you had to nip the thorax, and it
        would be quivering there. It wasn't easy like it was with a killing-
        bottle. And it was twice as difficult with her, because I didn't want to
        kill her, that was the last thing I wanted. (p. 40)

The difficulty in dealing with Miranda's entreaties is expressed in terms of a particular scenario derived from the BUTTERFLY source domain. In this scenario, Clegg catches a sought for butterfly with his hands and has to kill it with his fingers, rather than suffocating it in what he refers to as his 'killing-bottle'. The problem is that there is a fundamental incompatibility in the correspondence between the butterfly and Miranda. With the butterfly, Clegg's goals are achieved by killing, albeit in a more awkward way than he would like. With Miranda, his goals of possession and enjoyment cannot be achieved by killing her (which he explicitly says he does not want to do), since his pleasure mainly derives from watching her movements, her complexion, the effects of different hair styles and clothes on her appearance, and so on. However, Clegg's goals are also hard to realise with Miranda being alive. As a human being, Miranda cannot be fully controlled. In addition, Clegg is overwhelmed by her looks, charm and argumenta- tive power, which compounds his problems and frustration. The result is a situation of impasse and internal conflict. The BUTTERFLY metaphor has initially caused this impasse and is now used to perpetuate it and express it.

Cognitive metaphor theory can explain why and how Clegg makes sense of a variety of situations in terms of the BUTTERFLY metaphor, and account for the correspondence between Miranda and a butterfly and Clegg as a collector across a range of metaphorical expressions. However, this theory does not successfully explain the particular meanings of particular instantiations of the metaphor. My proposed interpretation of example (5) does not simply result from a unidirectional mapping of features and relationships from source to target domain: in the BUTTERFLY domain, there is no conflict or dilemma to be projected onto the target. The conflict arises in the attempt to merge together a scenario derived from the source domain and a scenario derived from the target domain.

Blending theory (also known as Conceptual Integration theory or Conceptual Blending theory) was developed precisely to deal with this kind of problem (Fauconnier 1997, Fauconnier and Turner 1996, Turner and Fauconnier 1999, 2000). Its aim is to account for the online construction of meaning in terms of networks of 'mental spaces'. [. . .]

> These spaces include two 'input' spaces (which, in a metaphorical case, are associated with the source and target of CMT [Conceptual Metaphor Theory]), plus a 'generic' space, representing conceptual structure that is shared by both inputs, and the 'blend' space, where material from the inputs combines and interacts.
>
> (Grady *et al.* 1999: 103)

In the case of example (5), the source input space is the scenario where Clegg awkwardly catches and kills a butterfly using his fingers. This space is derived from the larger BUTTERFLY domain in Clegg's conceptual structure. The target input space is the scenario where he has difficulties responding to Miranda and dealing with her pleas to be freed. This is part of the larger MIRANDA domain, which he is constructing as he is learning to deal with holding her captive. There is a partial cross-space mapping between source and target inputs (see the solid horizontal lines in Figure 26.1): Clegg as butterfly collector corresponds to Clegg as kidnapper, Miranda corresponds to the butterfly, capturing Miranda corresponds to catching a butterfly, Miranda's requests to be freed correspond to the butterfly trying to fly away, Clegg's inability to deal with Miranda's entreaties corresponds to the lack of a net, and the goal of possessing Miranda corresponds to the goal of possessing a butterfly. The main correspondences between these two mental spaces result from the BUTTERFLY metaphor which is part of Clegg's conceptual structure. However, the source input space has 'killing with fingers' as a solution to the problem with the butterfly. In contrast, in the target input space there is no solution for the problem, and Clegg declares that he does not want to kill Miranda. The generic space is an abstract scenario which consists of the basic structure shared by the two input domains: here Clegg captures a sought for living being and has difficulties dealing with its attempts to escape; no solution to the problem is specified.

The fourth space, the blend, arises from the fusion of material from the two input spaces into a single scenario, based on the cross-space correspondences and on their shared generic structure (in Figure 26.1, the correspondences between the generic space, the two input spaces and the blend are indicated by curved dotted lines). It is in the blend that, according to Blending theory, meanings are generated. The blend inherits the basic structure of the source input space: Clegg the kidnapper is Clegg the collector, Miranda is the butterfly, and so on. The notion of killing the captured being as a solution to the problem is projected from the source input space. However, this does

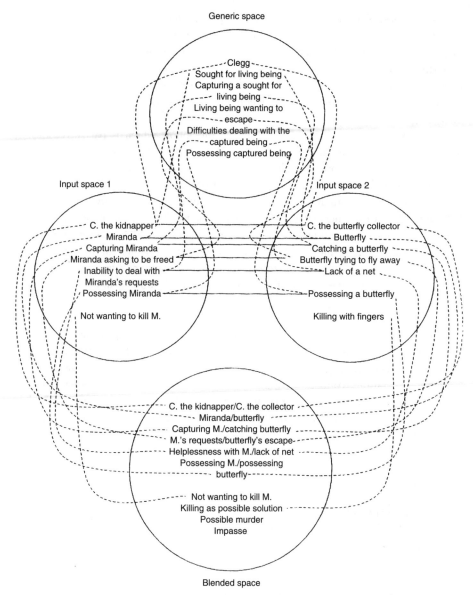

Figure 26.1 Conceptual network for example (5)

not provide an adequate solution to the problem in the blend, since it clashes with the desire not to kill Miranda which is projected from the target input space. Indeed, the target input space projects the feature '+ human' in relation to the captured entity, which results in the impasse I mentioned earlier: Clegg's goal of possession and enjoyment is incompatible with Miranda being alive (as is the case with the butterfly), but it is also incompatible with her being dead (unlike what is the case with the butterfly), even apart from any moral considerations. The notion of killing as a possible course of action is nevertheless projected from the source input space to the blend. In fact, Miranda's death would at least solve the immediate problem of dealing with her pleas and accusations. The blend has what is called 'emergent structure': Clegg's impasse does not exist in the source space and cannot therefore be explained in terms of the mapping of a feature of the source onto a feature of the target. Similarly, the killing of a butterfly in the source space is not problematic, as it is not criminal or illegal (although it may be seen as objectionable by some). It is in the blend, i.e. in the fusion of source and target spaces, that the decision whether to kill or not turns into an insoluble dilemma, and that the spectre of murder arises.

This example shows how the BUTTERFLY metaphor, which is partly responsible for Clegg's actions in the first place, cannot adequately serve him once he has captured a human being. [. . . H]owever, Clegg is unable to re-conceptualise the situation in a different way. Indeed, the final 'solution' to the problem posed by Miranda is the one provided by the source input space in example (5): although, technically, Clegg does not kill Miranda, he causes her death by not seeking the medical treatment she needs. This frees him to look for another victim who, he suggests, will be less confident and articulate than Miranda, and therefore easier to control. As readers, however, we know that the real cause of Clegg's problem is the attempt to map a non-human being onto a human being, so that the outcome of subsequent captures is unlikely to be different from that of the first.

[. . .]

In the case of Clegg's mind style, cognitive metaphor theory accounts for some idiosyncratic aspects of his conceptual structure and cognitive habits, while Blending theory accounts for his representations of particular situations, and for the way in which these representations contribute to the tragic end of the novel. Together, the two frameworks go a long way in explaining how metaphorical expressions are used in Fowles's novel to construct an insane and criminal, but apparently rational, mind.

[. . .]

References

Conradi, P. (1982) *John Fowles*. London: Methuen.

Cook, G. (1994) *Discourse and Literature*. Oxford: Oxford University Press.

Culpeper, J. (2001) *Language and Characterisation*. London: Longman.

Fauconnier, G. (1997) *Mappings in Thought and Language*. Cambridge: Cambridge University Press.

Fauconnier, G. and Turner, M. (1996) 'Blending as a central process of grammar', in A. Goldberg (ed.) *Conceptual Structure, Discourse, and Language*, Stanford, CA: Center for the Study of Language and Information, pp. 113–30.

Fowler, R. (1996) *Linguistic Criticism* (2nd edition). Oxford: Oxford University Press.

Fowles, J. (1998) *The Collector*. London: Vintage.

Goatly, A. (1997) *The Language of Metaphors*. London: Routledge.

Grady, J., Oakley, T. and Coulson, S. (1999) 'Blending and metaphor', in R.W. Gibbs, Jr and G.J. Steen (eds) *Metaphor in Cognitive Linguistics*, Amsterdam: John Benjamins: pp. 101–24.

Kövecses, Z. (2000) 'The scope of metaphor', in A. Barcelona (ed.) *Metaphor and Metonymy at the Crossroads: A Cognitive Perspective*, Berlin: Mouton de Gruyter, pp. 79–92.

Lakoff, G. and Johnson, M. (1980) *Metaphors We Live By*. Chicago: Chicago University Press.

Lakoff, G. and Turner, M. (1989) *More Than Cool Reason: A Field Guide to Poetic Metaphor*. Chicago: Chicago University Press.

Leech, G.N. and Short, M.H. (1981) *Style in Fiction*. London: Longman.

McIntyre, D. (2006) *Point of View in Plays*. Amsterdam: John Benjamins.

Olshen, B.N. (1978) *John Fowles*. New York: Frederick Ungar Publishing Co.

Palmer, A. (2004) *Fictional Minds*. Lincoln: University of Nebraska Press.

Ryan, M.L. (1991) *Possible Worlds, Artificial Intelligence and Narrative Theory*. Bloomington and Indianapolis: Indiana University Press.

Salami, M. (1992) *John Fowles's Fiction and the Poetics of Postmodernism*. London and Toronto: Associated University Presses.

Semino, E. (1997) *Language and World Creation in Poems and Other Texts*. London: Longman.

Semino, E. and Swindlehurst, K. (1996) 'Metaphor and mind style in Ken Kesey's *One Flew Over the Cuckoo's Nest*', *Style* 30 (1): 143–66.

Turner, M. and Fauconnier, G. (1999) 'A mechanism of creativity', *Poetics Today* 20 (3): 397–418.

Turner, M. and Fauconnier, G. (2000) 'Metaphor, metonymy, and binding', in A. Barcelona (ed.) *Metaphor and Metonymy at the Crossroads: A Cognitive Perspective*, Berlin: Walter de Gruyter, pp. 133–45.

Wolfe, P. (1976) *John Fowles, Magus and Moralist*. Lewisburg: Bucknell University Press.

Zunshine, L. (2006) *Why We Read Fiction: Theory of Mind and the Novel*. Columbus: Ohio State University Press.

Extracted from Elena Semino (2002) 'A cognitive stylistic approach to mind style in narrative fiction', in E. Semino and J. Culpeper (eds) *Cognitive Stylistics*, Amsterdam: Benjamins, pp. 95–122.

Chapter 27

Connectives in free indirect style: continuity or shift?

VIOLETA SOTIROVA

The stylistic feature of *free indirect discourse* has long been of interest to both stylisticians and traditional literary critics for its significance as a narrative technique that is central to the novel's capacity for expressing consciousness and subjectivity. In this chapter, Violeta Sotirova engages with the narratological theory by exploring the use of free indirect discourse in the writing of D.H. Lawrence. Aside from the intricate and precise analytical sensitivity to the text, Sotirova also pays attention to Lawrence's own manuscript revisions, and is not afraid to draw on this traditional literary-biographical factor in support of her stylistic argument. Historiographic and biographical contexts can also be seen as salient factors in stylistic analysis.

For more on the stylistics of consciousness, see Leech and Short (1981), Banfield (1982), Fludernik (1993), Lodge (2002) and Bray (2003).

Introduction

[. . .]

*F*REE INDIRECT STYLE FIRST presented a problem to linguists for its ability to blend deictic and modal features of two projected discourses: the narrator's and the character's. Having established a set of linguistic criteria for identifying the style, scholars became interested in sentences which do not overtly manifest the identified features but which nonetheless are interpreted as representing a character's point of view. This is the task pursued by Susan Ehrlich (1990) who explores the role of cohesive ties for viewpoint assignment and comes to the conclusion that just as these linking devices aid the creation of coherent texture in discourse, they act as devices sustaining the interpretation of point of view across sentences. Ehrlich builds her theory of cohesive ties as markers that help to sustain continuity of viewpoint on studies of cohesion by Halliday and Hasan (1976) and Reinhart (1980). In these works conjunctions are analysed as elements sustaining textual cohesion. The widely acknowledged role of conjunctions, then, is to hold texts together and contribute to their coherence. It is with a discussion of Ehrlich's position on this issue that this chapter begins.

Connectives and point of view

Ehrlich's semantic connectors comprise one set of items which trigger the reading of narrative sentences containing them as character-bound. She illustrates this effect with the following examples:

(1)   He was thinking of himself and the impression he was making, as she could tell by the sound of his voice, and his emphasis and his uneasiness. Success would be good for him. *At any rate they were off again.* Now she need not listen (Virginia Woolf, *To the Lighthouse*; cited in Ehrlich 1990: 55).

(2)   He thought, women are always like that; the vagueness of their minds is hopeless; it was a thing he had never been able to understand but so it was. It had been so with her – his wife. They could not keep anything clearly fixed in their minds. *But he had been wrong to be angry with her* [his daughter]; moreover, did he not rather like this vagueness in women? It was part of their extraordinary charm (Virginia Woolf, *To the Lighthouse*; cited in Ehrlich 1990: 55).

In passage (1) the first and second sentences are evocative of the viewpoint of the female character. The use of the progressive aspect in *he was thinking* and *he was making* makes the event unfold through the eyes of the character. This sense is heightened through the use of the modal verb *could* and especially the future-in-the-past *would* (was she thinking: 'I can tell by the sound of his voice . . . Success will be good for him'?). When we come to sentence three, it is the connecting phrase *at any rate* that hooks this sentence onto the preceding two, and the reader continues to interpret it as arising from the already established perspective of the protagonist.

In passage (2) the initial phrase *He thought* pinpoints the character's thought. For a few sentences thereafter the topic of women's minds is maintained, so the reading of the same point of view naturally follows. It is at the point of *But he had been wrong to be angry with her* that perspectives can potentially be switched and the sentence can be read as expressing the views of the narrator. Here we are faced with two interpretations: either the narrator is passing judgement on the character and is telling us that the character was wrong, or the character has changed his mind about himself. Ehrlich argues that the sentence will be interpreted as character subjective because the connective *but* prompts us to sustain our already established interpretation of point of view:

In all of these examples, the italicized sentences are connected to preceding discourse by the semantic connector beginning each sentence. Because the preceding discourse is identified as RST [represented speech and thought] by SCPs [sentences containing parentheticals] and/or other sentence-internal markers (e.g. root transformations, incomplete sentences), the sentences containing the semantic connectors receive the same interpretation in terms of point of view. For example, no syntactic feature of a sentence such as *But he had been wrong to be angry with her* of passage [2] identifies it as a character's judgement as opposed to the objective narrator's. Rather, it is

the inter-sentential linking achieved by the semantic connector *but* that
facilitates the RST interpretation.

(Ehrlich 1990: 55–6)

So one of the strengths of Ehrlich's approach lies in its ability to describe the style as
discourse not as isolated sentences.

Connectives: a problem in Lawrence

In this section I shall examine some passages of *free indirect style* which do not appear to
fit the model expounded up to this point. I have chosen my extracts from ones discussed
in relation to point of view by Helen Baron (1998) and Sylvia Adamson (1995).

(3)   (i) He had a high good time; (ii) and yet, when he remembered it, it
      seemed a pain. (iii) His mother was cool with him for a day or two.
      (iv) But he was so adorable – ! (v) And yet – a tinge of loneliness was
      creeping in again, between her and him (D.H. Lawrence 1992: 77).

(4)   (i) On the whole she scorned the male sex deeply. (ii) But here was a
      new specimen, quick, light, graceful, who could be gentle and who
      could be sad, and who was clever, and who knew a lot, and who had a
      death in the family [. . .] (iii) Yet she tried hard to scorn him, because
      he would not see in her the princess but only the swinegirl.
      (iv) And he scarcely observed her (D.H. Lawrence 1992: 174).

Baron sets out to explore one of Lawrence's major themes: the permeable boundary
between '*life* and *self*', and *self* and *other*; a theme, which she claims, is reflected in the
'narrator's unusual use of vocabulary and syntax' (1998: 357). This peculiar language
is embodied in *free indirect style* in (3) above. Baron (1998) believes that (3) begins with
the point of view of the Morel's eldest son, William; then the viewpoint shifts to that of
his mother, Mrs Morel. Baron (1998) suggests that halfway through the passage we are
already unsure of whose thoughts we are reading and the last sentence can apply to both
characters on stage.

Adamson's (1995) concern is of a different nature: her aim is to correlate linguistic
form and literary effect and to demonstrate that formal analyses can illuminate our
understanding of narrative meaning. Adamson quotes extract (4) as problematic
because, as an instance of editorial intervention, it demonstrates how the arrangement
of narrative sentences can radically change meaning in the novel. While in Lawrence's
manuscript the last two sentences appear separated by a paragraph break:

. . . Yet she tried hard to scorn him, because he would not see in her the
princess but only the swinegirl.
   And he scarcely observed her (author's manuscript; cited in Adamson
1995: 31).

In the first edition, *And he scarcely observed her* is added to the preceding paragraph, thus
producing:

. . . Yet she tried hard to scorn him, because he would not see in her the princess but only the swingirl. And he scarcely observed her (first edition; cited in Adamson 1995: 31).

Following Adamson's analysis we can see that the implications of this change are significant. If separated by a paragraph break, the sentence can be interpreted as the narrator's ironic comment on Miriam's qualms. As part of the preceding paragraph, the sentence adds to Miriam's reasons for scorning Paul. Adamson argues that the dividing line 'between what is subjectively true for the character and what is objectively true for the world of the novel' (1995: 32) is very subtle and a minor editorial correction can foreground this inherent indeterminacy of the *free indirect style* technique.

Extracts (3) and (4) were found problematic by these two scholars and both locate the problem in an inherent ambiguity in Lawrence's use of *free indirect style*. What is evident from a first reading is that both passages abound in connectives, and in Adamson's study the connective *and* also represents the crux of the problem. The questions raised by Baron's and Adamson's analyses of their respective passages can be phrased as: 1) what is the relevance of connectives to the study of *free indirect style*? and 2) is there any significant correlation between the presence of connectives and the two scholars' observations that point of view in these passages is problematic and ambiguous? In this instance Ehrlich's (1990) observations do not provide an answer. Connectives in extracts (3) and (4) are not used to sustain the same reading of perspective across sentences. As I shall argue a correlation between the use of these items and the analyses offered by Baron (1998) and Adamson (1995) is possible to establish. This will enable us to explain those occurrences of connectives that do not fit the Ehrlich model. What follows is my analysis of the role of connectives in the passages in question.

In extract (3) the first three sentences, as Baron has argued, arise from William's point of view: the phrase *high good time* is idiomatic, *it seemed a pain* implies William's interpretation of events; and *his mother* is a referring expression that can be attributed to him. As we read into sentence four, it can only be the expression of Mrs Morel's attitude: the semantically plausible option because only she can think that *he was so adorable*. An alternative interpretation is to read *But he was so adorable!* as William ventriloquising Mrs Morel's thoughts. Baron's perception of blurred point of view may therefore be explained more precisely by reference to the role of the connective *but*. The conjunction links the thoughts of the two characters, but rather than sustaining point of view it disrupts it.

Extract (4) poses similar questions. In sentences (ii) and (iii) the initial conjunctions sustain Miriam's thought and so remain unproblematic: this use agrees with the prediction of discourse analysts about their cohesive role. Sentence (iv), although formally linked to the preceding sentences by the coordinating conjunction *and*, is removed from them into a new paragraph. By opening the paragraph with *and* and by breaking with convention Lawrence changes the tone of narratorial voice, thereby signalling change in viewpoint. Failing to notice this, Lawrence's printers appended sentence four to the preceding paragraph, following the house-style of the publisher.

Given the theoretical predictions made in the literature on discourse analysis, how can we account for Lawrence's use of connectives at the interstices of perspectival shifts? Ehrlich (1990), a linguist who applies the discourse functions of connectives to the study of point of view, considers their role as primarily continuative. When a shift between viewpoints is effected: from character to narrator or from one character to another, it is surprising that these items of cohesion should be used.

An attempt to capture the functions of AND in a Lawrence short story

A fundamental reference point is Willie van Peer's study (1985) of the uses of the conjunction *and* in Lawrence's short story 'The Mortal Coil'. Van Peer classifies all instances of *and*, finding that of the total 201 occurrences of the conjunction, 19 (or 9.45%) do not readily belong to either of the four groups of meaning he has outlined (additive, temporal, causative, adversative). The first problematic case that van Peer quotes is (5):

> (5)   She looked in wonder for a few moments. '**And** what does it stand for now?' she said. 'A magnificent second-lieutenant!' (D.H. Lawrence, 'The Mortal Coil'; cited in van Peer 1985: 370).

[. . .]
    Van Peer is troubled by similar questions as the ones I raised [above]. If the function of *and* in passage (5) is not easy to classify under any of his four headings, there must be other textual reasons for using the conjunction at this point. Van Peer concludes that 'AND may not only be used to simply link two consecutive speech acts which follow each other immediately in the turn-taking position of the unfolding discourse, it may also and simultaneously be employed in order to bridge moments of silence' (1985: 371). Having established one of the pragmatic functions of *and* which directly stems from its use in conversation, van Peer then turns to a different set of problem-posing *and*s. For instance in (6):

> (6)   She stood watching as he sat bent forward in his stupefaction. The fine cloth of his uniform showed the moulding of his back. **And** something tortured her as she saw him, till she could hardly bear it . . . (D.H. Lawrence, 'The Mortal Coil'; cited in van Peer 1985: 371).

According to van Peer it is the 'change from the PERCEPTUAL to the MENTAL ACTIVITIES of the woman' (1985: 373) that necessitates the use of a conjunction in precisely this position. In van Peer's final example *and* is again analysed as linking different cognitive states in the character. Consider (7):

> (7)   He bent down **and** kissed her. **And** still her clear, rather frightening eyes seemed to be searching for him inside himself. (D.H. Lawrence, 'The Mortal Coil'; cited in van Peer 1985: 375).

The two uses of *and* here are described as registering 'a change from PHYSICAL to INTERACTIVE, and then from INTERACTIVE to MENTAL activities' (van Peer 1985: 375). Van Peer's insight is illuminating. We may add to his line of thought an explanation that relates the use of *and* to point of view. The description of action in the first sentence in extract (7) can only be supplied by the narrator, while the second sentence could be interpreted as the man's perception of the woman. There is textual evidence for such an interpretation: the evaluative *rather frightening*, the vague *seemed* and the reflexive *himself*. So, here we are not only confronted with an example of linking different states of the character, it is also different personae's viewpoints that are being linked with the conjunction. This use of connectives to set viewpoints in opposition is more apparent in a passage I have selected from the same story:

(8) 'Ha!' she cried suddenly. 'It wouldn't come to that, either. If they kick you out of the army, you'll find somebody to get round – you're like a cat, you'll land on your feet.'

But this was just what he was not. He was not like a cat. His self-mistrust was too deep. Ultimately he had no belief in himself, as a separate isolated being. He knew he was sufficiently clever, an aristocrat, good-looking, the sensitive superior of most men. The trouble was, that apart from the social fabric he belonged to, he felt himself nothing, a cipher . . . (D.H. Lawrence 1990: 175).

Here the bridging conjunction *but* links the woman's words with either the man's view of himself, or the narrator's insight into the real nature of the man's character. Apart from contrasting ideas in this instance the connective also contrasts the viewpoints of two narrative voices. Ehrlich's model (1990) does not account for this situation. Van Peer's observations (1985) strongly suggested to me the conversational aspect in the uses of conjunctions. In order to pursue further my intuitions regarding connectives and point of view in *free indirect style* it is helpful to learn from the findings of conversation analysis.

The evidence from conversation analysis

The group of connectives that I am interested in does not seem to fit into the discourse model which assigns cohesive functions to these items. An alternative source of explanation for the interpretation of connectives in *free indirect style* may be sought in conversational practices. The coordinating conjunctions (*and*, *but*) and the conjunctive adverbs (*yet*, *still*) which appear in my passages, have all received attention by conversation analysts, who group them under the heading of discourse markers, a larger set of items which also includes interjections (*well*, *oh*) and phrases, such as *you know*, *you see*, *I mean*, etc. What all these disparate items have in common in conversation is that they contribute to the organisation of talk in some way, i.e. their meaning is not only (although it may be derived from) their established lexical and grammatical meaning; they exhibit functional properties that contribute to some interactional aspect of communication. So, the connectives *and* and *but*, in their role as discourse markers, retain their respective semantic core meanings of addition and contrast, but they also acquire the pragmatic meaning of continuing actions and contrasting actions in conversation (Schiffrin 1986, 1987). [. . .]

So, connectives are interactionally significant. They signal the commitment of the current speaker to the joint building of ideas and they help acknowledge the interlocutor's point of view. We can now return to our Lawrence data and pursue the relevance of the claims made by conversation analysts to the presentation of point of view.

A conversational model for free indirect style

The new paradigm is dialogical. In this section we look at two more examples of viewpoint shifts in *free indirect style*. Both examples involve the struggles of Paul (*he*) and Miriam (*she*) in *Sons and Lovers*.

(9)   (i) 'You make me so spiritual'!' he lamented. 'And I don't want to be spiritual.' (ii) *She took her finger from her mouth with a little pop, and looked up at him almost challenging.* (iii) **But still** *her soul was naked in her great dark eyes, and there was the same yearning appeal upon her.* (iv) *If he could have kissed her in abstract purity he would have done so.* (v) **But** *he could not kiss her thus –* <u>and</u> *she seemed to leave no other way.* (vi) **And** *she yearned to him* (D.H. Lawrence 1992: 226).

After Paul's direct speech the reader is inclined to interpret sentence (ii) as Paul's perception of Miriam; an interpretation also strengthened by the use of the evaluative, but vague, *almost challenging*. Sentence (iii) is readily interpreted as a continuation of Paul's viewpoint: it contains two of Ehrlich's markers of continuation: *but* and *still*; it also makes use of the adjective *same* which would only be clear to a fellow participant in the narrative world, i.e. Paul. Sentences (iv) and (v) entertain a possibility in the narrative world and the hypothetical action of kissing Miriam and Paul's inability to do so are most logically the expression of his thoughts. It is at the point of sentence (vi) that the reader is jerked out of Paul's mind and is given an alternative interpretation of Miriam's state. While Paul thinks that Miriam is spiritual and thus blocks his desire for physical closeness, she is here revealed as *yearning* for him too. The same effect of blurred viewpoint which Baron (1998) and Adamson (1995) have noticed is felt here. This sentence disrupts the established viewpoint in the preceding discourse: it states that which Paul is unaware of and it states it in contrast to what he thinks. This comment, therefore, has to be external to Paul's consciousness and has to arise from the other character, or from the narrator, or from both of them. The use of the connective makes sentence (vi) sound as though the new viewpoint is orientated as a response to Paul's musings. The whole passage displays two viewpoints linked by the connective and made to stand in juxtaposition like rejoinders in dialogue. The connective links two viewpoints, which are incompatible with each other, but its presence signals their relatedness and the intention to make them sound as two sides of a whole: two angles from which the same problem is focused upon.

A similar use of connectives is found in the following extract in which the thoughts of the two characters, Paul and Miriam, interact again:

(10)   (i) Miriam shuddered. (ii) She drew him to her; she pressed him to her bosom; she kissed him and kissed him. (iii) He submitted, *but it was torture.* (iv) *She could not kiss his agony.* (v) *That remained alone and apart.* (vi) *She kissed his face, and roused his blood, while his soul was apart, writhing with the agony of death.* (vii) **And** *she kissed him and fingered his body, till at last, feeling he would go mad, he got away from her.* (viii) *It was not that he wanted just then – not that.* (ix) **And** *she thought she had soothed him and done him good* (D.H. Lawrence 1992: 435).

In passage (10) I have italicised the sentences (or clauses) that can potentially be read as *free indirect style*. What is obvious is that sentence (viii) expresses Paul's discomfort. Through a sudden move in the next sentence (ix) a counter-claim is made which contrasts Miriam's experience. Imagining this as a conversation helps us to perceive the structure of *free indirect style* more clearly. *And* here corresponds to what in conversation would be turn-initial position and it initiates the turn of the other protagonist to express herself. But in this case it sounds as if it initiates three simultaneous turns: the narrator's, Paul's and Miriam's.

The examples discussed so far display connectives at strategic points of shift to a new perspective. In most cases we witness dramatic conflicts between two characters which Lawrence transcribes effectively through rapid movement of the camera between the characters' respective minds. Part of the poignancy of these conflicts resides in the way in which characters experience each other's thoughts and feelings and are affected by them. The remarkable fact is that Lawrence manages to encode these inner and outer dialogues in a variety of *free indirect style*, which ensures that the narrative glides dialogically between minds. At this point what remains to be answered is how deliberate and how systematic Lawrence's use of connectives is.

Revisions of connectives: the evidence from manuscripts

In this section I will consider the revisions of conjunctions made by Lawrence himself, and the corrections introduced by his editor and printers which might affect the role of conjunction for the interpretation of *free indirect style*.

[. . .]

Lawrence's [. . .] thorough revisions of longer passages [. . .] reveal his ability to evoke contradictions through the use of sentence-initial connectives. The [following] revision was introduced by the writer in the final manuscript. First he had:

(11) *She felt she could bear anything for him. Her love was in the pure spirit of sacrifice.* She put her hand on his knee as he leaned forward in his chair. He took it and kissed it with his mouth. *Strangely enough, his heart also was now full of sacrifice. He loved her.* **But** *it was in a sacrificial, not a creative spirit. In loving her, he sacrificed himself.* Slowly, he drew her to him and kissed her (C. Baron and H. Baron 1992: 563, note 326: 11).

In the final manuscript Lawrence revised the passage to:

(i) *She felt she could bear anything for him, she would suffer for him.* (ii) She put her hand on his knee as he leaned forward in his chair. (iii) He took it and kissed it. (iv) **But** *it hurt to do so.* (v) *He felt he was putting himself aside.* (vi) *He sat there sacrificed to her purity, which felt more like a nullity.* (vii) *How could he kiss her hand passionately, when it would drive her away, and leave nothing but pain?* (viii) **Yet** slowly he drew her to him and kissed her (D.H. Lawrence 1992: 326).

The conjunction *but* in the first passage introduces a continuation to Paul's thoughts. Its continuative function accords with Ehrlich's analysis (1990). In the second passage, however, two connectives are used at points of shift to a new viewpoint. Sentence

(iii) describes an action of the protagonist and will be read as narratorial report. Sentence (iv) contrasts the character's thoughts with the narrator's report of his actions. At another such junction, between (vii) and (viii), the connective enacts a shift from Paul's thoughts to the narrator's report of his action. Lawrence does this type of thing a lot merging narrative report of action with character viewpoint. The new connective *yet* introduced in this passage shows how conscious was Lawrence's sensibility to the technical aspects of *free indirect style*.

[It is clear from these examples and others that] Lawrence consciously introduced some revisions involving connectives. When interpreted, the revised passages show a tendency towards a deepening of the conflict within a character's mind, or between characters, or between character and narrator. The revisions also make the psychological portraits of characters more poignant. The different viewpoints are not only presented next to each other, they are persistently wrought together and played off against each other in a dialogue of minds. As regards the changes made by editors and printers, these are instructive in showing us even more clearly the innovativeness and unconventionality of Lawrence's mastery of *free indirect style*.

[. . .]

The different narrative personae discourses are so juxtaposed as to suggest a dialogic probing of each theme: it finds no ultimate solution; instead, it is left open to be explored from different angles, each of them as valid as the other. Bakhtin's idea (1984) that a dialogue is inscribed in novelistic discourse, not only in formal exchanges of direct speech, seems to provide a powerful explanation of *free indirect style* if we approach it as discourse, not as a group of isolated sentences. This implicit dialogism, Bakhtin suggests, constitutes the aesthetic value of the novel. I have shown that the internal dialogue inscribed in Lawrence's text is also formally encoded in the linguistic structure of *free indirect style*. The evidence from conversation analysis, paired with Bakhtin's notion of dialogism, can now help us arrive at a meaningful interpretation of viewpoint shifts, meaningful both linguistically and aesthetically.

Part of the artistic task of the novel *Sons and Lovers* lies in the portrayal of Paul's personal development. In the process of growing-up he has to resolve several relationships with people he loves and also resolve conflicts within himself. All this naturally presupposes an intense sensitivity towards the other which we witness in every character. Corresponding to the content and the aesthetic aims of *Sons and Lovers* is Lawrence's peculiar deployment of *free indirect style*, the narrative technique that allows him to cast light on people and objects inhabiting his narrative world from numerous angles. The presentation of more than one perspective often produces the effect of merging perspectives. Connectives as linguistic markers of *free indirect style* enhance the sense of dialogic relatedness between viewpoints and minds.

References

Adamson, S.M. (1995) 'Empathetic narrative: a literary and linguistic problem', in W. Ayres-Bennett and P. O'Donovan (eds) *Syntax and the Literary Text*, Cambridge: Cambridge French Colloquia, pp. 17–42.

Bakhtin, M. (1984) *Problems of Dostoevsky's Poetics*. Ann Arbor: University of Michigan Press.

Banfield, A. (1982) *Unspeakable Sentences: Narration and Representation in the Language of Fiction*. Boston: Routledge and Kegan Paul.

Baron, H. (1998) 'Disseminated consciousness in *Sons and Lovers*', *Essays in Criticism* 48 (4): 357–78.

Baron, C. and Baron, H. (1992) 'Explanatory notes', in D.H. Lawrence *Sons and Lovers*, Cambridge: Cambridge University Press, pp. 509–80.

Bray, J. (2003) *The Epistolary Novel: Representation of Consciousness*. London: Routledge.

Ehrlich, S. (1990) *Point of View. A Linguistic Analysis of Literary Style*. London: Routledge.

Fludernik, M. (1993) *The Fictions of Language and the Languages of Fiction*. London: Routledge.

Halliday, M. and Hasan, R. (1976) *Cohesion in English*. London: Longman.

Lawrence, D.H. (1990) *England, My England and Other Stories* (ed. B. Steele) [original 1922]. Cambridge: Cambridge University Press.

Lawrence, D.H. (1992) *Sons and Lovers* (ed. C. Baron and H. Baron) [original 1913]. Cambridge: Cambridge University Press.

Leech, G. and Short, M. (1981) *Style in Fiction*. London: Longman.

Lodge, D. (2002) *Consciousness and the Novel*. London: Secker and Warburg.

Reinhart, T. (1980) 'Conditions for text coherence', *Poetics Today* 1: 161–80.

Schiffrin, D. (1986) 'Functions of *AND* in discourse', *Journal of Pragmatics* 10: 41–66.

Schiffrin, D. (1987) *Discourse Markers*. Cambridge: Cambridge University Press.

van Peer, W. (1985) 'Toward a pragmatic theory of connexity: an analysis of the use of the conjunction *AND* from a functional perspective', in E. Sözer (ed.) *Text Connexity, Text Coherence: Aspects, Methods, Results*, Hamburg: Helmut Buske Verlag, pp. 363–79.

Extracted from Violeta Sotirova (2004) 'Connectives in free indirect style: continuity or shift?', *Language and Literature* 13 (3): 216–34.

PART FOUR

Coda

Chapter 28

Stylistics: retrospect and prospect

RONALD CARTER AND
PETER STOCKWELL

A T THE END OF this Reader in Language and Literature, it might seem obvious to the non-specialist that literature, the most culturally valued and aesthetically pres-tigious form of language practice, is best studied using the resources developed in the field of linguistics. However, this truism has not always been obvious to a wide range of disciplines, all of which claim a different stake in the study of the literary. This situation has also been occasioned in part by the historical baggage accumulated by institutional-ised disciplines, out of territorial self-interest, and (it must be said) out of intellectual laziness, as well as legitimate arguments around the validity and scope of linguistics. Stylistics is the discipline that has bridged these areas, and stylisticians have found themselves engaged in arguments not only with literary critics, cultural theorists, philo-sophers, poets, novelists and dramatists, but also with practitioners of linguistics.

As an academic discipline stylistics has tended to be seen, pretty much throughout the twentieth century, as neither one thing nor the other, or, possibly worse, as all things to all men and women, as sitting therefore uncomfortably on the bridge between the linguistic and the literary. Some linguists have felt stylistics is too soft to be taken too seriously, tending to introduce irrelevant notions such as performance data and readerly interpretation; some literature specialists, by contrast, have felt that stylistics is too mechanistic and reductive, saying nothing significant about historical context or aesthetic theory, eschewing evaluation for the most part in the interests of a naive scientism and claiming too much for interpretations that are at best merely text-immanent. For one group, stylistics simply and reductively dissects its object; for the other, the object simply cannot be described in a scientifically replicable and transparent manner. But, as we have seen in this volume, the discipline is now long-established, is still here and is growing exponentially.

The multivalent position of stylistics has its roots in the histories of language study and literary criticism, and the institutional make-up of modern universities and depart-ment divisions which fossilise particular disciplinary boundaries and configurations. Stylistics has therefore come to be regarded as an essentially interdisciplinary field, drawing on the different sub-disciplines within linguistics to varying degrees, as well as on fields recognisable to literary critics, such as philosophy, cultural theory, sociology, history and psychology. However, we would like to argue that stylistics is a single coherent discipline: in fact, that it is naturally the central discipline of literary study, against which all other current approaches are partial or interdisciplinary. In order to arrive at this position, we must consider the history of stylistics, the status of stylistic analysis, and review the latest paradigms and principles in stylistics research. We would also like to avoid a simply retrospective synopsis and to point beyond this Reader, in the form of manifesto, with a programme for the discipline of stylistics.

A brief history of stylistics

Broadly viewed as the analysis of linguistic form and its social effects, stylistics can be seen as a direct descendant of rhetoric, which constituted a major part of the training of educated men for most of the past two and a half millennia. Specifically, stylistics overlaps considerably with 'elocutio', the selection of style for an appropriate effect. (The other four divisions of rhetorical skill were: invention, the organisation of ideas, memory, and delivery.) It is important to note the dual aspect in the discipline: rhetoric was concerned not only with linguistic form but also inextricably with the notion of the appropriacy of the form in context. The context was typically and primarily for spoken discourse, though rhetorical discussion was also applied to written texts. In the course of the twentieth century, stylistics developed with an almost exclusive focus on written literature, while at the same time the link between formalism and readerly effects became weakened.

According to Fowler (1981), there were three direct influences which produced stylistics: Anglo-American literary criticism; the emerging field of linguistics; and European, especially French, structuralism. Early twentieth-century literary criticism tended to be variously an exercise in philology, historical in orientation, based in author-intention, or more focused on the texture of the language of literary works. The latter, though also encompassing textual editing and manuscript scholarship, mainly focused on the 'practical criticism' of short poems or extracts from longer prose texts. Such 'close reading' was largely informed by a few descriptive terms from the traditional school-taught grammar of parts of speech. This British practical criticism developed in the US into the 'New Criticism'. Where the former placed readerly interpretation first with the close reading to support it, the New Critics focused on 'the words themselves'. Famous essays by Wimsatt and Beardsley (1954a, 1954b) and others argued for the exclusion of any considerations of authorial intention or the historical conditions of contemporary production of literary works, and also against any psychologising of the literary reading experience.

Despite the rather uncompromising stance taken by New Criticism, the belief that a literary work was sufficient unto itself did not amount to a purely descriptive account of literary texts. Interpretative decisions and resolutions simply remained implicit in terms of the social conditions and ideologies that informed them, while being dressed up in an apparent descriptive objectivity. A more rigorous descriptive account was, however, being developed in the field of linguistics. As Fowler (1981) again points out, Bloomfieldian structural linguistics evolving between the 1920s and 1950s offered a precise terminology and framework for detailed analyses of metrical structure in poetry. Chomsky's transformational-generative grammar from 1957 onwards provided a means of exploring poetic syntactic structure with far more sensitivity to detail than had ever been possible in literary criticism. And Halliday's functionalism (Halliday 1973) added a socio-cultural dimension that began to explain how stylistic choices are meaningfully encoded in literary and non-literary texts (see also Halliday (Chapter 3) and Fowler (Chapter 6) in this volume).

The third area that influenced stylistics was European structuralism, arising out of Saussurean semiology and Russian Formalism through the work of Jakobson, Barthes, Todorov, Levi-Strauss and Culler, among others. Branded 'formalists' by their detractors, many of the main concerns of modern poetics were in fact developed by the Moscow Linguistic Circle, the St Petersburg group *Opayaz*, and later the Prague School linguists. These concerns included studies of metaphor, the foregrounding and dominance of theme, trope and other linguistic variables, narrative morphology, the effects of literary defamiliarisation, and the use of theme and rheme to delineate perspective in sentences. The Formalists called themselves 'literary linguists', in recognition of their belief that linguistics was the necessary ground for literary study (Jameson 1972, Selden 1984: chapter 4).

As Lodge points out in this volume (Chapter 2), stylistics began as a distinct approach to literary texts in the hands of Spitzer (1948) Wellek and Warren (1949), and Ullmann (1964), for example, but it really emerged from the 1960s onwards as the different influences mentioned above came to be integrated into a set of conventions for analysis. From Formalism and practical criticism came the focus of interest on literature and the literary, and from linguistics came the rigour of descriptive analysis and a scientific concern for transparency and replicability in that description. Though stylistic analysis could be practised on any sort of text, much discussion involved the specification of 'literariness' and the search to define a 'literary language' – this preoccupation dominated to such an extent that stylistics has come to be identified very strongly with the discussion of literature, with non-literary investigations of texts delineating themselves separately as 'critical linguistics' or 'critical discourse analysis' or 'text linguistics' and so on. (It is partly as a corrective to this development that we entitled the volume a 'Language and Literature Reader', rather than a 'Stylistics Reader', although in fact the term has been used interchangeably with 'literary linguistics' throughout this book.) Of course, the notion of literariness makes no sense within a formalist or structuralist paradigm, since a large part of what is literary depends on the social, institutional and ideological conditions of production and interpretation. Nevertheless, and as illustrated in the Foundations section of this Reader (Part One), stylistic analyses flourished in the 1970s, especially explorations of the metrics and grammar of poetry, and explanations of deviant or striking forms of expression in both poetry and prose.

Concerns with literariness, the investigation of artificial rather than natural language, and the spectre of capricious interpretation all served to make theoretical and applied linguists in other areas of linguistic study rather suspicious of stylistics. At a time when the other branches of linguistics were claiming prestige and institutional funding as social sciences, those who were interested in literary analysis tended to be regarded as operating at the 'soft' end of the discipline. Equally and contrarily, literary critics and philosophers tended to regard the practices of stylisticians as being mechanistic and reductive. Since stylisticians often worked in literature departments, the most heated debates occurred with literary critics: traditional liberal humanist critics attacked a perceived irreverence for literary genius and its ineffable product; critics excited by the rise of literary theory as a discipline attacked stylistics for claiming to be merely a method without an ideological or theoretical underpinning. Notorious examples of the antagonism include the debate between the stylistician Roger Fowler and the literary critic F.W. Bateson (see Fowler 1971 for an account), centring on the question of rigorous descriptiveness against literary sensibility; or the attack by Stanley Fish and defence by Michael Toolan (see Fish 1980 and Toolan 1990), circling around the status of interpretation in literary reading. (Stubbs in this volume (Chapter 23), returns again to the issue.)

Although vigorous defences of stylistics continued to be raised in the 1970s and 1980s, the field largely sidestepped the theoretical quagmire by taking an explicitly practical approach in the form of 'pedagogical stylistics'. This was a natural consequence of teaching (English) language using literary texts: foreign language learners took most readily to a linguistic approach to literature without importing any undue concern for theoretical niceties nor any misplaced reverence for the literary artefact. Teaching language through literature mirrored stylistics very clearly: texts tended to be those of contemporary literature; stylistically deviant texts were popular because they were fun and made it easy for the teacher to illustrate a specific point of usage; grammar and lexical choice were discussed as a motivating means of accessing the literature, rather than studied rather dryly for their own sake. Stylistics thus took itself out of literature departments and found adherents in education and modern language study around the world, enthusiastically supported by the international cultural promotion agency of the UK government, the British Council. (See Widdowson 1975, 1992; Brumfit 1983; Brumfit and Carter 1986; Short 1989; McCarthy and Carter 1994 and Cook, Chapter 17, this volume.)

At the same time, in the 1970s and 1980s traditional linguists (with their focus on grammar and phonology) began to feel threatened by rapid advances in pragmatics, sociolinguistics and discourse analysis (augmented by the dialogic philosophies of Bakhtin and Vygotsky). These developments allowed stylistics to move beyond the analysis of short texts and sentence-level phenomena and generated richer accounts of language in use and in context. Studies involving speech act theory, norms of spoken interaction, politeness, appropriacy of register choice, dialectal variation, cohesion and coherence, deictic projection, turn-taking and floor-holding all allowed stylistics the opportunity of exploring text-level features and the interpersonal dimension of literature, especially in prose fiction and dramatic texts. New labels for a host of sub-disciplines of stylistics blossomed: 'literary pragmatics', 'literary semantics', 'discourse stylistics', 'stylometrics', 'critical linguistics', 'schema poetics', and so on. Stylistics came to identify itself as virtuously interdisciplinary, though it should perhaps properly be seen in this period as 'inter-sub-disciplinary' (see Fowler 1996; Verdonk 2002).

By the early 1980s, stylistics had established itself as a coherent set of practices largely based in Europe, mainly in Britain and Ireland, with strong centres in the Germanic and Scandinavian countries, representation in Spain as a major English as a foreign language destination for British teachers, with a separate tradition of *stylistique* operating in France, Italy, Greece and Turkey. Stylistics also developed where teaching links to Britain were strongest: in Australasia, India, Japan, Southeast Asia (especially Hong Kong and Singapore), and parts of Africa in the Commonwealth. The term 'stylistics' was nowhere near as widely used in North America, where generative grammar maintained its paradigmatic hold on linguistics, and post-structuralist theory enthralled those literature departments that aspired to more than character-study and a simple historicism, although some literary critics began to feel threatened by the linguistic turn in the humanities and social sciences. At this time, too, there was a steady professionalisation of the subject of stylistics with the founding of the international Poetics and Linguistics Association (PALA) in 1980, and new journals and series devoted to the interfaces between language and literature were established with international publishers.

The status of stylistic analysis

One reason for the historical debates concerning stylistics has been the difficulty of defining 'style'. Even in its most simple sense of variation in language use, many questions instantly arise: variation from what? varied by whom? for what purpose? in what context of use? The different sub-disciplines that have been drawn on in stylistics have also brought along different senses of the term. Variationist sociolinguists treat style as a social variable correlated with gender, or class, for example, and have developed a cline of formality on this dimension. Anthropologists and ethnomethodologists have identified style with the contextual 'domain' in which the language variety is used, so that style has developed a wider sense close to that of 'register'. Style as an interpersonal feature involves psychological and socially motivated choices, so style can be seen as the characteristic pattern of choices associated with a writer's or projected character's 'mind-style', or the pattern associated with particular periods, genres or literary movements (see Semino, Chapter 26, this volume). Most broadly, since every dimension of linguistic expression represents a choice – whether idiosyncratic or socially determined – the limits of 'style' can be seen to be the limits of language itself, which is in itself a not especially helpful position.

One central tenet in modern stylistics has been to reject the artificial analytical distinction between form and content. Contrary to the practice of traditional rhetoric, style cannot be merely an ornamentation of the sense of an utterance, when it is motivated by personal and socio-cultural factors at every level and is correspondingly evaluated along these ideological dimensions by readers and audiences. Style is not merely free variation. Even utterances that are produced randomly are treated conventionally against the language system in operation, (as can be seen in surrealist and nonsense works, for example, Stockwell, Chapter 20, in this volume). Moreover, there can be no synonymy in utterances, since the connotations even of close variations are always potentially significant. Taking this argument to its logical end, even the same sentence uttered twice is 'stylistically' non-synonymous since the context of the second occasion of utterance is different from that of the first.

Clearly, the sense of 'stylistic' being used here has moved on a great deal from the earlier formalist sense of 'the words themselves'. The sorts of things stylisticians have been doing over the last twenty to thirty years have added more and more dimensions to the strictly 'linguistic' level, encompassing more of what language is while not losing sight of the necessity to ground descriptions in tangible evidence. Socio-cultural and psychological factors have become part of stylistic considerations.

Since the early 1980s, stylistics has continued in this expansive phase. Criticised for constantly focusing on deviant or odd texts, stylisticians shifted to the analysis of less stylistically striking writing, and presented variation in terms of norms and patterns that were internally marked in the literary work. The search for a linguistic definition of literariness was largely abandoned, with the literary being located in contexts of production and interpretation. The emphasis turned to examining the continuities between literary creativity and everyday creativity, and to how literary reading is continuous with the reception of language in general. Sociolinguistic findings informed literary analysis. Cognitive psychological aspects fed into stylistic exploration. Developments in pragmatics and discourse analysis continued to offer new tools and areas of investigation for stylistics. Insights into language use provided by corpus linguistics were drawn on, and computational techniques applied to literary works, enabling more extensive analysis of complete novels and plays. Through the 1990s, stylistics in its most broad sense became one of the most dynamic and interdisciplinary fields within applied linguistics, its confidence growing as a result of palpable progression in the descriptive power of its analytical resources.

In response to its invigorated position within literary studies, stylistic practice has recently attracted a new series of methodological attacks, as well as debates between stylisticians themselves around theoretical issues and ideologies. However, the key arguments and issues being discussed can still be seen as rehearsals of concerns that have been of interest throughout the history of poetics. For example, there have been several variations on the theme of the position of stylistics as a science or as part of a more artistic endeavour. Most stylistics adheres to the scientific practices of presenting rigorous and systematic method and being explicit about its assumptions. Studies mainly conform to a Popperian approach to scientific method: they are transparent, explicit in their hypotheses and expectations, and are therefore falsifiable. Because analyses are explicit and replicable, other readers can compare their own readings and see how they differ from those of the stylistician.

Language, literature and hermeneutics

The key issue here is the question of interpretation, and the importance of noticing a difference between the textual object, reading and interpretation. As one of us has argued elsewhere in response to the integrationalist critique (see Stockwell 2002b), stylistics can be regarded theoretically as a form of hermeneutics. Texts exist as autonomous objects, but the 'literary work' is an actualisation of that object produced only by an observing consciousness (in the terms used by Ingarden 1973a, 1973b). The object of stylistic analysis (the literary work as opposed to the material literary text) comes into existence only when read. Since readers come with existing memories, beliefs and both personal and social objectives, the context of the literary work is already conditioned by interpretation, even before reading begins (see Gadamer 1989). This means that reading is the process of becoming consciously aware of the effects of the text in the process of actualisation: reading is inherently an analytical process, in this sense. Stylistics is simply the formal and systematic means of recording the same process and making it available for comparison.

As Toolan (1990: 42–6, and Chapter 9 in this volume) points out, stylistics can be used for a variety of purposes, including, as we see in this book, the teaching of language and of literature. It can also be used as a means of demystifying literary responses, understanding how varied readings are produced from the same text; and it can be used to assist in seeing features that might not otherwise have been noticed. It can shed light on the crafted texture of the literary text, as well as offering a productive form of assistance in completing interpretations, making them richer and more complex. Stylistics can thus be used both as a descriptive tool and as a catalyst for interpretation.

These two possible functions of stylistics have been debated as if they were mutually exclusive: is stylistics a type of descriptive linguistics or is it a type of critical theory? The sense of exclusivity arises only if it is assumed that description is non-ideological. There are some stylisticians who argue that stylistics is simply a tool that can then be used in the service of a range of critical and interpretative positions. For example, it is an objective fact that a certain poem has a certain set of noun phrases from a particular semantic domain. Or it is a fact that the viewpoint in a certain novel is consistently a first person focalisation. There are examples of this position in the *Foundations* section of this Reader (Part One).

However, we would argue against this position, firstly on the theoretical dimension set out above that interpretation at least partly precedes analysis, and secondly on the practical dimension: since stylistics as a tool can only be manifest by being used; the fact that it is a descriptive tool in an ideal state is true but irrelevant in practice. As soon as stylistic analysis is undertaken, it partakes of ideological motivations, from the nature of the reading to the selection of the particular work and particular linguistic model for analysis. Examining noun phrases in the poem, rather than verb phrases, or describing them as a semantic domain, or choosing to explore focalisation are all matters of ideological selection and are not neutral. So we might as well admit the fact and accept the ideological foundations on which we are operating.

Such debates within stylistics indicate that the field is far from settled at the theoretical level. It is a strange fact that the emphasis on practical application has meant that stylistics has a generally accepted method and approach; theoretical disagreements about the status of the discipline have continued around what remains a relatively consistent analytical practice. Any differences in stylistic approach tend to arrange themselves along a cline from 'linguistic stylistics' to 'literary stylistics' (see Carter 1997), reflecting the motivations of the researcher rather than any programmatic political attachment. Linguistic stylisticians tend to be interested in exploring language using literature; literary stylisticians tend to be interested in exploring literature through analysis of its language. The former are more likely to be language teachers and the literary text is the equivalent of the data in applied linguistics. The latter are more likely to be cognisant of critical theoretical issues. However, the best stylisticians, in our view, are those who perceive an animating value in both positions.

Clearly, in setting out to explore the texture of novels, any stylistic analysis of readable length cannot possibly be exhaustive, and we have mentioned that a process of selection and excerpting of key passages is necessary. This unavoidable selection is also part of what makes stylistics an interpretative enterprise rather than a mechanistic or purely descriptive approach. Scenes or passages that appear intuitively to be key parts of the text, or which create oddities in readerly sensation, are often good places to begin a more systematic stylistic analysis. It could even be said that the mark of a good stylistician is someone who selects a particular analytical tool best suited to the passage in hand. Such orientations are central to the *Developments* section of this volume (Part Two).

New directions in stylistics: 1995 onwards

The third section of this volume provides examples where there is a growing body of work in stylistics that marries up detailed analysis at the micro-linguistic level with a broader view of the communicative context. Indeed it is this integrative direction that seems to us to characterise the various emerging concerns of the discipline. Of the numerous different *New Directions* illustrated in this Reader (Part Three), all have in common the basic stylistic tenets of being rigorous, systematic, transparent and open to falsifiability. All set out to draw the principled connections between textual organisation and interpretative effects. In short, they present themselves as aspects of a social science of literature, rather than a merely poetic encounter with the literary. Modern stylistics continues the century-old tradition of denying any separation of interpreted content from textual form.

In this respect, stylistics *necessarily* involves the simultaneous practice of linguistic analysis and awareness of the interpretative and social dimension. The act of application is what makes stylistics a fundamentally singular discipline of applied linguistics, arguing that formal description without ideological understanding is partial or pointless. If there is a paradigm in stylistics, it is this, and it seems to us to make stylistics a unified discipline at heart, with spin-offs into history, social study, philosophy and literary archaeology, as practised in literature departments around the world (van Peer, Chapter 12, this volume; Robson and Stockwell 2005).

The discipline of stylistics is currently drawing much of this work to itself. For example, studies of the sociolinguistics of writing have led to a renewed emphasis on the various literatures of the world in different international Englishes and other world languages (Fabb 1997; Talib 2002). As illustrated by this volume, the discipline has thus far been a largely Anglo-European and Anglo-American pursuit, with a focus on texts within a Western canon. However, the ways that writers use different vernaculars to represent a greater richness of cultural voices are being now explored stylistically. These studies include explorations of particular authors and communities around the world, as well as more theoretical work on how different 'voices' are represented in literature. (Bhaya Nair 2003)

Also along the readerly dimension, a major evolution in stylistics has been the development of 'cognitive poetics' (also called 'cognitive stylistics'). Applying the growing field of cognitive science to the experience of literary reading has been generating many interesting new insights into literature. These range from the almost purely psychological to the almost purely textual, but the vast majority of cognitive poetic studies combines our understanding of readerly cognitive processes with textual reality in the stylistic tradition (see Stockwell 2002a; Gavins and Steen 2003; and Semino and Culpeper 2002).

Cognitive poetics adds new facilities to stylistics, enabling the field to address key current issues such as a principled account of 'texture', an understanding of how the thematics of reading a literary text works, or how a piece of literature can generate and sustain emotion, or connecting different reading practices across the professional and lay or reading group divides. These developments simply extrapolate the continuing evolution of stylistics towards encompassing matters that were traditionally the ground of literary critics alone. Several studies in this newly developing tradition are represented in the *Language and Literature Reader* (see Chapters 24, 25 and 26 in this volume, by Emmott, Gavins and Semino respectively).

Underlying much of this principled interest in social and psychological context is a renewed sense of *ethics* in stylistic research. Non-literary stylistic analysis has developed through critical linguistics and critical discourse analysis alongside stylistics: the interaction between the two fields has been constant and close and consequently very productive (see Fairclough 1995; and Mills 1995, for example). Along with the ethical awareness that the literatures of the world ought to be studied sociolinguistically, fields such as feminist linguistics have worked to remind stylisticians (and all applied linguists) of our ethical responsibilities and the impossibility of an ideologically neutral linguistic theory.

Stylistics has also continued to draw on methodological innovations in linguistics. In particular, corpus linguistics and the use of computerised concordances and other empirical analytical tools have revolutionised the systematic study of literary texts (see Thomas and Short 1996; Mahlberg 2007, and Stubbs, Chapter 23, this volume). The continuities between literary creativity and the creativity apparent in everyday discourse have been revealed in all their complexity largely out of the fruitful interaction of stylistics and corpus linguistics (Carter 2004). New methods such as these can be used to explore levels of language from lexical collocations right up to metaphor patterning across a text and narrative organisation (Deignan 2005). At the same time, the pedagogical element in stylistics has also developed strongly. Stylistic methods are now the paradigmatic approach in the foreign language classroom, and the applied study of creativity is becoming standard in native-speaker language teaching too (see Durant and Fabb 1990; Hall 2005; Pope 1995, 2005).

Stylistics, as a discipline, is therefore very much in its heyday with a very wide range and reach (see in particular the annual 'Year's Work in Stylistics' review in the journal *Language and Literature*). It is a progressive approach in the sense that stylisticians strive constantly to improve their knowledge of how language works, while at the same time being aware of the useful insights of its own tradition. Its challenges arise from an apparently boundless appetite for drawing in the different disciplines and levels of language study, and the desire of its practitioners to be at once rigorously disciplined, theoretically reflexive and also engaged and passionate about verbal art. It is interesting to note that this position has some similarities with recent developments in 'post-theory' literary theory (Eagleton 2004; Cunningham 2001; Selden, Widdowson and Brooker 2005).

A stylistics manifesto

We conclude, a little more tendentiously and programmatically, with a manifesto. This is *a*, not *the*, stylistics manifesto. It represents one particular perspective and does not claim to be in any way definitive or to point a single way forward; indeed, we endeavour to embrace pluralism and eclecticism, creating space rather than setting boundaries. A *manifesto* is usually programmatic and revolutionary, pasted to lamp-posts or nailed to the doors of authorities. However, this manifesto presents a view of what we take to be common practice in stylistics, at the same time as seeking, in particular, to strengthen arguments for the discipline as a precise specification and exemplification of hermeneutics in action. Not all will agree with the concluding (and overlapping) points we raise here but we wanted to avoid a bland, retrospective synopsis and to conclude with a vision which may be, to some degree and for some at least, provocative.

1. Be theoretically aware

As stylisticians we should be alive to the theoretical foundations of the different inter-disciplinary domains on which we draw, as well as of linguistic theory. Stylisticians have rightly criticised literary critics for many years for being insensitive to the linguistic texture of literature, but stylistics should also continue to learn from the greater philosophical awareness and reflexivity of critical and literary theory.

2. Be reception-oriented

The literary 'work' only exists as a text in the mind of a reader; this fact should be at the forefront of stylistic practice. Interpretation is not an 'add-on' feature but is a foundational principle with texture at its analytical centre.

3. Be sociolinguistic

We should not neglect the broad sense of language study, taking account of the social, cultural and ideological dimensions of reading.

4. Be eclectic

Stylisticians should be eclectic as a matter of principle, in terms of analytical tools and analytical projects.

5. Be holistic

We should be aware that classification, categorisation and the focus on features are analytical conveniences, and we should always re-contextualise the products of our analyses. We now have the tools to make this a reality as well as a slogan. The pedagogic focus and experience of the subject is a particular help here, as is the increasing development of research methodologies that integrate the quantitative and the qualitative.

6. Be populist

Stylisticians should continue to challenge the literary canon, promote new configur-ations of literariness, appreciate and demonstrate their value. We can move beyond scholarly 'actualisations' to explore the richness of readings in the world. We can augment simply professional institutionalised readings and develop ways to describe the engagements of the plurality of readers and readings outside the academy.

7. Be difficult

Being populist does not exclude the courage to demystify obscurity and wilful inarticu-lacy in theory, nor avoid challenging works of literature. The difficult edges of literature are where we should stretch and test our frameworks rather than simply illustrate and demonstrate their effectiveness.

8. Be precise

Stylistics should continue to uphold the highest standards of analytical precision and transparency of practice. We must be rational, rigorous, systematic, thorough and open.

9. Be progressive

We should aim for a better account of things. Where an approach is shown to be faulty, it should be repaired or discarded. In other words, we should aim for a stylistics of falsifiability.

10. Be evangelical

Stylistics is the best approach to literary study. We should be unapologetic about this, and should deploy all our rhetorical resources to continue to draw in enthusiastic and committed researchers, teachers and students, and continue the development of the field.

Stylistics, it seems to us, is now sufficiently mature as a discipline to insist on these precepts. In its incipient foundational years the field of stylistics cast itself, understandably, in a more ancillary, supportive and sometimes defensive role; its developments thereafter produced a robust and confident discipline; our new directions, as we hope this volume illustrates, are now altogether more primary and necessary.

References

Bhaya Nair, R. (2003) *Narrative Gravity*. London: Routledge.

Brumfit, C.J. (ed.) (1983) *Teaching Literature Overseas: Language-based Approaches*. Oxford: Pergamon.

Brumfit, C.J. and Carter, R. (eds) (1986) *Literature and Language Teaching*. Oxford: Oxford University Press.

Carter, R. (1997) *Investigating English Discourse*. London: Routledge.

Carter, R. (2004) *Language and Creativity: The Art of Common Talk*. London: Routledge.

Cunningham, V. (2001) *Reading After Theory*. Oxford: Blackwell.

Deignan, A. (2005) *Metaphor and Corpus Linguistics*. Amsterdam: John Benjamins.

Durant, A. and Fabb, N. (1990) *Literary Studies in Action*. London: Routledge.

Eagleton, T. (2004) *After Theory*. Harmondsworth: Penguin.

Fabb, N. (1997) *Linguistics and Literature*. Oxford: Blackwell.

Fairclough, N. (1995) *Critical Discourse Analysis*. Harlow: Longman.

Fish, S. (1980) 'What is stylistics and why are they saying such terrible things about it?', in *Is There a Text in this Class? The Authority of Interpretative Communities*, Cambridge, MA: Harvard University Press, pp. 68–96.

Fowler, R. (1971) *The Languages of Literature*. London: Routledge and Kegan Paul.

Fowler, R. (1981) *Literature as Social Discourse*. London: Batsford.

Fowler, R. (1996) *Linguistic Criticism*. Oxford: Oxford University Press.

Gadamer, H.G. (1989) *Truth and Method* (trans. J. Weinsheimer and D.G. Marshall). New York: Crossroad Press [original 1965].

Gavins, J. and Steen, G. (eds) (2003) *Cognitive Poetics in Practice*. London: Routledge.

Hall, G. (2005) *Literature in Language Education*. London: Palgrave.

Halliday, M.A.K. (1973) *Explorations in the Functions of Language*. London: Arnold.

Ingarden, R. (1973a) *The Literary Work of Art: An Investigation on the Borderlines of Ontology, Logic, and Theory of Literature* (trans. G. Grabowicz). Evanston, IL: Northwestern University Press [original 1931].

Ingarden, R. (1973b) *The Cognition of the Literary Work of Art* (trans. R.A. Crowley and K. Olson). Evanston, IL: Northwestern University Press [original 1937].

Jameson, F. (1972) *The Prison-House of Language: A Critical Account of Structuralism and Russian Formalism*. Princeton, NJ: Princeton University Press.

McCarthy, M. and Carter, R. (1994) *Language as Discourse: Perspectives for Language Teaching*. Harlow: Longman.

Mahlberg, M. (2007) 'Investigating Dickens' style: a collocational analysis', *Language and Literature* 16: 93–6.

Mills, S. (1995) *Feminist Stylistics*. London: Routledge.

Pope, R. (1995) *Textual Intervention: Critical and Creative Strategies for Literary Studies*. London: Routledge.

Pope, R. (2005) *Creativity: Theory, History, Practice*. London: Routledge.

Robson, M. and Stockwell, P. (2005) *Language in Theory*. London: Routledge.

Selden, R. (1984) *Criticism and Objectivity*. London: Allen and Unwin.

Selden, R., Widdowson, P. and Brooker, P. (2005) *A Reader's Guide to Contemporary Literary Theory*. Harlow: Longman.

Semino, E. and Culpeper, J. (2002) *Cognitive Stylistics*. Amsterdam: Benjamins.

Short, M. (ed.) (1989) *Reading, Analysing and Teaching Literature*. Harlow: Longman.

Spitzer, L. (1948) *Linguistics and Literary History: Essays in Stylistics*. Princeton, NJ: Princeton University Press.

Stockwell, P. (2002a) *Cognitive Poetics*. London: Routledge.

Stockwell, P. (2002b) 'A stylistics manifesto', in S. Csábi and J. Zerkowitz (eds) *Textual Secrets: The Message of the Medium*, Budapest: Eötvös Loránd University Press, pp. 65–75.

Talib, I. (2002) *The Language of Postcolonial Literatures*. London: Routledge.

Thomas, J. and Short, M. (eds) (1996) *Using Corpora for Language Research*. Harlow: Longman.

Toolan, M. (1990) *The Stylistics of Fiction: A Literary Linguistic Approach*. London: Routledge.

Ullmann, S. (1964) *Language and Style*. Oxford: Basil Blackwell.

Verdonk, P. (2002) *Stylistics*. Oxford: Oxford University Press.

Wellek, R. and Warren, A. (1949) *Theory of Literature*. Harmondsworth: Penguin.

Widdowson, H. (1975) *Stylistics and the Teaching of Literature*. Harlow: Longman.

Widdowson, H. (1992) *Practical Stylistics*. London: Oxford University Press.

Wimsatt, W.K. and Beardsley, M.C. (1954a) 'The affective fallacy', in W.K. Wimsatt (ed.) *The Verbal Icon*, Lexington: University of Kentucky Press, pp. 21–39.

Wimsatt, W.K. and Beardsley, M.C. (1954b) 'The intentional fallacy', in W.K. Wimsatt (ed.) *The Verbal Icon*, Lexington: University of Kentucky Press, pp. 3–18.

Extracted and adapted from Peter Stockwell (2002) 'A stylistics manifesto', in S. Csábi and J. Zerkowitz (eds) *Textual Secrets: The Message of the Medium*, Budapest: Eötvös Loránd University Press, pp. 65–75; Peter Stockwell (2006) 'Language and literature: stylistics', in B. Aarts and A. McMahon (eds) *The Handbook of English Linguistics*, Oxford: Blackwell, pp. 742–58; and Ronald Carter (2007) 'Preface' in G. Watson and S. Zyngier (eds) *Literature and Stylistics for Language Learners: Theory and Practice*, Basingstoke: Palgrave Macmillan, pp. vii–xi.

INDEX

Note: This is a combined subject and author index. It does not offer comprehensive coverage of all the topics and authors cited but focuses on entries judged to be of especial significance in navigating the field.